Acts of charity have generally been interpreted as a response to socio-economic conditions or to spiritual and ideological movements. In *Charity and power in early modern Italy* the focus shifts from these impersonal forces to the everyday experiences of benefactors, from collective mentalities to subjectivity.

Drawing extensively on archival material, this study analyses the tensions within the individuals' personal and political milieus and shows that power and gender conflicts within the world of the elites were a crucial factor in encouraging charitable giving and even in shaping perceptions of the deserving poor. Special attention is given to the symbolic and metaphorical significance of charity rather than to the explicit aims of charitable activity.

Through its examination of a city marginal to the Italian tradition of communes and city-states and its concern with a relatively under-investigated period of Italian history, the book offers an extended reassessment of what has hitherto been regarded as the typical Italian model of welfare.

Charity and power in early modern Italy

Cambridge History of Medicine

EDITED BY

CHARLES WEBSTER
Reader in the History of Medicine, University of Oxford,
and Fellow of All Souls College

CHARLES ROSENBERG
Professor of History and Sociology of Science,
University of Pennsylvania

For a list of titles in the series, see end of book

Charity and power
in early modern Italy

Benefactors and their motives
in Turin, 1541–1789

SANDRA CAVALLO

University of Exeter

Published by the Press Syndicate of the University of Cambridge
The Pitt Building, Trumpington Street, Cambridge CB2 1RP
40 West 20th Street, New York, NY 10011–4211, USA
10 Stamford Road, Oakleigh, Melbourne 3166, Australia

First published 1995

Printed in Great Britain at the University Press, Cambridge

A catalogue record for this book is available from the British Library

Library of Congress cataloguing in publication data
Cavallo, Sandra
Charity and power in early modern Italy: benefactors and their
motives in Turin, 1541–1789/Sandra Cavallo
p.   cm. – (Camabridge history of medicine)
Includes bibliographical references and index
ISBN 0 521 46091 3
1. Charities – Italy – Turin – History. 2. Public welfare – Italy –
Turin – History. 3. Charities, Medical – Italy – Turin – History.
4. Italy – History – 1492–1870. I. Title. II. Series.
[DNLM: 1. Charities – History – Italy. 2. Medical Indigency –
History – Italy. 3. History of Medicine, Modern – Italy.
HV 290 C377c 1995]
HV295.T82C38 1995
361.8'0945'12–dc20
DNLM/DLC   94–17672   CIP
for Library of Congress

ISBN 0 521 46091 3 hardback
ISBN 0 521 48333 6 paperback

Contents

Illustrations

Plates

Tables

Acknowledgments

I am extremely grateful to the Wellcome Trust for supporting me over the years during which the research for this book was carried out. Much of the work was done at the Wellcome Institute for the History of Medicine, where academic staff, research students and fellows provided a stimulating environment for research and discussion. I am especially indebted to Bill Bynum, Roy Porter and Andrew Wear for their constant advice and support. Discussion with scholars whose interests touch on charity and poor relief in other countries has been a source of inspiration: I would like to mention in particular Michael Eve, Mary Fissell, Margaret Pelling and Colin Jones, my colleague at Exeter University, who has been particularly supportive and generous with information and suggestions. Finally, I would like to thank Giovanni Levi for his encouragement and invaluable comments over the years.

This book has benefited much from the opportunity to discuss my work in progress in seminars and conferences. I am indebted in particular to Stuart Woolf for inviting me to the stimulating forum of the European University Institute and to Richard Smith for involving me in the 1992 Annual Conference of the Society for the Social History of Medicine. Finally, special thanks go to Jonathan Barry, Marco Buttino, Bill Bynum, Michael Eve, Colin Jones, Marjorie McIntosh, Roy Porter, Brian Pullan and Andrew Wear who have read the manuscript of this book, or parts of it. Their constructive criticism and precious suggestions and references have greatly contributed to its improvement. Furthermore I would like to thank all the friends and colleagues who helped with the English text, in particular the research students and fellows of the Wellcome Institute, and Allan Husband who translated and revised parts of a first version of this manuscript. A great debt of gratitude is due to Clare Coope, who thoroughly revised the final version. Her contribution went well beyond language revision: with her perceptive remarks she helped me a great deal to clarify my thinking and strengthen the presentation of my ideas.

Equivalent weights and measures

Capacity (dry)

1 *sacco* = 5 *emine*
1 *sacco* = 138,33 litres (3,81 bushels)
1 *emina* = 23,055 litres (3,04 pecks)

1 *carra* = 4 cubic metres

Capacity (liquid)

1 *carra* = 10 *brente*
1 *carra* = 493,07 litres (130,27 gallons)
1 *brenta* = 49,31 litres (13,03 gallons)

Money[1]

The main unit of currency was the *fiorino* (divisible into 12 *grossi*, divisible in turn into 4 *quarti*) up to 1632, when it was replaced by the *lira* (divisible into 20 *soldi*).

Other units referred to

scudo: before 1600 it was worth 8 to 13 *fiorini*; in the following decades its value soared as a result of heavy inflation up to 35 *fiorini* in 1632. After this date its value oscillated between 3,5 and 9 *lire*.

ducatone: it was worth 12 to 19 *fiorini* before 1632, and 2,5 to 6 *lire* in the following period.

doppia: two *scudi*

[1] D. Promis, *Le Monete dei Reali di Savoia*, Turin 1841, vol. II; S. J. Woolf, 'Sviluppo economico e struttura sociale in Piemonte da Emanuele Filiberto a Carlo Emanuele III', *NRS*, 1 (1962), pp. 25–9.

Abbreviations

Archives

AAT	Archivio Arcivescovile, Turin
ACT	Archivio Comunale, Turin
AOC	Archivio Ospedale di Carità
AOSG	Archivio Ospedale S. Giovanni
AOSML	Archivio Ordine di S. Maurizio e Lazzaro
ASSP	Archivio Storico S. Paolo
AST, p.s.	Archivio di Stato di Torino, prima sezione
AST, s.r.	Archivio di Stato di Torino, sezioni riunite
BR	Biblioteca Reale

Archival funds

Ins.	Insinuazione di Torino (in AST, s.r.)
LPqM	Luoghi Pii di qua dai Monti (in AST, p.s.)
OPCB	Opere Pie Comuni e Borgate (in AST, p.s.)
Ord.	Ordinati del Comune di Torino (in ACT)
PCF	Patenti Controllo Finanza (in AST, s.r., art. 689)
T.P.	Testamenti Pubblicati dal Senato (in AST, s.r.)

Printed primary sources

Borelli	G. B. Borelli, *Editti Antichi e Nuovi dei Sovrani Principi della Real Casa di Savoia*, Turin 1681.
D.	F. A. Duboin, *Raccolta per Ordine di Materia delle Leggi, Editti, Manifesti . . . Emanate dai Sovrani della Real Casa di Savoia sino all' 8-12-1798*, 23 Toms, Turin 1818–69.

Periodicals

AHN	Acta Historica Neerlandicae
AHR	American Historical Review
AIIGT	Archivio dell'Istituto Italo-Germanico di Trento
Ann. Osp. M. Vitt.	Annali dell'Ospedale M. Vittoria di Torino
ARH	Archiv für Reformationsgeschichte / Archive for Reformation History
ASI	Archivio Storico Italiano
ASL	Archivio Storico Lombardo
BSSS	Biblioteca della Società Storica Subalpina
BISSSV	Bollettino dell'Istituto di Storia della Società e dello Stato Veneziano
BSBS	Bollettino Storico Bibliografico Subalpino
BHM	Bulletin of the History of Medicine
CC	Continuity and Change
EcHR	Economic History Review
ESR	European Studies Review
Giorn. Acc. Med.	Giornale dell'Accademia di Medicina di Torino
JIH	Journal of Interdisciplinary History
JMH	Journal of Modern History
Loc. Pop. St.	Local Population Studies
MH	Medical History
Mem. Acc. Sc. Tor.	Memorie dell'Accademia delle Scienze di Torino
NRS	Nuova Rivista Storica
QS	Quaderni Storici
RQ	Renaissance Quarterly
RSLR	Rivista di Storia e Letteratura Religiosa
RSI	Rivista Storica Italiana
SHM	Social History of Medicine
SS	Società e Storia
SMRH	Studies in Medieval and Renaissance History
TRHS	Transactions of the Royal Historical Society
Univ. Birm. Hist. Jl	University of Birmingham History Journal

Introduction

This book is an attempt to relate two objects of study which are usually treated separately: the identity of the dispensers and changing definitions of the recipients of charity. It is concerned with how changes in the social composition of donors and administrators affected policy towards the poor and with how shifts in the motivations for becoming involved in charity affected the social composition of those groups for which the relief was intended.

Within the social history of poor relief it has generally been assumed that the recipients of charity changed as a result of changes in the nature of poverty, a view which would suggest that new welfare policies were a reflection of, for example, shifts in the numbers, age and sex of the poor and in the extent of crime and vagrancy. This has meant that social historians have tended to attribute a crucial role to the nature of demand as the chief determinant of social policy – an approach which is problematic unless we assume that charity can be interpreted as simply a response to a lucid and rational analysis of the condition of the poor.

Those who have chosen instead to look at charity in terms of the actions of individuals and groups rather than of governments and institutions have focused more on what we might call the supply side. They have examined the factors (not always related to the actual conditions of the poor) which motivated the actions of benefactors in different periods and which influenced the structure and aims of their giving. Much has therefore been said about the impact of mendicant preachers and their calls for the rejection of temporal wealth in the Middle Ages; about the impetus for moral reform which prompted a wave of charitable activity from the late sixteenth century on; and also about the decline in voluntary charity caused by increased secularisation during the Enlightenment.[1] In addition there has been debate over the close link between theories of

---

[1] B. Pullan, *Rich and Poor in Renaissance Venice. The Social Institutions of a Catholic State, to 1620*, Oxford 1971; M. Vovelle, *Piété Baroque et Déchristianisation en Provence au XVIII siècle*, Paris 1973; C. Fairchilds, *Poverty and Charity in Aix-en-Provence 1640–1789*, Baltimore,

1

political economy and specific forms of welfare provision which set out ways to enforce social discipline, population policies and control of the labour-force.[2]

This 'supply' approach has been valuable in showing that policy towards the poor was not determined solely by the statistical extent of poverty. Too often, however, the sorts of explanation for charity which are given within this approach are over-generic and certainly cannot account for the concrete actions of individuals. Reference to spiritual or ideological movements which were in vogue at the time or to structural changes which slowly redefined collective mental attitudes certainly illuminates the context in which philanthropy took place, but historical analysis of the motivations behind measures for the poor should not stop there. It is always the case that certain social groups are far more receptive to these ideas and conditioning factors than others, perhaps women rather than men, or young people more than the old. The variety of possible responses to the same ideological stimulus becomes particularly evident when one shifts from generalisations about the influence of, say, the Counter-Reformation, or the subsequent process of 'de-Christianisation', to the analysis of specific situations. It becomes clear that the preaching of a given religious order in a particular local context might have stimulated some to charitable activity but also aroused the hostility of others. The spread of Counter-Reformation ideas was often encouraged by specific groups and circles who were pursuing wider aims in local politics (as will also be apparent in cases discussed in following chapters).

We need, therefore, to look for those more hidden motivating factors which might allow us to establish some pattern to the apparent randomness of different individuals' participation in charitable activity, and to find explanations for their involvement which are less remote from the concerns of their everyday experience. Motivations for charity, ranging from conflict over family wealth to the search for prestige, have occasionally been mentioned by historians (especially in descriptions of individual donors), but they have never been analysed systematically; above all, no attempt has been made to construct a periodisation of charity based on changes in the role that charity

Md. 1976; J. Chiffoleau, *La Comptabilité de l'Au-Delà: les Hommes, la Mort et la Religion dans la Région d'Avignon à la fin du Moyen Age*, Rome 1980; C. Jones, *Charity and Bienfaisance. The Treatment of the Poor in the Montpellier Region 1740–1815*, Cambridge 1982; K. Norberg, *Rich and Poor in Grenoble 1600–1814*, Berkeley, Calif. 1985; S. K. Cohn Jr., *Death and Property in Siena 1205–1800: Strategies for the Afterlife*, Baltimore, Md. 1988; S. K. Cohn Jr., *The Cult of Remembrance and the Black Death. Six Renaissance Cities in Central Italy*, Baltimore, Md. 1992.

[2] G. Himmelfarb, *The Idea of Poverty. England in the Early Industrial Age*, London 1984; D. Andrew, *Philanthropy and Police. London Charity in the Eighteenth Century*, Princeton, N.J. 1989; M. Lindemann, *Patriots and Paupers. Hamburg, 1712–1830*, New York Oxford 1990.

played in the secular circumstances of its dispensers.[3] The present study seeks
to go some way towards achieving this. Various forms of charity are examined
in the social context in which they took shape, firstly by establishing the
identity of the individuals and groups who introduced, controlled and funded
welfare provisions in various periods; and secondly by examining those
conflicts and social dynamics within the actors' social and political milieux,
as well as in their private lives, which may have affected their attitudes to
charity.

In the earlier period covered by this study (chapters 1 and 2) the predominance
of broadly based civic forms of charity tends to make individuals less evident
and the protagonists of the dynamics I describe are mainly social groups;
subsequently (with the exception of the period examined in the last chapter, in
which an impersonal subject, namely the state, returns) the stage is occupied
instead by individuals whose aim it was to ensure that their names should be
linked with the charitable acts they performed. It should be pointed out that in
this section not *all* those who contributed to the maintenance of the poor are
considered, but only those who gave substantial donations, either in the form
of dispositions made while they were still alive and intended to take effect
immediately, or in the form of dispositions within their wills. Because I am
chiefly interested in secular motivations for charity I have not taken small
donations into account since these were presumably motivated above all by
compassionate impulses towards the poor, by concern for the after-life and by a
wish to avoid the embarrassment of refusing the invitation – which notaries were
obliged to extend to all testators – to add a charitable clause to their will.[4] The
charitable acts on which I focus are those which, due to their size, represented a
public as well as religious and private act and clearly constituted a message to
one's peers.

For the purposes of this study, I have found wills and testaments to be a
particularly fruitful source of evidence concerning the context in which
charitable activity took place. When considered in their entirety, and not just –
as has often been the case – for the charitable bequests they contain, these
documents can reveal much about the lives of benefactors, their status, their
struggles to establish or enhance prestige, their social networks and their family

---

[3] One exception is represented by Cohn's attempt to link different pious attitudes to the changing
meaning and use of property. However his concern is with 'strategies for the afterlife' in general
rather than with provisions for the poor specifically. Cohn, *Death and Property* and *The Cult of
Remembrance*.

[4] For the same reason this study does not deal with casual charity, with those occasional contributions to alms-boxes for the poor which, though they may have been made as public acts,
have remained anonymous. This sort of giving can only reveal changes at the rather vague level
of collective mentalities. For the criteria used to calculate donations and bequests see chapter 3,
note to figure 1.

ties and conflicts.[5] Wherever possible I have supplemented this data with additional biographical details which throw light on the public appointments and economic activities of benefactors and administrators of charity.[6] Finally, I also consider the material celebrations of charity: changes in the architectural form of hospitals and institutions and other figurative representations of charity have proved a particularly valuable source for tracing shifts in the symbolic implications of charitable acts.

My study thus focuses less on the explicit aims which administrators and donors declared and more on the indirect and symbolic meanings which charity embodied for its dispensers. Special attention is given to the various patterns of power and of conflict within the elite groups in which differing charitable practices developed. Two types of conflict have been identified as particularly significant: firstly, conflict resulting from shifts in the influence, status and access to power of different social groups in the arena of city politics and, secondly, conflict caused by changes in the configurations of family and gender relationships. Following these two main threads, different chapters examine the clash between the representatives of civic power and the ducal entourage in the later sixteenth and early seventeenth century (chapters 1 and 2), the tension between new economically successful groups and the older court elite which held the monopoly of prestige in the mid seventeenth century (chapter 3), the attack by state functionaries on traditional corporate forms of hospital administration in the eighteenth century (chapter 5) and its outcome (chapter 6). Chapters 4 and 5 pay particular attention to the redefinition of marital relationships and control over family property within the upper classes and to the emergence of new patterns of family and kinship among the dispensers of charity in the late seventeenth and eighteenth centuries.

These various patterns of conflict among the elites largely explain the predominance of particular groups in charitable initiatives at particular times,

---

[5] This research was greatly facilitated by the existence in the Archivio di Stato of an index, arranged alphabetically and by year, to the Turin Insinuazione (Ins.), which contains all notarial acts drawn up in the city. This collection, together with that of the Testamenti Pubblicati dal Senato (T.P.), also in the Archivio di Stato, made it possible to consult complete copies of wills once a list of the names of benefactors and details of their charitable acts had been drawn up from collections of bequests and donations housed in the archives of charitable institutions. In order to be legally valid, in fact, it was required that a will be either recorded by a notary or deposited with the Senate if written by hand without a notary and witnesses. Only wills made outside Turin are not found in these sources (but they were a small minority).

[6] These include notarial acts drawn up on behalf of the individuals in question which reveal their financial transactions and social networks; Patenti Controllo Finanza (PCF), or authorisations for payments from the state treasury for public offices held, for repayments for loans to the duke, etc.; and finally, lists of members of various institutions such as the City Council, the confraternities and the boards of governors of hospitals.

and also the particular forms which charity took.[7] For example, the shift from outdoor relief to institutional care – something which is often explained by reference to an emerging ideology of *renfermement* – seems in fact to have been more closely linked to a shift away from an idea of charity as a civic duty (and therefore away from a tendency to care for the poor within the community), which was dominant as long as the City Council retained its monopoly over welfare issues. In a period characterised by fierce rivalry between elites, this broad and impersonal idea of charity gave way to a more personal and voluntary one which attributed new importance to hospitals as theatres for the public display of the benefactors' prestige.

Even shifts in the definition of the deserving poor – in other words of those categories of the needy seen as especially worthy of assistance – seem to have been related to changes in the social identity of benefactors or administrators – or rather, in the discourses and sets of values which those controlling charity endorsed. For example, the introduction of discrimination against outsiders to the town in the second half of the sixteenth century was an aspect of the political rise of the City Council and the related construction of a rhetoric in which citizens came to be given special prestige. Similarly, state employees became the object of special charitable concern precisely during the period when the special dignity of state service was being emphasised by functionaries who were appropriating power in crucial areas. In the late seventeenth century, concern for women who suffered marital violence or desertion and for widows and young women unable to marry, came above all from women benefactors – a pattern which can be linked to the acute awareness of female vulnerability and to the anti-marriage rhetoric which were widespread among aristocratic women in a period in which gender conflict was rife within families of rank.

These kinds of dynamics contributed towards shaping the very perception of poverty itself and thus influenced definitions of the worthy recipient to a much greater extent than has previously been recognised: in many cases, the definition of who was and was not deserving of relief can be seen as a metaphorical transposition of discourses which reflected tensions within the world of the elites.

Measures for the poor have been studied primarily in cities in the small states of the North and the Centre with a strong communal tradition and a sophisticated system of urban government which developed further in the Renaissance. It is these studies which have provided the basis for a picture of the principal

[7] I use the word 'elites' loosely to indicate not only those at the very top of the social hierarchy but also the affluent and those involved in the exercise of power in the various urban institutions and government bodies; in other words those who were in an economic and political position to influence substantially the resources available for the poor and the policies adopted towards them.

characteristics of the 'Italian system' of poor relief: the importance of the charitable activities of the confraternities; the existence as early as the fifteenth century of large hospitals with hundreds of medical patients; and the early appearance of a policy of *renfermement* in the form of legislation which confined beggars and other categories of outcast in institutions.[8] It is usually assumed that these elements combined to make the charitable system existing in certain parts of Italy exceptional in the European context. Thus the towns of the Veneto, of Tuscany and Lombardy – which had already led the way in adopting public health measures against the plague after the Black Death – continued in the early modern period to be admired by foreign observers and governments of the time and the measures adopted with regard to the poor and the sick to be taken as examples to emulate.[9]

But what was the situation in those numerous areas of Italy (covering most of the South, but also many parts of the North and Centre) whose economies were feudal and rural in nature rather than urban and industrial, and where towns were essentially creations of the early modern period? Turin is an ideal place to examine this question because it is not generally held to have been part of the Italian tradition of *comuni* and Renaissance city-states. The Duchy of Savoy, of which Turin was officially made capital in 1560 (though it had effectively functioned as such from the end of the fifteenth century onwards), is usually thought to have been characterised by a form of economic and social organisation which, being predominantly feudal, was closer to that prevailing in the nearby kingdom of France than it was to that in neighbouring Italian states.[10]

Certainly the economy of this small state which straddled the Alps (consisting

---

[8] Surveys of the numerous works on poor relief published in the last two decades (most of them on single institutions or single aspects of relief) are in: M. Rosa, 'Chiesa, idee sui poveri e assistenza in Italia dal Cinque al Settecento', *SS*, 10 (1980); G. Assereto, 'Pauperismo e assistenza. Messa a punto di studi recenti', *ASI*, 141 (1983); A. Pastore, 'Strutture assistenziali fra Chiesa e Stati nell'Italia della Controriforma', *Storia d'Italia, Annali 9, La Chiesa e il Potere Politico* (edited by G. Chittolini and G. Miccoli), Turin 1986; S. J. Woolf, *The Poor in Western Europe in the Eighteenth and Nineteenth Centuries*, London and New York 1986 (Introduction); B. Pullan, 'Support and redeem: charity and poor relief in Italian cities from the fourteenth to the seventeenth century', *CC*, 3 (1988). Among the most significant studies to be published after these surveys are C. F. Black, *Italian Confraternities in the Sixteenth Century*, Cambridge 1989, P. Gavitt, *The Ospedale degli Innocenti, 1410–1536*, Ann Arbor, Mich. 1990, and S. Cohen, *The Evolution of Women's Asylums since 1500*, Oxford 1992. On medical charity in particular see also J. Henderson, 'The hospitals of late medieval and Renaissance Florence: a preliminary survey', in L. Granshaw and R. Porter (eds.), *The Hospital in History*, London 1989; K. Park, 'Healing the poor: hospitals and medicine in Renaissance Florence', in J. Barry and C. Jones (eds.), *Medicine and Charity before the Welfare State*, London 1991.
[9] E. Chaney, '"Philanthropy in Italy": English observations on Italian hospitals, 1545–1789', in T. Riis (ed.), *Aspects of Poverty in Early Modern Europe*, Stuttgart 1981; K. Park and J. Henderson, '"The first hospital among Christians": the Ospedale di Santa Maria Nuova in early sixteenth century Florence', *MH*, 35 (1991).
[10] The most authoritative account of this influential view is F. Gabotto, 'Le origini "signorili" del "comune"', *BSBS*, 8 (1903).

of Piedmont on the Italian side and part of Savoy on the French side) relied
mainly on agriculture: grapes from the wine-growing areas of the pre-Alps,
cereals and rice from the plains of the Po river and livestock raised on the slopes
of the Alps constituted resources sufficient both to satisfy domestic requirements
and provide a modest surplus for export. It was only in the second half of the
seventeenth century that any significant industrial development took place. In
particular, the manufacture of raw and unfinished silk thread rapidly established
itself throughout the region as a natural extension of the cultivation of mulberry-
trees and silk-worms which had flourished in the Piedmontese countryside since
the end of the fifteenth century. Before long, the silk threads exported by the
Duchy, especially the famous Piedmontese organzines, came to be regarded as
the best in Europe – a reputation which was to remain unchallenged for decades,
until oriental silks became widely available at the end of the eighteenth century.
This expansion was in part the result of government policies which, like
Colbert's experiments in France, saw the development of traditional domestic
manufacturing skills as the most 'natural' way to increase the industrial output
of the state; it was also, however, related to the contemporary expansion of the
silk-weaving industry in nearby Lyon. Indeed, together with England, this
French city was to establish itself as the chief market for almost all the
unfinished silk produced in Piedmont.[11]

Yet even the rapid growth of the silk industry (and that, less pronounced, of
the wool, hemp and linen industries) did not alter the fundamentally economic
and social character of the Duchy. The forms of production which were
developed fitted readily into the traditional economy of the peasant family and
gave rise to a predominantly rural industry. Silk spinning became widespread in
the countryside but was carried out in small domestic units within the home,
while the spinning-mills which turned the raw thread into organzines became
numerous not in the big cities but in the larger rural centres and market-towns.

It will be clear that both the history and character of the Duchy of Savoy are
substantially different from those of the oligarchic republics and principalities of
the Centre and North of Italy, which have attracted the attention of historians.
In terms of its urban structure too, the Duchy follows a particular form of
chronological development characterised not by continuity between the age of
the *comuni* and the early modern period but by dramatic shifts in the relative size
and importance of its urban centres.[12] The towns and cities of Piedmont which
had been important commercial and manufacturing centres in the Middle Ages
went into decline in the fifteenth and early sixteenth century while the towns and

---

[11] S. J. Woolf, 'Sviluppo economico e struttura sociale in Piemonte da Emanuele Filiberto a Carlo
Emanuele III', *NRS*, 46 (1962).
[12] G. Levi 'Come Torino soffocò il Piemonte', in his *Centro e Periferia di uno Stato Assoluto*, Turin
1985; M. Ginatempo and L. Sandri, *L'Italia delle Città. Il Popolo Urbano tra Medioevo e
Rinascimento (Secoli XIII–XVI)*, Florence 1990.

cities that flourished in the early modern period were those whose rise to
prominence was relatively recent. Turin is the most obvious example of this
phenomenon. In the Middle Ages the city was very small (with no more than
3,000 inhabitants in the fourteenth century) and lagged considerably behind
centres which had a more highly developed industrial base such as the woollen
cloth-producing towns of Asti, Vercelli and Pinerolo, and Chieri, famous for
its fustian. By the end of the fifteenth century the city had assumed a more
important role as a university town, episcopal seat and headquarters of the
Duchy's administration, and its population had risen to between 5,000 and
6,000.[13] This sustained expansion continued in the following two centuries, and
became particularly intense at the turn of the seventeenth century. The population had more than doubled by 1571 and underwent a rise of 70 per cent in the
next forty years (growing from around 14,000 to over 24,000 between 1571 and
1614). The number of inhabitants then increased again by 100 per cent over the
next hundred years (reaching 49,000 in 1712). This last increase was especially
remarkable given that during this period the city had to withstand the plague of
1630, the dynastic civil war (1637–42), and the devastating effects of wars
fought on Piedmontese soil in the 1650s and, almost without interruption,
between 1690 and 1706. During the eighteenth century Turin continued to grow,
albeit at a more moderate rate, and by the 1790s the population had reached over
78,000 (table 1).[14] The rate of physical expansion of the city itself also gives a
useful indication of the chronology of growth in the numbers of inhabitants.
There were three main phases in which additions were made: to the South in the
first half of the seventeenth century (with the creation of the so-called Città
Nuova – New Town), to the East in the 1670s and 1680s and to the West from
1730 on (see plate 1).[15] As a result, the number of *isole* (i.e. the groups of
dwellings bounded by four streets characteristic of the Roman grid on which the
plan of the city is based) doubled between 1631 and 1705, from a total of sixty-
nine to over 130.[16]

---

[13] A. Barbero, 'Una città in ascesa', in *Storia Illustrata di Torino* (ed. by V. Castronovo), vol. II,
Torino Sabauda, Milan 1992.

[14] For the 1571 and 1614 figures Ministero dell'Agricoltura Industria e Commercio, *Statistica del
Regno d'Italia. Censimento degli Antichi Stati Sardi e Censimento della Lombardia, di Parma
e di Modena*, vol. I, P. Castiglioni, *Relazione Generale con una Introduzione Storica sopra i
Censimenti delle Popolazioni Italiane dai Tempi Antichi sino al 1860*, Turin 1862; for the 1702
to 1792 figures G. Levi, 'Gli aritmetici politici e la demografia piemontese negli ultimi anni del
Settecento', *RSI*, 86 (1974).

[15] V. Comoli Mandracci, *Torino*, Bari 1983, and, recently, M. D. Pollak, *Turin 1564–1660: Urban
Design, Military Culture and the Creation of the Absolutist Capital*, Chicago, Ill. 1991.

[16] There were 126 in 1705, excluding the Città Nuova. Ord. 7.6.1592; F. Rondolino, 'Vita torinese
durante l'assedio (1703–1707)', in Regia Deputazione di Storia Patria, *Le Campagne di Guerra
in Piemonte (1703–8) e l'Assedio di Torino (1706)*, Turin 1909, vol. VII. The calculation of the
number of *isole* excludes all those which were entirely occupied by ducal palaces or by public
buildings.

Table 1. *Population of Turin and suburbs,*
1571–1792

1571	14,244
1614	24,410
1702	43,866
1712	49,102
1722	52,989
1732	59,558
1742	59,320
1752	62,356
1762	66,103
1772	71,680
1782	73,984
1792	78,514

Source: See note 14

The expansion of the city was undoubtedly linked to its new status as capital and to its increased appeal, as the seat of the court and the administrative centre of the state, for immigrants, industry and commerce. In the second and more dramatic phase of its development, however, a significant part was also played by its transformation into a centre for the manufacture of cloth and other silk products. Indeed, from the end of the seventeenth century on, the government stubbornly pursued mercantilist policies whose aim was to ensure that not only the production of raw and unfinished silk but also the final stages of silk manufacture were to be kept strictly within the confines of the state (even if this were at the expense of the profitable export of organzine threads). Turin was the city in which these policies produced their best results: in 1702 there were already 432 working looms in the city, exclusively for the manufacture of silk cloth; by the middle of the century this number had risen to 1,150 (out of a total of 1,510 in the whole of Piedmont).[17]

The history of Turin is thus very different from that of Italian cities which had strong manufacturing, trade and guild traditions and where systems of relief generally regarded as pioneering developed. The city began to flourish only in the early modern period at precisely the time when, in Piedmont as well as in other parts of Italy, the foremost urban centres of the late Middle Ages and the Renaissance saw their role decline and experienced difficulty in maintaining their populations.[18] A substantial expansion in the number of employees in services and manufacturing industry occurred only from the mid seventeenth century onwards and, accordingly, the numerical importance and role of craft

[17] G. Prato, *La Vita Economica in Piemonte a Mezzo del Secolo XVIII*, Turin 1908.
[18] On these different chronologies of urban development, see E. Fasano Guarini, 'La politica demografica delle città Italiane nell'età moderna', in Società Italiana di Demografia Storica, *La Demografia Storica delle Città Italiane*, Bologna 1982.

organisations and devotional associations became significant only from the late decades of the century on.[19]

A study of the case of Turin makes it possible, therefore, to shift the focus from the Italian cities of the Renaissance, which have so far attracted the attention of historians of charity, to those of the early modern period. This may allow us to glimpse what things were like in that neglected other half of Italy but I hope that this research will also have wider implications and contribute to a reappraisal of what has come to be regarded as the 'Italian model' of measures for the poor and sick.

The story begins in 1541, the year in which the first comprehensive plan for relief was issued by the municipal authorities; it then traces the history of welfare provision offered by different charitable agencies for just over two centuries, up until the eve of the French invasion of Piedmont.[20]

It seeks to give as comprehensive a picture as possible of initiatives taken on behalf of the poor, including policy towards the sick, a subject which the now numerous monographs on relief in various European cities usually omit as belonging to the separate domain of the historian of medicine.[21] The tendency to see poverty and disease as separate areas of investigation reflects a recent distinction which certainly does not hold for the early modern period (and even today is often inappropriate): as has been demonstrated elsewhere and as my study confirms, illness, together with marital status, gender and age, was at this time one of the components of contemporary definitions of poverty.[22]

The period covered by the book is one which has been insufficiently explored by studies of charity and welfare facilities in Italy. Histories of medical provision in particular have focused either on the Renaissance or on the enlightened despotism of the later eighteenth century while the intervening years

---

[19] On the late development of guilds, S. Cerutti, 'Corporazioni di mestiere a Torino in età moderna: una proposta di analisi morfologica', in *Antica Università dei Minusieri di Torino*, Turin 1987 and *La Ville et les Métiers. Naissance d'un Langage Corporatif (XVIIe–XVIIIe Siècle)*, Paris 1990. On lay religious associations, by contrast, there are no recent studies. See G. Martini, *Storia delle Confraternite Italiane con Speciale Riguardo al Piemonte*, Turin 1935.

[20] The only aspects of relief and social policy I do not touch on are policy towards lunatics (the main initiative in the period seems to have been the mad-house called the Pazzarelli, which had an elite clientele) and measures dealing with converted heretics (Jews and Waldensians). Both are characterised by features which distinguish them significantly from other forms of social policy. On converted heretics in Turin L. Allegra 'Modelli di conversione', *QS*, 78 (1991). I have also been obliged to exclude the House of the Orfanelle, an institution (founded in the mid sixteenth century) for young girls who had lost their fathers, since its Archives were not open to consultation when the research for this book was carried out. They are now available at the Archivio di Stato di Torino, prima sezione.

[21] For an exception to this tendency see C. Jones, *The Charitable Imperative: Hospitals and Nursing in Ancien Régime and Revolutionary France*, London 1989.

[22] See, for example, M. Pelling, 'Illness among the poor in an early modern English town: the Norwich census of 1570', *CC*, 3 (1988); M. Fissell, 'The "sick and drooping poor" in eighteenth century Bristol and its region', *SHM*, 2 (1989).

have been largely overlooked.[23] This lack of interest may in part be due to an enduring view of the history of Italy in the early modern period as a history of decline. However, the persistence of a tendency to impose the classic three-fold periodisation of Renaissance, Counter-Reformation and Enlightened Absolutism onto explanations of charitable activity and assistance in general in Italy has also played its part in excluding consideration of developments which appear to sit uncomfortably within these categories. Thus little is known about what became of measures for the relief of the needy and sick which were adopted between the later Middle Ages and the Renaissance and equally little is known about the long interval which elapsed between the burst of charitable activity during the Counter-Reformation and the assumption of responsibility for welfare provision by the enlightened governments of the later eighteenth century.

In carrying out my research on Turin I have tried to avoid forcing events into preconceived periods, seeking instead to adopt a periodisation which was more intrinsically linked to my material and based on the question: who controls charity? It is this question which also accounts for the way in which I have structured the narrative: different chapters chart the shift of control of charity from the municipality to corporate bodies and then to the state, and from women to men, and bring out the different definitions of poverty and forms of assistance that these various configurations of control implied. This approach is one which interprets the emergence of new attitudes towards the poor as a process rooted in patterns of conflict within the elite and, as such, I hope it will perhaps contribute to bring the subject of motivations for charity back into the domain of social relations and away from the elusive territory of the history of ideas and *mentalités*.

---

[23] A somewhat whiggish emphasis on the eighteenth century 'reforms', seen as the precursor of 'modern' medical treatment, has prevailed among most Italian medical historians. See, for example, *Storia d'Italia, Annali 7 Malattia e Medicina*, edited by F. Della Peruta, Turin 1984.

1

Sixteenth-century municipal plans for poor relief

The 1541 plan in Turin

At the beginning of May 1541, an announcement was trumpeted through the streets of Turin. It invited all the poor, be they 'men or women, young or old, healthy or infirm', to congregate a few days later at the cathedral, where they were to see a committee of the 'reverend suffragan [the archbishop's delegate], the reverend canons and several gentlemen and merchants of the city'. When the poor had assembled at the cathedral on the appointed day, they were asked to file past the committee one by one. The committee had brought two white books and a bag of money and, while one of them handed out a coin of small value (*un quarto di re*) to each pauper, another recorded in the first book the names of 'the orphans, the infirm and the disabled who had no dwelling in Turin' and in the second book the names of 'those who have rooms'. Those entered in the first book were taken to the hospital of S. Giovanni, where they were given 'sufficient food, drink, clothing and a place to sleep'. As for the others, 'careful investigations were made by religious and secular persons delegated by the above mentioned gentlemen in order to ascertain their requirements'. A dole varying 'according to their state of need' was established on the basis of these inquiries. It consisted partly of bread and partly of money and every Sunday the poor were to collect it from the hospital; 'some were given 12 good sizeable loaves and one Piedmontese *grosso*, others were given four loaves and two *grossi*, others thirty-six loaves and three *grossi* and still others sixty loaves and five *grossi*'. On Sunday, hospital officials would also deliver the agreed amount of alms to the homes of the *poveri vergognosi* (the respectable poor who were ashamed to go in person).

This account is just the first part of a long document which describes in detail the charitable system operating in Turin in 1541.[1] A lack of records for the

---

[1] ACT, C.S.657. All quotations in the following pages will refer to this document, unless otherwise specified.

previous period prevents us from ascertaining to what extent the document marked the introduction of a new relief plan in that year, or merely gave written and statutory form to a set of measures already enforced in the capital, possibly re-enacting provisions which had fallen into neglect. Despite this uncertainty, the document represents an important source and gives a comprehensive picture of attitudes towards the poor at this early date and of the methods employed in their relief. It certainly testifies to the desire for a permanent and well-ordered organisation of welfare, capable of meeting the different needs of the various categories of the poor in the city.

The system laid down in 1541 attempted to provide for all those who were really in need by identifying them through a thorough and regular examination of the poor in the town. The hospital's governors had the duty of visiting the city, house by house, every six months, in order to update the records of those qualifying for assistance and to adjust the amount of relief on the basis of the current circumstances of the recipients, 'providing everyone according to his needs'. But the system also aimed at 'uprooting the true cause of trickery'. Begging was therefore unnecessary and was in fact outlawed; the regulations considered anyone caught begging an impostor and instructed that they should be punished accordingly. The document concluded with the order – which was to be proclaimed throughout the city – that no pauper, whether from the city or outside, 'should dare ask for alms, under pain of being irremissibly whipped'.

The statutes also provided for the hospital's internal life and defined the roles and duties of staff, and the procedure for day-to-day management. As far as medical treatment was concerned, it was stated that a doctor and a surgeon should attend the hospital regularly, visiting the sick twice a day, and that a male nurse should constantly watch over the sick and provide them with 'medicines, ointments and whatever may be necessary'. The chaplain had a crucial role in assisting the sick and supervising the running of the hospital, as well as conducting Sunday mass and administering the sacraments to the patients. He had to visit the sick four times a day and twice at night, to give them food and medicines, and to provide 'generally for all their needs'. He was responsible for furniture and equipment, kept the accounts of charitable gifts received, purchased the necessary food and provisions, 'corn, wine, firewood, meat, fish and other things', and submitted the accounts to the treasurer. The chaplain was assisted in these activities by an 'agent', 'a diligent and trustworthy man who receives an honest salary'.

Provision of poor relief thus appears to have been mainly the responsibility of the hospital of S. Giovanni which, following the union in 1440 of twelve small medieval hospitals, constituted in 1541 the only hospital in the city. Not only did this hospital receive the sick and disabled, and provide outdoor relief to the needy through the weekly distributions of bread and money, but it also had a duty to take in foundlings. In the first years of the latter's lives they were sent to the country for wet-nursing at the expense of the City Council; they then returned to the hospital. The 1541 document also laid down regulations for the education of the foundlings, by stating that a teacher had to be hired 'to teach the alphabet to the boys' and 'an honest woman' to teach the girls spinning, sewing 'and other womanly activities'. As soon as possible, the hospital had to send the boys to an artisan for apprenticeship and place the girls in service or arrange a marriage for them, in which case it had also to supply the dowry.

We do not have much information on the hospital building prior to 1545, when the move took place to a larger establishment, after receipt of a legacy. The new house, which was in the very centre of the city and close to the cathedral, had two floors: on the ground floor were a chapel and a pharmacy (this was already mentioned in the 1541 document), as well as the service rooms (kitchen and refectory, bakery and stable); the first floor was divided into seven large rooms into which the patients were segregated according to sex. The patients were also housed separately from the foundlings.[2] The overall capacity of the hospital was probably quite limited, but we have to consider that much of its relief activity consisted of outdoor provisions.

The measures issued in Turin in 1541 have many points in common with the municipal plans for poor relief which emerged in the first half of the sixteenth century all over Europe. They share the same naive idea that it was possible to eradicate begging by setting up a permanent and all-embracing system which would provide aid to the deserving poor and punishment to able-bodied impostors and idlers. One of the best known sets of provisions of this kind had been drawn up in nearby Lyon a few years previously,[3] and published in a 1539 pamphlet which could easily have been known in Turin.[4] However, regulations of this type were much more widespread. From the information currently available, it would appear that similar measures were adopted in German cities such as Nuremberg, Augsburg, Strasbourg, Wittemberg, Leipzig in the early 1520s, and in many towns of the Low Countries, such as Lille (1506), Bruges (1512), Mons, Anvers (1521), Ypres (1525) and Valenciennes (1531).[5] For the

---

[2] T. M. Caffaratto, *L'Ospedale Maggiore di San Giovanni Battista e della Città di Torino. Sette Secoli di Assistenza Socio-Sanitaria*, Turin 1984, p. 12.

[3] J. P. Gutton, *La Société et les Pauvres: l'Exemple de la Généralité de Lyon*, Paris 1971; N. Zemon Davis, 'Poor relief, humanism, and heresy: the case of Lyon', *SMRH*, 5 (1968).

[4] *La Police de l'Aulmosne de Lyon*, Lyon 1539.

[5] H. J. Grimm, 'Luther's contributions to sixteenth century organization of poor relief', in *ARH*, 61 (1970); R. Jutte, 'Poor relief and social discipline in sixteenth century Europe', *ESR*, 11 (1981). On the Low Countries, H. Pirenne, *Histoire du Belgique*, Bruxelles 1923 (first edition 1907), vol. III, pp. 273–80; J. Nolf, *La Réforme de la Bienfaisance Publique à Ypres au XVIe Siècle*, Gand 1915; P. Bonenfant, 'Les origines et le caractère de la bienfaisance publique aux pays Bas sous le règne de Charles Quint', *Revue Belge de Philologie et d'Histoire*, 5 (1926) and 6 (1927).

1530s and 1540s there are documented examples in Spain: in the Basque Country (1535), and in Zamora, Salamanca, Valladolid, Madrid and Toledo.[6] In this period there were also countless French cities where municipal initiatives reorganised and centralised poor relief under *bureaux des pauvres* or *aumônes générales*.[7] In Italy, Venice remains the best known-example, thanks to Brian Pullan's exhaustive study: in that city comprehensive poor relief schemes made an early appearance in 1527 and 1529 and were further developed in 1545.[8] But there is some evidence that municipal systems of poor relief existed elsewhere in Italy, particularly in the Po Valley. Apart from the cases of Verona, Brescia and Salò (which are mentioned by Pullan), Modena had its charitable provisions centralised under civic control during the 1530s and 1540s.[9] In Genoa, by 1540, an office for the poor was responsible for keeping a list of all those requiring relief who had been resident in the city for at least six months, and handed out bread and money.[10] In Lucca, two bodies were created in the 1540s by the Municipal Council to deal with the different categories of the poor, the Offizio dei poveri foretani e forestieri (for the non-resident poor) and the Offizio dei poveri vergognosi (for the local respectable poor).[11] In England too, the early decades of the sixteenth century seem to have been a crucial experimental period in the local administration of poor relief and the suppression of begging. At the beginning of the century, a number of towns initiated campaigns to expel vagrants and the poor originating from other areas, and this wave of activity was particularly intense between 1517 and 1521. At the same time there were attempts to regulate begging by granting the deserving local poor licences to beg. In many parishes individual charity was discouraged and donors were enjoined to make use of communal collection boxes for the poor in the churches –

[6] L. Martz, *Poverty and Welfare in Habsburg Spain. The Example of Toledo*, Cambridge 1983, pp. 14–15, 21–2; M. Flynn, *Sacred Charity. Confraternities and Social Welfare in Spain, 1400–1700*, London 1989, pp. 91–4.

[7] M. C. Paultre, *De la Repression de la Mendicité et du Vagabondage en France sous l'Ancien Régime*, Paris 1906, vol. I, pp. 55–115; C. Bloch, *L'Assistance et l'Etat en France à la Veille de la Révolution*, Paris 1908, p. 44; M. Fosseyeux, 'La taxe des pauvres au XVIe siècle', *Revue d'Histoire de l'Eglise de France*, 20 (1934). The system operating in Paris is described in the pamphlet *La Police des Paouvres de Paris*, about 1555, published by E. Coyecque in *Société de l'Histoire de Paris et de l'Ile de France Bulletin*, 15 (1888).

[8] B. Pullan, *Rich and Poor in Renaissance Venice. The Social Institutions of a Catholic State, to 1620*, Oxford 1971.

[9] Ibid., pp. 270–8; S. Peyronel Rambaldi, *Speranze e Sogni nel Cinquecento Modenese. Tensioni Religiose e Vita Cittadina ai Tempi di Giovanni Morone*, Milan 1979, pp. 153–61.

[10] E. Grendi, 'Ideologia della carità e società indisciplinata. La costruzione del sistema assistenziale genovese (1470–1670)', in G. Politi, M. Rosa, F. Della Peruta (eds.), *Timore e Carità. I Poveri nell'Italia Moderna*, Cremona 1982, p. 68.

[11] S. Russo, 'Potere pubblico e carità privata. L'assistenza ai poveri a Lucca tra XVI e XVII secolo', *SS*, 23 (1984). It should be pointed out that in this period, the expression '*povero vergognoso*' does not necessarily refer to people who had lost their previously high social status but often instead to members of the labouring classes in difficulty. See for example, chapter 2, p. 57 and chapter 3, p. 111.

the alms from which were redistributed by specially nominated officials. In the following decades, it increasingly became the practice to keep an up-to-date record of all the poor in a given town, and to establish the obligation for parishioners to contribute regularly to their support through the payment of voluntary or compulsory poor rates.[12] Such measures seem to have become even more common in the 1550s and 1560s, at much the same time as the first provisions from central government to encourage their adoption were issued.[13]

Many scholars have seen all these civic plans for relief as embodying a radical shift in attitudes and in the policy towards the poor.[14] The measures adopted were largely repressive in nature and implied the abandonment of traditional unselective charity and the last vestiges of the sacredness which had been attributed to poverty in medieval society. Other features are also seen to have marked a new departure. For the first time, poor relief provision was made more efficient by centralising its administration and its financing: existing charitable funds were put at the disposal of the new scheme, attempts were made at channelling voluntary donations into a common chest and, in a few cases, at imposing poor rates on various corporations and the tax-paying population. Finally, the new provisions were usually secular in origin. City Councils, in particular, were often the prime movers (although the launching of the initiative was often backed by the religious sermons given by professional preachers). This last aspect has led historians to see the sixteenth-century urban relief schemes not only as a 'rationalisation' of the action towards begging, but as a move towards a 'secularisation' of charitable activity, which supposedly, up to that time, had been primarily in the hands of the Church.

All these features which are normally considered to have revolutionised sixteenth-century policy towards the poor can be found in the Turin case. Not only did the plan adopt measures regarded as characteristic of the new, more discriminating attitude (the prohibition of begging, the expulsion and punishment of transgressors, the investigation and census of the poor, etc.), but it shows the same attempt at centralising the management and financing of charity under secular control. While the overall organisation of relief was apparently in the hands of the governors of S. Giovanni, the reality was that the City Council was by now the major force in the hospital's administration. More generally, the

---

[12] P. Slack, *Poverty and Policy in Tudor and Stuart England*, New York 1988, pp. 115–19, 123; M. McIntosh, 'Local responses to the poor in late medieval and Tudor England', *CC*, 3 (1988).

[13] For examples in Suffolk, McIntosh, ibid., p. 229 and note 81; for Essex, F. G. Emmison, 'The care of the poor in Elizabethan Essex', *Essex Review*, 62 (1953).

[14] This view has prevailed since the very first works on the history of poor relief, e.g. Bloch, *L'Assistance*, p. 39. More recently R. M. Kingdon, 'Social welfare in Calvin's Geneva', *AHR*, 76 (1971); Zemon Davis, 'Poor relief'; C. Lis and H. Soly, *Poverty and Capitalism in Pre-Industrial Europe*, Brighton 1979.

City Council had been responsible for the formulation of the scheme and for imposing the financial arrangements which funded it.

1541 did in fact mark the secularisation of the hospital of S. Giovanni. According to the version repeated by many of Turin's historians, the hospital fell into decline in the 1530s, when Piedmont was hit by the plague and then became the battleground for French and Spanish armies. In 1536, the Duke of Savoy finally abandoned his territories and the Duchy was divided between the two contenders. A long period of foreign occupation then commenced. Turin remained subject to the French for nearly 30 years (1536–63) and, like the rest of Piedmont, it suffered, especially in the early years, from the disastrous consequences of the military taxation imposed by the occupiers which caused considerable impoverishment, the abandonment of properties and vast areas of cultivated land and the flight of much of the population. According to the conventional account, these dramatic circumstances also took their toll on the capital's hospital and eventually induced the City Council to come to its aid by donating the income of twelve lay confraternities which it administered in the city. The hospital was then able to re-establish itself following this considerable improvement in its financial situation. In return for bailing the hospital out, the City Council obtained a majority control in its administration: four of the six governors were to be City Councillors, while the other two were to be canons of the Cathedral Chapter, the body which had originally founded the hospital and which had administered it up until that time.[15]

The historians of Turin present this change in the hospital's administration as an erosion of the powerful hold of the Church over charitable institutions and they attribute it mainly to the late medieval Church's financial difficulties and the faltering of its authority. This interpretation, which is the one commonly given for the secularisation of charity in other parts of Europe also, is questionable for many reasons and will be discussed later. For the moment, I wish to focus on one of the factors to which this view gives insufficient importance, namely the strength of local governments which, quite independently of any supposed weakness of the Church, lay behind the 1541 plan in Turin and also behind similar plans in other European towns.

[15] F. M. Ferrero di Lavriano, *Istoria di Torino*, Turin 1679, pp. 533, 696–7; G. B. Semeria, *Storia della Chiesa Metropolitana di Torino*, Turin 1840, p. 415; L. Cibrario, *Storia di Torino*, Turin 1846, vol. I; S. Solero, *Storia dell'Ospedale Maggiore di S. Giovanni Battista e della Città di Torino*, Turin 1859; and more recently M. Grosso and M. F. Mellano, *La Controriforma nella Diocesi di Torino*, Vatican City 1957, vol. II, p. 100. A few decades later, the hospital government came to be shared by four canons and four councillors. This probably occurred in the 1570s after a conflict between the board of governors and the archbishop (who in those years was the Duke's man) over the management of the institution. This dispute has to be seen in the context of the clash between municipality and ducal power which was rife at the time, as we will see further on.

Civic ideology and provision for the poor

It may come as some surprise that a city like Turin, which according to traditional interpretations was, in the late Middle Ages, no more than an appendage of a feudal lord or an episcopal authority, could possibly have developed welfare systems comparable to those of the Italian cities which already boasted a long tradition of urban culture and autonomous government. This somewhat stereotypical view of the city is however in need of revision.[16] Very little is actually known about the organisation of urban life in Turin in the late Middle Ages and even less about the twenty-five years during which the city was subject to French domination (1536–62). This lack of interest is largely due to the dynastic-centred approach, which has characterised much historiography of Turin and the Savoy kingdom: even in recent works, the Dukes, and among them the most determined centralisers, are often seen as the moving force behind major initiatives.[17] According to this view, the real history of the city is taken to have begun in 1563, the year in which the House of Savoy officially returned to the newly created capital after more than two decades of Piedmont's domination by a foreign power. The period before this is regarded instead as a period of stagnation: nothing of any significance could have occurred during these years of tyranny and plunder, in the absence of the legitimate rulers. The introduction of social policies too could only have taken place after the restoration and as a result of the intervention of the first absolute sovereigns of the House of Savoy.[18]

In keeping with this view, the city's early historians discussed the 1541 document only in terms of the changes it introduced in the composition of the administrative board of the hospital, and they did not pay attention to the extensive system of relief that this implied nor to the major organisational and financial commitment that the enforcement of this plan required on the part of the City Council. The first step had been to centralise the funds to be used for charitable purposes, by transferring all the income that had originally been managed by the confraternities to the hospital. But the City Council also managed to persuade the other authorities present in the town, both secular and

---

[16] For the long-dominant 'feudal' interpretation, Gabotto, 'Le origini', and, recently, G. Chittolini 'Cities, "city-states", and regional states in north-central Italy', *Theory and Society*, 18 (1989). Some recent studies, however, argue against this view: G. Sergi, *Potere e Territorio Lungo la Strada di Francia*, Naples 1981, and 'Le città come luoghi di continuità di nozioni pubbliche del potere. Le aree delle marche d'Ivrea e di Torino'; and R. Bordone, '"Civitas nobilis et antiqua". Per una storia delle origini del movimento comunale in Piemonte', both published in *Piemonte Medievale. Forme del Potere e della Società*, Turin 1985.

[17] See for example the recent synthesis of the history of the city, *Storia Illustrata di Torino*, in particular the contributions on the early modern period in vol. II, *Torino Sabauda*, Milan 1992.

[18] A. Erba, *La Chiesa Sabauda tra Cinque e Seicento. Ortodossia Tridentina, Gallicanesimo Savoiardo e Assolutismo Ducale (1580–1630)*, Rome 1979.

religious, to pay regular poor rates. The French administration agreed to pay a fixed levy, which supposedly – in a gesture which was not without symbolic meanings – was to take the form of a deduction from the pay of the occupying troops, at the rate of one *soldo* per soldier. In addition the excise officer responsible for the salt duty, which was the direct tax that hit the poor hardest, had to supply the hospital every year with one measure of salt. On 1 September 1541, some four months after the introduction of these financial agreements, it was decided to add further taxes on the religious authorities possessing the richest benefices.[19] The archbishop undertook to pay two *scudi del sole* every week, plus two *sacchi* of corn, two *carre* of firewood and twelve of wine every year. The Abbot of S. Solutore also committed himself to two *carre* of corn, two of wine and ten of firewood every year. The parish priest of S. Andrea and prior of the Consolata was to supply the same amount, while the parish priest of S. Dalmazzo was to give eight *sacchi* of corn, a *carra* of wine and five of firewood every year.

It is clear that the City Council enjoyed considerable prestige if it was able to bind both ecclesiastical and secular authorities to such an agreement.[20] It is particularly striking that it managed to exact recognition of its authority even from the occupying forces and obtain the latter's support for a civic enterprise. An episode that occurred a few years later reinforces this impression: in 1556 the hospital governors won the judicial support of the French government in a dispute with the new archbishop, who had refused to honour his predecessor's undertakings concerning the annual payment of the poor rates. The Conseil du Roi sitting in Turin immediately accepted the governors' complaints and instructed the archbishop to fulfil the agreement. Six months later, as the latter continued to refuse to pay, the King himself issued an order which authorised his Conseil in Turin to proceed against the archbishop's property and income.[21] Besides confirming the strength of the City Council, this incident also points to a lack of concern for welfare matters in the upper ranks of the Church. This was a period in which the Turin diocesan seat was in the hands of absentee archbishops interested only in cashing their revenues, and not at all inclined to expend energies and resources on behalf of the poor. In 1515 the local Cathedral chapter lost the right to nominate the archbishop, who was henceforward to be appointed by the pope: this meant that, until 1563, when the Duke gained this right for himself, the archbishops of Turin were foreigners and totally uninvolved with local power and social policy. In this kind of context, it is very plausible that the ecclesiastical authority was foreign to the process of reshaping

[19] ACT, C.S.658.
[20] Significant of the leading role played by the City Council in setting up these agreements is also the fact that this was the only urban authority which was not bound to give a fixed contribution to the hospital but instead was free to send alms as it wished.
[21] Sentence carried on 17.1.1556 and Henry II's letter of 27.6.1556. Semeria, *Storia*, p. 283.

poor relief which culminated in the 1541 plan. The scheme should therefore be seen as an expression of the power of the civic government and of the secular and ecclesiastical elites represented in it.

However, the project did not only rely on the regular fixed payments which had been agreed with the religious authorities and the occupying forces. The entire citizenry was involved in making the plan work. Collection-boxes were supposed to be handed out to merchants and inn-keepers with instructions to request alms from the clients visiting their shops and inns. Larger collection-boxes were to be used in each of the four districts into which the city was divided. A citizen was to be entrusted with the collection-box and required 'to go every Saturday from house to house and from shop to shop, asking for alms for the poor. After a month he is to give the collection-box to his neighbour, and so on until everybody has done his turn.' A few days before the Christmas festivities, the governors were to make a further collection for the poor by visiting houses and shops, and at Easter, with the help of some of the more affluent citizens, they were supposed to go to various churches around the city, set up a table and request alms from passers-by. The poor, too, were employed in the process of raising funds for the scheme. A new kind of beggar was created who was authorised to beg on behalf of the hospital: an iron box was to be placed at the entrance to the more important churches, with the inscription 'Donations for the poor'; there was always supposed to be a certified pauper present, who would ask all the passers-by to contribute. Two other paupers from the hospital were authorised to beg once a week throughout the city. At harvest time, groups of poor people assisted by the hospital were repeatedly to visit the farms within the city's territory in order to collect donations of corn, wine and vegetables.

The plan to assist the poor and eliminate begging was therefore a community-wide initiative, and an expression of municipal self-government. The involvement of all the citizens, and not just the governors or the City Councillors, turned it into a civic enterprise. This aspect was ritually highlighted by the annual procession, which displayed to the citizens the results of all their efforts: on the eighth Sunday after Whitsun all the poor receiving relief, 'whether resident at the hospital or dependant on its charity', paraded through the streets of the city, two abreast, and divided into groups according to age and sex, 'the girls first and then the boys and men'.

In Turin the prohibition on begging was not accompanied by a ban on alms-giving, as occurred in some other cities. This was a matter on which there was a great deal of caution since such a ban could be resented by the Church: the argument that any restriction of voluntary charity was contrary to Christian doctrine as it limited the freedom to carry out acts of mercy had repeatedly been championed by churchmen in this period. In fact these reservations mainly reflected worries about harming the mendicant orders and those religious institutions which derived part of their income from the collection of alms.

Otherwise the Church was not at all against the policy of limiting charity to the deserving poor. The Sorbonne theologians, for example, when requested to give their opinion on the new schemes for poor relief, concluded that they were perfectly acceptable, but exempted the mendicant orders from the prohibition against begging.[22]

It seems likely that the compromise solution adopted in Turin was similar to those commonly adopted elsewhere: although provisions for relief did not outlaw almsgiving, they attempted indirectly to discourage face-to-face charity by arranging regular opportunities for giving to the deserving poor (i.e. those accepted by the centralised organisation of welfare), and thus directed the citizens' charitable impulses towards the municipal system of poor relief.

Radical solutions were also avoided with regard to taxation. Strictly speaking, no taxes for the support of the poor were levied on the citizens of Turin, as they were in a number of other towns. However, a sort of obligation to contribute to the city's scheme was established, due to the continuous pressure exerted on citizens. Again, this was the most common strategy adopted at the time, since there was strong resistance to any attempt to impose compulsory poor-rates.[23] Where there was compulsion, it was usually limited to crisis years. In some localities a compromise was reached by which the citizens were required to register the amount of money they were willing to give.[24] Failure to pay the rate they had committed themselves to could result in prosecution. It is possible that such a system was at work in Turin too at this early date, although no documentation of this practice survives for the mid sixteenth century. Certainly this kind of voluntary self-taxation for the poor was endorsed by the City Council at the end of the century, as we will see further on, and was still in force a hundred years later.

The comprehensive plan for poor relief drawn up in 1541 thus relied not only on a well consolidated civic authority but also on a widely accepted civic ideology which stressed citizens' obligations towards their own poor and urged them to involve themselves practically and financially in the implementation of the scheme. The combination of these two factors made the project work: for it did not remain simply on paper but was put into practice up until the late 1560s,

---

[22] B. Geremek, 'La réforme de l'assistance publique au XVIème siècle et ses controverses idéologiques' in *Domanda e Consumi Livelli e Strutture (nei secoli XIII–XVIII)*, Florence 1978.

[23] There was similar resistance to early attempts to introduce poor rates in England, which in some cases continued after the Elizabethan Poor Law came into force. P. Slack, *Poverty and Policy*, pp. 125–8.

[24] For example, a tax was imposed in Venice from March to August of 1528, in order to deal with the emergency caused by famine and plague. Pullan, *Rich and Poor*, pp. 247 and 251. Examples of temporary taxation have also been noted in France, in Abbéville, Poitiers, Dole and Nantes; while more regular impositions of poor-rates (although the exact amount to be paid normally remained voluntary) were found in Limoges, Angers, Nîmes, Orleans, Avignon, Lectoure and in Paris from 1525. Fosseyeux, 'La taxe'.

when action towards the poor took on new characteristics, as we will see in the next chapter. For about three decades, therefore, the hospital of S. Giovanni continued to care for the poor along the guidelines established in 1541. In the absence of direct sources on the hospital's activity, figures for the consumption of victuals give some idea of the scale and nature of the relief provided. The complete series of accounts in the period 1541 to 1549, and the fragmentary information available for the following two decades, shows high expenditure on bread: it appears that the institution consumed between 325 and 429 *sacchi* of wheat every year, which enabled the governors to distribute as charity up to 84,000 pounds of bread (an average of 230 pounds per day) 'both inside and outside the hospital'.[25] This represented a substantial quantity of food for a city which at that time had not reached a population of 15,000 (table 1). Although we do not know how much of this food was consumed in the hospital and how much was given to the poor outside in the weekly distributions of bread, there can be no doubt that outdoor relief figured very prominently in the charitable activity of the hospital, given the modest size of the institution. Again we do not possess definite information about the number of those assisted within the hospital but some indication can be obtained from the consumption of wine: this stayed at a very stable 32–34 *carre* per year, which is equivalent to about 45 litres a day. Given that the staff numbered about ten, and that there was always a significant number of foundlings living in the hospital, following their return from wet-nurses, we can reasonably assume that there were no more than a couple of dozen patients.[26] A substantial amount of the bread consumed by the hospital thus went to relieve the poor outside.

The financial arrangements contained in the 1541 plan also continued to be honoured in the years that followed: the lists of receipts record the arrival of wheat, wine and firewood from the various institutions and authorities committed to maintaining the hospital. Even the Savoy ducal family had to accept the existing system after it regained its territories in 1563. Shortly after his return to Turin, the Duke was asked to specify what his contribution to poor relief would be, and in 1566 an agreement was reached which committed him to making a yearly payment of 30 *scudi* to the hospital. Six years later, following complaints by the governors about the continuing failure of the Duke to meet the undertaking, this was guaranteed by linking it to the excise duty on meat, and by having it paid directly by the tax collectors involved.[27]

---

[25] AOSG, Cat.11, 'Protocollum aliquot instrumentum 1541–1589'. After 1549, the accounts only record receipts on a daily and no longer on an annual basis. However, the partial information available after this date suggests that there were no drastic changes in consumption.

[26] In wine-producing regions such as Piedmont wine was one of the main constituents of the diet amongst the lower classes. Consumption of a litre a day was common also for those assisted in charitable institutions, as later regulations reveal.

[27] Caffaratto, *L'Ospedale*, pp. 18–19.

The fact that the Council was the force pressing for the financing of poor relief even after the return of the House of Savoy is particularly interesting because it casts doubt on the long-prevailing view which sees the central government, if not the Duke in person, as the main agent of social policy, and largely ignores the contribution made by other political forces. The local nature of initiatives for poor relief does not, incidentally, seem to be a peculiarity of Turin, but seems to characterise the entire wave of activity and concern for the poor that spread across European cities in the early sixteenth century. Even the body of provisions that eventually constituted the Elizabethan Poor Law issued in 1598–1601 was not the outcome of a reorganisation of poor relief emanating from central authority, but rather the product of a long interaction between experimentation at the local level and legislation.[28] This close connection between sixteenth-century plans for poor relief and municipal governments with their civic ideology has not received sufficient attention in the various arguments which have sought to explain the origins of these initiatives.

New methods and conceptions of poor relief?

The idea that a profound reorganisation of the welfare system was brought about as a result of urban schemes in the sixteenth century has for long been a leitmotiv in the historiography of poor relief. As I have already mentioned, these plans are seen as having introduced a twofold reform, consisting of the removal of poor relief from the control of the Church and of a break with the traditional Christian view of the poor. Various arguments have been put forward to support the idea that measures for the poor which were adopted in the towns of sixteenth-century Europe represented a break with the past. One of the most widespread has linked their appearance to the Protestant ethic and therefore to the teaching of the Reformation.[29] This connection between religious doctrine and poor relief policy was first suggested in Germany towards the end of the last century, and was explored again in the interpretations of the history of welfare which developed within the English and German Christian-socialist circles in the second and third decades of this century.[30] Already in this period, however,

---

[28] For an emphasis on the local precedents of legislation on poor relief see McIntosh, 'Local responses'. For the classic view from above, G. R. Elton, 'An early Tudor poor law', *EcHR*, 6 (1953).

[29] On this debate Pullan, *Rich and Poor*, pp. 11–13, 197–200; B. Geremek, *La Pietà e la Forca: Storia della Miseria e della Carità in Europa*, Bari 1986, pp. XIV–XVII; Grimm, 'Luther's contributions'.

[30] E. Troeltsch, *The Social Teaching of the Christian Churches*, London and New York, 1931 (German edition 1911); R. H. Tawney, *Religion and the Rise of Capitalism*, London 1926. See also B. and S. Webb, *English Poor Law History*, part I, *The Old Poor Law*, London 1929.

Belgian historians, adopting a more pragmatic approach, were able to undermine the idea that different models of charity operated in Catholic and Protestant countries.[31] They showed that municipal relief plans similar to those introduced in reformed German towns in the 1520s had been formulated in the same period in the Catholic Low Countries, quite independently of the German experience. Though accepting the idea of a sixteenth-century reorganisation of poor relief, these historians argued that it took place as a result of developments in economic relations, and in particular of the capitalist ethos and humanist culture that inspired the new urban mercantile bourgeoisie.[32] The case for Christian humanism inspired by Erasmian ideas being the moving force behind the sixteenth-century reform of poor relief has been argued with renewed vigour in more recent studies, and rests in part on changed approaches to the Reformation, the purely 'heretical' view having given way to an emphasis on the call for spiritual renewal from within the Catholic world itself both before and in parallel with Luther's preaching.[33]

The significance of the part played by humanist teachings should not however be overstated. For instance, the key role usually ascribed to Juan Luis Vives' pamphlet *De Subventione Pauperum* in inspiring the European welfare reform movement needs to be put into perspective: it was published only after the city of Ypres' famous provisions, which have long been seen as constituting a pioneering urban relief scheme.[34] Moreover, important precedents to this plan can be found in the Low Countries and elsewhere in the previous two centuries.[35] Humanist views certainly created an ideological context favourable to the formulation of a more sophisticated policy but to say that they revolutionised attitudes to the poor is an exaggeration. A similar criticism can be made of another approach that has become dominant in recent years. According to this view it is economic and demographic circumstances and their social consequences which should be seen as the real causes

---

[31] More recently, this view has been fully discredited by B. Pullan, 'Catholics and the poor in early modern Europe', in *TRHS*, 26 (1976). A recent study on Geneva provides new evidence for comparison: J. E. Olson, *Calvin and Social Welfare. Deacons and the Bourse Française*, London 1989.

[32] Nolf, *La Réforme*; Bonenfant 'Les origines'; Pirenne, *Histoire*, pp. 273–80.

[33] In particular Davis 'Poor relief'; M. Todd, *Christian Humanism and the Puritan Social Order*, Cambridge 1987; and, for a survey of old and new approaches to this period of religious history, A. Jacobson-Schutte, 'Periodization of sixteenth century Italian religious history: the post-Cantimori paradigm shift', *JMH*, 61 (1989).

[34] M. Bataillon, 'Juan Luis Vives, réformateur de la bienfaisance', *Bibliothèque d'Humanisme et Renaissance*, 14 (1952). The *De Subventione Pauperum* originally appeared in Latin (Bruges, 1526), and was subsequently translated into German (Strasbourg 1533), Dutch (1533) and Italian (Venice 1545). C. G. Norena, *Juan Luis Vives*, The Hague 1970, p. 302.

[35] Nolf, *La Réforme*; Bonenfant, 'Les origines'; W. P. Blockmans and W. Prevenier, 'Poverty in Flanders and Brabant from the fourteenth to the mid-sixteenth century: sources and problems', *AHN*, 10 (1978); Fosseyeux, 'La taxe' and, for Southern France, *Assistance et Charité*, *Cahiers de Fanjeux* 13, Toulouse 1978.

of the sixteenth-century shake-up in ideas and policies for dealing with the poor.[36] Certainly population growth and pressure on resources in the sixteenth century, together with the devastation caused by war, famines and epidemics – and the consequent explosion of begging, vagrancy and crime – encouraged a harshening of attitudes towards the poor. But these factors fail to provide a precise chronology for the emergence of specific provisions: it has been noted, for instance, that in Venice the adoption of measures against famine preceded demographic growth and immigration.[37]

The very idea that there was in fact such a radical reform of welfare in this period becomes tenuous if the measures adopted in the sixteenth century are compared with those enforced in the previous period. On the whole, however, such comparisons have been avoided, even though there has long existed a substantial body of literature on late medieval welfare which points to significant areas of continuity between earlier and later centuries. With regard to the French situation for example, nineteenth-century historians had already shed light on the efforts made in the late thirteenth and in the fourteenth century by local authorities (*échevins* and canons of the cathedral chapters) to create permanent and organised welfare systems. In many French as well as Dutch towns, *tables des pauvres* or *tables du Saint Esprit* were set up to centralise alms and charitable revenues, and to provide shelter, pensions and medical treatment for the various categories of worthy poor living in the parish or neighbourhood.[38] More recently, Belgian historians have been able to document extensive municipal and parish welfare systems operating in the main centres of Flanders and Brabant from 1300. These relief structures, which operated via regular distributions of food, clothing, footwear and firewood, and provided home medical assistance, represented a not inconsiderable resource for the local poor.[39]

It emerges from these and other studies that many of the features that were supposedly introduced in the sixteenth century were already characteristic of the charitable practices of late medieval society. In the first place, it appears that medieval charity too was selective. Since the fourteenth century in particular, provisions for controlling begging, the inspection of the poor, and the issuing of badges or tokens to licensed beggars had become common practice in most

[36] For examples of this approach, Lis and Soly, *Poverty and Capitalism*; Geremek, *La Pietà*; this line of interpretation is particularly common in English studies on which see Slack, *Poverty and Policy*, in particular pp. 46–9, 54–5.

[37] B. Pullan, 'The famine in Venice and the new Poor Law 1527–1529', *BISSSV*, vols. 5–6 (1963–64).

[38] See the studies referred to in Fosseyeux, 'La taxe'. These structures often evolved into the sixteenth century *bureaux des pauvres* or *aumônes générales*. See also A. Vauchez, 'Assistance et charité en Occident XIII–XV siècles' in *Domanda e Consumi*.

[39] Blockmans and Prevenier, 'Poverty'.

of Europe.[40] It also emerges that the involvement of secular authorities in charitable initiatives was already widespread. They were responsible for setting up the network of hospitals and almshouses that had sprung up all over medieval Europe, albeit at different times, between the twelfth and fourteenth centuries.[41] Equally, the volume of poor relief provided by lay confraternities should not be underestimated. In Italy and France the growth of these organisations reached its peak in the fourteenth century, while in England this probably occurred a century later.[42] Often, their charitable activities were restricted to providing relief to their own members and their families, and to ritual distributions of food (particularly in association with religious events, or during times of famine). But there are important examples of some of the larger confraternities being in charge of civic welfare, and giving assistance on a regular basis to those considered to be deserving cases.[43] Finally, the desire to rationalise and centralise the management and financing of poor relief cannot be seen as a sixteenth-century innovation. Examples of centralisation of charitable funds in the hands of bodies comparable to the French or Belgian *tables des pauvres* can be found already in the twelfth and the thirteenth centuries in Northern Italy, and somewhat later in England. These bodies administered holdings of land and livestock which had been gradually built up by bringing together legacies

[40] Vauchez, 'Assistance'; B. Tierney, *Medieval Poor Law: a Sketch of Canonical Theory and its Application in England*, Berkeley, Calif. 1959. In particular for the situation in England, Slack, *Poverty and Policy*, p. 22; for France and Belgium, Bonenfant, 'Les origines'; for German towns Grimm, 'Luther's contributions'; for Spain, Martz, *Poverty and Welfare*, p. 12. On token issued by Italian confraternities W. J. Courtenay, 'Token coinage and the administration of poor relief during the late middle ages', *JIH*, 3 (1972–73).

[41] J. Imbert, *Les Hôpitaux en Droit Canonique*, Paris 1947, pp. 58–66; E. Nasalli Rocca, *Il Diritto Ospedaliero nei suoi Lineamenti Storici*, Milano 1956; P. Bonenfant, *Hôpitaux et Bienfaisance dans les Anciens Pays-Bas des Origines à la Fin du XVIIIe Siècle*, Bruxelles 1965, pp. 13–32; M. Rubin, 'Development and change in English hospitals, 1100–1500', in L. Granshaw and R. Porter (eds.), *The Hospital in History*, London 1989, pp. 46–7, 54–6. For a comparative overview, P. Horden, 'A discipline of relevance: the historiography of the later medieval hospital', *SHM*, 1 (1988).

[42] The literature on confraternities is now vast. For an overall view see A. Vauchez, 'Les confréries au moyen age: esquisse d'un bilan historiographique', in *Les Laics au Moyen Age. Pratiques et Expériences Religieuses*, Paris 1987. On Italy R. Rusconi 'Confraternite compagnie e devozioni', in G. Chittolini and G. Miccoli (eds.), *Storia d'Italia, Annali 9, La Chiesa e il Potere Politico*, Turin 1986. On England, C. M. Baron, 'The parish fraternities of medieval London', in C. M. Baron and C. Harper-Bill (eds.), *The Church in Pre-Reformation Society: Essays in Honour of F. R. H. Du Boulay*, Suffolk 1985; G. Rossen, 'Communities of parish and guild in the late Middle Ages', in S. Wright, *Parish, Church and People. Local Studies in Lay Religion 1350–1750*, London 1988.

[43] To date, the Florentine case is the best known example in this regard. See C. M. De la Roncière, 'Pauvres et pauvreté à Florence au XIVe siècle', in M. Mollat (ed.), *Etudes sur l'Histoire de la Pauvreté*, Paris 1974, vol. II, pp. 691–5, 714–22; J. Henderson, 'Piety and charity in late medieval Florence: religious confraternities from the middle of the thirteenth century to the late fifteenth century', unpublished Ph.D. dissertation, Westfield College, University of London 1983, J. R. Banker, *Death in the Community: Memorialization and Confraternities in an Italian Commune in the Late Middle Ages*, Athens and London 1988.

and donations. The purpose was to create a regular income to distribute to the poor belonging to the community.[44] An important example of centralisation (to which we will return later) was brought about by the unification of the small medieval hospitals, thus creating larger and more functional institutions to deal with the sick. This phenomenon, which is particularly well documented for the cities of Northern Italy, predates by nearly a hundred years the kinds of re-organisation of charity which were to take place in the sixteenth century.[45]

Even though there is now a considerable body of research into medieval poor relief, there is still considerable reluctance to follow through the implications of its findings and thereby modify our understanding of early modern systems of poor relief. In the periodisation of welfare history the theory of a radical shift from medieval forms of charity to the forms of relief adopted in the early modern period persists. Why has this interpretation proved so resistant?

It is possible that some part at least has been played by the contemporary arguments over proposals for dealing with the poor. Historians may have accepted these controversies at face value, believing the clamour that accompanied the anti-begging policies to be proof of their innovative nature. It is well known that during the 1520s and 1530s, urban plans for poor relief became the object of wide debate and theological dispute. In 1531, theologians at the Sorbonne scrutinised the scheme for poor relief enacted by the city of Ypres, to check that it conformed to Christian doctrine. Vives' *De subventione pauperum*, which was to be seen as the ideological manifesto of poor relief 'reform', also aroused criticism and misgivings. It was discussed by Cellarius and Jacques De Paepe at Louvain University and elsewhere; but, on the whole, the comments were favourable and the threat to declare it heretical never materialised.[46] Vives had intentionally made his pamphlet doctrinally water-tight, taking 'every possible precaution' (as he confided in a letter to his friend Cranevelt) to avoid linking the problem of begging in general to that of monastic begging – aware as he was of how explosive the issue could be in that particular period.[47] The polemic over measures towards begging broke out with more violence in Spain, in the dispute between the Dominican friar De Soto and

[44] In Piedmont and in Savoy these properties were known as *beni di Santo Spirito*. P. Duparc, 'Confréries du Saint Esprit et communautés d'habitants au moyen-âge', *Revue d'Histoire du Droit Français et Etranger*, s.4, vol. 35 (1958); F. Bernard, 'Les confréries communales du Saint-Esprit, leur lieux de réunions et leurs activités du Xe au XXe siècle dans la région Savoie Dauphiné', *Mémoires de l'Academie des Sciences, Belles-Lettres et Arts de la Savoie*, s.6, 7 (1963); Erba, *La Chiesa*, p. 237. For the English case, McIntosh, 'Local responses'.

[45] Nasalli Rocca, *Il Diritto*, pp. 81–9.

[46] C. Cellario, *Oratio Contra Mendicitatem Pro Nova Pauperum Subventione*, Louvain 1531. On the dispute over Vives' work and other fifteenth-century welfare plans see Geremek, *La Pietà*, pp. 196–210; Martz, *Poverty and Welfare*, pp. 22–30; Flynn, *Sacred Charity*, pp. 94–102.

[47] Vives was afraid he might be reported by the Franciscan Nicolas De Bureau, vicar to the Bishop of Tournai, who had accused him of Lutheranism. The quotation from the letter to Cranevelt is taken from Bataillon's 'Jean Luis Vives', p. 143.

the Benedictine Juan De Robles (or De Medina), in Lyon in the hostility of the
Dominican inquisitor, Nicolas Morin, towards the priest Jean de Vauzelles who
supported the civic plan for poor relief, and in Bruges where, as late as 1560, the
Augustinian Lorenzo de Villavincencio attacked Wyts' pamphlet on welfare.[48]

We must however ask what these polemics were really about, whether the
violent reactions to the civic relief plans really reflected a clash between
traditional views of charity and innovative proposals, or whether they had a
metaphorical significance. In the turbulent climate of the early sixteenth century
– created, as has been pointed out, not only by Luther's attacks on religious
conventionality, but also by evangelical and reformist tendencies within
Catholicism itself – attitudes to begging took on the value of symbolic stands on
the burning issues of the day (namely the autonomy of the mendicant orders and
the patrimony and authority of the Church). Controversy over the first issue
was already dividing the Catholic world at this time and the emergence of
ambivalent attitudes towards the mendicant orders certainly predates Luther's
attack on them. The renewed growth of monastic radicalism, asceticism and
itinerant preaching was the cause of the growing hostility which was to affect
both ecclesiastical and secular authorities. At the beginning of the sixteenth
century, the governments of Venice and other Italian cities were already
manifesting their impatience with the number of religious orders that were
springing up, complaining about the conflicts between the various orders and
about their increasing influence on local politics.[49] The cities were already
trying therefore to contain the expansion of this ungovernable force. Not by
chance did the policy enforced later in the century by the Council of Trent aim
at confining the orders within the monasteries. Indeed, it actually succeeded in
imposing strict seclusion on tertiary orders and nuns, and made missions and
sojourns in the outside world subject to the issuing of special permits ('licentia
extra standi'). In spite of the declared intention of encouraging the monastic
vocation, the Tridentine directives introduced restrictions on recruitment which
were aimed at containing the expansion of the orders and cooling the fervour for
evangelical beliefs and absolute poverty.[50]

Secondly, the clear formulation of non-ecclesiastical control over poor relief
embodied by the civic plans of the sixteenth century, although not in itself new,
had alarming implications given the particular moment. This was the period in

[48] J. de Medina, *De la Orden qu en Alqunos Pueblos de Espana se ha Puesto en la Limosina: Para Rimedio de los Verdadores Pobres*, Salamanca 1545; D. de Soto, *Deliberación en la Causa de los Pobres*, Salamanca 1545; L. de Villavincencio, *De Oeconomia Sacra circa Pauperum Curam*, Anvers 1564; G. Wyts, *De Continendis et Alendis Domi Pauperibus et in Ordinem Redigendis Validis Mendicantibus*, Anvers 1562.

[49] G. Zarri, 'Aspetti dello sviluppo degli ordini religiosi in Italia tra '400 e '500. Studi e problemi', in P. Prodi and P. Johanek (eds.), *Strutture Ecclesiastiche in Italia e Germania prima della Riforma*, Bologna 1984, in particular p. 207.

[50] Ibid., pp. 214–15.

which the Roman Church was attempting to establish its control over local ecclesiastical authorities and to regain its usurped estate. As a consequence, the conflicts between central and local Church figures, and between city or state governments and the papacy, became particularly acute.[51] In this context, provisions made by the cities to deal with the poor, which in the Middle Ages had been regarded simply as measures to preserve public order, or as famine prevention, now appeared to be questioning the extent of Church authority and jurisdiction. The controversy which came to surround provision against begging in the sixteenth century should not be taken literally, as the result of a merely doctrinal dispute, but as an expression of the struggle which at the time saw secular and religious powers, mendicant orders and ecclesiastical and secular authorities, locked in conflict with each other.

A secularisation of charity?

The idea that a radical reform of welfare took place in the sixteenth century was originally formulated in the context of the belief that Church institutions underwent impoverishment and degeneration in the late Middle Ages.[52] This financial and moral decadence is also supposed to have affected the institutions responsible for poor relief which were presumed to be under the control of the Church. According to the established view, it was inefficiency and corruption in the administration of charity that forced the secular authorities to take action. Indeed, it is usually maintained that because of a general break-down in the organisational structure of the Church and because of the moral decadence of the clergy, hospitals and other charitable institutions almost ceased to carry out the welfare duties they had originally been given. Charities are thought to have fallen victim to voracious administrators, often belonging to the clergy, who diverted revenues to their own orders or even for personal or family gain. Under increasing pressure from the growth of poverty, the secular forces (civic authorities or groups of leading citizens) are then said to have taken over responsibility for poor relief, removing the existing hospitals from Church control and founding new institutions. This is thought to have heralded a brief period of secular control over welfare organisation before the Council of Trent reasserted the Church's charitable mission in Catholic countries, prompting a revival of Catholic initiative and the proliferation of provisions for the poor in the Counter-Reformation age.

[51] G. Chittolini, 'Stati regionali e istituzioni ecclesiastiche nell'Italia centro-settentrionale del Quattrocento', in *Storia d'Italia, Annali 9*.
[52] As an example of this widespread view, see the influential work of G. Le Bras, *Histoire du Droit et des Institutions de l'Eglise en Occident*, vol. I, *Prolégòmenes*, Paris 1955, pp. 162–4; also J. Imbert, 'L'Eglise et l'Etat face au problème de l'assistance', in *Etudes d'Histoire du Droit Canonique dédiées a G. Le Bras*, T.I, Paris 1965.

The image of a crisis-ridden Church at the end of the medieval period was long accepted among historians.[53] The predominance of this view helps to explain why both Catholic and secular historians have vigorously supported the thesis of a reorganisation and secularisation of poor relief in the sixteenth century.[54] Only in the last twenty years has such a stereotype been questioned. Renewed interest in religious life in the late Middle Ages has also undermined the simplistic image of widespread stagnation and corruption and encouraged study of poor relief activity in this period. Indeed, this very period from the late fourteenth to the beginning of the sixteenth century is now seen as an age of considerable religious vitality. While it is true that ecclesiastical authorities were troubled by serious economic and organisational problems, and that the papacy, undermined by the Great Schism, lacked direction, this was also a period in which religious initiative found new expressions. The laity took on a more active role in religious life, and there was an extraordinary expansion of pious organisations (in the form of companies of penitents, confraternities and prayer groups).[55] Indeed it has been said that this was the golden era for lay piety and religious activity.[56] But much was also happening inside the Church; at the same time as ancient orders were falling into decay, new orders were being founded in the fifteenth century, especially mendicant orders coming out of the observant movement.[57] So while it is important to emphasise the contribution made by the laity in the spread of religious awareness in the late Middle Ages, one should not exaggerate the gap between lay religious experience and the activity of ecclesiastical institutions. At the local level religious initiatives were often the product of intermingling between laity and clergy, between political and religious power, which makes it difficult clearly to distinguish the sphere of the Church from that of temporal authorities. One of the most useful contributions that recent developments in religious history have offered to historians of poor relief is the removal of an over-sharp distinction between secular and ecclesiastical domains.

Groups of layfolk and secular institutions encouraged and financed the establishment of new orders and the building of churches and monasteries. They controlled nominations to ecclesiastical positions and associated benefices in the locality, often right up to the level of bishop or archbishop. The links between political and ecclesiastical power were often made even closer by family ties, for

---

[53] The theme can still be found in recent literature, for instance M. Carlin, 'Medieval English hospitals', in L. Granshaw and R. Porter (eds.), *The Hospital in History*, London 1989.

[54] Compare, for example, the works of the secular historian Bloch and the Catholic Lallemand: Bloch, *L'Assistance*, pp. 39–46; L. Lallemand, *Histoire de la Charité*, vol. IV, Paris 1906, pp. 1–29.

[55] For an overview, Prodi and Johanek (eds.), *Strutture*. On the confraternities, G. G. Meersseman, *Ordo Fraternitatis: Confraternite e Pietà dei Laici nel Medioevo*, Rome 1977.

[56] Vauchez, *Les Laics*, 'Avant-propos'.

[57] Zarri, 'Aspetti'.

the majority of the city's ecclesiastical authorities came from the local patriciate – particularly the canons who made up the influential metropolitan chapters. This allowed the most prominent families not only to consolidate their power but also to control much of the Church's property. Up until the Council of Trent (whose directives were aimed at changing the bishops into real representatives of papal policy), a bishop was often a distant figure who did not set foot in his diocese. Bishops who were active and well-versed in local politics were mainly to be found in the cities where canons still maintained their ancient rights to nominate the bishop.[58]

Initially, it was thought that this situation in which local power was unchallenged in its leadership of a city's religious life was mainly a character-istic of those cities of Northern and Central Italy where the independent tradition of medieval communes and city-states was strongest. Recent studies, however, show that symbiosis between political power and religious initiative – or 'civic religion', as it has come to be known – was not only a vestige of the period of the *comuni*; it received a further impetus between the late fourteenth and the early sixteenth centuries due to the weakness of the Church's central authority.[59] In the late medieval period, religion increasingly became an aspect of local politics. Princes, powerful clans and factions, and especially municipal governments instigated campaigns to defend Christian morals or to attack heretics and set themselves up as the upholders of the faith and religious precepts. They guided the reform of the Church through their support for observant movements, oversaw the reform of life within the religious com-munities, and encouraged confraternities and the establishment of new devotional cults. The ideological purpose of these initiatives was to reassert the autonomy and unity of the 'civitas', and therefore the legitimacy of the municipal authorities. But religious initiatives were also used in the struggle for influence and prestige. In the fifteenth century in particular, private interests expanded their control over rights of patronage and over appointment to the main ecclesiastical positions in parishes, abbeys and monasteries. Private religious foundations multiplied to such an extent that large religious buildings like cathedrals and convents were to be divided by the most powerful families into their personal chapels and cells.[60]

Increased religious awareness was also accompanied by greater interest in

[58] G. Miccoli, 'La storia religiosa', in *Storia d'Italia*, part II, vol. I, Turin 1974; S. Bertelli, *Il Potere Politico nello Stato-Città Medievale*, Florence 1978; G. Chittolini, 'Stati'.

[59] L. Donvito, 'La "religione cittadina" e le nuove prospettive sul Cinquecento religioso italiano', in *RSLR*, 19 (1983). On civic religion in the communal period see M. Orselli, 'Vita religiosa nella città medievale italiana tra dimensione ecclesiastica e "cristianesimo civico". Una esemplificazione', in *AIIGT*, 7 (1981); M. Ronzani, 'La "chiesa del comune" a Pisa nel '200–300', in G. Rossetti (ed.), *Spazio, Società, Potere nell'Italia dei Comuni*, Naples 1989.

[60] Donvito 'La "religione cittadina"'; Chittolini, 'Stati'; G. Zarri, 'Monasteri femminili e città (sec.XV–XVIII)', in *Storia d'Italia. Annali 9*.

charitable activities. In particular there was a wave of reform of existing institutions; the composition of their administrative bodies was altered, management regulations were reorganised and funds which had originally been intended for assisting the poor, but which had fallen into private hands, were recovered. One of the better known results of this religious and charitable activity was the unification of several smaller hospitals founded in the twelfth or thirteenth centuries into one larger and richer hospital (often called *ospedale maggiore*). However, this was not the only form of welfare reorganisation taking place in this period. In fifteenth-century Italy there are various examples of ancient confraternities and other sorts of charitable funds being brought together in order to finance systems of outdoor relief. In Mantua, for example, revenues for the poor had already been centralised by the beginning of the century, and entrusted to a Consorzio di cittadini (whose members were appointed by the town council) which examined and assisted the poor district by district.[61] Scholarly attention, however, has so far concentrated on fifteenth-century unification of hospitals. Between the 1430s and the beginning of the following century, this phenomenon affected most of the cities of Northern Italy. The amalgamation of medieval hospitals took place in Cuneo (1437), Casale (1440), Turin (1440), Brescia (1447), Mantua (1450), Cremona (1451), Reggio Emilia (1453), Milan, Bergamo and Lodi (all in 1459), Como and Crema (both in 1468), Piacenza (1471), Genoa (1471), Parma (1472), Ferrara (1478), Novara (1482), Modena and Imola (both in 1488), Ravenna (1513).[62] In the majority of cases it was the municipal government that initiated the changes and took control of the new institution created through incorporation. The local ecclesiastical authorities often gave their full support, although on occasion the bishop could be extremely hostile. In any case, the bishop's attitude reflected his personal views and his relationship with the local Church and power groups, rather than any policy in relation to charitable action emanating from the papacy.[63]

Recent research into urban religious life in the late Middle Ages thus confirms the impression that provision for the poor adopted in the sixteenth century drew on a wealth of experiences in poor relief administration accumulated over the previous two centuries. These studies also cast doubt on the notion of a sixteenth-century secularisation of the management of charity. Far from being the monopoly of the Church, responsibility for poor relief was already shared to

---

[61] R. Navarrini and C. M. Belfanti, 'Il problema della povertà nel ducato di Mantova: aspetti istituzionali e problemi sociali (secoli XIV–XVI)', in Politi, Rosa, Della Peruta (eds.), *Timore*, in particular pp. 125, 130–1.

[62] Nasalli Rocca, *Il Diritto*; A. Pastore, 'Strutture assistenziali fra Chiesa e Stati nell'Italia della Controriforma', in *Storia d'Italia, Annali 9*. On the Milan case see Leverotti's fine analysis of the struggle between various temporal and religious authorities that led to the establishment of the *Ospedale Maggiore*. F. Leverotti, 'Ricerche sulle origini dell'Ospedale Maggiore di Milano', *ASL*, 107 (1984).

[63] Leverotti, 'Ricerche'.

a very considerable extent by layfolk and by secular authorities in the late medieval period.

Turin's 'civic religion' in the late Middle Ages

The picture of civic initiative in the field of religion and charity which has been observed in some of the late medieval Italian cities in general applies also to fourteenth- and fifteenth-century Turin. Unfortunately, there exist only very dated accounts of the city's social policy in this period. Tied to the traditional interpretation – according to which municipal power in Piedmontese towns was an expression of feudal relations rather than of the urban patriciate – these studies show a purely anecdotal interest in the activities of civic authorities and therefore provide very incomplete, and often indirect, information. Even from these sketchy accounts, however, a picture of 'civic religion' emerges which is very similar to that found in Italian cities which had stronger traditions of independence as medieval *comuni*.[64]

In Turin as elsewhere, therefore, there appear to be some important precedents to the 1541 municipal plan for poor relief. Certainly, this was not the first time that the city authorities had become involved in welfare matters. More than a century earlier, they had played a key role in carrying out the hospital reform, which after repeated attempts finally reached completion in 1440. This led to the incorporation of the ten hospitals situated on the city's perimeter into the hospital of Santa Maria del Duomo (later named hospital of S. Giovanni after the city's patron saint), situated in the very heart of the city, next to the cathedral. It is interesting to note, in passing, that the hospitals which were merged on this occasion originated in lay initiative: they had been founded in the twelfth and thirteenth centuries by single families or groups of affluent citizens and entrusted to religious orders or, less often, to keepers appointed by the benefactors.[65] In the

---

[64] Unless it is stated otherwise the following pages are based on the information found in Ferrero di Lavriano, *Istoria*; Semeria, *Storia*; T. Rossi and F. Gabotto, *Storia di Torino, BSSS*, 82 (1914); Grosso and Mellano, *La Controriforma*.

[65] The hospitals involved were as follows: S. Dalmazzo run by the friars of S. Antonio; S. Biagio which was founded by four citizens in 1208 and which benefited from further private donations in 1226 and 1228 – this was run by the order of the Crociferi; S. Cristoforo founded in 1244 by the citizen Giovanni Cane and run by the Umiliati; the Maddalena founded by the Arpini family in 1196 and run by the canons of Rivalta; S. Giacomo di Stura founded in 1146 by two citizens and later enriched by new donations by Ardizzone Borgesio and Uberto Caccia (1214 and 1244), run by the Vallombrosani; S. Severo and S. Brigida run by the Templars and later by the knights of Jerusalem; S. Andrea run by the Benedictines; Santa Maria del Duomo reputed to have been founded by a canon of the cathedral; Santa Maria di Pozzo Strada; S. Lazzaro founded to assist lepers; S. Benedetto; S. Bernardo. See Semeria, *Storia*; G. Borghesio and C. Fasola 'Le carte dell'Archivio del Duomo di Torino (904–1300) con appendice 1301–1433', *BSSS*, vol. 106, 1931, pp. 50–2, 65–80, 107–8, 190–1; A. Cognasso, 'Cartario dell'abazia di San Solutore di Torino. Appendice di carte varie relative a chiese e monasteri di Torino', *BSSS*, vol. 44 (1908), pp. 299–308.

second half of the fourteenth century, when the City Council started to campaign for hospital reform, most of the religious orders had fallen into decay, the families of the original benefactors had died out and – so the municipal officials complained – the hospitals had fallen into the hands of corrupt administrators. A further strain was put on the system by population increase, which was quickly making up for the losses of the Black Death, and by the migration which occurred during this phase of revival.[66] The hospitals, which were generally very small and in a state of disrepair, had become totally ineffective. These were the arguments (very similar to those generally employed in such cases of incorporation) that the City authorities put to the bishop, who held formal jurisdiction over the hospitals. It is not possible to reconstruct the events in detail, but it would appear that the first move was the petition from the city authorities presented to Bishop Giovanni di Rivalta in 1378, in which they offered the co-operation of their own officials in a plan to reform the hospital administration. We do not know the outcome of this initiative, but in 1385 we find another appeal to the bishop by the City Council, which again refers to the bad management of the town's hospitals. Four years later the municipality proposed that the administration of the hospital of Santa Maria del Duomo be turned over to the lay confraternity of the Battuti and its accounts be regularly checked by a committee of canons and councillors. After considerable pressure from the City, the hospital reform was finally carried out in 1440 with the suppression of ten of the twelve existing hospitals. Their incomes were used to increase the funding of the hospital of Santa Maria (soon renamed hospital of S. Giovanni), which became the only institution for the sick continuing to operate within the city walls (outside the walls the hospital of S. Lazzaro continued to be run for skin diseases but for a short time only).

Lay involvement in welfare administration thus occurred well before the sixteenth century. It was not the 1541 agreement between the canons and the councillors on the administration of the hospital of S. Giovanni that led to the introduction of the laity into an area previously dominated by the clergy. The municipal authorities had had a role in the reorganisation of the city's welfare system in the fourteenth and fifteenth centuries and it may well be that they already played an active part in the administration of the two hospitals which remained after the amalgamation. It is significant for instance that in the message sent to the bishop thanking him for his cooperation in the reorganisation of the hospitals, the City defined itself as the 'patron' of the two resulting hospitals. In any case, the Council certainly controlled the

---

[66] In the plains of Piedmont there had been an 80 per cent increase in the number of hearths between 1420 and 1450 and this trend continued in the second half of the century. The growth of the Piedmontese population between 1415 and 1571 has been estimated at around 240 per cent. R. Comba, *La Popolazione del Piemonte sul Finire del Medio Evo. Ricerche di Demografia Storica*, Turin 1977, pp. 76–92.

management of charity on other occasions. In periods of famine, for example, it was the municipality which took emergency measures, approving and administering special provisions for the poor. Thus in 1375 the Council allocated 200 *fiorini* to finance a daily distribution of bread and wine to the poor. It also decreed that the confraternities should be obliged by the City officials to contribute to the scheme, as did the bishop who supplied money and grain.

It appears in any case difficult to make a clear distinction between the lay and the ecclesiastical administration of poor relief, given the markedly civic nature of the local church. The canons who administered the city hospital were mainly members of the leading patrician families, as in many cases was the bishop who formally held jurisdiction over the hospitals. Throughout the fifteenth century and for part of the sixteenth, the city chapter retained the right to nominate the bishop. In Turin we therefore find the classic situation of a shared identity between the local church and the urban ruling class, which seems to have been a typical feature of the late medieval city. This becomes particularly clear in the decades between 1483 and 1515, during which, for three generations, the diocesan seat was held by the Della Rovere family, one of the four most prominent families in the city. The outstanding position of these families was so obvious that it found symbolic recognition in the privilege of carrying the four poles that supported the canopy under which the consecrated host was kept during processions and major public ceremonies.

Such symbiosis between secular and ecclesiastical power was partly upset in the period between 1515 and 1563 when the archbishops were nominated by the pope. And in fact conflicts arose in this period between the absentee archbishops, who were principally interested in protecting and increasing their own revenues, and a City Council deeply involved in religious and welfare matters. The diocesan authority made itself heard only when money was involved: in 1550 for example, Archbishop Cesare Cibo refused to contribute towards the expenses incurred when the City Council invited preachers to give sermons against heresy in the city's churches. This conflict, like the refusal to finance the charitable activity of the hospital a few years later, ended in a judgement that obliged Cibo to pay.[67] Obviously the pope's appointees were not in the least interested in influencing religious life at the local level – a task which in any case was virtually impossible due to the number of benefices and dioceses that they had to govern – and control remained firmly in the hands of the municipality. In some cases, they would happily delegate the running of the diocese to a suffragan fully conversant with the

[67] Semeria, *Storia*, p. 283.

city's politics, reproducing in this way the traditional pattern of civic religion.[68]

The sermons against heresy mentioned above suggest that, in a number of domains, secular responsibility over religious matters extended further than that of the ecclesiastical authority. First of all, it appears that the confraternities were under the control of the City Council: this supervised the employment of their revenues and could force them to make special payments to the poor in times of food shortage. It was the municipal authority and not the archbishop that had taken control of the incomes of those extinct confraternities which, in 1541, the councillors were to incorporate into the hospital of S. Giovanni. More generally, the Council carried out the role of guardian of the faith and of religious orthodoxy much more vigorously than the Church authorities. It was the City Council that passed laws in 1421 to ensure that Sundays and religious holidays were respected, banning markets, the opening of shops, the baking of bread and grinding of corn on those days. The Council encouraged the introduction of new religious orders into the city, by providing them with a church and monastery or mediating with the bishop in order to obtain his protection;[69] and it repeatedly took up the struggle against heresy, not just by paying for preachers to campaign against heretics but also, as in 1561, by expelling priests who showed sympathy for heretical views. In the fifteenth century, the influence of the municipal authorities on the religious life of the city can also be seen in the successful introduction of the cult of Corpus Domini which in a very short time was transformed into a civic ritual and became the religious symbol of the city's unity and of its municipal power.[70] The origin of this cult was the miracle of the Host that occurred in Turin in June 1453. The event took place shortly after a battle with the French on the border between Piedmont and the Dauphinée where the Duke of Savoy had been trying to prevent the French from crossing into Italy to assist his enemy, the Duke of Milan.[71] During the plunder which ensued, a soldier stole a silver monstrance from the village church of Exilles but when, on the way to Lombardy, he arrived in Turin with his booty, the monstrance miraculously escaped from the bundle in which it was wrapped. The Host floated into the air where it remained suspended, emitting an intense light, above the heads of the crowd which had by then gathered. From

---

[68] For example, another Della Rovere was appointed by archbishop Innocenzo Cibo (uncle of Cesare) as his suffragan in the administration of the diocese. Cibo (who was the pope's nephew) was invested with various bishoprics and archbishoprics at the same time. In the thirty years that he was archbishop of Turin (1520–49) he never resided in the diocese.

[69] As in the case of the Capuchin friars for whom the City built the monastery of S. Maria del Monte in 1538, or that of the Minori Osservanti who were given the parish of S. Tommaso following the intercession of the Council in 1542.

[70] On the growth of the cult of the Corpus Domini in fifteenth century Italy and its characteristics of civic devotion see Rusconi, 'Confraternite', p. 479 on.

[71] Semeria, *Storia*, p. 245; Cibrario, *Storia di Torino*, p. 186.

that time on the Corpus Domini became the principal object of the citizens' worship.

Whatever the meaning of the miracle, it should be noted that this legendary event was immediately appropriated by the secular and ecclesiastical authorities of the city. According to legend, the miraculous Host was carried to the cathedral in a procession made up of the bishop, canons and most eminent citizens, but not, it should be stressed, of any representatives of the House of Savoy or of the court. A magnificent tabernacle was built to house it and soon the Councillors had a chapel erected for it in the cathedral. On this they lavished considerable attention, turning it into the most popular urban place of worship and the only one where the consecrated Host was always present. It was decided too that there should be an annual Corpus Domini procession in the month of June and this became the most important public event in the city's calendar. The City also created a fraternity of the same name which rapidly established itself as the religious association most favoured by the elite involved in urban government. This municipal cult was given new impetus in the following century when, in 1521, the Council built a separate chapel dedicated to the Corpus Domini on the spot where the miracle had taken place. In 1606 this was turned into a church as a votive offering following the end of the plague and the war which had oppressed the city in the closing years of the sixteenth century.

The information we have on this period, although patchy, clearly demonstrates the strength of Turin's municipal institutions in the late Middle Ages and the significant role that the Council played in directing and governing religious and charitable activities in the city. The welfare plan that was supported by the Council in 1541 – and which was the starting point for this chapter – did not represent a radical change of direction in the management of poor relief, but just one more expression of the tradition of municipal initiative in the City's social policies. These findings obviously clash with the long-prevailing tendency to see as incompatible the consolidation of an urban ruling class capable of having a significant impact on the organisation of city life and the persistence of feudal relations and seigneurial power in Turin. A challenge to this view, however, and support for the thesis that the municipal government was a key player in the social policy of the city, comes from Koenigsberger's work on the Piedmontese Parliament. This study – whose implications have been largely ignored – shows that municipal structures retained a very important role in Piedmont for much longer than they did in other Italian states.[72] Indeed, until 1560 Piedmont had an assembly of the three estates endowed with considerable powers (the Cismontane Council), while similar representative bodies had for long been suppressed in other Italian states since they were deemed incompatible with the

[72] H. J. Koenigsberger, 'The Parliament of Piedmont during the Renaissance, 1450–1560', in his *Essays in Early Modern European History*, Ithaca, N.Y. 1971.

growing despotism of the prince. It was a powerful body with a decisive voice in all the important decisions taken in the country; above all it carried out the delicate task of assessing the fiscal contributions to be made by each city and considering requests by the duke for special levies. Contrary to what one might expect, the nucleus of this assembly was made up of members of the urban elite, elected by the Town Councils, rather than by the feudal class.

The persistence of the assembly of the three estates and the lasting importance of its role are indicative not only of the weakness of the House of Savoy during this period ('a landowner among the others', in Koenigsberger's words) but also of the unexpectedly powerful part played by municipal governments in Piedmont. It is clear that considerable influence was exerted by an urban ruling class which, even though it controlled significant manufacturing industries in only a few cities, nevertheless derived substantial economic power and status from the control of trade in foodstuffs and from the direct possession of land in the city countryside.

Even the Italianisation of this state, which was for a long time more Savoyard than Piedmontese, and of its conspicuously 'French' overlords, began in response to pressures from the Piedmontese elites. In the 1490s, the Cismontane Council was involved in a lengthy tussle with the regent, demanding that it should have more representatives among the state officials – the majority of whom had hitherto been Savoyards – and that the exorbitant tax burden, which had until then fallen mainly on the 'Italian' territories, should be alleviated. These years of head-on conflict also marked the beginning of a more comprehensive shift of policy towards Italy on the part of the House of Savoy, traditionally more oriented towards France.[73] This change in direction, given its clearest expression in the promotion of Turin as the regular seat of the central administration, which, having been itinerant, was in these years gradually becoming fixed, was not to be abandoned and was resolutely pursued by subsequent Dukes, both in their domestic policy and in their expansionist foreign policy.[74] There is little doubt that the impact which the municipal government had on the history of Turin merits far greater attention than it has hitherto received. The authority of this body made itself felt not only in the late Middle Ages but also well after the restoration of the Dukes to their territories. When the House of Savoy regained its sovereignty over the territory in the mid sixteenth century, it found a capital with a long tradition of self-government – which, far from having been subdued by French rule, may even have been reinforced during the thirty years of foreign occupation.[75]

---

[73] Ibid., pp. 62–3.
[74] A. Barbero, 'Savoiardi e Piemontesi nel ducato sabaudo all'inizio del cinquecento. Un problema storiografico risolto?', *BSBS*, 87 (1989).
[75] Ibid., pp. 70–1; Barbero, 'Una città in ascesa', p. 320.

2

Civic charity in the age of state formation

The growth of municipal poor relief

Even those who have recognised the vitality of the local welfare systems which developed in late medieval towns hold that municipal control over poor relief ended in the sixteenth century. It is generally assumed that the formation of nation states had dire consequences for municipal autonomy. Allegedly, civic power (of which the organisation of local welfare was a manifestation) went into decline, as did the social and communal dimension which had characterised it and found expression in the intense devotional and charitable activities typical of Italian cities in the fifteenth century. The cities then lost control of poor relief, which increasingly became the responsibility of central government.[1] In fact, however, very little is known of what became of municipal systems of relief in the early modern period. Despite the existence of scattered evidence suggesting that municipal leadership over poor relief often lasted well beyond the sixteenth century, and even expanded in the following periods,[2] the fate of civic welfare systems has not been a focus of interest.

The study of sixteenth-century urban relief schemes has largely been motivated by a desire to test the influence of the Reformation on attitudes to the poor; hence investigation has been limited to the decades most affected by the spread of Protestantism, and has shown less concern for the subsequent evolution of local systems of charity.[3] On the other hand, studies of poor relief in the later period have had a completely different focus, for they concentrate heavily on the emergence of government schemes for the internment of the poor (of the type given clearest expression in the project for the French *hôpitaux généraux*), i.e. on the development of forms of intervention which centred on

---

[1] Donvito, 'La "religione cittadina"'.
[2] Fosseyeux, 'La taxe', pp. 411–12, 424; J. Imbert, 'La bourse des pauvres d'Aire-sur-la Lys à la fin de l'Ancien Régime', *Revue du Nord*, 34 (1952).
[3] Kingdon, 'Social welfare'; Pullan, 'Catholics'; Davis, 'Poor relief'; Jutte, 'Poor relief'; Martz, *Poverty and Welfare*.

institutions. As in the case of studies on Italy too, interest has focused on only one aspect of the policy towards the poor of the late sixteenth and seventeenth centuries – on the hospitals for beggars which became widespread throughout the country.[4] Locally managed forms of poor and medical relief, often provided outside the hospital, have been largely neglected. This approach reflects the prevailing tendency to see the state as an agency that suffocated previous centres of power. As a consequence of this view, more attention has been given to the policies of central government while the activities of civic administrations in the early modern period have been overlooked.

In this chapter I shall examine the changing patterns of the Turinese system of assistance to the poor in the period between the restoration of the House of Savoy (in 1563 in the wake of the French occupation) and the emergence, in the mid seventeenth century, of a welfare policy more heavily centred on institutions. I wish to focus, in other words, on the decades usually neglected by studies of poor relief. Analysis of this period produces several surprises in relation to the established view. First of all, it suggests that the consolidation of central power did not bring a decline, but rather an expansion, of the welfare system administered by the municipality. Secondly, it shows that this policy of expansion and improvement was aimed almost entirely at the growth of outdoor provision for the poor and sick, whereas municipal investment in institutionally based care and aid was very limited. For nearly a century into the first phase of state-formation, the welfare system operating in the city would remain municipally run, sustained by a strong civic ideology and characterised by non-institutional provision.

For decades after its reinstatement, the ducal government did not interfere in local social policy. Indeed, the City Council even strengthened its direct control over the organisation of poor relief and medical care in this period. Up to the late 1560s, provision for the poor was still centred on the hospital of S. Giovanni and managed by the governors according to guidelines which were established during the French occupation and officially laid down in 1541. However, over the following couple of decades, responsibility for the welfare of the poor was gradually removed from the (already largely municipally controlled) hospital to become more directly one of the tasks of the local authorities. As the City Council took over full control, resources for poor relief and the care of the sick expanded considerably. New services were created – such as a system of outdoor medical relief, which provided treatment at home and free medicines for those who lacked the means to obtain them. This system was built up between 1569

---

[4] B. Geremek, 'Renfermement des pauvres en Italie (XIV–XVIIe siècle). Remarques préliminaires', in *Mélanges en l'Honneur de Fernand Braudel. Histoire Economique et Sociale du Monde Méditerranéen 1450–1650*, vol. I, Toulouse 1973 and the studies surveyed in Rosa, 'Chiesa', and Pullan, 'Support and redeem'.

and 1587 and included provision for a doctor, a surgeon and an apothecary 'for the poor'. At the same time, the health and welfare system underwent a major administrative reorganisation and was divided into a large number of specially created departments subject to the management of specific officials. Many new positions were created for this purpose, and entrusted either to salaried officials or to City Councillors. From 1568 a *Cavaliere di virtù e polizia* (an officer for the protection of public morality and order) was hired, with the task of expelling from the city all beggars who did not qualify for assistance; for this purpose he was aided by a number of constables.[5] The position was not permanent, but was frequently renewed on those occasions, for example, when orders were issued to keep beggars away. A few years later, the census and classification of the poor – which up till then had always been carried out by the governors of the hospital of S. Giovanni – also passed into the hands of City officials. Initially this task was entrusted to the *Conservatori di sanità* (municipal Health Office), a body of Council officials created in 1577 with the principal aim of preventing and fighting epidemics, particularly the plague. Later, in 1586, the task of keeping records on all the poor living within a particular *cantone* (or *isola*) shifted to the City Councillors appointed to the new office of *Cantoniere*, each *Cantoniere* carrying out the census for the *cantoni* assigned to him.[6] The municipal authority also extended its control over the management of abandoned children who, after being brought to the hospital, were sent to wet nurses outside the city. The Council insisted on stricter controls over this activity and arranged that it should be supervised by a new body, also made up of City Councillors. This was the Foundlings Office (*Conservatori degli esposti*) which was established in 1585 and whose task it was to keep the accounts for wet-nursing, and visit the villages and towns where the wet-nurses lived to check for any abuses that might occur.[7]

At the same time, the Council reorganised the administration of those measures that dealt more directly with public health. This activity was undoubtedly given added impetus by the return of the plague to almost the entire Italian peninsula after fifty years of partial respite in which it had been restricted to a few localities (Turin's last serious outbreak had been in 1523). In 1577, when the news arrived that the plague had spread to neighbouring regions, it was decided – as was usually done in these circumstances – to appoint a *Visitatore dei cadaveri* (a corpse inspector) who looked into any suspicious deaths. But on this occasion the threat of plague also led to the creation of a health board – the *Conservatori di sanità* – which was to become a permanent body dealing with

---

[5] D., T. XIII, p. 248, *Lettere di Sua Altezza colle quali nomina un cavaliere di virtù e polizia con autorità di scacciarne gli oziosi mendicanti*, 5.4.1568.

[6] Ord., 21.8.1577, 10.9.1586. In 1592, there were 52 *Cantonieri*, ibid., 7.6.1592. For a description of *isole* see above, p. 8.

[7] Ibid., 14.11.1585.

routine provisions for sanitation in normal times as well. The number of
Conservatori (once again, City Councillors) sitting on this board varied from
five in normal times to twenty-five during epidemics. Although their regular
duties times are poorly documented, it seems that a series of public health
measures concerning slaughter-houses, street-cleaning, rubbish removal, drains,
the control of those who might carry infectious disease, etc. were adopted in this
period and that they remained in force after the plague had passed. For example,
a system of rubbish collection was organised between 1584 and 1588, and a new
official paid by the City, the *Soprastante alle strade* (a streets supervisor), was
placed in charge of workmen who removed the rubbish in large carts. This
official also had the duty of enforcing the municipal regulation requiring each
household to keep its own stretch of street clean. Households were required to
pay a tax to maintain the service, based on the amount of rubbish they produced,
and set by the City authorities.[8]

While it has been mainly anti-plague legislation which has interested, and
fascinated, historians, it should be realised that these years were also marked
by a growing concern for wider questions of public health. One major preoccupation was the threat of syphilis and an important task of the *Conservatori*
was in fact to combat its spread. On various occasions in the sixteenth century
the City engaged a *Visitatore delle meretrici* (Inspector of prostitutes), a surgeon
who was supposed to identify those prostitutes who had been infected with the
'French disease', and report them to the *Cavaliere di virtù* who would then see
to their expulsion.[9] The inspections and expulsions of prostitutes were applied
with increased vigour whenever it was felt there was any danger of plague, but
they were also enforced in other times, reflecting the concern over the harm
thought to be caused by these women who 'infected the youth and wrought their
perdition', leaving many 'crippled' and forcing the City to pay for their treatment in the hospital.[10] The extent of this concern is also attested by other sources:
from a petition presented to the Council by the hospital governors in 1598, in
which permission was requested to sell property in order to construct a larger
building, we learn that most of the patients in the institution were suffering from
'French disease'.[11]

The years between 1568 and 1588 were thus crucial in Turin for the
emergence of a body of civic legislation concerning public health, welfare and
public order. These provisions were formally set down in the *Ordini politici*
(municipal regulations governing almost every aspect of city life) which were
first published in 1573, and republished on several successive occasions with

---

[8] Ibid., 8.3.1584, 22.2.1588, 21.9.1588, 29.1.1589.
[9] Ibid., 21.8.1577, 29.9.1591, 1.3.1602; ACT, C.S. 4834, 16.8.1588.
[10] D., T. XII, p. 248, 5.4.1568.
[11] Ord. 20.4.1598.

minor amendments.[12] Even though we cannot rule out the idea that similar measures had to some extent been experimented with by the local government in the preceding period, there can be little doubt that they were considerably extended and rationalised in the second half of the sixteenth century. The nature of these later developments also deserves attention since it was not primarily a matter of institutionalisation or internment of the sick and poor. The city's hospital did undergo some expansion in these decades, and in fact moved twice to larger premises between the 1560s and the 1590s; but its size remained modest throughout the period (it could house some twenty patients by 1601) and its services were largely directed to a rather elite clientele, as we will see.[13] Its impact on the needs of the poor was marginal if compared with the amount of medical service provided by the municipal system of outdoor medical relief, which constantly expanded from the 1580s on. Similarly, policy towards beggars and the indigent – which underwent a good deal of experimentation in these decades in response to outbreaks of dearth – did not involve any plan for confinement, but was based on the distribution of bread and money and on monitoring the poor in their houses or in the streets.

The case of Turin thus suggests that the classic image of continental systems of charity providing a highly institutional type of relief, in contrast with the community-based care provided by the English Poor Laws, requires qualification, at least with regard to the earlier decades of the early modern period. The importance of forms of outdoor relief has probably been underestimated largely as a result of the scant attention paid to the activities of local charitable agencies. The existence of municipal doctors for the poor, for instance, has also been documented in other Italian and European cities in the late Middle Ages. Historians have tended, however, to insist on the temporary and marginal nature of this service, which supposedly died out with the growth of the centralised state and the weakening of local governments at the turn of the sixteenth century.[14]

In the next three sections, I will discuss the characteristics of this non-institutional system of charity, focusing on three areas of activity: the management of the emergency situations created by the plague; the provisions taken to deal with famine; and the organisation of poor relief and sick care in 'normal times'. In the remaining two sections I will discuss the dynamics behind the growth of the municipal welfare system. The overall aim of the chapter is to suggest an alternative approach to the one which is commonly adopted to explain the emergence of new forms of intervention in public health and poor relief.

---

[12] D., T. XI, pp. 1173–5 and 1104. In 1545, 1569 and 1571 there is already mention of a set of *Ordini politici* but they have not been preserved. Ibid., p. 1099 and D., T. III, p. 1455.

[13] In 1601 there were twelve male patients (Ord., 19.12.1601); in 1609, ten beds for female patients (AOSG, Cat.2, Cl.5, 'Inventari 1609–1797').

[14] A. W. Russell (ed.), *The Town and State Physician from the Middle Ages to the Enlightenment*, Wolfenbuttel 1981.

Attempts are usually made to establish a strict correlation between the devising and trying out of new kinds of health and welfare provisions and the eruption of new kinds of crisis (such as the plague or outbreaks of syphilis). Similarly, new measures are seen as closely related to problems such as those created by population growth and food shortage. Explanations of this sort often seem inadequate, however, and certainly cannot account for the chronology and geography of the new policies. It is still a matter of debate, for example, as to why many countries and communities were unable to enforce anti-plague legislation until the late sixteenth or seventeenth centuries, despite the fact that the main principles of protection had already been tried out in Italy in the wake of the Black Death and that by the fifteenth century they constituted a recognised and well-known corpus of measures.[15] In the pages which follow I would like to focus on the extent to which internal political dynamics determined the relatively early or late appearance of these welfare measures. On the one hand I will investigate the part that municipal governments played in consolidating public health and relief policy. It should be noted that the enforcement of emergency provisions to cope with the event of plague or dearth, and the establishment of regular welfare schemes in general, required access to large-scale financial resources and the development of a complex bureaucratic apparatus that not many communities could boast. In other words the degree to which local power was established was a crucial factor, as was the degree of civic identity which the municipal government could count on. After all, these municipal initiatives relied mainly on the generous support of the citizenry which had to be mobilised to provide the necessary practical and financial resources. On the other hand, I hope to show the crucial part played by political conflicts at the local level and by the ideological climate which this struggle created. In Turin, the development of civic measures in relation to welfare and public health benefited substantially from the growth of a rhetoric celebrating the values of self-government. This was fostered by the Council as a means of counteracting the rival power of the Duke and not only sanctioned the expansion of the municipal authorities' fiscal powers and administrative autonomy, but also contributed to enhance the notion of civic obligation implied by the image of the city as a commonwealth.

Responses to the plague

The emergence of regulations designed to limit the spread of the plague and minimise the damage where it had already occurred is generally attributed to central government initiative. Italy is considered to have been at the forefront of

---

[15] For a summary of the most recent and stimulating interpretations see Paul Slack's Introduction to the volume *Epidemics and Ideas: Essays on the Historical Perception of Pestilence* (edited by T. Ranger and P. Slack), Cambridge 1992, pp. 18–20.

this development, and the measures taken by the Visconti in Milan, by the Venetian state and by the Grand Duke of Tuscany in the fifteenth and sixteenth centuries are considered prime examples.[16] This early appearance of anti-plague measures in the northern Italian states is usually attributed to a centrally coordinated network of local health boards under the direction of a chief authority (frequently referred to as the *Magistrato di Sanità*) based in the various regional capitals. The corpus of regulations resulting from this system is therefore perceived as an administrative victory and a demonstration of the efficiency and advanced centralism of the small Italian states. According to this view, the Italian case appears similar to that of England, since, in both, provisions against the plague are supposed to have spread 'from centre to periphery', rather than originating from local experiments – although this process occurred much later in England. In France and Spain, by contrast, policy towards the plague is thought to have evolved as a consequence of initiatives taken by individual cities, while orders issued by the central government prescribing the establishment of health boards, which were also to include state officers, started to appear only in the seventeenth century.[17]

Piedmont does not conform to this characterisation of the Italian model since in Turin and other Piedmontese cities and towns measures against the plague were developed and put into practice by local authorities.[18] By the fifteenth century, some communities had already adopted forms of provision which were similar to (albeit less sophisticated than) those enforced in the second half of the sixteenth century.[19] Local experimentation in anti-plague policy thus existed more than a century before central government took any interest in public health questions, for the central office of the *Magistrato di Sanità* (with responsibility for the whole of Piedmont) was not created until 1576.[20] In any case, even

---

[16] On the chronology of these measures and the events leading up to them, see: C. M. Cipolla, *Public Health and the Medical Profession in the Renaissance*, Cambridge 1976; R. Palmer, 'The Control of the Plague in Venice and Italy 1348–1600', unpublished Ph.D. thesis, University of Kent, 1978; A. Carmichael, 'Plague legislation in the Italian Renaissance', *BHM*, 57 (1983), and 'Contagion therapy and contagion practice in 15th century Milan', *RQ*, 45 (1991).

[17] On the English case, see: P. Slack, *The Impact of the Plague in Tudor and Stuart England*, Oxford 1985, in particular p. 200; on France and the rest of Europe, see: J. N. Biraben, *Les Hommes et la Peste*, Paris 1975, vol. II, pp. 106, 138–43.

[18] For examples of communities only a few miles from Turin, see: M. Abrate, *Popolazione e Peste del 1630 a Carmagnola*, Turin 1972, and T. M. Caffaratto, *Il flagello Nero*, Saluzzo 1967 (which deals with the situation in Moncalieri).

[19] The practice of checking where travellers have come from, and which territories they had passed through already existed in the fifteenth century, but the system was based purely on the sworn statements of those being questioned. Moreover, checks were restricted to the movement of people, and still did not cover the movement of property and goods. I. Naso, *Medici e Strutture Sanitarie nella Società Tardo-Medievale. Il Piemonte dei Secoli XIV–XV*, Milan 1982, pp. 59–72.

[20] The precise make-up of this authority is unclear. Most of the documents relating to it refer only to one principal officer, called the *Magistrato di Sanità*. It seems likely however that he was assisted by a small number of other state officials, collectively referred to by the same name.

the constitution of this body did not bring about a great deal of change. In Turin, for example, the activities of the office (whose duties, significantly enough, were not formally defined until 1723) appear to have been restricted to the issuing of orders confirming and systemising local authority decisions and to establishing penalties for offenders; the *Magistrato* did not enact legislation on its own or take independent initiatives. By and large its role seems to have been that of giving greater legitimacy to the regulations adopted locally to deal with the plague, by putting the Duke's authority and his more extensive legal powers at the disposal of the City's public health administration. Only occasionally did the *Magistrato* oppose the City's policies (see for example differences over the disinfection phase, discussed below), when decisions taken by it seemed to threaten the interests of the Duke's subjects more generally.

Probably the most important contribution that the *Magistrato di Sanità* made was its monitoring of the areas afflicted by the plague. It was naturally much better placed than the City to carry out this activity because of the information it received through the state diplomatic network. The fact that in the 1570s and 1580s the region avoided the plague that broke out with such virulence in other parts of Italy and in neighbouring Savoy must also have been due to the activities of the newly created office – which on several occasions banned all movement between Piedmont and infected territories.[21] However, all other aspects of the struggle against disease were in the hands of the City authorities.

As I have already mentioned, the office of *Conservatore di sanità* was created in 1577, when the plague was raging in Savoy. On that particular occasion, however, Piedmont avoided the plague and the *Conservatori* only had to take preventive measures, although the region remained in a state of alert for two years. They had a much more active role between 1596 and 1598, and again in 1629 and 1631, years in which there were particularly severe outbreaks in the capital. Under their direction, all the measures which were by then typical of the methods used by Italian cities to fight the plague were adopted. The complexity of the *Conservatori*'s tasks is reflected in the amount of administrative documentation they produced. For the two-year period 1598–99, in particular, this documentation is so rich that it allows us to follow step by step the measures adopted by both the municipal and ducal

---

[21] Movement from Sicily, Calabria, Venice and its mainland territories, Milan and many other cities in the Po Valley, Trento and the Tyrol was banned on 26.8.1576; the ban was extended to various regions in Italy and the Near East, to Asti and surrounding area, Savoy, Lyon and surrounding area, Auvergne, Languedoc, Provence, Cévennes and Alès on 11.8.1579. Lièges, Namur and other Flemish cities were also included on 19.8.1579. The Dominion of Genoa was added to the list in 1580, Savoy in 1585, and Ivrea and all the towns on the other side of the River Orco in 1589. D., T. X, pp. 254–73.

authorities.[22] Obviously there was a wide gap between the ideal situation envisaged by these provisions and what really went on, between the regulations on paper and their implementation. If one wants a description of the reality of city life in time of plague one should turn to a different type of source.[23] In this section, however, my concern is not with lay attitudes to the plague but precisely with those administrative responses which, in the last two decades, have provided the focus for debate about the disappearance of the plague. The measures adopted by the authorities to fight the disease have been seen as evidence for the idea that it was human intervention rather than biological transformations which played the key role in the defeat of the plague.[24] Most scholars now maintain that public health provisions, which centred around the principle of separating infected areas, goods and human beings from the unaffected, were indeed a success and were instrumental in expelling the plague from western Europe. It is certainly true that, although based on a contagionist view of the transmission of the disease, these measures did also have the effect of barring the way to fleas, and possibly to rats, which were the real carriers. It seems to me, however, that while a positive evaluation may make sense in relation to the *cordons sanitaires*, i.e. the ban on contacts with infected territories, it is not justified when applied to the elaborate segregation and disinfection measures adopted within cities. These undoubtedly had an important role on a symbolic level (based as they were on notions of physical contamination and purification), and on a ritual level (contributing for example to preserve a sense of community and to discourage anti-social behaviour). But these aspects of the question are yet to be analysed, while most studies of the plague tend instead to look at anti-plague practices from the point of view of the impact they had on the disease itself. This functional view has often led scholars to interpret the anti-plague programme set out in the regulations too literally and to see any 'abuses' of them as merely freak exceptions to rules whose efficacy they tend to idealise. It is well known in fact that there was, quite regularly, a total collapse of the whole protective apparatus, especially when the plague was at its height. Furthermore, the selling and granting of exemptions from the regulations – practices typical of the old regime – certainly did not cease during times of plague. Indeed one could go so far as to say that the

---

[22] See in particular volume 148, I of the Ordinati of the commune of Turin ('Libro delle congregationi et ordinati del Consiglio di Torino e de' signori deputati sovra gli occorrenti della contagione'), largely published in Caffaratto, *Il Flagello*. Unless otherwise stated, I refer to this register for the information presented in the following pages.

[23] Of the kind, for instance, employed by G. Calvi in her *Histories of a Plague Year*, Chicago, Ill. 1989.

[24] See in particular A. B. Appleby, 'The disappearance of plague: a continuing puzzle', *EcHR*, second series, 33 (1980), and P. Slack, 'The disappearance of plague: an alternative view', Ibid., 34 (1981); also, Biraben, *Les Hommes*, and D. Panzac, *Quarantaines et Lazarets. L'Europe et la Peste d'Orient (XVIIe–XXe Siècles)*, Aix-en-Provence 1986.

regulations really constituted no more than a framework within which bargaining could take place. One clear example of this is provided by the quarantine rules which, as they were applied in Turin, did not indicate, as one might assume, a strict period of forty days isolation but simply 'a period of isolation' whose duration was determined on an *ad hoc* basis according to various pressures such as the power relations between the parties concerned and so on. There is, then, a tendency within the approach outlined above to overstate the effects of anti-plague legislation and, while emphasising the benefits it brought, to underestimate the costs. There is, then, little mention, for example, of the long disinfection phase which endlessly protracted the state of emergency well after the infection had disappeared; nor is sufficient weight given to the administrative and financial burden which the classic anti-plague measures implied and to the repercussions they had on citizens' lives *after* the plague.

It may be useful therefore to provide a detailed chronicle of the measures adopted day by day by the authorities in times of plague in order to see what exactly they consisted of. It is hoped that this account will allow a more complete picture to be drawn and thus contribute to a more balanced assessment of the impact of anti-plague legislation.

The action taken in Turin can be clearly divided into three phases, in each of which different types of provisions were implemented: a prevention period, one of direct confrontation with the epidemic, and finally one of disinfection.

In Turin, as elsewhere, preventive measures were introduced very early on. In May of 1596, after being informed of an outbreak of plague in Savoy, the City appointed an official to check that those coming to the town had certificates of health, and that they did not come from a banned area. The state of alert lasted all through 1597.[25] In April 1598, a decree issued by the *Magistrato* tightened up the regulations concerning contacts with Savoy, by ordering surveillance of the Alpine passes and prohibiting the use of minor or roundabout routes to evade these road-blocks. There was considerable concern that the infection would be brought back by soldiers returning from Savoy, after the Treaty of Vervins (2 May 1598) had brought about a temporary pause in the hostilities with France. A further order of the *Magistrato* therefore requested all communities to put soldiers returning home in quarantine for twenty days.[26]

On 26 May, even though the threat of plague was still distant, the City proceeded to nominate ten special deputies to deal with the risk of epidemic; these were supposed to co-ordinate the activities of the *Conservatori di sanità* and the *Cantonieri* if outbreaks should occur. It was not until July that deaths possibly due to the plague occurred in towns close to Turin. At this point the City immediately sent two doctors from the College of Physicians to ascertain

---

[25] Ord., 5.8.1596, 19.7.1597 and 10.9.1597.
[26] D., T. X, p. 285, 16.5.1598.

whether the plague really was the cause of death, and two days later, following confirmation, the *Magistrato* banned all contact with those towns.[27]

The City authorities immediately took precautions to fight the plague when it made its appearance. Even though the first cases did not appear in the city until the middle of September, the two intervening months saw the introduction of a whole series of measures to set up and equip the organisation which was to defend the city from the disease.[28] Surveillance at the city gates was tightened up: one *Conservatore di sanità* took responsibility for each gate, with the assistance of two subordinates and two gatekeepers. All except a few roads leading to the town were blocked with tree trunks and other barricades. To further ensure that nobody attempted to enter the city by any unauthorised route, some citizens were organised into foot patrols while others scoured the boundary roads on horseback.

A series of repressive measures were taken against those groups and activities that were considered likely to spread the plague, and these measures were later confirmed by decrees from the *Magistrato*. Begging was prohibited and some of the beggars were sent back to their home towns, while others were confined to places outside the city where they were maintained at the expense of the Council. A *Chirurgo delle meretrici* (a surgeon responsible for prostitutes) was appointed to keep a register in alphabetical order of all prostitutes, to visit them every eight or fifteen days, and to report the development of any suspicious symptoms. All public gatherings were cancelled, including those for religious purposes. All activities involving contact with livestock, meat or skins (dyeing, tanning, slaughtering and the sale of meat) were either banned or moved outside the city, as they were considered responsible for infecting the air with 'putrid fumes'. An official was appointed to remove from the city all dead cats and dogs found in the street.[29]

Lastly, a complex system of controls was set in motion to monitor any changes in the health of the population, and prevent the concealment of anybody suspected of plague. On 15 August, the Council took on a doctor and a surgeon to visit any of the poor suspected of having contracted the disease.[30] Controls were also imposed on public and private medical practitioners in the attempt to impede collusion between doctors and patients. All doctors practising within the city, even if privately, were obliged to send a written report to the City

---

[27] Ord., 26.7.1598.

[28] The sense of urgency was maintained by the appearance of further cases in the neighbouring towns and indeed one case on the city boundaries. The authorities reacted with drastic measures to this last case: the furniture was burnt, the cats and dogs killed and the eight people living in the house were put in quarantine. Ord., 26.8.98.

[29] Ibid., 28.7.1598, 29.7.1598, 3.8.1598 and 4.8.1598.

[30] Ord., 15.8.1598, 'Contratto con Pasquasio Dobbesio e Nicola Auxilio'. These men also undertook to continue their duties even if the city became infected with the plague; in these circumstances their salaries were to be increased by a factor of five (from ten to fifty *scudi*).

authorities on the state of health of all their patients. Ten doctors appointed by the City, working in pairs, were required to see the patients of these private doctors, every two weeks, 'in order that no cases of plague be incorrectly diagnosed or kept secret'. At the same time the *Cantonieri* were instructed to visit the entire population of their block (*cantone*) every Monday and Thursday, and to turn in all those found to be ill. Failure to do so would incur a fine of twenty-five *scudi*. Even civic officials were not immune from suspicion and were subjected to the same kind of surveillance. In September, the *Magistrato di Sanità* extended to the entire citizenry the obligation of notifying his office of any cases of illness, under the threat of various punishments. These could include the death penalty in cases where the sufferer had clear physical signs of the plague.[31]

At the same time, the Council was stockpiling corn, wine and medicines, in case the gates had to be shut and the city sealed off from the outside world. It recruited *monatti* – the people responsible for transporting the dead and those suffering from plague, and for dealing with infected houses and property. Carts were provided for this work. The hospital of San Lazzaro (originally for lepers), outside the walls, was made ready to receive patients infected with the disease.

Even before the plague actually reached Turin, therefore, the local government put considerable financial and organisational resources into the lengthy preventive procedures that they considered necessary to protect the city. Once the disease had actually broken out, the councillors' workload and local expenditure increased dramatically.

The plague started in Turin in mid September, with the death of two Franciscan friars. This was the first occasion on which quarantine was required: the remaining friars were isolated in their monastery for twenty-two days. As no more cases were reported during this period, the city was declared free from the plague on 5 October. But after another case had been discovered on 2 November, the *Magistrato* wrote to the other communities in Piedmont informing them that Turin was still in danger. At this point, the City started to prepare special quarantine facilities. Temporary shelters ('huts') were constructed outside the town walls for those who were to be placed in quarantine, and the generous diet that the council was to supply daily was agreed upon. This consisted of 'two and a half pounds of bread, one jug of wine, three ounces of cheese, and eight ounces of meat on days that meat is allowed'. In November, the plague broke out with full force. 'For the general good', all government activity was transferred to other Piedmontese towns not affected by the plague. All state officials left by the same road that had been taken by the Duke and his court some time before.[32] All those citizens who had relatives

---

[31] Ibid., 9.9.1598, 12.9.1598 and 20.9.1598.
[32] D., T. X, p. 287, 8.11.1599.

elsewhere, and the economic means to travel, lost no time in leaving the city. The City authorities then became completely absorbed by the management of anti-plague operations.

At this stage, most of the measures were aimed at separating the sick from those who had been in contact with them, and segregating these two latter categories from the completely healthy. Any contact between these three groups was prohibited. The sick were sent to pest-houses outside the city walls. The 'suspect cases' (those who had been in contact with the sick or had uncertain symptoms) were sent to the quarantine camps if they were poor or, if better off, were permitted to stay at home for the duration of the period required to establish their state of health. This was on condition that they could undertake to pay for their own maintenance, medical treatment and the guard that was placed on their house. These measures imposed enormous administrative pressures on the Council. The special records which had to be kept were, by themselves, a considerable burden for the City officials. They were expected to keep a register of all the sick and suspect cases, and keep track of the latter group's health, releasing them on termination of the quarantine or transferring them to the pest-houses. They were required to register the dead and arrange for their burial, to seal infected houses and draw up an inventory of their contents. They had to find notaries for those wishing to leave a will, and to retain a copy in order to deal with any future claims of inheritance. They also had to keep records of citizens able to pay for their quarantine, and to collect the payments from them.[33]

These provisions were not only complex, but also extremely expensive. The City was obliged to take on a vast number of extra employees: doctors, *monatti*, gravediggers, guards and staff for the pest-houses. Their wages were a notable drain on the Council budget. Thirty-seven people, for example, were employed in the two quarantine camps outside the city, including workmen, butchers, bakers, water-carriers, wine-carriers, horse-drivers, porters, attendants and clerks. The *monatti* and their families numbered about 300 people.[34] In addition, the Council was obliged to feed thousands of people – not only the sick and those in quarantine, but also the increasing numbers of destitute. For the isolation of the city, which prohibited all movement of people and goods, had also brought all commercial and manufacturing activity to a standstill. The misery of the plague was compounded by the poverty resulting from unemployment, which drastically undermined living conditions and considerably reduced the City's financial resources. The municipal authority in fact had to maintain nearly all those who had stayed in the town (presumably the poorer citizens). We can get some idea of the vast numbers involved from the fact that on 4 January, after

---

[33] See 'Istruzione da osservarsi dal controllor deputato per tutti quelli che saranno in quarantena' published in Caffaratto, *Il Flagello*, pp. 53–7.
[34] See Ord., 19.7.1599; D., T. X, p. 325, 23.11.1599.

only two months of widespread plague, the City was complaining of quarantine costs in excess of 26,000 *scudi* (nearly twice the City's entire annual income).[35] It was then decided to reduce the quantity and quality of the food distributed. Wine was restricted to three days a week. By February, it was no longer possible to keep to the rules that stipulated white bread for the sick and '*pane secondo*' (bread of lower quality) for those in quarantine, since there were already complaints about unfair distribution. It was therefore decided to distribute only one kind of bread, made of a mixture of white and brown flour. The central government also intervened in this emergency, and the *Magistrato* was authorised to call upon other parts of the territory to supply food and other provisions, which were to be left at the gates of the capital. However, the order, in spite of being repeated twice, was widely ignored.

For a few months, the epidemic subsided and the emergency regulations were relaxed. But as the weather became hotter, the plague returned with even greater severity. The city authorities were not caught completely unawares, however. By the late spring, they had recalled all the special deputies and these had set up the whole organisational structure again. The *Magistrato* once again gave the City his full support, and re-published the regulations in force a few months before.[36] However, by July when the plague was at its height, the whole of this complex organisation for combating it was falling apart. Only one doctor continued to practise, in spite of the threat to confiscate the property of those who ignored instructions not to leave the city, and the promise that even if suspected of being infected they would not be segregated or put in quarantine.[37] By this time, in any case, nearly all the councillors had either fled or died, and not enough remained to make up a quorum.[38] The Duke had to authorise the mayors to carry motions with only two councillors present, but on 21 July the mayors themselves also abandoned the city. Due to deaths and defections, Turin was left for forty days without a proper government, and in a state of chaos. This pattern was fairly typical, and is to be found again in the plague of 1630. In that year, according to the memoirs of one of the few officials who did stay in the city, any kind of control over the epidemic ceased. The rule of law lapsed in the absence of the *Magistrato di Sanità*, and criminals, extortionate doctors and other unscrupulous elements took over the city. The citizens were at the mercy of the greed of the *monatti*, even for such essential services as the removal of bodies from the street. The few doctors that stayed in the city abandoned the pest-houses in order 'to vend their services to the highest bidder'. Even the pest-houses were only

---

[35] Information concerning the city budget has been taken from M. Chiaudano, 'La finanza del comune di Torino ai tempi di Emanuele Filiberto', *Torino Rassegna Mensile*, 1928, p. 915.

[36] D., T. X, pp. 292–4. The order of 12.5.1599 brought back into force those of 12.9.1598 and 20.9.1598.

[37] Ibid., p. 305, 16.6.1599.

[38] Ord., 1.7.1599.

accessible to those who could bribe the keeper 'with money, jewellery, house-keys, legacies, donations or trusts'.[39]

The city government only managed to reassert its control after the plague had begun to wane, and it was then able to introduce the third phase of its plague policy – the disinfection programme. The procedures involved in this were as arduous and costly as the preceding provisions for isolation and quarantine. Teams of City officials and doctors were set up in each district, to direct the job which was actually carried out by *monatti*. They unsealed, cleaned and perfumed houses that had been infected or suspected of infection, room by room. An inventory was made of the furniture and utensils in each house; these were then boiled in cauldrons, washed by laundresses, and left in the sun. They even ordered the money to be boiled, as it was considered particularly dangerous for the spread of the disease. The only concession was that they did allow this part of the operation to be carried out in private, in the presence of two witnesses. The zones that had been cleansed – the so-called 'clear' (*nette*) areas – were cordoned off, and guards placed so as to prevent any contact with the contaminated zones – referred to as 'foul' (*brutte*) areas. Fires were lit at every crossroads and outside the pest-houses, in order 'to purge the air that had conceived the infection'.[40]

Thus the disappearance of disease did not bring back normality, nor did it end the financial and administrative burden on the City. Once again, City officials devoted all their time to the onerous record-keeping that arose with such large-scale operations. The expenses incurred by twenty-four teams of *monatti*, laundresses, perfume-spreaders, doctors and surgeons, must have been very high. In 1630, the City employed 200 people in similar cleansing operations, plus twenty-five cart horses and six oxen for transporting personal effects to the cauldrons.[41] Worst of all from the point of view of the city's economy, isolation continued. The process of disinfecting the city lasted for a month and a half. This was followed by a period of 'post-plague' quarantine (*quarantena compita*), a trial period in which the city was still cut off from the outside world, but worked quite normally within its walls in order that 'all things be handled and all houses lived in, so that the disease would show itself, if it was still hidden (may God prevent it!)'.[42] Before the city could be freed from restrictions or 'released' (*liberata*), it had to prove its return to good health by reopening all the houses and having them lived in for a period of twenty-two days. If the owners did not wish to reoccupy their house, they had to send proxies called '*prove*'.[43]

[39] G. F. Fiocchetto, *Trattato della Peste et Pestifero Contagio di Torino dell'Anno 1630*, Turin 1631, pp. 51–5.
[40] D., T. X, pp. 308, 317 and 321 (19.9.1599, 19.10.1599 and 29.10.1599).
[41] Fiocchetto, *Trattato*, p. 65.
[42] D., T. X, pp. 321 and 329, 29.10.1599 and 11.11.1599.
[43] Ibid., p. 308, 14.8.1599.

However, those who had fled the plague were frightened to return, and even though the *Magistrato* repeatedly ordered all citizens to come back under threat of severe punishment, the City had great difficulty in persuading inhabitants to return.[44] The moment of 'release' was thus continually postponed, as one post-plague quarantine followed another, protracting the hardship of those who had not been able to leave the town. It was not until the February of 1600 that the City authorities finally freed Turin from all restrictions.[45]

For a full five months after the last cases had been reported within the walls, the city therefore continued to be isolated. The economic ruin inflicted by a year's interruption to normal trade was compounded by every passing day. Increasingly, during the disinfection phase, the civic authorities became more concerned with poverty and the number of mouths to feed, than with the plague and the number of dead. They were aware that the city's hardship and financial difficulties were far from over; disease was to give way to destitution. This cruel legacy was discussed in a letter from the Council to the Duke, dated 4 October. 'In matters of health' things were said to be 'improving day by day', so that in the city itself there were 'no more sick of any kind' and very few in the pest-houses outside the walls; of the latter six were dying, while four to five hundred people were in 'clear' quarantine of twelve days, without showing signs of disease. However, a month and half after the disappearance of the epidemic, the City Council still had to distribute three thousand rations of food every day – not to the sick but to the destitute, since 'the end of the disease does not entail the end of the poverty'.[46] Feeding 3,000 people from the public purse – in a city which had less than 15,000 inhabitants even before the advent of the plague and which had been decimated by deaths from the disease and the exodus of many of its inhabitants – plainly constituted a major crisis.

It has to be asked, at this stage, whether the measures taken by the City to fight the epidemic did not contribute to this state of affairs. Historians have usually been interested in these provisions only for what they tell us about the medical rationale behind them and they have therefore looked favourably on the emergence of regulations intended to isolate the infected and on the new interpretation of the plague as a contagious disease which these reflected. They perceive these developments as denoting a departure from the traditional humoral and miasmatic theory which by its very nature discouraged attempts to defeat the epidemic.[47] It is difficult to share this enthusiasm, however, if we

---

[44] Ibid., pp. 325–7, 23.11.1599 and 14.12.1599.
[45] Ibid., p. 330, 12.2.1600.
[46] AST, Corte Paesi per A e per B, no.7, Fasc. 9, 'Rappresentanza dei Sindaci della città di Torino', 4.10.1599.
[47] For a review of the various positions concerning the interpretation of the disease in medical literature, see Palmer, 'The Control'; V. Nutton, 'The seeds that fell among thorns? The reception of Fracastoro's theory of contagion', *Osiris*, 1990.

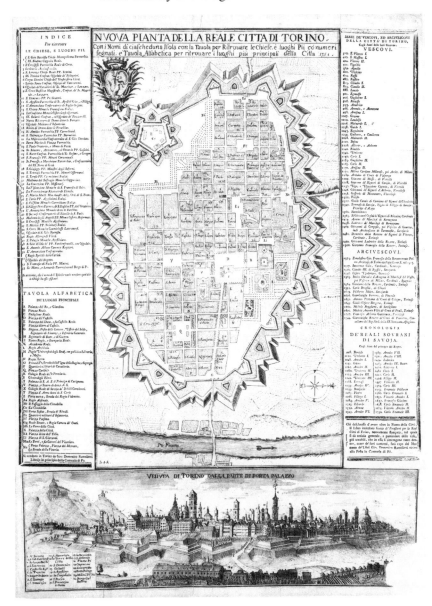

Plate 1. Bernardo Antonio Re, view and plan of Turin, 1751, engravings
(BR INC.IV.96).

consider the overall consequences of anti-plague legislation – the havoc it wreaked on the economy and on trade. The isolation procedures might have been marginally effective in confining the spread of the disease, but they certainly had other effects which, over time, could be devastating. Apart from reducing many citizens to indigence, and causing prices to soar, they led to an enormous increase in public expenditure, which continued to have negative repercussions on the poor long after the epidemic had passed.[48] It should not be forgotten that the municipal government was the principal source of poor relief; the drain on financial resources caused by the plague left the competent authorities indebted, and limited their ability to assist the poor, provide medical care and carry out normal public health measures. On 4 October, the City, in its struggle against the plague, had already contracted debts in excess of 125,000 *scudi*, an enormous figure if one considers that less than 15,000 *scudi* entered their coffers every year.[49]

City officials were well aware of this link between traditional anti-plague policy and increasing poverty. Not surprisingly, isolation procedures were a recurring source of dispute between civic and central government. On the surface, there was general agreement over what kind of policy to adopt. As we have seen, the *Magistrato* supported the tenor of the City's anti-plague initiatives. However, the general principles of this policy were mere abstractions. For instance, the term quarantine applied to an undefined period of isolation, whose length had to be specified case by case on each occasion, probably as a result of negotiation between the interests and requests of different parties. As has been seen in the course of this account, quarantine rarely lasted for forty days; more usually it was twenty-two, twelve or even just eight days long. When the disease appeared to be dying out, the conflict over the exact length of time the city was to remain cut off brought the two authorities more directly into conflict. Once disinfection operations had been completed, the civic government immediately wished to reopen the city to the outside world, whereas the *Magistrato* adopted a stricter and more literal interpretation of the regulations. In November 1598, the City authorities were vehemently opposed to 'his highness's desire and that of his excellency the *Magistrato sopra la*

[48] The negative effects that the block of trade and industry had on the poor were partly mitigated by the opportunities for emergency employment that the plague created (in providing services for the sick, disposing of the dead, etc.). As has been pointed out recently, for some of the poor, the epidemic was an occasion for high salaries and enrichment. B. Pullan, 'Plague and perceptions of the poor in early modern Italy', in T. Ranger and P. Slack (eds.), *Epidemics and Ideas: Essays on the Historical Perception of Pestilence*, Cambridge 1992. For reasons which remain to be investigated, however, the people who specialised in these menial functions often came from abroad.
[49] 'Rappresentanza dei Sindaci'. The figure given by the City was perhaps exaggerated. According to Chiaudano debts amounted to 97,000 *scudi*. Chiaudano, 'La finanza del comune di Torino ai tempi di Carlo Emanuele I', *Torino Rassegna Mensile*, 9 (1930), p. 925.

Sanità' that the city remain shut for the period of 'post-plague' quarantine, 'in order that it could more speedily free itself of the contagion'. They protested that:

> the city has no wine, salt, wheat or firewood for the maintenance of the poor and the needy, beggars and *poveri vergognosi* (shamefaced poor), who, at present, number five thousand, and are still increasing, owing to the state of beggary to which poor artisans have been brought. After fourteen days of quarantine, the City has used up all the victuals that it had put in store, and his Excellency the *magistrato di Sanità* has made no provision to send the supplies necessary for its maintenance, in spite of our repeated requests.[50]

The City was at pains to point out the side-effects of the public health measures. These arguments should not be mistaken for irresponsibility or lack of concern for the public good, in contrast to central government's supposed greater awareness of the health risks. Rather, it was that local government knew, through its own experience, that the sequence famine–epidemic, that recent scholars have emphasised,[51] could as easily be reversed. Poverty was not only one of the causes of the plague; it also increased during an epidemic partly as a result of the action taken to combat it, and continued long after it was over. The city government was also the main agency which had to bear the expenses incurred by the isolation of the city. While it had run up debts around 100,000 *scudi*, the Duke had made only a limited contribution to the cost of the epidemic. He had donated 3,000 *scudi*, and promised 2,000 sacks of corn, to cover the costs of billeting the soldiers in the fortress within the city walls. However, by 4 October 1599, only 1,406 *scudi* had been paid. Central government also empowered the City to impose a death duty on its citizens, but a few months after the end of the plague, the *Camera dei Conti* (Chamber of Accounts) reduced the total the City could exact to the sum of 10,000 *scudi*.[52]

Anti-famine policy

Turning our attention to poor relief, we will now examine the system that emerged as a result of the expansion and bureaucratisation of the 1570s and 1580s. What resources did these developments make available to the poor? What effect did they have on definitions of poverty and on attitudes to begging?

The treatment of the destitute and beggars seems to have been based on the same principles as those drawn up in 1541. The duties of the new officials responsible for poor relief were not dissimilar to those that had been previously

---

[50] Ord., 25.11.1598.
[51] This sequence is widely discussed in J. Walter and R. Schofield (eds.), *Famine, Disease and the Social Order in Early Modern Society*, Cambridge 1989 and in A. De Waal, *Famine that Kills: Darfur, Sudan, 1984–85*, Oxford 1989.
[52] This limitation was stipulated on 31.1.1600. D. T. VII, p. 267, 19.10.98.

carried out by the governors of the hospital of S. Giovanni, when this had been the principal relief agency. The *Ordini politici* published by the City in 1587 specified that the *Cantonieri* had to pay visits twice a week to all the inhabitants of the group of dwellings they were responsible for. They were to take down the Christian names, surnames, places of origin, ages and addresses of all 'the beggars, the needy and the shamefaced poor (*vergognosi*)', and record the reason for each one's destitution – whether due to 'youth, old age, or other factor making it impossible for him to earn a living'. The lists were then submitted to the City mayors who could order the hospitalisation of the sick and the disabled, and the issue of permits to beg for those who 'have no means by which to help themselves, other than that which is necessary for sleeping and to clothe themselves'. By contrast those deemed unworthy of any assistance were to be expelled from the city and severe penalties were fixed for those caught begging without permits (a lashing, the rack or banishment according to the persistence with which the offence was committed). The *Ordini politici* also provided for the dismissal of gatekeepers who did not stop vagabonds and destitute 'foreigners' (from outside the city) from entering, and a twenty-five *scudi* fine for those householders who took in such people.[53]

On paper therefore, the regulations set down in the second half of the sixteenth century show a notable intransigence towards beggars and poor outsiders. They drew a clear-cut distinction between the really needy who qualified for assistance and the undeserving who were made liable to severe punishment; and they established a permanent and minute form of control of the poor and their needs, aimed at stamping out all begging. However, if the implementation of these measures is taken into account, attitudes towards beggars and outsiders appear highly ambivalent. The census of the poor and the expulsion of beggars who did not qualify for assistance were only enforced when the Council recognised that there was a threat of dearth, and that the city had to defend itself against an influx of poor. In normal times, these measures were dropped and beggars were not only tolerated but even protected. In addition, even in times of emergency, attitudes were much more complex than legislation would lead us to think.

From 1586 on, a state of alert caused by food-shortages recurred with extreme frequency, at times even on a two-yearly basis: crises are recorded in the City's minute books in 1592, 1596, 1598, 1601, 1603, 1611, 1620, 1623 and 1629.[54] We do not know whether this pattern reflects a recrudescence of dearth or rather a more interventionist attitude on the part of the City. The list of dates of crisis

[53] ACT, C.S.4701, *Ordini politici formati dal Consiglio della Città*, 1.8.1587 and *Ordini politici da osservarsi dalli Signori Capi de' Cantoni e dal Cavaliere di Virtù . . . per ordinare li poveri mendici . . .*, 29.5.1592, in Borelli, pp. 228–9.

[54] Ibid., 7.6.1592 (and, for the measures taken from then on 27.9.1594), 8.12.1596, 11.2.1598, 20.4.1598, 30.11.1601, 14.12.1603, 27.12.1611, 19.7.1620, 9.8.1623, 16.5.1629.

years is based on years in which anti-dearth measures were taken by the Council. Obviously, action of this kind does not simply reflect a situation of need but could be the result of a number of different factors. These might range from the pressing need to respond to the threat of disorders from below or to pressure from above; to more ideological and strategic aims such as that of gaining consensus in a situation of competition with other agents of power; or to a desire to divide the population and isolate certain sections of it through the selective distribution of aid.[55] All we can do is to note that more crises were recorded during years which – as we will see in the section on poor relief and city politics – were characterised by the strengthening of the City's authority and that emergencies on account of dearth became rarer during the course of the seventeenth century as the conflict between municipal and ducal powers intensified.

If we take the volume of anti-famine measures as evidence of the severity of the crisis, the most serious outbreak of dearth affecting Turin seems to have been that of 1586–87. This was also, however, the first occasion on which the City experimented with its anti-famine provisions and it is possible that the high costs incurred persuaded the City to limit itself to a more prudent policy on subsequent occasions. From September 1586, when the first signs of dearth were noted, the *Cantonieri* carried out their duties on a regular basis. Their twice-weekly visits resulted in the banishment of 'idle outsiders' and the realisation of a massive operation to assist the poor who qualified for aid. The first expulsion took place in September, that is to say after the harvest had been gathered in and it was evident that there were likely to be problems of shortage the following year. A second expulsion was enforced in April 1597, and a third in August, after the new harvest, in order to clear the city of the poor 'who had been tolerated during the period of greatest need'.[56] This pattern of expulsions therefore shows the prevalence of relatively compassionate attitudes towards beggars and outsiders even during food crises. The authorities tried to deal with the shortage several months in advance, using early expulsions to discourage the poor from the countryside from flocking to the city; but they were then reluctant to send the poor back to the countryside when conditions there were worse.[57] Expulsions were suspended during the most acute shortage and were resumed only well after the new harvest. Meanwhile, considerable assistance was given to the needy who

---

[55] P. Slack, 'Dearth and policy in early modern England', *SHM*, 5 (1992); for examples from the modern period see A. De Waal, *Famine that Kills*; M. Buttino, 'Politics and social conflict during a famine: Turkestan immediately after the Revolution' in (ed.), *In a Collapsing Empire. Underdevelopment, Ethnic Conflicts and Nationalisms in the Soviet Union*, Annali della Fondazione Feltrinelli, Milan 1993.

[56] Ord., 10.9.1586, 8.4.1587, 1.8.1587.

[57] The countryside did not have, to the same extent as the city, the benefit of controlled retail prices (the setting of which was carried out by the civic authorities) nor of stocks imported from outside. In 1586, for instance, Turin was supplied with grain from Sicily. M. Chiaudano, 'La finanza . . . ai tempi di Emanuele Filiberto'.

had been allowed to remain in town. Unfortunately, gaps in the records only allow us to have precise figures for emergency expenditure on the indigent for a limited period. But in just forty days, from 19 May to 30 June 1587, the City distributed 28,000 pounds of bread made from 145 *sacchi* of wheat: 382 pounds a day in the first week, 573 pounds on each of the following ten days and 764 on each of the last twenty-five.[58] It is clear that these amounts would keep several hundred people from starving. To this expenditure we must add a further four *scudi* per day allocated for medicines for the poor who were sick, and the cost of the bread given to the poor who were expelled, to eat on their journey back.[59]

On this occasion, the City engaged in a tremendous effort which left it with a debt of 30,000 *scudi* (more than double its overall budget) once the emergency had passed.[60] More limited operations were carried out during the shortages that recurred at the turn of the century. Generally speaking these consisted of the distribution of relief in the form of money allocated on the basis of the *Cantonieri*'s visits and sometimes granted for periods as long as a year; the usual expulsions of undesirable beggars; and the issuing of permits to beg.[61] The large-scale distribution of bread was repeated only during the terrible dearth of the late 1620s, which preceded the serious plague outbreak of 1630. Even though the City became more cautious in its policy after the experience of the 1580s, there is no doubt that it was eager to show the paternalistic and caring side of its power in these years, and was willing to engage in major financial outlay to protect its poor citizens (and occasionally outsiders) from starvation. This attitude appears to be one aspect of a wider sense of civic obligation that the City actively tried to inculcate; in effect the City was expecting all members of the community who had some means to take part in its policy towards the poor, through regular financial support or even through more direct involvement in their relief. The high costs of special expenditure were partly covered by voluntary levies of the kind we have already encountered in the previous chapter. A great deal of pressure was brought to bear on the citizenry to make them contribute regularly to these levies for poor relief. In times of emergency, the *Cantonieri* were required to visit all house-owners and better-off members of their block, and to register the contribution they were willing to make during the period of hardship.[62] The donator was subsequently repeatedly reminded of his under-taking. Another form which the extraction of semi-voluntary charity took was

[58] Ord., 19.5.1587, 27.5.1587, 7.6.1587.
[59] Ibid., 22.4.1587, 11.8.1587.
[60] Chiaudano, 'La finanza . . . ai tempi di Emanuele Filiberto', pp. 922–3. According to Chiaudano, the price of a sack of wheat increased from 30 florins in May to 48 in September of 1586, and then to 58 in February and 60 in June of 1587. If this information is correct, then just in the forty days we have been discussing here, the City spent more than 1,500 *scudi* in exceptional expenses to provide bread to the poor, on an overall budget of nearly 12,000 *scudi* (1587 figure).
[61] For example in 1591–92, Ord., 12.1.1592, 26.1.1592, 29.5.1592, 7.6.1592, 12.7.1592, 1.11.1592.
[62] For example, ibid., 8.4.1587.

that of sending groups of the poor assisted by the municipality every day to the houses of those 'who had said they were willing to donate the left-overs from their lunch and dinner'.[63] These systems, although not compulsory, were probably reasonably efficient, given that they called into question the reputation of the richer citizenry. Records of who had paid and who had not clearly appeared in the *Cantonieri*'s registers and became part of public knowledge. Refusal to donate was cause for scandal, and could lead to a reprimand from higher authorities. In 1602, following a period of famine, the Duke, perhaps at the instigation of the Council, publicly rebuked his courtiers and officials 'who had refused to pay the levy requested for the poor', and asked the City for a list of their names.[64]

It is often suggested that a more selective attitude towards beggars emerged in the sixteenth century in response to the public order problems created by demographic growth, famine and war. Begging was increasingly identified with culpable idleness, and the idle were more vigorously sought out, distinguished from the genuine cases of disability, and then punished. Citizens became particularly intolerant towards outsiders who arrived with stories of unproven misfortunes.[65] However, the idea of increasing harshness towards begging does not appear very convincing in the case of Turin, where attitudes were extremely ambivalent even during the dearth emergency, and easily switched from repression to leniency and more positive aid. Once a crisis was over, the prohibition on begging would fall into abeyance, and expulsions would cease. Paradoxically, those categories of the poor who (at least on paper) had been hardest hit by the repressive measures might become the recipients of special welfare provisions. In September 1588 for example, just a year after the previous expulsion, an order was issued instructing that 'accommodation should be given to destitute foreigners and vagabonds'.[66] Again, in September 1591, measures were taken to protect 'the many poor who go wandering and have no place to rest themselves at night', and two councillors were appointed 'to find rooms whose rent they will agree with the owners for one year, engage a suitable person for the protection and care of said poor persons and have twelve straw mattresses made at the City's expense'.[67] Measures of this kind that provided shelter and warmth for 'destitute beggars' were very common, especially in wintertime when it was feared that those who 'naked and barefoot sleep at night on the bare earth' would freeze to death.[68] It is a curious fact that the homeless

[63] Ibid., 27.12.1601.
[64] Ibid., 1.3.1602.
[65] See for instance N. S. Davidson, 'Northern Italy in the 1590s' in P. Clark (ed.) *The European Crisis of the 1590s*, London 1985, pp. 168–9.
[66] Ibid., 21.9.1588.
[67] Ibid., 29.9.1591.
[68] Ibid., 3.1.1623.

and the incomers, the primary target of the expulsion orders, were now the major beneficiaries of this compassion. The terms 'foreigner and vagabond', which usually had such negative connotations, were considered here as denoting states of acute vulnerability and caused widespread concern. This reversal of attitude cannot be explained merely in terms of a survival of very different attitudes towards begging. Rather, we need to ask whether orders against begging have not been interpreted in too simplistic a fashion. There has perhaps been a tendency to take the harsh invectives against idlers and vagabonds from outside the city at face value and to focus too much on the negative and repressive nature of sixteenth-century legislation against begging. Instead we need to know more about the way in which it operated in practice.[69]

The existence of two lists of destitute persons to be expelled in 1601 allows us to compare the policy actually put into practice towards beggars with the picture that emerges from the anti-begging decrees. On 30 November 1601, with dearth threatening the city, the *Cantonieri* were instructed by the Council to carry out a census of 'the destitute persons who go begging around the city streets', listing all those who turned out to be 'foreigners from outside the city or from other states'.[70] Here a definition of the undeserving poor seems to be given, which corresponds to non-citizens and those from other states. Further examination of the implementation of this order, however, shows that the interpretation of the term 'foreigner' is not as obvious and straightforward as one might assume.

Two separate lists were drawn up by the *Cantonieri*, one consisting of 226 poor people who were either *oltremontani* ('those who came from the town of Susa and beyond') or from 'foreign states';[71] and the other consisting of 123 poor people originating from various Piedmontese localities (including five from Turin itself). On 18 December, those on the first list were all expelled from the city, each having been given six pounds of bread and an amount of money which varied from 1 to 3 *ducatoni* according to the size of their family.[72] The treatment meted out to the second group was very different. In most cases the expulsion order was not enforced. For 84 of the 123 Piedmontese poor (68.3 per cent), the sentence was commuted to an undertaking not to beg. This undertaking was

---

[69] There are only a few studies (all on the situation in England) which have analysed who precisely the poor really affected by the legislation against vagabonds were: J. Pound, 'An Elizabethan census of the poor: the treatment of vagrancy in Norwich, 1570–80', *Univ. Birm. Hist. Jl*, 8 (1962), A. L. Beier, 'Vagrants and the Social Order in Elizabethan England', *Past and Present*, 64 (1974), P. A. Slack, 'Vagrants and vagrancy in England, 1598–1664', *EcHR*, second series, 27 (1974); J. R. Kent, 'Population Mobility and Alms: Poor Migrants in the Midlands during the Early Seventeenth Century', *Loc. Pop. St.*, 27 (1981).

[70] Ord., 30.11.1601.

[71] The Susa valley leads to the Mont Cenis pass, which at that time was the principal Alpine crossing point between Piedmont and Savoy, and Italy and France. Susa was the last centre of some importance on the Piedmontese side of the state.

[72] Ord., 18.12.1601.

made by the individuals themselves or – in nearly half of the cases – by other people resident in the city, on their behalf. If the undertaking was breached, the beggar would be flogged and the guarantor fined. In this case, then, the expulsion order was not rigidly applied, but used to force relatives, neighbours, fellow townspeople and house-owners to take on responsibility for those reduced by the shortage to destitution and begging. As in the case of the voluntary levies squeezed out of the citizens to tackle the emergency, the Council policy was to prompt a sense of obligation towards the less fortunate, by using indirect methods of compulsion. In other cases, the duty of assistance was simply made obligatory. Those who sheltered much younger siblings (probably on the basis of some agreement with their family) were quite simply ordered to restrain their charges from begging, under threat of punishment. The Councillors themselves set an example of charity and solidarity with the poor, by taking into their houses some of the worst cases of destitution and those without relations, undertaking to keep them for eight or fifteen days, or until they regained their health.[73]

It would appear, then, that the primary function of expulsion orders was often both to deter, and to set an example. They had the effect of containing the problem of begging by increasing public awareness and responsibility towards the poor, but only in a few cases did they lead to physical expulsion from the city. Yet only a few days before, 226 *oltremontani* had been expelled without remission. How do we explain this discrimination between the two groups of poor? According to the language in which the legislation was expressed, the repression of begging was directed against people who refused to work, and against foreign vagabonds who used up the charity intended for the city's own poor. The *oltremontani*, however, did not generally resemble the stereotype of those voluntarily idle or the dangerous vagabonds who were the target of the expulsion orders (table 2). In the first place, families were more common than single people. Of the ninety-five units expelled, fifty-eight (60 per cent) were families. Of these, as many as twenty-six (nearly half) had a woman as head of family, twenty were made up of siblings, six were fathers with their sons, and a further six were complete nuclear family units consisting of both parents and their children. Unfortunately, the ages of the poor are not stated, only the sex and the relationship to the head of the family. However, the fact that nearly a quarter of the children (24 per cent) are defined as *creature* (infants) and 40 per cent are registered as *figliolo* (child) or *figlio piccolo* (small child) implies that in many cases they were young families, with small children. Even amongst the high number of family units made up of siblings, the most common pattern seems to be of an elder teenager (generally a girl) who would go begging, taking along younger brothers and sisters. The beggars who were expelled therefore seem

[73] Ibid., 26.12.1601.

Table 2. *Family composition of* oltremontani *beggars expelled in 1601*

Singles F	Singles M	Mothers and children	Fathers and children	Parents and children	Siblings	Comrades	Relatives	Total of family groups
13	19	26	6	6	20	2	2	95

to be principally the most vulnerable categories: widows (or widowers) with children, orphaned adolescents and children. Given that age was not recorded, the identity of the thirty-two single people (nineteen men and thirteen women) is more obscure. The possibility that they too may have belonged to vulnerable categories like the old or the disabled cannot be excluded. Finally, there were the five remaining family units, three of which consisted of couples with the same surname and unspecified relationship, and two of which consisted of couples of the same sex (two women and two men) defined as 'comrades'.

The majority of these people would appear to have been reduced to penury by family disasters (the loss of their spouse or parents) or by other adversities. This impression is further confirmed by their places of origin. Most of them (66 per cent) came from the impoverished region of Maurienne just on the other side of the Mont Cenis pass, which up until a few months previously had been the theatre of war against the French. The other family units (12 per cent) came from Alpine villages just on the Italian side of the pass, in the Susa and Lanzo valleys. The origin of the *oltremontani* was therefore from the same kind of ecological area. The economy of these mountainous regions was essentially based on the income earned by mule-drivers from the transit of goods and people across the Mont Cenis pass, and from sheep-farming and the use of common land. However, the protracted conflict with France (which had stricken this area intermittently for fifty years) had had disastrous effects. The interruption of normal commercial traffic, together with the burden of war taxation, not infrequently produced cases of depopulation.[74] Given the beggars' extremely localised area of origin, it is reasonable to speculate that in some cases they were part of a mass exodus. And in fact we find that seventy-three of the ninety-five family units came from neighbouring hamlets in a very limited area spanning the Mont Cenis pass (plate 2).[75] Of these, as many as thirty-six (twenty-two family groups and fourteen single persons) came from the same village, Bessans. The

[74] Savoy was subject to fifty years of war between 1580 and 1630, and two total occupations in 1600 and 1630. See J. P. Leguay (ed.), *Histoire de la Savoie*, vol. III, *La Savoie de la Réforme à la Révolution Française*, Rennes 1983–86. On the economic situation: P. Guichonnet (ed.), *Histoire de la Savoie*, Toulouse 1984, pp. 135–47.

[75] For twenty of the ninety-five family units the place of origin was not specified, but it is probable that they came from the same area; in ten cases they had the same surnames as other families for whom the place of origin was registered.

Table 3. *Family composition of Piedmontese caught begging in 1601*
(in brackets those expelled)

Singles F	Singles M	Mothers and children	Fathers and children	Parents and children	Siblings	Comrades	Relatives	Total of family groups
11(4)	32(24)	3(2)	3(1)	10(—)	3(—)	—	—	62

departure of several score people from villages and hamlets that usually counted only a few hundred inhabitants gives an idea of the dramatic situations that these migrants left behind. In this context, the Council's decision to return them to their lands would appear particularly lacking in compassion. Their rejection was total and a priori; no exceptions were entertained.

The treatment of the second group (the Piedmontese), by contrast, was much more circumspect. In this case, harsher treatment was reserved mainly for single people, who were expelled in much greater numbers than the families (table 3). Twenty-eight of the forty-three single people (65 per cent) were expelled, against only three of the nineteen family units (16 per cent). Gender also seems to have been taken into account in the case of the single persons: twenty-four of the thirty-two men were expelled as against only four of the eleven women. This does not seem to have been the case for the families, however, two of which had a woman as head.

It is interesting to observe that the discrimination against the *oltremontani* was explicitly justified on the basis of their foreignness. Significantly, the census distinguished them from other beggars, registering them on a separate list. This attribution would seem completely unjustified, however. The *oltremontani* were simply inhabitants of certain Alpine regions of the Savoy state. Only one of the expelled beggars came from a 'foreign state' (Casale). From a political point of view, they were all the Duke's subjects, just as much as the Piedmontese beggars who were to be allowed to stay only a few days later. Nonetheless, the use of the term *forestiero* (foreigner, outsider) evidently did capture a genuine foreignness in social terms. As far as the movement of goods and men was concerned, these territories had traditionally been more linked to the French than to the Italian side of the Dukedom. In the sixteenth century, migrants from Savoy went to various parts of France, Switzerland and Germany, but not yet to Piedmont and its capital.[76] The *oltremontani* therefore were considered foreigners by the city authorities, because they did not belong to the city's social space, to that territory which was defined not by political borders, but by links of commerce and migration. Such an hostility was also exacerbated by the longlasting conflict

---

[76] J. P. Leguay, *Histoire*, vol. III. A century later, by contrast, the Maurienne region contributed massively to the seasonal migration to Turin. Levi, 'Come Torino', pp. 41, 53.

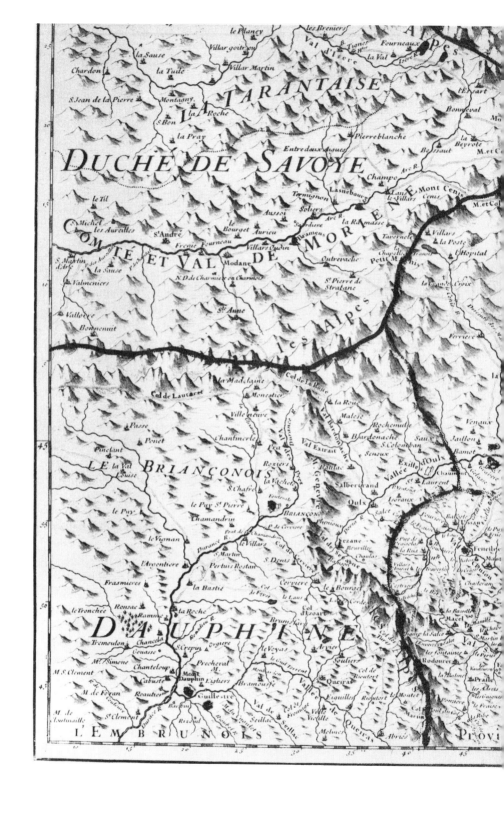

Plate 2. D. De L'Isle, *Carte du Piemont et du Monferrat*, Paris 1707 (detail).

for political supremacy between the Piedmontese and the Savoyard element of the elite, a conflict which, in the early sixteenth century, had led to many violent attacks against Savoyard courtesans and their servants sojourning in Turin.[77] The social foreignness of the *oltremontani* is further confirmed by the fact that they were not able to produce relatives willing to give guarantees on their behalf and protect them from expulsion. Their flight to the capital had evidently been motivated by desperation; it was a disorganised form of immigration, not one in which immigrants arrived via sponsors in the town of destination. It was these factors that worried the City – which did not want to take on people with whom it had a purely relief relationship. It totally rejected this new influx, which risked becoming an uncontrollable wave of people who, in addition, could not count on friends and relations who could ease their integration into the capital. The situation of the 123 destitute Piedmontese was very different: half of them could count on uncles, brothers, or fellow-townspeople who were working in Turin as, for example, servants to the aristocracy, tailors and butter-sellers. In some cases, they themselves were able to declare an occupation that they had previously carried out in the capital (wine-carrier, fruit-seller, worker at the powder-magazine), thus proving their roots in the city.

The analysis of the treatment received by the poor in the two lists thus demonstrates that those definitions of the unworthy poor which appear in the orders against begging, and which have often been the main focus of historians' interest, were really just convenient compartments into which the groups that at that moment appeared most unwelcome could be slotted. In the case examined, a strict definition of idler might in part explain the distinctions made within the Piedmontese group, but it in no way accounts for the treatment of the *oltremontani*, in whose case so many of the expelled were women and children. Yet a simple identification of the unworthy poor with the foreigner would also be misleading: as we have seen, there were times when their condition as vagabonds without possessions and without a place to sleep provoked greater compassion. The demarcation between the worthy and unworthy poor was unquestionably influenced by conjunctural factors, such as food shortage, but more important still was the way in which the groups to which the poor belonged were perceived by the citizenry. Their degree of familiarity or extraneousness in relation to the city seems to have played an important role in defining attitudes towards beggars. In addition, attitudes were also influenced by indirect factors, such as the pattern of social or political conflict – which might have the effect of boosting a given ideological discourse. In the section on poor relief and city politics, I will examine just such a case, and show how the condemnation of foreigners grew with the rhetoric that exalted the status of citizen.

---

[77] Barbero, 'Una città in ascesa', p. 315.

Charitable resources for the poor and sick in 'normal times'

Further clues as to the mechanisms used for selecting the recipients of relief can be inferred from an examination of patterns of access to other forms of assistance offered by the local system of welfare. We have already seen that mass assistance in periods of shortage gave way, when the emergency was over, to *ad hoc* provisions to assist the city's beggars, and to a general tolerance of the practice of begging. In addition, the City handed out assistance *ad personam*, in the form of money in response to petitions presented by the poor, often via the mediation of a *decurione* (a City Councillor). In 1581 the responsibility for the decisions over petitions was delegated to the two mayors of the city, who were given discretion to distribute alms as they wished from a budget which generally amounted to eight *scudi* a month. If the mayors kept to this sum, no report was required by the Council.[78] Only if alms payments exceeded the budget were additional grants discussed in the Council. We can obtain some idea of who the beneficiaries were by examining some of these cases. The recipients appear to belong to two categories. First of all, there were the *poveri vergognosi* who largely consisted, in this case, of those who had enjoyed a certain status or affluence, but had fallen on hard times. In February 1598, for example, ten poor in this category received a special payment on top of the sum already allocated; they included a notary, a doctor in law, a soldier and a French gentlewoman.[79] In April, it was the turn of '*messer* Perrachia', 'once a wealthy merchant and now without the means to feed or clothe himself', who, on the recommendation of Councillor Magnano, obtained twenty-three *fiorini*.[80] The other group of recipients seems to have consisted of destitute people somehow connected to the Council – having been either directly employed by the municipality (as bailiffs, janitors, etc.) or holding some other kind of contract. Thus in 1584 Margarita Grosso, who rented a stall from the Council in the market square, obtained thirty florins in alms and the suspension of rent payments for the stall for a year, on becoming a widow responsible for four small children. Access to this kind of assistance was therefore restricted to selected categories, who could boast past social distinction or the existence of patrons and intermediaries. Social contacts, which we have seen play an important part in deciding who the deserving poor were, even in times of shortages, were still more crucial in normal times.

The same kind of 'selective' access to charity, channelled through personal contacts and patronage, also seems to have operated at the hospital of S. Giovanni. Unfortunately we have only very limited records for the hospital in the second half of the sixteenth century. However, administrative records do exist for the three-year period from 1585 to 1588, and they give some hints as to

---

[78] Ord., 17.12.1581.   [79] Ibid., 11.2.1598.   [80] Ibid., 20.4.1598.

the nature of the assistance given.[81] It appears that the decision to accept the sick into the hospital was taken by the governors, quite often on the basis of a petition presented by an intermediary known to the hospital. So on 14 September 1586, it was agreed that Giò Nigra, the hospital agent, could bring in his brother-in-law for treatment for three days; on 4 January 1587, the governors accepted the proposal made by Giò Marco Invinceraio, an apothecary from Turin, to bring in Alessandro Cisari of Turin who was sick. However, the most common route for entry into the hospital was through a bargain struck directly between the governors and the patients. The latter would commit themselves to leaving the hospital a legacy in property or money, and would receive in return the right to be cared for as long as they lived. On 12 May 1585, Gioannino Perreto of Ceres, resident on the outskirts of Turin, and at that time in the care of the hospital of S. Giovanni, 'not wishing to be ungrateful for the assistance given', donated to the hospital 'were he to die while within its walls' the sum of ten *scudi*. On 29 September, Antonio Martina of Dronero, a mule-driver in Turin, donated a white mare to the hospital, once again were he to die while in its care. Martina was to pass away three months later and the mare, when sold, brought in fourteen *scudi*.[82] It was normal practice for the hospital to expect some kind of recompense from patients whose treatment was liable to be lengthy, either because of the nature of the illness, or because they were old or had no relations to assist them. Even when no agreement had been made, the patient and his family were considered to have incurred a debt to the hospital which they had to pay before they could benefit from any further assistance. On 23 June 1585, Claudio Madis of Borgaro repaid a debt of this kind by donating a piece of land of about half a hectare, owed by his brother Giovanni, who had died in the hospital some three years before, 'as the said Claudio was himself in need of the hospital'.

This kind of contract covered caring arrangements which were very similar to those made between private citizens, whereby solitary persons in need of care or custody would be entrusted to a keeper who in turn would be paid an allowance for his or her services.[83] Typically, these individuals were drawn from among the poorer sections of society (in particular widows) and their role as carers provided them with a valuable source of income. Inn-keepers, too, feature prominently among those who undertook this kind of activity. They would either offer a

---

[81] ACT, C.S.662, 'Volume Congreghe tenute dalla direzione dello Spedale dal 26.3.1585 al 18.12.1588'.

[82] Ord., 5.1.1586.

[83] Agreements of this kind were common in England in the same period, and were even provided for in the Poor Law. See M. Pelling, 'Healing the Sick Poor: Social Policy and Disability in Norwich, 1550–1640', *MH*, 29 (1985); A. Wear, 'Caring for the Sick Poor in St. Bartholomew Exchange: 1580–1676', in W. F. Bynum and R. Porter (eds.), *Living and Dying in London*, *Medical History Supplement n.11*, London 1991.

complete service consisting of board and lodging or would send meals daily to the homes of the needy. At the same time they would keep an eye on their charges' health, calling upon the doctor or buying medicines when necessary. In wills, debts to inn-keepers for these kinds of services are frequent, as are words of gratitude for the care provided.[84] Old single or widowed persons, orphans or children whose parents were away, and young women without close relatives were the most common candidates for the services described. Either the family (usually distant relatives) entrusted the person to a keeper, or the person himself/herself arranged to invest in care what little revenue or savings he/she had.

The hospital thus provided care in exchange for payment in the same way as private keepers did. Admission to institutional care was not free but open only to those who could offer some significant recompense. It was not in competition with, but rather an extension of, the care on payment available in the community. Further evidence for this lies in the fact that it was often to the hospital that private keepers addressed themselves when something went wrong and they were no longer able to keep to an agreement. On 15 September 1585, for example, a woman named Caterina Genta approached the hospital's governors asking to admit a ten-year-old girl, Angela, daughter of the late 'messer Hercole' Begiamo of Savigliano. Up to that time Caterina had looked after the girl, who had been entrusted to her by her father. But the father was now dead, and Caterina was unable to collect the agreed 'expenses for food', and being 'poor, old and sick' herself could no longer afford to look after the girl (who was also goodlooking and thus exposed to particular danger). The governors accepted the petition and took Angela in, assuming, in a certain sense, responsibility for the contract made between Caterina and messer Begiamo. We would be wrong, however, to interpret the decision as an act of charity. Angela was no destitute but had a dowry of fifty scudi that the father had left to her; in exchange for the services provided to the girl the governors secured for the hospital the annual income deriving from this sum.

The cases discussed above point to the existence of a paying long-stay clientele within the hospital made up of people in need of care and protection (as in the case of the young Angela) rather than just medical treatment. They thus invite us to question the classic antagonism between institutional care and care available in the community. In the late sixteenth and early seventeenth century residence within the hospital was complementary rather than alternative to care in the community, since it intervened when the latter had failed or had become

---

[84] There is evidence suggesting that some of the residents in the hospital might have lived on private care before entering it. Domenica Pianlono, for instance, in the will she dictated from a hospital bed in 1622, mentioned two substantial debts to two different inn-keepers for food delivery. AOSG, Cat.4, Cl.1, Fasc.5, vol.38, 12.9.1622.

inadequate to the seriousness of the case. The importance of the caring function of the hospital is confirmed by information found in a different source, namely a small number of wills left by members of this paying section of the hospital's clientele. It is a precious source for, whereas minute books only mention the portion of the will which refers to bequests to the hospital, the documents themselves register all the provisions made by the testators to the benefit of relatives and friends. They therefore provide a picture of the patients' ties within and outside the family and give some hint of what determined them to opt for hospital care. In the course of my research into the activities of the hospital, nine wills came to light for the period between 1587 and 1667: three of them were drawn up in the decade 1587–97; five between 1620 and 1640; and only one after that period. This chronological distribution is in itself interesting for it suggests that the caring functions of the hospital became less important from the mid seventeenth century onwards when its major expansion started to take place. The striking feature of these wills is that they are all made by women. This partly indicates that women tended to be more exposed to the need for shelter, but it also reflects the limited power that lower class women had over their property, so that, unlike men (whose donations to the hospital usually take the form of contracts having immediate effect), they could only leave instructions as to how their patrimony was to be disposed of after their death. The wills show clearly that it was the critical family situation of these women that lay behind their need to resort to the hospital. Women on their own predominate: five of the nine testators were widows, one was an unmarried woman, and only three were married with a husband who was still alive. The wills made by widows and by the single woman mention only the existence of distant relatives. Thus Caterina Rossatto left 12.5 *scudi* in the eventuality that two grandsons, for many years in Flanders, should come back and make claims over her property; the other women refer briefly to a brother-in-law, two 'female relatives' not otherwise identified, and a *nipote* (nephew or grandson) as beneficiaries of small legacies, or as having rights over their goods.[85] Even when a closer member of the family was still alive, however, there does not seem to have been a close relationship. In 1635 Caterina Cossola, a widow, left her dowry (secured on a cottage and some land) to the hospital 'for the good services received' during the two months of her stay, whereas in the case of her daughter, she recognised only her right of *legittima* (the minimum she was entitled to from her mother's property).[86] Cristina Morello was a similar case, since she left to her husband (whom the staff of the hospital witnessing the will declared they could not identify), the mere interest on her dowry, whereas all her goods (after the payment of small legacies to three religious confraternities) went to the hospital.[87] All the

---

[85] Ibid., vol.44, fasc.2, 7.6.1597.
[86] Ibid., Cl.2, vol.7, fasc.1, 23.8.1635.   [87] Ibid., vol.34, fasc.1, 21.2.1640.

examples seem to indicate that the persons taken in by the hospital for long stays were not in a position to benefit from family care either because of the absence of close relatives or because of conflicts with them. In two cases, in particular, the existence of a violent conflict seems to be the crucial factor leading the women to seek admission to the hospital. On 2 March 1587, the last wishes of Mattia were recorded. She had been in the hospital for ten months and during this period, she had been 'fed, treated, and given all necessary things, having been gravely ill and continuing to be so'. The principal reason why she had resorted to the hospital was the negligence of her husband, who had not only ignored her medical needs and left her unattended during her infirmity but had even taken a concubine and had severely beaten his wife 'so that she would have died had she not been admitted to the hospital'. The grateful Mattia therefore bequeathed the hospital her dowry which amounted to the tidy sum of 100 *scudi*.[88] Maddalena Barbero was a similar case, having been forced on three occasions to take refuge in the hospital following mistreatment by her second husband and negligence of her illness. The governors had received her 'with love and charity', and had twice arranged reconciliation with the husband who had promised to mend his ways. On the third occasion, after having been beaten 'with sticks and cut with a scythe', Maddalena returned to the hospital to stay, and in December 1590 she revoked the deed of gift made over to her husband at the time of her wedding and transferred all her wealth to the hospital poor.[89]

The hospital does not appear as provider of medical services alone but also offered the protection and care lacking in the community; on the other hand it did not function as an indiscriminate refuge but had a well-defined medical profile. With only a single exception, that of the young Angela, all the patients mentioned in the surviving documents were seriously ill, although infirmity had not been the only reason why they had been accepted: their medical needs were aggravated by isolation, and desertion by children, spouses, or relatives. We must note, in addition, that admission to the hospital was not restricted to the poor, since some of the patients were far from indigent. Both in the case of the poor and of the better-off, however, the hospital intervened *only* when family relationships and other forms of solidarity had broken down, and also when disability and dependence were too advanced to rely on private caring arrangements: all the patients taken in on the basis of a contract or a promise (in the case of women) to repay the services dispensed survived only a few months (from two to three in most cases). As in private care, they continued to pay in order to be assisted. This requirement might appear harsh on the most unfortunate, an exploitation of the needs of the poor, and might even lead us

[88] 'Volume Congreghe'.
[89] AOSG, Cat.4, cl.2, vol.2, fasc.2, 14.10.1590.

to question the image of the hospital as a dispenser of charity. It is possible, however, that it represents above all a recognition that care was not simply a right and that it implied both financial outlay and personal commitment on the part of those who offered it. According to this view, the relatives of needy individuals should not be expected to provide care only on the basis of family ties and obligations.[90] A share in the patrimony of those they looked after was taken to be just reward for services rendered. On the other hand, if for some reason family members were unable or unwilling to care for their relations, it was accepted that their entitlement would pass instead to the hospital, which took over the responsibility. We have more than one example of such transfers of rights in the wills examined. Money, however, was by no means the only concern. That charity did indeed play its part is evident from the fact that patients were required to pay only according to their means. The governors accepted 100 *scudi* from the affluent Mattia Ruspa, but in the case of Antonio Martina they were content with a mare, which was probably all the mule-driver could offer. The patients were not, in other words, expected to pay on the basis of a fixed charge but to help, as best they could, to meet the expenses of their maintenance.

It would seem that the number of these long-stay patients exceeded by far those admitted for short-term treatment. I have come across only three cases of patients accepted free of charge on the basis of (unspecified) physical ailments.[91] However, the fact that the brevity of their stay was emphasised – 'for three days', 'for a few days' – and that they were all accepted thanks to the intercession of an intermediary known to the governors, points to the special nature of these admissions; these patients were different from the usual cases dealt with by the hospital and were only exceptionally accepted. Only one other group of patients figure prominently and they, unlike the long-stay cases, seem to have been admitted precisely because of the particular nature of their medical complaints. These were the syphilis sufferers who, as becomes clear from the discussion (which took place in the years 1597–98) over the needs to move the hospital to a larger building, made up a large proportion of the residents:

> Since the hospital building is small and cramped, the sick, most of whom suffer from the French disease, fail to recover, because there is little room to carry out the purges. And what is worst, given that it is only possible to put four patients at a time on the cure for French disease, because of the lack of space, it is necessary to

[90] This argument has been reiterated by D. Thomson in several works. For a recent summary of his views, 'The Welfare of the Elderly in the Past, a Family or Community Responsibility?', in M. Pelling and R. M. Smith (eds.), *Life, Death and the Elderly: Historical Perspectives*, London 1991.

[91] 'Volume Congreghe'.

keep other patients suffering from the said disease for many months, before treatment is available, incurring extra-costs for the hospital.[92]

This testimony allows us a better understanding of the role of the hospital in relation to medical treatment and care available in the community. Admission to the hospital was reserved on the one hand for cases that ordinary medical assistance could not handle, e.g. syphilis patients, and, on the other hand, for extreme cases for which the usual solutions arranged within the family and the community to cope with old age and sickness had become inadequate.[93] The rationale behind this system is more evident if one considers that help was provided to the poor who were still partly independent and could count on some support in the community, through the regular supply of free medicines and free medical assistance, and the distribution of bread in times of shortage. The City made a considerable investment in the expansion and improvement of these latter types of charity, encouraging therefore the development of forms of support in the community rather than institutionalisation.

Until the second half of the seventeenth century, when the hospital of S. Giovanni began to expand significantly, the impact of hospital care was insignificant in Turin. Charitable provisions for the sick poor have to be found elsewhere – in the municipally funded outdoor medical relief schemes. This system was initiated with the agreements drawn up with the hospital physician (1569) and blood-letter (1581), according to which these received supplementary salaries from the city for assisting those without means. In 1587 a third agreement was concluded with the apothecary to supply the medicines prescribed by the doctor free of charge.[94] The Council then attempted to improve access to the system by publicly displaying on every street corner the name of the doctor and the barber engaged by the City 'in order that the poor should know to whom they should turn in times of need'. In 1612 the surgeon for the poor was offered the shop next to the town hall tower in Piazza del Municipio, so that his activity could be seen by all, and would be in a place which was easy to find.[95]

The municipal medical service was substantially enhanced during the seventeenth century, mainly in response to the increased demand. At the beginning of the century complaints had been recorded about the high number of prescriptions, but numbers continued to rise, reaching startling levels by mid

[92] Ord. 20.4.1598. There is no reference to this category of patients in the minute book mentioned above. This leads us to assume that syphilis cases were probably admitted through a different procedure from the ordinary sick, i.e. without having to be discussed at board meetings. There is also evidence that some of them (mainly prostitutes and youth infected by them) were sent to the hospital (and paid for) by the municipality, as part of its overall public health policy. See above, note 10.
[93] On the variety of these arrangements, M. Pelling, 'Old age, poverty and disability in early modern Norwich', in Pelling and Smith, *Life*.
[94] Ord., 11.3.1569, 12.2.1581, 8.4.1587.
[95] Ibid., 5.8.1586, 9.3.1612.

century. The annual expenditure on medicines rose 'to several hundred *lire*' by 1653, but already by 1662 we find a proposal to fix an annual ceiling of 1,000 *lire*. In 1679, there were complaints that expenditure, which, until a few years previously, had been around the 1,500 or 2,000 *lire* mark, had now exceeded the enormous figure of 7,000 *lire*.[96] In 1675, a second doctor was engaged, as a result of protests made by the one already employed by the City that he had an excessive number of patients.[97] In 1678 the number of doctors was increased to four, and three young surgeons were also appointed to back up the surgeon for the poor by carrying out minor duties, such as 'visiting the sick, blood-letting, and putting on poultices and bandages', thus freeing the senior surgeon for more serious operations. Up to that time, the surgeon had used three apprentices who, however, had not been sufficient to allow him to carry out all his duties.[98] This sharp rise in the expenditure on medicine and health care at the end of the 1670s coincided with an enlargement of the city boundaries, although demographic pressure was not the only reason for the expansion of the system. This can be seen by the fact that the consumption of medicines very quickly levelled off, and that during the following century expenditure mostly stayed within the 6,000 to 7,000 *lire* range, in spite of a steady increase in the city's population (table 4). It may be that this relative decline was in part due to the expansion of the hospital, which commenced in the last quarter of the seventeenth century. But above all, the medical service was affected by the City Council's loss of independence in the management of local government. Already in the first half of the eighteenth century there were protests that the post of doctor for the poor had become little more than a sinecure. The doctors collected their salaries without having their activities checked up on, and they put most of their energies into private practice.[99] From the 1740s on, in particular, the functions of the municipal health system did gradually change and it adjusted its services to meet the demands of the state institutions (prisons and reformatories), while neglecting the treatment of the poor in their homes.

For at least the century and a half before this, however, municipal medical outdoor relief was the principal charitable resource available to the City's poor. It is impossible to establish precisely how the numbers of recipients varied over the period, since the earliest figures date from the eighteenth century. In 1735, free medicine was distributed to 5,792 patients (in a city of over 65,000

[96] Ibid., 13.9.1602, 20.4.1653, 29.5.1662, 30.9.1679.
[97] Armano left the post of city doctor in 1675 for this very reason. But even the two doctors together found the workload too heavy, and complained that they had twice fallen ill through overwork and requested to be replaced. Ibid., 31.12.1675, 6.8.1678.
[98] Ibid., 29.9.1678.
[99] In May 1748, as a result of this concern, the numbers of doctors and surgeons were increased to four and nine respectively. This was not an attempt to expand the service, merely to save it. The doctors were allocated smaller areas of the city in the hope that they would find it easier to reconcile their duties for the City with their private practices. ACT, C.S.4793.

Table 4. *Civic medical outdoor relief*

	Annual expenditure (*lire*)	Number of patients	
1662	1000 approx		
1679	7000 and over		
1687	7778		
1705	7318		
1710	6556		
1711	6956		
1718	8581		
1719	7464		
1729	6574		
1730	6512		
1735	8675	5792	
1740	5336		
1749	6287		from 1743 expenditure also includes
1750	5785		medicines to prisoners
1759	6597	4454	
1760	6520	4310	
1761	6281	3889	
1762	6178	4539	
1769	8596		
1770	6618		
1779	9737		from 1776 expenditure also includes
1780	10100		medicines given to the inmates of the
1783	10387	6065	Ritiro Martinetto (for prostitutes).
1789	12485		
1790	13245		

Note: The table shows the expenditure on medicines at the turn of every decade as well as all the available information about the number of recipients. For the eighteenth century the information is drawn from the annual *Conti del Tesoriere* (in ACT). Scattered data derive from the Ordinati of the City Council. On the extension of the service to prisons and houses of correction, ACT, CS4796 and Coll.IV, fasc.6.

inhabitants) and between 1759 and 1763, the number of recipients averaged 4,200 a year (table 4). Given that the level of expenditure on medicine remained steady from the late 1670s on, it seems reasonable to argue that the figures available for the eighteenth century could also be extrapolated back to the preceding period.[100] If this is accepted, we may surmise that already by the late seventeenth century, the recipients of municipal medical assistance numbered some several thousand. Obviously, backdating the figures cannot take account of fluctuations in the cost of medicines or of changes in medicines prescribed. However, we can find further evidence that the volume of medical assistance supplied by the Council must have been high if we compare it with the hospital's

[100] Unfortunately we do not know how these figures were calculated – whether the poor who received assistance several times in a year were counted only once, or every time they resorted to the service.

expenditure on medicines. In 1693, a year in which war and famine must have crowded the hospital with patients, expenditure amounted to 3,329 *lire*, about half the average figure that the Council paid for the poor treated at home.[101] Although we do not know the overall number of patients treated yearly in the hospital of S. Giovanni, we do know that by this time the latter had some ninety beds and so no longer constituted a small refuge for extreme cases, but an important centre for medical care.[102]

The extraordinary expansion of the municipal medical service was certainly not planned nor welcomed by the City Council. The reasons for its growth probably lay in the fact that, unlike other forms of assistance we have examined, the selection of recipients was not centralised but very much at the discretion of the doctors. The doctors probably found it hard to send away the poor who came to their shop without a prescription. It is also very likely that the apothecaries themselves prescribed medicines to the poor, since it seems unlikely that the few practitioners paid by the City could be responsible for the thousands of prescriptions figuring annually in the bills of the apothecaries of the poor (even if we assume that their duties were largely carried out by their apprentices and pupils). The salary received by the doctors was not affected by the number of patients but we certainly cannot exclude the possibility of some kind of agreement between doctors and apothecaries, aimed at sharing the profit deriving from the high number of prescriptions (given the frequency of this type of practice at the time). The service may therefore have expanded under the pressure of demand and because of the tolerance (and avidity) of doctors and apothecaries. The City made repeated attempts to establish its control over access to this form of assistance. In 1653 a committee of six councillors was set up to ascertain whether those who benefited from free medicines were 'truly poor and destitute'. In 1672 it was stipulated that the poor had to obtain a *fede di povertà* ('certificate of poverty') from the parish priest (plate 3), and this remained an obligatory requirement throughout the period. However, the length of validity of these documents is not stated and it is likely that, once the poor person had obtained the certificate, he could refer directly to the doctor any time he was in need of medical treatment. On several occasions, the doctors were exhorted to make out prescriptions 'only in the most serious cases and where there was urgent need', to avoid expensive medicines, and to treat only those who were really poor and, in particular, to avoid treating servants of any kind, as they were the responsibility of their employers.[103] Detailed guidelines about how to keep the expenditure low can be found in the *Istruzione per i dottori dei poveri* ('Instructions to doctors for the poor') which the City commissioned the

---

[101] Caffaratto, *L'Ospedale*, p. 179.
[102] AOSG, Ord.13.7.1692.
[103] Ord., 29.9.1653, 10.9.1672. See also ibid., 1.6.1648, 29.5.1662, 30.9.1679 and 21.12.1679.

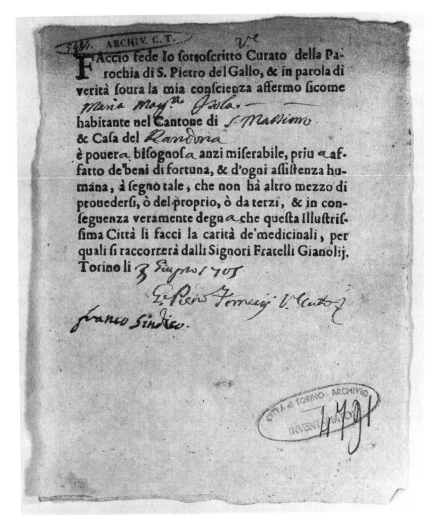

Plate 3. *Fede di povertà* (certificate of poverty), 1705 (ACT, C.S.4791).

Protomedico to write in 1679, and which was reprinted on several occasions (plate 4).[104] However, the doctors retained their control over this form of assistance, largely because the scale of the operations meant that any supervision could be only very cursory. Unfortunately, we have no information as to the identity of the poor who benefited from the medical treatment at home. It may

[104] ACT, SI/C 10838, *Avvertimenti per la cura de' poverelli infermi, nella città di Torino*, Turin 1680.

well be that, as the City complained on several occasions, the consumption of medicines was increased by corrupt practices, and that some of the recipients did not really qualify on the grounds of destitution, but these protests seem to have been mainly an expression of alarm over increasing costs.

Partly against the Council's wishes, medical assistance had grown considerably from the end of the sixteenth century and had become the core of the municipal welfare system. Of the various forms of aid offered by the City, it was certainly the one which affected the greatest number of poor, partly because it was a permanent service, not just one which appeared in times of crisis, and partly because it operated relatively independently from the channels of patronage and privilege that dominated other forms of aid. Medical relief also proved extremely durable, and continued to operate after the hospital expanded and the City had lost its control over other aspects of the urban charity system.

Poor relief and city politics

By the end of the sixteenth century, the civic government had increased its control over Turin's charitable system, which had expanded its scope considerably in the space of a few decades. The system was able both to deal with emergencies caused by famine and epidemic, and to give extensive aid to the poor in normal times. In the following pages I will argue that this expansion of welfare was closely linked to the pattern of city politics which characterised the first decades after the return of the Duke. The extension of the relief system controlled by the City was not an isolated tendency but an aspect of a wide-ranging consolidation of civic powers and privileges which occurred in this period. This statement would appear to clash with the long-prevailing view, according to which, after repossessing his territories, Duke Emanuele Filiberto immediately engaged in a policy of centralisation in all areas of government, including welfare,[105] stamping out all local obduracy and rival power structures, and earning his reputation as one of the first examples of an absolute monarch.[106] Yet there is substantial evidence of a very different story. The Duke had difficulty asserting his authority, and encountered constant hostility from the myriad local administrations whose autonomy had become consolidated during the period of French domination (which had lasted more than twenty years).[107]

---

[105] Erba comments on the implications for welfare in *La Chiesa*.

[106] P. Anderson, *Lineages of the Absolute State*, London 1974, pp. 170–1; E. Stumpo, 'I ceti dirigenti in Italia nell'età moderna. Due modelli diversi: nobiltà piemontese e patriziato toscano', in A. Tagliaferri (ed.), *I Ceti Dirigenti in Italia in Età Moderna e Contemporanea*, Istituto di Storia dell'Università di Udine, Udine 1984. Even Koenigsberger accepts this interpretation, although he adopts a more negative attitude to the Duke, whom he describes as despotic; 'The Parliament'.

[107] Numerous examples are referred to in W. Barberis, *Le Armi del Principe. La Tradizione Militare Sabauda*, Turin 1988.

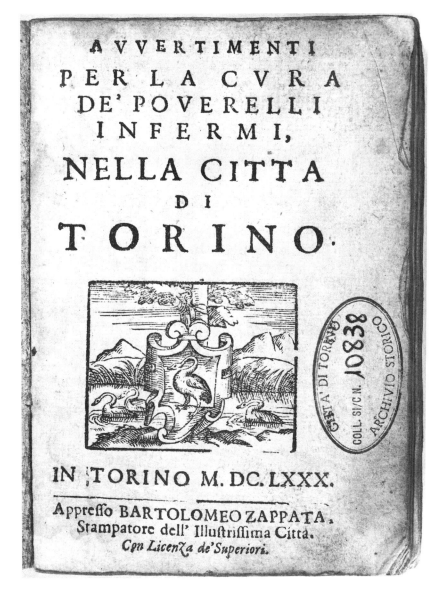

Plate 4. *Instruction for the doctors of the poor*, front cover, 1680 (ACT, Coll.SI/C 10838).

As far as the capital is concerned, some well-documented (although largely ignored) studies show that, for several decades, the City authorities were far from submissive towards the Dukes.[108] Indeed, the key to understanding the relationship between central and local powers in this period seems to be the Duke's isolation and lack of authority, rather than his strength and determination. This would help to explain the desperate attempts – which strongly characterise the rule of the first Dukes – to shore up their image, creating new areas of patronage. The bestowal on a grand scale of gifts, titles, enfeoffments (mainly taken out of state property) and fiscal incomes all show, in my opinion, that the sovereign was on the defensive, trying to buy consensus and support and not, as has usually been suggested, that he was successfully executing a plan to replace the established, unreliable nobility with a group of loyal new men.

The Duke was particularly unpopular in Turin where, as we have seen, local autonomy had not only been recognised but strengthened by the French occupation. As the new capital of the Duchy of Savoy, Turin often found itself in disagreement with the sovereign's requests; indeed the very presence of his entourage was cause for continuous clashes. The disputes began as soon as Emanuele Filiberto entered the city, and were to last for several decades. The citizens were reluctant to accept the authority of his officials, and hostile to his requests for accommodation for his family, soldiers and courtiers. Nor did they take kindly to the imposition of new taxes or to the request that they provide men for the formation of a militia. The City contended that these demands were incompatible with its traditional immunity and administrative independence. Continual remonstrances on the part of the Council led to drawn-out negotiations on various issues, which ended with concessions being made by both sides. The City donated large sums to central government, which was in major financial difficulties, in exchange for exemption from the taxation and other obligations that the Duke wished to impose. In this way, the City increased its fiscal and administrative privileges, while the Duke obtained recognition of the legitimacy of his requests. For a few decades, ducal and municipal power, therefore, grew together, the one reinforcing the other. Contrary to the traditional view of the state-building process, the affirmation of central government did not imply the weakening of local power, but to a certain extent its enhancement.

---

[108] Besides the already cited articles by Chiaudano, see on the first Dukes, D. Bizzarri, 'Vita amministrativa torinese ai tempi di Emanuele Filiberto', *Torino Rassegna Mensile*, 7–8, 1928, and 'Vita amministrativa torinese ai tempi di Carlo Emanuele I', ibid., 9, 1930; for the following period, G. Claretta, *Storia della Reggenza di Cristina di Francia, Duchessa di Savoia*, 3 vols., Turin 1868; and *Il Municipio di Torino ai Tempi della Pestilenza del 1630 e della Regente Cristina di Francia*, Turin 1869. This view has been recently taken up and developed by S. Cerutti. See in particular 'Cittadini di Torino e sudditi di Sua Altezza', in G. Romano (ed.), *Figure del Barocco in Piemonte. La Corte, la Città, i Cantieri, le Provincie*, Turin 1988.

In its attempts to reinforce its powers and status, the City leant heavily on reassertions of its claims to ancient privileges. However, this was a classic case of the 'invention of tradition', for the extension of municipal prerogatives in this period went well beyond the powers which had been enjoyed in the Middle Ages. On the basis of supposed ancient rights, the citizens of Turin obtained exemption from all direct and extraordinary taxation imposed by central government,[109] exemption from the land registry of all land and property within the commune, and crucial rights of jurisdiction. The Duke conceded, in fact, that all civil and criminal cases involving citizens of Turin should be tried, both in the initial and in the appeal stage, before one of two municipal officials, the *Giudice* and the *Vicario*.[110] From 1575, the right to nominate these judges passed from the Duke to the City itself;[111] and from 1577 onwards the City was allowed to keep the whole of its income from fines, whereas previously central government had had the right to a quarter.[112] But the municipal authority not only reinforced its administrative independence, it also extended the scope of its activity: for example, it obtained recognition of its role in the management of urban police[113] – that is in the system of public order and law enforcement that was expanding in this period and was codified in the *Ordini politici* to which I have already referred.[114] These orders were intended to regulate many different aspects of city life: from commercial activities (controlling weights and measures, prices, the baking of bread, in order to prevent speculation, fraud and hoarding), to working conditions, building, sanitation and public health; from education, moral standards and public order to public holidays and festivities.

The city administration also obtained recognition of its rights to the income raised from customs and excise within its territory. Some of these rights had indeed existed since time immemorial, and they were confirmed by the Duke. They included the tax on wine sold in the city, and duty on the wine that was imported, the tax on meat butchered in the city, and (most profitable of all) the duty on milling (that is on all flour used to produce bread consumed in the town). The Duke also confirmed the City's rights to the rents from the stalls in the

---

[109] D., T. XX, *Atto pubblico di convenzione*, 30.4.1567, pp. 1071 and 1076 ff. provide a summary of successive acts confirming the tax exemption obtained in exchange for City donations to state coffers.

[110] The *Giudice*, whose court was held in the Palazzo Comunale, was responsible for all first instance jurisdiction in civil and criminal cases; the *Vicario* was responsible for first appeals while the Senate heard cases which reached the second appeal stage. The *Vicario* in addition was required to pass judgement in cases concerning public order and the police. In these two areas, controlled by regulations in the *Ordini Politici*, the *Vicario*'s responsibilities were administrative and supervisory as well as judicial. Bizzarri, 'Vita . . . ai tempi di Emanuele Filiberto', p. 441.

[111] The local authorities had, however, to present the Duke with a choice of three candidates. Ibid., p. 442.

[112] ACT, C.S. 94; C.S. 103, 1580; C.S. 114, 1582.

[113] Ibid., C.S. 94, 1569; C.S. 103, 1575.

[114] See this chapter p. 43 and note 12.

market square and the tax on the goods sold there.[115] New rights were obtained on the other hand in this period of rivalry with central authority, such as the right to introduce new taxation. New taxes included charges on the river-crossings and on the use of water from the Po (1570), two new taxes on meat sold in the city (1564 and 1566), and the salt duty previously held by the Duke (1587).[116] Other concessions obtained during negotiations included the right to increase the duty on milling (1564), the doubling of wine duty (1578), and the right to income from the taxes paid by the commune of Grugliasco (1567).[117] The City also obtained permanent exemption from the most unpopular of all its obligations to the sovereign, namely the cost of billeting the Duke's entourage and of providing men for the town garrison.[118] It is clear that the City's budget was considerably enhanced by these concessions. The growth in fiscal powers and the income from increased police and judicial activities, in particular, brought the City's finances to an unprecedented state of prosperity.

The municipality also obtained symbolic recognition of its enhanced status as a political institution. From 1574, the City Council was represented in public ceremonies in a position immediately behind the most illustrious of the bodies representing the Duke's power, the *Camera dei Conti* (Chamber of Accounts).[119] Moreover, from the 1570s, city officials could use the emblem of civic identity and power (a bull) as a symbol of the dignity of their office. The symbol of the bull was displayed on councillors' coats of arms and on their doors, and carried by the municipal usher, who walked through the streets in front of the mayors.[120] Finally, in 1597 the councillors were given all the rights associated with feudal status, including the carrying of weapons.[121]

There can be little doubt, then, that the privileges and status of civic authority increased enormously in these three decades at the end of the sixteenth century. As I have mentioned, this was the result of intense bargaining between the interests of the City and those of central authority. Like the spectacular cases of social mobility which became frequent in this period, permitting individuals of modest background to attain large fortunes and high office, the growth of the City's powers originated in the fragility of the Duke's authority, and in his willingness to concede privileges. In both cases, the Duke's quest for consensus interacted with the strategies of groups and individuals who aimed to exploit his weakness.

---

[115] ACT, C.S. 86, 1564–66; C.S. 91, 1567; C.S. 101, 1575; C.S. 106, 1578.
[116] Ibid., C.S.86; C.S.95, 1570; on the transfer of the salt duty, see Chiaudano 'La finanza . . . ai tempi di Carlo Emanuele I', p. 913.
[117] Chiaudano, 'La finanza . . . ai tempi di Emanuele Filiberto', and 'La finanza . . . ai tempi di Carlo Emanuele I'.
[118] ACT, C.S.106, 1578.
[119] Ibid., C.S. 100, 1574 and C.S. 106, 1578.
[120] Ibid., C.S. 100, 1574.   [121] Ibid., C.S. 145, 1597.

The developments which affected poor relief in the second half of the sixteenth century were inextricably linked to this increase in the influence of the municipal government. Investment in welfare was not only a consequence of the enhanced political identity of the City, but also an instrument for its formation; for the expansion of the civic welfare system boosted the authority of the municipal government, and support for it. The definitions of deserving poor that were formulated in this period were themselves partly an outcome of the ongoing political conflict. In its negotiations with the Duke, the City strongly emphasised the privileged status of its citizens; policy towards the poor became a vehicle for reinforcing this civic identity and awareness of the rights associated with the condition of citizen. At least in terms of the rhetoric employed in the legislation, it was in precisely this period that access to welfare was restricted to citizens of Turin. We should recall that, previously, no distinction had been made between citizens and non-citizens in the distribution of poor relief. Indeed, in 1541 the poor who 'had no rooms' in the city were entitled to favourable treatment – a place in the hospital of S. Giovanni – whereas residents could receive assistance only at home.[122] Or again, in 1568 and 1571, the distinction between beggars to be expelled and to be assisted depended on their ability to work, and not on their citizenship.[123] Foreignness appeared as a negative attribute only in 1586. For the first time, the City Council ordered 'the expulsion of the indolent foreign vagabonds who steal bread from the mouths of the city's poor'.[124] However, the uncertainty surrounding the criteria used to distinguish who was and who was not a citizen demonstrates that the concept was still alien and ill-defined. In July of 1587 the new edition of the *Ordini politici* stated that all the poor who arrived in the city after Christmas were to be considered non-citizens, and those who arrived before Christmas, citizens. A further edition of the *Ordini*, published in the autumn of 1592, changed the cut-off date from Christmas to Michaelmas (i.e. to autumn and the beginning of the cold season).[125] In subsequent years, orders for the expulsion of beggars usually mention the distinction between citizen and non-citizen as one of the principal criteria for their selection, but without further clarification.

The reasons for the emergence of a discourse which discriminated against non-citizens are to be found in that political clash which prompted the City to define its own borders and to play heavily on the rhetoric concerning the privileges and status of citizenship. As I have already suggested, this does not mean that rules concerning citizenship were applied to the letter. They were, in fact, widely inconsistent with the dynamics of immigration which sustained the

---

[122] Ibid., C.S. 657, 1541.
[123] D., T. XIII, p. 248, *Lettere di Sua Altezza con le quali nomina un Cavaliere di virtù*, 5.4.1568, and ACT, C.S. 3234, 1571.
[124] Ord., 10.9.1586.
[125] ACT, C.S. 4701, 1587, and Borelli, pp. 228 ff., *Ordini politici*, 29.5.1592.

expansion of the city in those years and its transformation into a capital. In practice, the rules concerning citizenship were applied in a fashion which reinforced social rather than geographical discrimination. However, the distinction between citizen and non-citizen did contain an important ideological message. During the struggle against the Duke's authority, the inclusion of this distinction in legislation must have reinforced the City's identity and the image of a body with its own rights and privileges.

The rise of ducal charity

Initiatives taken in the field of poor relief thus have to be understood within the context of local politics. This becomes even clearer if we examine the changes in the Duke's initiatives in welfare, since these appear to be closely related to shifts in the local balance of power. Three phases can be detected. In the 1570s and 1580s, the Duke set up two welfare institutions of his own (the hospital of San Maurizio and Lazzaro and the Albergo di Virtù), and generously funded them from his coffers. Ducal policy at this stage was extremely cautious and mainly orientated towards the creation of separate areas of influence. At the turn of the century, there were the first attempts at more direct interference with municipal charitable activity, but these were easily resisted by the City. It was not until the 1620s, when ducal authority had become more established, that a more determined attack was made on the City's control over welfare. In the Dukes' attempts to develop their own welfare system and, subsequently, to challenge the municipal monopoly, a key role was played by the knights of the Ordine di San Maurizio e Lazzaro, made up of the Dukes' closest courtiers. A religious congregation dedicated to San Maurizio had been founded by Duke Amedeo VIII of Savoy in 1434, but it had subsequently fallen into decline. After the restitution to the House of Savoy of its territories, however, the fact of its formal existence was used as a pretext for a purely political project to establish an order of knighthood under the control of the Dukes. In 1572, after complex diplomatic manoeuvres, Emanuele Filiberto did in fact obtain a papal bull which united the existing order of San Maurizio with the order of San Lazzaro of Jerusalem which possessed substantial benefices *in commendam*.[126]

---

[126] The order of San Maurizio was established by Pope Gregorio XIII in a papal letter of 16.9.1572, and Papal Bull of 13.11.1572 brought about the union with the order of San Lazzaro (D., T. I, pp. 271 ff. and 275 ff.); privileges and the incorporation of the property of the order of San Lazzaro were confirmed in the *Breve di papa Clemente VIII* of 9.9.1603 (ibid.). With the Letters Patent, 22.1.1573 Emanuele Filiberto founded the Sacra Religione di San Maurizio e Lazzaro (ibid., p. 399). Histories of the order include: G. Baldesano, *La Sacra Historia di S. Mauritio Arciduca della Legione Thebea . . .*, Turin 1604 (second edition); G. B. Ricci, *Istoria dell'Ordine Equestre de' SS. Maurizio e Lazzaro col Rolo delle Comende*, Turin 1714; L. Cibrario, *Breve Storia degli Ordini di S. Maurizio e di S. Lazzaro Avanti e Dopo l'Unione Loro*, Turin 1844; G. Claretta, *Dell'Ordine Mauriziano nel Primo Secolo della Sua Costituzione*, Florence 1890.

Initially, the foundation of a hospital of San Maurizio e Lazzaro was merely a consequence of the fact that the ancient order of San Lazzaro had originally been dedicated to the care of the sick (in particular lepers). And in fact, although the hospital formally existed from 1575, in a house donated by the Duke together with other property,[127] it did not actively involve itself with welfare until the following century.[128] The hospital only started to carry out its duties once the status of the order had been firmly established. In the mid seventeenth century it underwent its first major reorganisation and expansion; then, in the 1670s, a newly constructed building of 'greater dignity' replaced the original group of medieval buildings. The later decades of the century saw the fastest expansion of the institution – which grew from fourteen to fifty beds between 1656 and the end of the century.[129] After this period, however, the hospital seems to have suffered a kind of paralysis, and there was no significant expansion in the eighteenth century. The growth of the hospital therefore reflected the rise and fall of the prestige of the new order much more closely than the changing requirements of the city's population.

Originally, the creation of the order of knighthood was aimed at establishing the dynasty's status in relation to other ruling families – as the high number of foreign knights testifies. So in the first few decades, knighthoods were conferred in order to foster relationships with other courts. But after the turn of the century, the order was used increasingly for internal political purposes as a means of bolstering the pro-Savoy camp. The knights now came mainly from within the state.[130] At the same time, members of the order received an impressive list of privileges – such as tax exemptions, special jurisdictions, rights of precedence, and the right to carry arms – which placed them at the highest level of the social hierarchy.[131] The status of the order was further enhanced by the decision, taken in 1603, to declare St Maurice's Day a

---

[127] The donation (effected on 27.4.1575) included, along with the house, an income of 600 *scudi* per year and some land in the territory of Poirino. See T. M. Caffaratto, 'Storia dell'Ospedale Maggiore di Torino della religione e ordine dei SS. Maurizio e Lazzaro', *Ann.Osp.M.Vitt.*, vol. 22 (1979), p. 366.

[128] In the early decades of the seventeenth century the building was used as a convent for the friars of Santa Teresa. Ibid., p. 379.

[129] Caffaratto, 'Storia dell'ospedale', p. 371.

[130] See the list of the investitures which, although incomplete, does make it possible to observe how the trend was inverted, in Ricci, *Istoria*.

[131] On 8.1.1608 the knights were exempted from the payment of duty, tolls, personal taxation (except the registration of property) and payments for the upkeep of the garrison, and from service in the guard; they were given precedence over doctors, lawyers and craftsmen in public ceremonies, and, with their servants, were granted the right to carry all types of arms. On 12.4.1608 legal privileges which had already been accorded to the knights in 1572 were extended. Not only was jurisdiction over religious affairs to be in their hands, but so too were criminal and civil cases (including debt). All such cases were now to be heard by a special court presided over by the Auditor of the Order. In 1609 the knights and the hospital were given the right to keep their own slaughter-house, where the meat was to be free of duty. Borelli, *Editti*, pp. 245 ff. and D., T. I, pp. 428 and 454.

public holiday. The prosperity gained in the same year from its union with the order of San Lazzaro allowed it to grant its knights wealthy benefices *in commendam*.[132]

The boosting of the order's prestige constitutes a typical example of the way the Duke sought to enlarge his following and increase his influence by introducing new forms of social advancement under his direct control. However, the opposition that this policy encountered from other political bodies points to the weakness of the Duke's position and the climate of political barter that still characterised the period at the turn of the century. On three occasions, the Senate refused to pass the edict granting privileges to the order of San Maurizio e Lazzaro, even after having already forced the Duke to accept a whole series of amendments to the previous draft. Despite the concessions they had won, the Senate continued to obstruct ratification of several clauses, especially one that granted the knights precedence over doctors, lawyers and trade guilds in public meetings. In the end, the Duke was obliged to justify this precedence in terms of the religious status of the knights, and to assure his opponents that it did not imply any slight to the professions or trades. On 8 February 1608, the Senate finally had to capitulate, but it insisted on putting its continued opposition on record and stating that ratification was the result of pressure from their sovereign.[133]

One of the Duke's aims in building up the order was to create a nucleus of loyal officials invested with his direct authority. This notion of loyalty was central to the rituals of the order and to the propaganda surrounding it; the knights' devotion to the Duke even appeared to have the seal of religious vows. Before very long, a clear distinction was to emerge between court offices and governmental duties, and this confined the order within the boundaries of the court so that it came to have a merely ceremonial role.[134] For a brief period before these developments took place, however, the knights were given positions of considerable responsibility as the Duke's representatives. It was in this context that, at the end of the sixteenth century and in the early decades of the seventeenth, 'the knights of our order' took on the task not just of administering the new charitable institutions established by the Duke (which I shall come to shortly) but of implementing a plan for what was presented as a reorganisation of poor relief throughout the entire territory of the state. From 1609 to the 1630s the Duke repeatedly attempted to expropriate the considerable charitable resources belonging to the Confraternities of the Holy Spirit and to put

---

[132] Ibid., p. 285.
[133] Ibid., p. 245.
[134] In the following decades, the order was increasingly identified with court circles, and court protocol attributed particular importance to its role in public gatherings. See T. De Gaudenzi, 'Torino e la corte sabauda al tempo di Maria Cristina di Francia', *BSBS*, part 1, vol. 18 (1913), pp. 41 and 43, and ibid., part 2, vol. 19 (1913), p. 53.

them under the control of the order. These resources mainly consisted of landed property which, in the Middle Ages, had provided the revenue for the communal organisation of poor relief and existed in virtually every Piedmontese and Savoyard community.[135] The order to expropriate these *beni di Santo Spirito* and take them out of the hands of the lay confraternities which had hitherto administered them was justified on the usual grounds of a desire to put an end to current abuses and, by putting them under the control of the knights, to restore an important source of revenue to the poor. It seems however that profits accruing from the small proportion of *beni* which they managed to sell (in spite of the community's opposition to the Duke's action) were used to provide benefices *in commendam* and pensions for the knights of the order. Although there are no studies specifically on the subject, there seems little doubt that the Duke's attempt to take control of these funds was a failure. The plan was never sanctioned by the local community, nor did it have the approval of the Roman Curia (necessary given the charitable status of the *beni*), but above all, it never achieved its declared aim of establishing a network of hospitals stretching right across the country.[136]

The knights of San Maurizio were also involved in the administration of another ducal initiative for the poor, the Albergo di Virtù. This had been founded in 1580 by a number of members of the Compagnia di S. Paolo (Turin's most important lay congregation),[137] but it existed only on paper until Duke Carlo Emanuele I took it over in 1587, and entrusted it to the order, which, together with the members of the Council of State and the Auditor of the *Camera dei Conti*, was to manage it.[138] The Albergo di Virtù was also made the beneficiary of a considerable transfer of financial resources. On paper at least it was to receive an annual cheque for 600 *lire* derived from three sources: the revenues from the *gabelle*; one-tenth of the income from fines imposed in all criminal and fiscal cases tried in courts of the Piedmontese side of the Alps; and, finally, profits previously reserved for the Duke from the state monopoly on playing cards and *tarocchi* (it should be added, however, that in practice, the Albergo had a struggle to extract these dues from the tax-farmers). In addition, the Albergo was given a large building outside the city walls called the Palazzo delle Poste, which for many decades was to be the centre of the Duke's activities in the field of welfare. Here, under the auspices of the Duke, the brothers of S. Gio' di Dio later established their hospital and this was also where the first hospital for

---

[135] See above, chapter 1, note 44. Duparc, 'Confréries du Saint Esprit'; Bernard, 'Les confréries communales'.

[136] Erba, *La Chiesa*, pp. 242 ff.

[137] D., T. XIII, pp. 198 ff., *Letters Patent*, 18.12.1580.

[138] AST s.r., Albergo di Virtù, scat. 3, 'Atto di remissione dalli direttori della casa dell'Albergo al Duca Carlo Emanuele I . . . ', 29.6.1587; Borelli, *Editti*, p. 205, *Eretione e autorità del consiglio dell'Albergo*, 8.7.1587.

beggars was to be set up.[139] Right from the beginning the institution thus bore the marks of ducal patronage. It is no surprise, therefore, to learn that the inauguration was a stately occasion with a full procession, arranged to coincide with the Duke's birthday in January 1588.

The Albergo has generally been seen as an attempt to favour the formation of a class of artisans, and encourage the spread of manufacturing activities at a time when Piedmontese industry was extremely limited.[140] The Albergo took in a few dozen children aged between twelve and fifteen (mostly boys) and trained them under resident master craftsmen.[141] In the early period at least, most of these craftsmen were recruited from outside the state, in order to introduce new skills. Yet the institution was also an important vehicle for the Duke's policy of establishing spheres of influence. Given the privileges that it entailed, admission to the Albergo was desirable both for the apprentices and for the craftsmen who opened shops there. The institution paid for the maintenance of the boys and girls and all the costs of their six-year apprenticeship.[142] At the end of this period they were supposed to be experienced enough in their craft to be able to enter the labour market, and spread the new skills they had acquired.[143] The Albergo also committed itself to the maintenance of the artisan, his family and any workers he might take on, and to supplying the workshop (and in some cases even the equipment) free of charge.[144] The institution also shared the risk of the enterprise in that it advanced the capital for the raw materials (this capital was then reimbursed from sales). Finally, the covenant often provided for the concession of monopolies in the production of specific articles; these might last a number of years, and sometimes covered the whole of the state's territory.[145] Membership of the Albergo therefore not only created favourable working conditions, but also guaranteed access to a number of privileges and rights not enjoyed by the other artisans in the city. In 1587, the Albergo and all those who worked in it

---

[139] Ibid., *Fondazione dell'Albergo*, 24.7.1587. By way of comparison, it should be remembered that the duke's contribution to the maintenance of the hospital of S. Giovanni was 30 *scudi* a year.

[140] D., T. XIII, p. 198; G. Ponzo, *Stato e Pauperismo in Italia: l'Albergo di Virtù di Torino (1580–1836)*, Rome 1974.

[141] AST. s. r., Albergo di Virtù, Scat. 47, 'Ordinati del Consiglio di amministrazione', 1, 1587–98, 26.12.1587 and 15.12.1587. Sixty children (forty boys and twenty girls) were accepted at the inauguration. The total number of inmates remained at about a hundred.

[142] On 21.6.1594, following consultations with the Duke and Duchess, it was agreed that, in order to avoid excessive spending, the master craftsmen would take on responsibility for the maintenance of the apprentices, and would be paid an annual lump sum for each one. Minutes of 21.6.1594.

[143] Some children were admitted for no charge, but in many cases the family paid a modest fee. Especially in the early period, there were limited openings on the labour market outside the institution, and the ex-apprentices stayed on as employees in the workshops run in the Albergo, where they received free board and a small salary.

[144] Some examples are found in the minutes of 25.6.1589, 16.12.1589 and 23.12.1590.

[145] For example, the minutes of 24.1.1593 and 7.8.1594, and the covenant with Pattino, in D., T. XIII, p. 203, 15.9.1587, *Letters Patent*.

came under the Duke's direct protection, which meant that all civil and criminal cases concerning the governors, the master craftsmen, their servants and workers were removed from ordinary jurisdiction and put under that of the institution's own governing council.[146] This policy of granting special privileges continued in the following century. In the mid seventeenth century, the governor and craftsmen were granted exemption from personal and military taxes, and further concessions were obtained in the eighteenth century.[147] The Albergo was therefore a kind of free port zone. It enjoyed immunity from the duties imposed by the Duke on 'all goods, livestock, fruit, and any other items in transit across the state' for use by the institution, and in 1636 it was exempted from the tax on the silk bought in Racconigi.[148]

The establishment of the Albergo constituted an important political act at this particular moment in the late sixteenth century when the Duke found himself in such a vulnerable situation. His initiative did not interfere directly with the charitable institutions managed by the City, nor did it create a system of patronage in competition with that of the municipality. By and large the Duke's strategy for creating consensus did not even, at this stage, involve the capital, as can be shown by the fact that most of the apprentices came from the provinces. Admission was nearly always arranged through the intercession of the provincial nobility or members of the court, and only very rarely did the governing body admit candidates whose families petitioned directly. Very often the Dukes themselves were the mediators. They would receive the petitions, check them through and pass them onto the governing council of the Albergo for acceptance.[149] It would thus appear from the minute books that in the first few decades the Duke and his wife, the Infanta, managed the Albergo almost directly, and continually concerned themselves with questions of internal organisation, to the extent that the governing council seems to have consulted them before taking even the most petty decisions. The main impact of the institution upon the balance of power in the city was the influence that the Duke was able gradually to extend over a class of artisans who had been trained in the Albergo or who had been granted special privileges. In other words, the Albergo encouraged the creation of a network of entrepreneurs and artisans tied to the Duke by links of dependence, and therefore an area of support that he could count on.

It was only at the end of the century that the Duke openly attempted to subvert

---

[146] *Letters Patent*, clause 9.
[147] Ponzo, *Stato e Pauperismo*, p. 99. With the development of craft guilds, the apprentices were assured of the title of master craftsman free from the charges and conditions usually imposed by guilds. The master craftsmen were granted the right to sit with the leaders of their guild once a year. AST, p.s., LPqM, m.16, *Albergo di Virtù*, fasc.3.
[148] See the *Letters Patent* referred to above, 15.9.1587, and Ponzo, *Stato e Pauperismo*, p. 120.
[149] See the minutes of 22.4.1593 and 19.2.1594 in AST, s.r., *Albergo di Virtù*.

the autonomy and prestige of the charitable institutions run by the municipality. In 1597 he attempted to set up a new hospital in competition with the City's hospital of S. Giovanni. Prior to this the Duke had supported a proposal put forward by the brothers of the order of S. Gio' di Dio (the Fatebenefratelli) that they should establish themselves in Turin, and take over the management of the hospital of S. Giovanni. This project would have involved the exclusion of the City Council from the running of the hospital, given that the members of this order were obliged by their statute to submit the accounts of their management only to the archbishop.[150] The City had refused a similar proposal put forward by the same brothers some four years earlier, and this second plan met with the same fate, in spite of the fact that this time it was openly supported by the Duke and the archbishop. Faced with a blank refusal by the City Council, the Duke backed away from the plan, and gave the friars a wing of the building used by the Albergo di Virtù, until they were able to establish their own hospital under the name of Santissimo Sudario. The inauguration ceremony of this new institution was held in May and attended by the Duke and the Infanta, together with their officials and courtiers, in order to emphasise the importance attached to the event. Even the City Councillors could not refuse the Duke's request that they send two delegates to the ceremony. However, the municipality was able to impose rigid conditions on the order, which were stipulated in a notarial act on the very day of the inauguration. These conditions effectively subjected the new hospital to the City's supervision. A particularly significant clause was the one which limited the maximum number of friars to six, thus blocking any plans the order and the new hospital might have for expansion. Moreover, the friars could be sacked in cases of malpractice, and any items acquired by dubious means would remain the property of the hospital.[151] By December the City was already exercising its rights and ordering two councillors to carry out an inquiry into allegations that the friars were not using all the alms collected to help the sick, but were sending them out of the country. Further investigations of this kind were carried out in the decades that followed, constantly to remind the brothers of their unstable position in town and their dependence on the local authority.

In 1598 the Duke was still using the hospital of Santissimo Sudario in his attempt to limit the expansion of the hospital of S. Giovanni, and to move it outside the city walls. The governors of the latter had just purchased a building in order to enlarge the hospital further, when the Duke asked them to exchange their new building with that occupied by the brothers of S. Gio' di Dio. This

---

[150] For the sources on this episode, see G. Radice and C. Marpelli, *I Fatebenefratelli*, vol. V, *I Conventi. L'Ospedale del S. Sudario di Torino e di S. Michele di Asti*, Milan 1977 (pp. 13–48), which contains a good part of the documentation.

[151] The covenant is published in D., T. II, pp. 1–3.

request was rejected out of hand, and sparked off a lengthy polemic between the ducal authorities and the municipality. The Duke argued that outside the city walls the air was healthier and the hospital would be better placed in time of epidemics; the governors replied that a central position was more essential if they and the doctors were to carry out their duties properly, and argued that the hospital's existing position offered gentlemen and gentlewomen the opportunity to exercise their piety by visiting the sick. They further argued that the presence of the sick within the town itself encouraged charity amongst the citizenry.[152] Although this conflict was presented as a noble struggle between the protection of the health of the poor on the one hand and the economic interests of the hospital on the other, it was essentially a political dispute, centred on the decrease in prestige that would have resulted from the transfer outside the city walls of the hospital of S. Giovanni, which had been at the very heart of the city since the fifteenth century.

This attempt to shift the City's hospital to a less central place on Turin's social map was successfully resisted, and when he was forced to concede defeat the Duke seems to have abandoned the plan to create an alternative centre for the care of the sick. The hospital of Santissimo Sudario never had anything more than a marginal role in the city's welfare system. Until the 1620s it was housed in a building which was totally unsuitable for the care of the sick, due to its state of disrepair and to the fact that the hospital was not sealed off from the manufacturing activities in the adjacent institution. As a consequence of this, its patients and staff were constantly disturbed by the noise of the spinners and 'the terrible smell' produced by the silk worms.[153] In 1628, after the hospital had been transferred to a new building built by the friars, there were still only five patients. At the end of the century, in the final building, completed in the 1680s after further enlargement, the infirmary consisted of only ten beds.

In the first decades after the restoration of the House of Savoy, the development of Turin's welfare system therefore reflected the continuing weakness of the duke's authority, in contrast with the increasing prestige of the municipality. The institutions protected by the duke remained largely ineffective. They were unable to provide a significant focus for the local poor; isolated from city life, they retained all the characteristics of a fief of the dukes. This also helps to explain the fact that, as we will see, they were unable to attract significant amounts of private charity, unlike other hospitals and institutions.

The municipality's dominance of the welfare scene was not seriously challenged until the 1620s. After that date, however, the conflict became more acute. The Duke started to meddle more often in the treatment of beggars. His

---

[152] AOSG, Cat. 1, cl. 1, cart. 5, 69, 'Ragioni d'addursi acciò che l'Hospitale no' si muti fuori della città', 1598.
[153] Radice e Marpelli, *I Fatebenefratelli*, p. 48.

delegates would frequently present the City Council with censures which bitterly attacked its policies. He denounced the municipality's inefficiency and its inability to free respectable citizens from the nuisance of begging. He sought the adoption of measures that 'imposed order and stopped destitute beggars from wandering the streets'.[154] The civic government was accused of being too lax towards beggars, and even of exposing the city to the risk of contagious diseases:

> His Highness protests at the terrible state of affairs and the way the poor in the city live, their scandalous lifestyle, atrocious sins, licentiousness, the constant contact between men and women day and night, with the ensuing danger of some infection.[155]

But at the same time, the councillors were denounced for their lack of compassion for the poor:

> who at night suffer the cold, which has caused three deaths, and the City has demonstrated little charity in assisting them, and must quickly provide somewhere for them to shelter at night to avoid death from cold [. . .] and if they do not do this His Highness will, in disgust at the City's lack of responsibility provide for the poor himself.[156]

The accusations of lack of proper Christian charity to the poor who were left to die of cold, or driven from the city's territory without any assistance, were intended to acclaim the sovereigns' piety and solicitude, their willingness to protect *all* their subjects and their ability to interpret their needs:

> and a great number of exhausted and destitute people come to the city, and many die in the city and just outside, and the doctors say that these deaths are caused by the terrible sufferings they undergo, which has caused His Highness great affliction upon hearing of it.[157]

The attack on the municipal management of welfare was in fact based on arguments implying a universal and indiscriminate attitude towards charity, in opposition to the corporative nature of the measures taken by the City Council. The Duke argued strongly against any distinction between citizen and non-citizen – the element which by then constituted the basis of the municipality's rhetoric. He opposed expulsions of beggars, and put forward plans to assist all the needy in the city without distinction. In 1627 this policy of extending welfare to all subjects in need was acted upon with the establishment of the hospital for beggars of the Annunziata, which the Duke entrusted to the knights of San Maurizio e Lazzaro. The new hospital invited 'all the poor of whatever situation who come from our territories and happen to be in the city' to seek

---

[154] Ord., 17.8.1623 and 19.7.1620.   [155] Ibid., 30.8.1624.
[156] Ibid., 7.2.1622.   [157] Ibid., 5.6.1629.

shelter within its walls.[158] However, the establishment of this hospital did not mark a turning point in the overall policy towards begging. The hospital had a short and difficult existence. This was in part caused by the serious outbreak of plague three years after its foundation, and then by the dynastic civil war (1637–42), which broke out following the death of Duke Vittorio Amedeo I, over who was to succeed him. The hospital finally ceased to function at the end of the 1630s.[159]

The City continued to oppose plans for universal charity, but its power had at last been eroded. Welfare initiatives increasingly resulted from difficult negotiations between the Duke and the municipality. When the City Councillors carried out the traditional collections from the wealthier citizens, or distributed daily hand-outs to the poor, they were often flanked by the knights of the order of San Maurizio e Lazzaro in their capacity as representatives of the Duke.[160] The controversy over the 1629 anti-famine measures (in a period of dearth that was the prelude to a dramatic outbreak of plague) clearly demonstrates the nature of the conflict. The anti-famine policy was administered jointly, instead of being organised by the City autonomously as had been the case previously, but this situation had to be forced on the municipality and was a source of serious conflict. The City allocated ten *scudi* a day to finance relief, but the Duke demanded that it should commit itself to pay half the bill, whatever this should come to. The City replied that the policy of indiscriminate aid which the Duke wished to enforce was too extravagant, and would have involved 'undertaking the impossible'. It therefore requested the adoption of selective measures. The two authorities eventually reached a compromise by which the City committed itself to pay a thousand *scudi* for another three months, but the Duke had to concede that no non-citizens would be assisted. On 26 May, hundreds of poor were expelled from the city, although the municipality was obliged to pay a further 125 *scudi* to supply them for their journey.[161]

In spite of the arbitrary nature of the distinction between citizen and noncitizen, the municipality attempted, in these years of intense conflict with the Duke, to impose it with the utmost rigour. This was clearly a dispute with wider symbolic implications, since any attack on the notion of citizenship, which the City had employed to justify its hegemony, was an attack on the ideological basis

---

[158] Borelli, *Editti*, p. 232, *Eretione di un hospitale per i mendicanti*, 10.3.1627. The hospital of the Annunziata as it was called was initially housed in the disused building belonging to the ancient hospital of S. Lazzaro outside the city, and later in the Albergo di Virtù, after the brothers of S. Gio' di Dio had moved.

[159] No documents have survived recording the activities of this first hospital for beggars. However the dates of the duke's provisions in its favour (payment of the donations and incomes allocated to it) cease in 1638, suggesting that the hospital was closed around this time. D., T. XII, pp. 254 ff.

[160] Ord., 4.6.1628, 5.6.1629.

[161] Ibid., 21–22.6.1629 and 26.5.1630.

of municipal power. It challenged the privileges enjoyed by citizens, and opposed the principle with an alternative perspective based on the equality of all subjects' rights and on the sovereignty of central government.

It is important to note that the Dukes were able to take on a more active role in welfare policy at a time when the court was expanding and gaining a privileged position in the urban social hierarchy. In other words, at a time when the sovereign's power was becoming consolidated. Again, the attack on municipal hegemony over charitable provision was very much an outcome of this new political context and of the changing balance of power. Nor was the offensive restricted to the field of welfare, for in this period the City's immunities and privileges generally were attacked with renewed vigour.[162] In the 1620s, for the first time, the imposition of war taxation did not respect the capital's privileged status. Turin was requested to make large contributions to the special levy for military expenses, and was obliged to borrow heavily, incurring unprecedented levels of indebtedness. Meanwhile the City was deprived of some of its revenues (such as the salt duty). In addition, Turin's citizens were now threatened with ordinary taxes from which they were supposed to be exempt. The Duke simply ignored the agreements drawn up in previous decades, not to mention the once-and-for-all payments which the City had made to acquire its immunity. The Duke's edicts now quite explicitly and blatantly disregarded the myth of Turin's special status, and continually equated the capital with his other territories.

Many other privileges were lost at this time; in 1616 the citizens of Turin were called to arms for the first time (once again this was a measure which put them on a par with other subjects). The City resisted this violation of its privileges for a long time, but in the end it had to capitulate. It soon became clear that this was no isolated incident; in 1620, even though the state was at peace, the citizens again had to 'bow their heads' before the order to provide a permanent militia for the city, and accept 'something that had never occurred in centuries gone by, even in time of war'.[163] Compulsory military service was extended to the entire territory of Turin. In the following decade, even the ancient rights over milling were questioned (1629).[164] On numerous occasions, the City's dignity as an institution was slighted, and its position in public ceremonies usurped.[165]

As we will see in the next chapter, profound changes were taking place in the relative status of the various elite groups, and these were leading to a

[162] Chiaudano, 'La finanza . . . ai tempi di Carlo Emanuele I', pp. 926–31; Bizzarri, 'Vita amministrativa . . . ai tempi di Carlo Emanuele I', pp. 869–76; Cerutti, 'Cittadini', pp. 268–71.
[163] Bizzarri, 'Vita . . . ai tempi di Carlo Emanuele I', p. 876.
[164] Ibid., p. 894, note 15.
[165] Ibid., in particular p. 885.

redefinition of the pattern of power. The confrontation between the Duke and the municipality which had dominated the scene for many decades, causing even charitable institutions to be split into two well-defined camps, now gave way to a more complex distribution of power and a more complex pattern of political initiative in the capital.

3

Motivations for charity

From civic to voluntary charity

1649 saw the founding of an institution which eventually took over a considerable part of the charitable functions of the City Council. This was the Ospedale di Carità, which, after a shaky beginning, went on to become a large poorhouse which housed 2,000 inmates and gave bread to hundreds of families outside. This new hospital marked a significant watershed, for some of the poor who until that time had been assisted principally by means of outdoor relief provided by the City Council now came to be segregated in an institution set up specifically for the purpose. Unlike the hospital for beggars that had been started in 1627, but had never taken off, and soon closed, the Ospedale di Carità was to become the main focus for Turin's charitable activity.

How can we explain this transformation? The appearance of forms of confinement of the poor has normally been seen as a result of new attitudes towards poverty which led to it being increasingly perceived as blameworthy and synonymous with crime and sin. According to this view, beggars were no longer regarded with compassion but aroused fear, annoyance and revulsion among the respectable ranks of society. The poor were therefore cast into secluded institutions where they were supposed to receive the moral and religious education they lacked and forced to do what they would not have done spontaneously – that is, work.[1] In this chapter, I would like to draw attention to a different kind of development which took place at the same time and which may have played a considerable role in prompting the emergence of the institutionalisation of the poor.

The advent of institutions for beggars should be seen in the context of the

---

[1] M. Foucault, *Folie et Déraison. Histoire de la Folie à l'Age Classique*, Paris 1961, Première Partie; Gutton, *La Société et les Pauvres*, chapters 2–3; O. H. Hufton, *The Poor in Eighteenth Century France 1750–1789*, Oxford 1974, pp. 139–59; Fairchilds, *Poverty and Charity*; Norberg, *Rich and Poor*, chapters 3–5; R. M. Schwarz, *Policing the Poor in Eighteenth Century France*, Chapel Hill, N.C. and London 1988.

98

rapid expansion of prestigious charitable building which is noticeable in many
parts of Europe, especially from the mid seventeenth century on.[2] This period
saw a wave of new construction and of rebuilding of existing institutions not
only for the indigent, but also for the sick and other categories of needy. Newly
founded institutions were established in grandiose edifices and existing
foundations left their old, modest buildings (which had often originally been
designed for some other purpose) and moved into new purpose-built premises.
Hospitals and other institutions came to be modelled on the splendid lines of
noble domestic architecture.[3] In Italy, the baroque style in architecture provided
them with an imposing and ornate appearance. Turin was no exception to
this trend; in the last quarter of the seventeenth century, all its main charitable
institutions moved to new premises: the Ospedale di Carità in 1683, the hospital
of S. Giovanni in 1680, the Albergo di Virtù in 1682, the hospital of San
Maurizio e Lazzaro in the late 1670s, and that of S. Gio' di Dio in the early
1680s. The first two, in particular, were built as real civic monuments; even at
the time, they were recorded in guides to noteworthy buildings in the town (see
plates 5–6).[4]

The fact that the 'houses of the poor were coming to resemble palaces' (to use
the expression adopted by one contemporary commentator)[5] is an important
phenomenon, which deserves more attention than it has received. In Turin, this
architectural change combined with the development of a series of rituals and
celebratory practices centred around charitable institutions which turned the
latter into something much more complex than simple places of shelter or
confinement of the poor. Hospitals became a grandiose stage on which new
forms of celebration of the prestige of governors and benefactors were enacted,
a theatre where hundreds of poor inmates could be employed to praise the virtues
of the wealthy. Moreover, they provided new opportunities for the acquisition of
power and influence. The multiplication in this period of hospitals for beggars –
and of charitable institutions in general – not only reflects a change in policies
towards the poor and sick, but shows that charity was now actively employed as
an instrument in the strategies of the rich. The appearance of large institutions
for the poor was also accompanied by an ever-increasing growth in charitable

[2] D. Leistikow, *Ten Centuries of European Hospital Architecture*, Ingolheim 1967; J. D.
Thompson and G. Goldin, *The Hospital: a Social and Architectural History*, New Haven, Conn.
1975; A. Scotti, 'Malati e strutture ospedaliere dall'età dei Lumi all'Unità', in *Storia d'Italia,
Annali 7*.

[3] S. Coppo, 'L'edilizia assistenziale ospedaliera nell'urbanistica torinese del Sei e Settecento', in
A. Cavallari Murat (ed.), *Forma Urbana e Architettura nella Torino Barocca*, Turin 1968,
vol. I, part II, p. 854.

[4] Ibid. The dates cited are those when works began; in some cases, several years elapsed before
completion. The new wave of building was made possible by the eastward extension of the city
limits in the 1670s.

[5] Cited in Jones, *The Charitable Imperative*, p. 37.

Plate 5. Hospital of S. Giovanni, entrance to the male infirmary (Archivio Museo Civico, Turin).

donations. Evidently, the institutionalisation of the poor – by creating an arena in which city elites could put their prestige on display through their charitable acts – stimulated their generosity considerably. In fact, the end of the century is marked by a large increase both in the number of legacies (see figure 1) and in their average size. There is no comparison between the few *scudi* which for decades was all the hospital of S. Giovanni could hope for in the way of charity and the generous donations and legacies which started to rain down at the turn of the century. In the earlier period bequests and donations were often given by long-term inmates in return for services they received, whereas well-off citizens contributed to the hospital's maintenance mainly through small, though perhaps frequent, alms. This type of giving, modest in size and above all anonymous, constituted the main form of charity that the hospital received. At the beginning of the seventeenth century the minutes carefully record the income obtained from the various boxes placed at the hospital's gates and at those of various churches, the result of the alms-collections carried out by single governors and by the Ladies of the Compagnia delle Umiliate (who did their charitable work in the hospital) during the Christmas festivities and during the Lent period, and the alms entrusted to the chaplain or to a governor by a 'pious person' who did not want to be mentioned. As the century proceeded, this impersonal form of

Plate 6. Hospital of S. Giovanni, staircase (Archivio Museo Civico, Turin).

charity lost importance, whereas larger but *una tantum* donations and bequests made by recognisable benefactors became the common practice of Turin's elites.[6]

This generalised voluntary giving was also very different from the practice of contributing to municipal special levies for the poor which had previously sustained the City Council's upkeep of the needy. A related change which took place in the last quarter of the seventeenth century was, in fact, in the shift of the greater part of financial assistance for poor relief, away from the City government to private charity. From this time on, the financial needs of the institutions – including the enormous costs of constructing the new buildings – were covered almost entirely by private donations. A revolution in the meaning of charity and in forms of giving had taken place. Charity had been transformed from a civic duty – administered by the City Council – into a voluntary and personal act bestowing prestige on the giver.[7] This change and its chronology is

---

6 Alms-collection declined in the late 1620s, and only had a short-lived revival between 1658 and 1664. See AOSG, Ordinati, 1.9.1658, 19.3.1660, 8.5.1661, 24.2.1662, 22.6.1664.
7 Dinges finds a similar shift from forms of giving based on an *esprit de réciprocité* to ones intended to display the social status of benefactors, in seventeenth-century Bordeaux. M. Dinges, 'Attitudes à l'égard de la pauvreté aux XVIe et XVIIe siècles à Bordeaux', *Histoire, Economie et Société*, 10 (1991), p. 362.

illustrated by the comparison between two lists of contributors to the relief of the poor which exist for 1683 and 1739.[8] In both cases, the Ospedale di Carità tried to overcome its financial difficulties by means of a voluntary tax on citizens – a practice which is reminiscent of the City's sixteenth-century imposition of taxes to which I have just referred. However, whereas the 1683 charge still managed to obtain contributions from a substantial number of citizens who had resources of some kind, the 1739 list is a much shorter one including only a couple of dozen contributors. In 1683, in the ten parishes for which the tax register survives, 508 citizens committed themselves to giving money or goods to the hospital. If we assume that another hundred contributors may have been obtained in the two parishes for which we have no register,[9] we can calculate that around 15 per cent of heads of households contributed.[10] Even though this is not an extraordinarily high percentage, it is not an insignificant one. The wide-ranging status of contributors is also worth noting. These included innkeepers, shopkeepers and artisans, as well as state officials and prominent aristocrats. Likewise, the contributions varied from a few *soldi* to hundreds of *lire*, from a few pairs of shoes or a piece of cloth to large quantities of corn or wine. On paper (for we do not know if all the contributors fulfilled their commitments), our ten parishes gave a total of 4,165 *lire*, plus 720 *emine* of cereals (mostly wheat), 257 *brente* of wine, and various quantities of bread, shoes, cloth, oil, etc.[11]

The response to the charge levied in 1739 was very different. Despite the notable growth of the city's population since 1683, the register lists only 32 subscribers, all of whom belonged to the most exclusive ranks of the City's aristocracy. It may well be that this restriction to a much more elite group was not the sign of a decrease in levels of Turinese generosity, but rather a sign that this form of charity had become unpopular. The majority of affluent citizens appear to have refused to contribute to what was in effect a semi-imposed form

---

[8] AOC, Cat.V, Parte I, Busta 1, fasc.1, 'Libro delli concorsi dei benefattori alla tassa fattasi da ciascuno per il sostentamento dell'Hospedale della Carità, 1683'; fasc.2, 'Libro delli particolari tassatisi, 1739'.

[9] One of the parishes for which the register is missing (S. Pietro del Gallo) contained the Duke's palace and thus was the main area of residence for members of the court; in theory, at least, it should have provided a high number of wealthy contributors.

[10] I obtain this figure by multiplying the 600 contributors listed by four (estimated average size of household) and dividing it by the total city population, which at the time was around 40,000. Some idea of the distribution of wealth in Turin can be gained from the fact that in 1705, there were 974 owners of private houses in the city, of whom 843 owned only one house and 131 two or more. E. Casanova, 'Censimento di Torino alla vigilia dell'assedio', in Regia Deputazione di Storia Patria, *Le Campagne di Guerra in Piemonte (1703–8) e l'Assedio di Torino (1706)*, vol. VIII, Turin 1909.

[11] Some donors committed themselves for just one year, others for three years; it seems probable, therefore, that the charge was imposed for three years. This supposition seems reinforced by the fact that in 1685 the governors noted that 'payment must be solicited of alms which citizens have committed themselves to making and bills sent out', AOC, Ordinati, 30.12.1685. I have found no reference to any other charge between that made in 1683 and that of 1739.

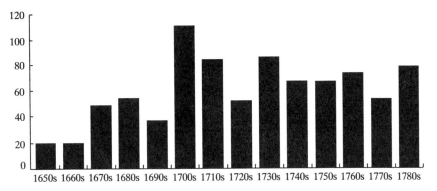

Fig. 1. Charitable institutions. Number of bequests and donations by decade,
1650–1789.

Note on the criteria used to calculate bequests and donations (in figures 1, 2, 3 and 4):
I have included in my calculations only substantial legacies and donations, i.e. those of
500 *lire* and above (to gain some sense of the value of these figures we should bear in
mind that throughout the eighteenth century, the cost of maintaining a poor person at the
Ospedale di Carità was estimated at circa 100 *lire* per year, while the annual pension
requested in the second half of the seventeenth century from older 'persons of quality'
who decided to withdraw to live in the hospital of S. Giovanni varied from 400 to
750 *lire*). Apart from the reasons given above (Introduction, p. 3), this choice is
determined by the need for accuracy: it would have been difficult to arrive at a precise
calculation of very small donations because for those, especially if they were made while
the donor was alive, no notarial act was required.

Repeated donations by the same individual have been considered separately, even if
made to the same institution. I have excluded donations and bequests which did not come
into effect, because subject to conditions which did not materialise (such as the absence
of heirs) or because the amount of the estate was not as expected. The date is that of the
donation or will, not that of the payment. When there was more than one testament, I have
considered only the last one (if this amended wishes laid down in previous ones).

of giving, and one which by this time did not seem sufficiently personalised.
Only the thirty or so names at the top of the social hierarchy – those, in other
words, who took part in every public initiative – were on the list.[12] Whereas the
1683 levy was still in the tradition of the municipal poor rates discussed in the
previous chapters, the contribution called for four decades later was just an
unsuccessful attempt to revive a custom by now totally anachronistic.

Private charity in Catholic countries has usually been seen as an expression of
religious sentiment and linked in particular to the Counter-Reformation

12 Contributions to the 1739 charge were standardised as contributors were asked how many
poor they were prepared to support (the annual cost of maintaining one poor person having been
calculated at 90 lire). Contributions thus went from 90 *lire* 'for one poor person' to the Marquess
Tana's 600 *lire* 'for 6 and 2/3 poor persons'.

Church's encouragement of charitable action. In Turin, however, it became important only towards the end of the seventeenth century – too late, in other words, to be ascribed in any direct way to the influence of the Counter-Reformation. Moreover, there was a continued rise in this form of charity (figure 1) in the middle decades of the eighteenth century, which are usually seen as years in which the grip of religion – and hence also charity inspired by concern for the afterlife – declined.[13] The chronology of this trend becomes meaningful, on the other hand, if we relate it to changes in social stratification and to changes in the structure of local power. On the one hand, the expansion of private charity seems to be linked to a changed political context in which the City Council lost many of its prerogatives, and the previously dominant bipolar pattern of power gave way to the emergence of a corporate pattern which entailed a widespread involvement of elites in the boards of the charitable institutions. On the other hand, the growth in charity seems to be related to the more elitist configuration of social prestige that was emerging – which made it essential for large sections of society to seek alternative ways of gaining recognition of their status. In the middle of the seventeenth century a widening gap emerged within the Turin elite. The top of the social scale came to be occupied by an aristocracy which consolidated its position in the space of a few decades thanks to the Dukes' spoils system and to financial speculation. This aristocracy gradually closed in on itself, becoming increasingly centred around the life of the court, which by this time had come to be formalised in exclusive rituals, and, more generally, around the figure of the Duke. The court circle cut itself off from the rest of the elite both through inter-marriage and by abandoning most of its involvement in the administration of the state in favour of specialisation in diplomatic and military careers and in the role of the Duke's immediate counsellors. In this way the court became a clearly separate entity, whereas earlier it had been common to find the combination of court functions and various bureaucratic offices in the same individuals and the same families.

Historians of Piedmont have traditionally seen the seventeenth-century court as an ancient hereditary nobility.[14] In fact however this aristocracy was not so much the heir of an uninterrupted tradition as the beneficiary of rapid upward mobility. The families which made up the exclusive court aristocracy in the later seventeenth century came from very varied backgrounds. Some could boast

[13] Vovelle, *Piété Baroque*.
[14] The idea that the distinction between ancient nobility and new nobility, and between nobility and bourgeoisie, was the basis of the system of social stratification is to be found in G. Quazza, *Le Riforme in Piemonte nella Prima Metà del Settecento*, 2 vols., Modena 1957; also, in more contradictory form, in L. Bulferetti, 'L'elemento mercantilistico nella formazione dell'assolutismo sabaudo', in *BSBS*, 54 (1956); and 'Sogni e realtà del mercantilismo di Carlo Emanuele II', *NRS*, 37 (1953); E. Stumpo, *Finanza e Stato Moderno nel Piemonte del Seicento*, Rome 1979, pp. 228–9, 277, 293. Although Bulferetti and Stumpo refer to processes of social mobility, they do not develop any alternative criterion of stratification.

noble origins, but even these families were often modest or obscure vassals who in any case owed their current privileged position to processes of social mobility set in motion by the restoration of the Savoy family's rule. A few came from the legal profession, and many from the ranks of financiers. The often cited case of the Turinettis – bankers and jewellers who became wealthy through dealing in foreign currency exchanges and loans to the Duke, and achieved prominent positions in the court aristocracy – was not an isolated case. A similar trajectory characterised the rise of financiers, like the Coardis (who became Counts of Carpenetto), the Biancos (Counts of San Secondo) and others.

Entry into the uppermost ranks of society was relatively easy in the early and middle decades of the seventeenth century and made possible first of all by the prodigality of the Duke, eager to win supporters and continually needing to bestow favours in exchange for the loans he depended on. Further opportunities for enrichment and promotion were created by the difficulties of the public treasury, which, between the late sixteenth century and the mid seventeenth, had to maintain the direct and indirect costs of almost permanent war by constant borrowing from private financiers. The combination of the obligation to reward favours rendered, and of the attempt to obtain support in the future, led to the widespread creation of new noble titles, to the concession of feudal land (converted from the royal demesne), and to the selling of fiscal rights.[15]

In the earlier period, the opportunity of plunging into court life seems to have been just one of the alternatives available to families who had been involved in this widespread experience of social mobility. Some families chose instead to focus their investment in state offices, or in a career in the City Council. After the mid seventeenth century, however, the court succeeded in establishing itself as an altogether superior level in the Turinese hierarchy of status. This change was no doubt made possible by that more restricted access and increased tendency towards inter-marriage to which I have referred. But the creation of symbolic boundaries was also an important factor.

The court built up its image and its self-identity as a separate body through a series of exclusive rituals and practices which created a deep divide between itself and other elite groups. As we have seen, the ruling family had long been trying to build up a circle of loyal servants, pressed as it was by the difficulty of asserting royal authority in the capital city. But it was not until the regency of Cristina (1637–61) that a distinctive court culture really consolidated itself, crowning the efforts already made along these lines by the two previous Dukes. Under Cristina, a precise court ceremonial emerged, with its rituals and

---

[15] In 1625 there were 106 'new' fiefs – a third of the total; Barberis, *Le Armi*, p. 116. By 1688 rights to over half of the *tasso* – Piedmont's main source of fiscal income – had been ceded to private individuals; see L. Bulferetti, 'Assolutismo e mercantilismo nel Piemonte di Carlo Emanuele II', *Mem.Acc.Sc.Tor.*, series 3, T.II (1953), pp. 21–2.

mechanisms for emphasising internal hierarchies and distinctions.[16] Grandiose new ducal residences were built in these years outside the town, which, along with the rebuilding of the ducal palace in the centre of Turin, provided new opportunities for the development of a court life.[17] At the same time, there was a sharp increase in the number of occasions on which the ducal family appeared in public against a highly emotive baroque backdrop. Ceremonies of religious piety had a central place here. Already in the first decades of the century the Dukes had asserted their leadership in the taking of religious initiatives, and it was they who were mainly responsible for the introduction of Counter-Reformation practices into the city. Thus the new religious orders started up in Turin under the direct patronage of the ducal family, and under its direction the orders which were already established in the city were reformed. Turin's architecture was transformed in this period by an explosion of church-building: thanks to aid from the ducal coffers some eleven convents with their accompanying churches were built or re-built in the thirty years between 1620 and 1649 alone.[18] These buildings provided the infrastructure around which the rituals characteristic of the Counter-Reformation – the flagellations, public confessions, processions of the Way of the Cross, and other forms of mortification and penitence – developed. The ducal family, and especially its female members – the Infanti Maria and Caterina (the Duke's daughters), and subsequently the regent Cristina – were, with the ladies of the court, the principal promoters of these expressions of religious fervour.[19]

[16] De Gaudenzi, 'Torino e la corte'; I. Massabò Ricci and C. Rosso, 'La corte quale rappresentazione del potere sovrano', in Romano (ed.), *Figure.*

[17] In the 1650s the Vigna di Madama Reale was built on the hill outside Turin, and the Valentino palace (christened Little Versailles), on the banks of the Po, was finished. In 1660 work was started on the hunting palace of Venaria. See A. Pedrini, *Ville dei Secoli XVII e XVIII in Piemonte*, Turin 1965; also M.Viale Ferrero, *Feste delle Madame Reali di Savoia*, Turin 1965.

[18] L. Tamburini, *Le Chiese di Torino dal Rinascimento al Barocco*, Turin 1968, which also gives extensive details of the contributions made by the ruling family to building costs. On the contributions Cristina in particular made to costs of construction and decoration, see Claretta, *Storia della Reggenza*, vol. II, pp. 547–70, and P. Codreto, *Memorie di Alcune Opere Pie fatte da Madama Reale Christina di Francia, Duchessa di Savoia, Regina di Cipro*, Turin no date.

[19] See the numerous references to these religious activities of court ladies in De Gaudenzi, 'Torino e la corte' and Claretta, *Storia della Reggenza*. See also *La Virtù Educata in Corte, Perfettionata nel Chiostro, Descritta dal Padre Fr. Alessio di Santa Maria, Carmelitano Scalzo, nel Doppio Stato Secolare e Religioso della Venerabile Serva di Dio Suor Anna Maria di S. Gioachino, nel Secolo Donna Caterina Forni*, Turin, 1692. On the Infanti Maria and Caterina, see P. Codreto, *Spreggio del Mondo. Vita e Morte della Serenissima Infanta D. Francesca Caterina Figlia del Gran Carlo Emanuele*, Mondovì, 1654; A. A. Codreto, *La Fragranza dell'Amaranto. Istoria Panegirica della Serenissima Infanta S. Maria Figlia del Gran Carlo Emanuele*, Turin 1657; B. Alessio, *Vita della Serenissima Infanta Maria di Savoia*, Turin 1663; M. Arpaud, *Vita dell'Infanta Caterina di Savoia Religiosa del Terz'Ordine di S. Francesco*, Annecy 1670. On Cristina, see also *Harangue Funèbre de Madame Chrestienne de France, duchesse de Savoie et Reyne de Cypre Prononcée par le R. P. De Barenne de la Compagnie de Jésus*, Paris 1664, 'Il Conte Fulvio Testi alla corte di Torino negli anni 1628 e 1635', in D. Perrero, *Documenti Inediti*, 78, Turin 1865.

I will discuss the particular role that women fulfilled in this flowering of religious enthusiasm in the following chapter. For the moment I wish only to point out that these ceremonies played a crucial part in creating a distinctive shared language and an exclusive set of rituals that helped to make the court a more homogeneous entity, with a culture of its own.

The court also separated itself spatially from the rest of the population. In the 1650s and 1660s the most prominent families at Cristina's court nearly all moved to the noble houses which had sprung up in or around the new royal square and along the road (Contrada Nuova) which connected the square to the ducal palace.[20] The new mansions gave the appearance of forming one entity together with the ducal palace, which was itself rebuilt during these years along much more grandiose lines, to replace the modest and relatively small structure of 1584.[21] In this way, the architecture, and the plan of this new part of the city, visually symbolised the unity of sovereign and court and, at the same time, the new gulf existing between the court and other social strata.

This process of the formation of a court, its turning in on itself, and its elevation in Turin's hierarchy of prestige would seem to have encouraged the emergence of a configuration of power which placed greater emphasis on membership of a corporate body. Certainly this tendency became prevalent at least in the management of charity; as we will see, the court was henceforth represented in charitable institutions and initiatives as a separate body in its own right and with its own delegates. Other groups had an equally corporatist form of representation.

The growth in importance of the court also had the effect of encouraging the search for, and creation of, new ritual arenas in which the prestige of members of other sections of the elite could be asserted. This phenomenon seems particularly important in explaining the rapid expansion of private charity. It is important to bear in mind at this juncture that the consolidation of a court aristocracy by no means implied that other forms of social mobility were cut off. Up until the early eighteenth century in fact it continued to be possible to make a fortune and to experience rapid advancement through exploitation of the state's financial needs. Merchants and financiers continued to rise socially by means of tax-farming, making loans to finance wars, or working state monopolies. Titles of nobility and feudal properties were still being handed

---

[20] The royal square and the Contrada Nuova were built on the southward expansion of the city. It is interesting to note that the repeated invitations to build on this land, which had been issued since the end of the sixteenth century, had fallen on deaf ears for decades; Comoli Mandracci, *Torino*, pp. 26–8, 34–9. On the explosion of prestige building in Turin in the mid-seventeenth century, M. Abrate, 'Elementi per la storia della finanza dello stato sabaudo nella seconda metà del XVII secolo', *BSBS*, LXVIII (1969).

[21] For descriptions of the original ducal palace, see N. Carboneri, *Ascanio Vitozzi. Un Architetto tra Manierismo e Barocco*, Rome 1966, pp. 117–25; A. Scotti, *Ascanio Vitozzi, Ingegnere Ducale a Torino*, Florence 1969, pp. 26–9.

out.[22] However, even though these routes to upward mobility – through commerce, finance, offices (especially financial offices) within the state bureaucracy, the acquisition of noble titles and feudal land – were the same paths which in the first half of the seventeenth century had led to spectacular cases of rise in status, it had by now become more difficult to achieve assimilation into the very top levels of the social hierarchy, where the court elite sat in splendid isolation, divided from the rest of society by rigid barriers. It was this exclusion which had such a stimulating effect on private charity; for it was precisely these upwardly mobile strata whose social aspirations were frustrated that plunged into charitable works in the second half of the seventeenth century. It was they who cast the institutions in a new mould and introduced new forms of encouragement to private giving which led to a sharp upturn in the volume of charitable donations and legacies.

In the remainder of this chapter, I shall explore the forces which help to explain the great expansion of charity to institutions which took place in the late seventeenth century. Although charitable giving is usually described in terms of spontaneous reactions of brotherly feeling, or in terms of obedience to religious injunctions, I will try to link it to more secular concerns and to social processes. In the following section, I will examine the various attempts to defend status which formed a constant leitmotiv in private charity. In the section on corporate control over charity, I will look at the new pattern of control over the administration of charity which emerged in the mid seventeenth century. In the section on the internment of the poor I will discuss the relationship between the new patterns of charitable behaviour and the move towards confinement of the poor which found expression in the creation of the Ospedale di Carità. In the final three sections, I will examine the transfer of prestige, patronage and influence entailed in the charitable act and participation in the running of an institution.

Charity and the defence of status

The flow of charitable funds was directed overwhelmingly towards certain institutions and ignored others. Above all, those institutions which were well funded by ducal finances (described in the previous chapter) received a negligible quantity of private funds. Donations to the hospital of S. Gio' di Dio[23] were virtually non-existent, and the Albergo di Virtù seems to have been completely ignored by benefactors. By contrast the hospital of San Maurizio and

---

[22] After a brief gap, new fiefdoms began to be created again from the 1670s on to pay for war, and continued during the wars of the 1690s and 1703–13. Bulferetti, 'Assolutismo', p. 18; Woolf, 'Sviluppo economico'.

[23] The hospital's historians mention only one donation from Antonio Vagnone in 1602 and one from Abbot San Martino d'Aglié in 1678. Radice and Marpelli, *I Fatebenefratelli*, p. 68ff.

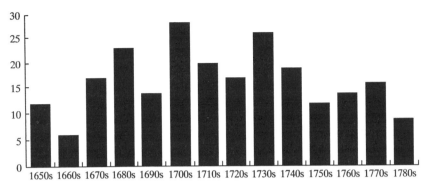

Fig. 2. Compagnia di San Paolo. Number of bequests and donations by decade,
1650–1789

Lazzaro was characterised by numerous legacies, although these were extremely
small in size. This can be explained with reference to the special privilege this
institution had obtained from the Duke, which obliged notaries to ask all those
drawing up a will whether they wished to leave something to the hospital. A fair
number of testators – in a situation in which they were face to face with
the thought of their death – did leave a few *lire*. We may therefore think of the
hospital of San Maurizio and Lazzaro as the recipient of acts of charity genuinely
linked to concerns about one's fate in the afterlife. The hospital was much less
successful, on the other hand, in attracting donations which sprang from more
secular impulses (and generally involved much larger sums of money).[24]
The increase in the overall number of legacies (figure 1) mainly reflects the
combined amount of charity received by the three major institutions, the
Compagnia di San Paolo, the Ospedale di Carità, and the hospital of S. Giovanni
(see figures 2, 3 and 4 for the bequests and donations they received singly).[25]

The Compagnia di San Paolo, which has already been mentioned as the
body which made the original proposal to found the Ospedale di Carità, was
established in 1563 as a congregation of laymen for the defence of the Catholic
faith. After a period of decline, the company grew increasingly important in the
seventeenth century, partly thanks to the vigorous preaching of the Jesuits who

---

[24] Between 1650 and 1780, the hospital of San Maurizio e Lazzaro received only about forty
legacies over 100 *lire* (or 20 *scudi* before 1632), and most of these were quite modest. AOSML,
m.2 and m.3 da ordinare.

[25] In the overall estimate (figure 1) I have also included institutions founded in the eighteenth
century (such as the House of the Provvidenza and the Opera Bogetti) which I will discuss in
chapter 5. I have excluded, however, the small female institutions of Santa Maria Maddalena
and Santa Pelagia, since these had an ambiguous status – half way between nunneries and
shelters for women. I will deal with their case in chapter 4 and look at what kind of donations
they attracted.

became the company's spiritual counsellors in 1605.[26] It quickly developed into one of the main centres of Turin's charitable activity; not only did it administer a number of charitable initiatives and institutions which attracted considerable funds, but it became the favourite body for testators to designate as executors of their wills, when these included charitable or pious legacies not made out to institutions.

One reason why so many testees entrusted their affairs to the company may have been that it counted among its members a large number of jurists (lawyers, senators and other magistrates). In the closing decades of the seventeenth century, it seemed in fact to be teeming with that bureaucracy *de robe* which was to gain increasing prestige (especially from the 1720s on) in the city's social structure. However, the company also boasted numerous representatives of the mercantile and financial elite, prominent state officials, and a few members of the court.[27] To a considerable extent, therefore, it was characterised by a social mix similar to that found in the administration of the Ospedale di Carità, which I describe below. This merging of individuals from different social milieux and, often, of differing status, who usually had few contacts with each other in public life, was especially noticeable in one of the areas of activity promoted by the company, namely the spiritual exercises. These took the forms of retreats under the spiritual guidance of the Jesuits and became a crucial focus for the city's elites. They grew so popular that, from 1683 onwards, a series of benefactors began to leave legacies which would constitute funds enabling also those who were not brothers of the company to take part.[28]

At first glance, the company may appear to be a typical Counter-Reformation organisation (similar in its purposes to the French Company of the Holy Sacrament), given its constant concern with the conversion of heretics, with morality and the preservation of female honour, and its initiatives to encourage religious piety. In fact, the charitable works it administered included funds to provide poor girls with dowries and clothes, two women's institutions – the House of the Soccorso and the Deposito – and funds to pay for missions in valleys where heresy had a hold.[29] On closer examination, however, the most

---

[26] Two very valuable works exist on the Company – the contemporary *Istoria della Venerabile Compagnia della Fede Cattolica Sotto l'Invocazione di S. Paolo*, by E. Tesauro, published in Turin in 1654 and in an enlarged edition in 1701; and the more recent work of M. Abrate, *L'Istituto Bancario S. Paolo di Torino*, Turin 1963.

[27] ASSP, 5, 'Elenchi degli ufficiali e dei confratelli', 1, 1668–1783.

[28] These retreats usually consisted of a stay of eight days in a house outside the town which the company had equipped especially for the purpose. Every day four different themes were proposed for participants to meditate on, from 5 am to 9 pm. The Turin city archives contain the guide to the spiritual exercises held in 1732 (ACT, Coll. SI/n.8991).

[29] Besides the works I have listed, the company also managed a pawnshop (Monte di Pietà), set up in 1579, which gave loans in exchange for pawned goods at a low rate of interest (2 per cent). A large number of Monti di Pietà were founded in Italy in this period (adding to those which had been set up in the first wave, in the fifteenth century) with the stated aim of giving aid to tide

distinctive characteristic of the company's activities seems to have been the tendency to favour those whose poverty was linked to a fall from a position of economic prosperity and social distinction. The company's work in fact was directed at a clientele which was quite different from that assisted by the Ospedale di Carità: its recipients were those for whom poverty was a disgraceful condition and who could not, for reasons of status, either resort to humble occupations such as domestic service or beg, even if in serious need.

It is interesting to note that this specialisation in the defence of status became more marked as the years went by. At the time of the company's foundation, the concept of *povero vergognoso* had been understood as meaning 'those who, by reason of their standing, do not beg'. Well into the seventeenth century, we still find that the expression was used to denote the honest and respectable poor in general: during the food shortage of 1670 for example, the number of 'poveri vergognosi' in the town was estimated at 8,000![30] From the last decades of the seventeenth century on, however, the interpretation grew more and more restrictive, gradually coming to refer solely to an elite clientele.

The company organisation which was specifically aimed at dealing with the *poveri vergognosi* was the Ufficio Pio, which was set up in 1589. This distributed money and goods regularly through members elected to the office of 'almsgivers' (*elemosinieri*): each of them was responsible for a particular area of Turin and, functioning in much the same way as the *Cantonieri* of the City Council, they made frequent visits and kept up the company's records of the needy. The other function of the Ufficio Pio was to distribute dowries and clothes to poor girls, and here too it was the respectable poor who were the target. Thus one of the prerequisites for being included in the draw from which winners were selected at random on the feast-days of St Paul and the Assumption was that they should never have been employed as servants.[31] Just as occurred with the distribution of alms, however, dowry funds gradually came to impose ever more stringent restrictions, limiting applicability to either the daughters of the old nobility, or those of state officials, or those of impoverished merchants, etc.

Another noteworthy phenomenon is the considerable expansion of charitable

the poor over a difficult time. Historians, however, have usually been sceptical about the truly charitable nature of their activities. In those towns where the records have survived, the diversion of capital to a favoured few, or at any rate to social strata which were far from poor, seems to have been the rule. Pullan, *Rich and Poor*, vol. III, especially chapter 6; Pastore, 'Strutture', pp. 451–6.

[30] Ord. 2.1.1670. A similarly broad definition is found in Florence in the fifteenth century. A. Spicciani, 'The "poveri vergognosi" in fifteenth century Florence', in T. Riis (ed.), *Aspects of Poverty in Early Modern Europe*, Stuttgart 1981.

[31] In addition, they had to be of legitimate birth, Turinese (this condition was waived in the case of converted heretics or converted Jews), of good morals, and had not to have any other dowry. See D., T.XIII, pp. 42–4.

resources for the shamefaced poor which accompanied this increasingly specialised provision. By the middle of the eighteenth century, the budget of the Compagnia di San Paolo was roughly equal to that of the two main hospitals (the Ospedale di Carità and the hospital of S. Giovanni). At this time, it had an annual income of over 10,000 *lire* to distribute in alms to the shamefaced poor alone (to get an idea of what this meant, we may recall that the annual cost of maintaining one poor person in the Ospedale di Carità was estimated at 90 *lire*); in addition, it had 7,800 *lire* per year to spend on dowries.[32]

Research dealing directly with provisions to the shamefaced poor has so far concentrated predominantly on the late medieval period, giving the misleading impression that concern over the problem of relative poverty was not important in the following centuries.[33] Evidence from Turin, however, suggests that aid motivated by the desire to defend status was a fundamental aspect of the city's system of relief and one which took up a significant part of total charitable resources throughout the period considered in this work. Indeed, in Turin this kind of charity reached its major expansion during the eighteenth century. As we will see further on, a series of changes in the pattern of social stratification in the early decades of the century led both elites in decline, and, at the same time, new elites looking for a firmer group identity and social recognition, to establish charitable funds reserved for specific social categories – thus symbolically asserting the prestige of their particular group.

A similar preoccupation with the defence of status can be found in the working of the institutions for women administered by the company, although the explicit discourse here was that of female 'honour'.[34] The Casa del Soccorso, founded by the Company in 1589, was an asylum for girls 'in danger' – who, that is, were thought to run the risk of becoming corrupted or falling into bad ways. According to the chroniclers of the institution, the first girls admitted were naive and physically attractive, they had no fathers and were neglected by their mothers; as such, their virtue was besieged by fraudulent protectors and

---

[32] AST, LPqM, m.18 d'add., fasc.2, 'Bilancio dell'opera dei vergognosi', 1747; ibid, fasc.1, 'Ristretto dei redditi', 1745.

[33] R. C. Trexler, 'Charity and the defense of urban elites in the Italian communes', in F. C. Jaher, *The Rich, the Well-Born and the Powerful*, Urbana, Ill. 1973; G. Ricci, 'Povertà, vergogna e povertà vergognosa', *SS*, 9 (1979); Spicciani, 'The "poveri vergognosi"'.

[34] The literature on institutions for women in Italy is by now very large. See among the many works L. Ciammitti, 'Fanciulle, monache madri. Povertà femminile e previdenza a Bologna nei secoli XVI–XVIII', in *Arte e Pietà. I Patrimoni Culturali delle Opere Pie*, Bologna 1980; and 'Quanto costa essere normali. La dote nel conservatorio femminile di S. Maria Barracano a Bologna (1630–1680)', *QS*, 53 (1983); L. Ferrante, 'L'onore ritrovato. Donne nella Casa del Soccorso di San Paolo a Bologna (sec.XVI–XVII)', *QS*, 52 (1983) and 'Malmaritate tra assistenza e punizione (Bologna sec. XVI–XVII)', in *Forme e Soggetti dell'Intervento Assistenziale in una Città di Antico Regime*, Bologna 1986; D. Lombardi, *Povertà Maschile e Povertà Femminile. L'Ospedale dei Mendicanti nella Firenze dei Medici*, Bologna 1988, pp. 135–209 and, recently, Cohen, *The Evolution*.

unworthy knights.[35] These hagiographic accounts seem to indicate that originally the company planned a form of charity designed for intervention in emergencies; once it heard of critical cases, it would step in to prevent the downfall of the girls in question. At first in fact, the regulations of the Casa del Soccorso specified a stay of a few months, up to a maximum of one year.[36] However, it was not long before the aims of the institution altered. The girls 'in danger' became a minority, and most of the girls (who were allowed to enter from the age of fourteen) left only when they were eighteen and when the House had found them some sort of social position to go to.[37] Of the various requirements for eligibility laid down in the regulations, only that of father-lessness was normally adhered to; conditions of being 'in danger' and being physically attractive remained at the level of rhetoric. Entry was via direct application of the family or friends, and many of the girls paid fees.[38] The inmates were mainly girls without close relatives able to look after them, who were relatively poor but still had some property or a small income – which was not, however, sufficient to keep up the standard of living necessary to preserve their social status. The circumstance of belonging to some branch of a once distinguished family fallen on hard times was invariably one which those who decided on applications took into very serious consideration.[39]

Despite the supposed taboo on manual work, the institution's inmates were far from inactive. The girls were taught to 'manage a house' and to 'starch, cut and sew shirts, collars and similar things'. In fact they worked almost all day for outside merchants, and the assessment the institution made of their behaviour gave a central place to the girls' skill in their work.[40] A system of commen-dations, rewards and small percentages of the profits on their work encouraged them to become more skilled and productive. It is noteworthy that high 'profit' in work was also an essential requisite in order to obtain a dowry.[41] Evidently, it

[35] Tesauro, *Istoria*, pp. 76–87.

[36] ASSP, 249, Casa del Soccorso, fasc. 9, 'Regola Antica, 1589'.

[37] If a marriage was arranged, they had the right to a dowry provided by the Ufficio Pio, without having to go through the draw. D., T.XIII, p. 58.

[38] They paid a sum which fluctuated over time between 13 and 18 *lire* a month. The House then paid the 'mother'(the matron) 80 *lire* per year for the maintenance of every inmate (1683 figure). In addition, the mother was entitled to the proceeds of the girls' work. ASSP, Rep. Lasc. 161, Soccorso.

[39] ASSP, 251, Casa del Soccorso, 'Ordinati 1665–1699'.

[40] According to the 1679 regulations book, the girls rose at 7 am in winter, and at 5 am in summer; after mass they worked up until lunch, and after a break they worked again until 8 pm in winter, and until 7 pm in summer. See 'Regole 1679' in ibid., Rep. Lasc. 161.

[41] Medals and rewards were given out by the ladies of the lay religious confraternity called Compagnia delle Umiliate (on which see chapter 4). Ibid. In the early years, the girls worked for the institution all week but for themselves on Saturday. But from 1682 the custom was introduced of giving the girls a fixed proportion of the return from their work. This was made possible by the legacy of a brother of the Company (Marquis Pallavicini), which made up the sum lost by the matron. ASSP, Busta 120, n.190.

was not the association between manual work and respectable status which was perceived as socially destabilising but the circumstances in which women deprived of a family setting would be obliged to work. Entering the institution spared girls of respectable origin the humiliation of having to sell their labour in the market place and working in a dependent position as waged labourers, and provided a protective domestic environment where their work could be appropriated without offending anyone's dignity, just as normally took place within the family of origin and in the marital home. The institution also provided a skill and a general training which enabled the inmates to marry or to be reintegrated in a family environment more easily: it is not an accident that the girls often went on to marry within the artisan and low mercantile class, or were accepted as higher ranking domestic servants in the house of some distant relative.

At the Casa del Soccorso, therefore, the original aim of preventing or redeeming from sin soon became subordinate to the more secular concern for the preservation of social status; most of the girls admitted were soon more respectable – both morally and, above all, in terms of their social background. The other institution for women administered by the Compagnia di San Paolo – the Deposito – followed a similar pattern of development. The original intention was that this institution, founded in 1684, should devote itself to three categories of women: 'those who live through the public prostitution of their modesty'; 'those who have fallen but are not exposed to public shame'; and 'those in danger of falling or suspected of having already fallen'. In other words, the apparent aim seems to have been to take up the type of cases which the Casa del Soccorso had come to neglect. In reality, however, the Deposito also restricted its attentions to the last two categories. In addition, it seems that many women abandoned by their husbands or with unfortunate marriages – the *malmaritate* – were also admitted to the Deposito as paying inmates.[42]

In this case, too, therefore, there was a notable divergence from the original aims. This seems in fact to have been the fate of all similar projects. Despite the preoccupation with female sexual behaviour that contemporaries showed, provisions for the protection and rehabilitation of women's honour were inextricably entangled with concern for social honour. In other words, such provisions were restricted to women of a certain social station. Once again in the 1740s, a plan to provide for women of ill repute but also of low origin encountered strong opposition. In 1741 a benefactor promised to leave the company a large legacy if it finally agreed to set up 'a refuge for poor fallen women, of any social condition'. The proposal, which was backed by the government, forced the company to examine the possibility of opening up the Deposito to 'women, whether repentant or not, even public prostitutes'. But

---

[42] ASSP, 252, Opera del Deposito, 'Ordinati 1742–1800'.

in spite of the favourable terms of the arrangement – which would have saved the Deposito from the grave financial difficulties into which it had fallen – the company rejected the plan, arguing that the brothers were more inclined to 'rid themselves for ever of the taint of said sinners, which various brothers found tiresome and unpleasant'.[43] It was decided instead to set up a separate institution, called the Forzate, where women could be compulsorily interned at the request of their family or other citizens. However, even this institution encountered the same difficulties in putting its original aims into practice and in the end restricted its entry to 'sinners of respectable birth'.[44]

It was thus not until the later eighteenth century – a period when state action in the field of public order had become well established – that an institution aimed at ordinary prostitutes appeared, in the form of a house of correction set up and administered by state delegates (see chapter 6). Although Counter-Reformation rhetoric was trumpeted in official statements of aims, so long as social policy was dominated by private charity, the redemption of sinners took effect only when the fact that they belonged to a family of distinguished status made their behaviour particularly embarrassing, or when, if the women themselves were of low origin, their sin embroiled men of higher rank. This second instance is illustrated by the case of an inmate in the Forzate whose admission to the institution was instigated (and the financial costs met) by the Marchioness of Angrogna, in order to put an end to the adulterous relationship the woman entertained with the lady's son. As soon as her daughter-in-law died, however, the Marchioness of Angrogna lost interest in the case and gave up paying the woman's pension, leaving her free to go back to her sinful habits.[45] The aim of protecting male immoderate behaviour from scandal was a no less potent motive behind the working of women's institutions than that of preserving women's honour.

Corporate control over charity

In 1649 the Compagnia di San Paolo put forward a proposal to establish a refuge for beggars 'based on the example of Lyon', which would provide not only for 'the upkeep of poor mendicants, men, women and children, ill as well as healthy, but also for the collection of information and support of the needy persons of the city'. The healthy were to be employed in 'worthy works' and the sick to be 'aided with charity'. The new hospital – the Ospedale di Carità – planned to institutionalise the poor, but this does not seem to have been the crucial point

---

[43] OPCB, m.221, fasc.3, 'Atto presentato dalla Compagnia di S.Paolo', 7.5.1741; D., T.XIII, pp. 5–6.
[44] ASSP, Casa del Deposito, 250, 'Memoria sul ritiro delle Forzate, 1777'.
[45] ASSP, 252, Ordinati, 6.3.1754.

under discussion. The proposal mentioned only briefly and in very general terms
the activities that the new institution was meant to carry out; it dwelt at length,
on the other hand, on the structure that the governing body was to assume. The
plan reiterates a number of times that 'all orders in the city' were to be involved
in the new project, and that 'all the parts of which this city is composed' should
be represented in the administration.[46] The document thus makes explicit
reference to the need to overcome the opposition between the Duke and the City
Council which had dominated the Turin scene for around a century, and which
was even reflected in the organisation of charitable institutions, rigidly divided
as they were into areas of ducal and areas of municipal influence.

The patents for foundation contain the same message. Here again, little
consideration is given to the actual functions which the hospital was supposed to
perform, whereas great care is lavished on the form that the administration
should take, on how various responsibilities should be shared out and rotated,
and on the political equilibria thus expressed.[47] In both documents, therefore, the
project is presented as a political event of some importance rather than a reform
in the treatment of the poor.

The power balance contained in the regulations for administration did indeed
contain novel elements. For the first time, a mixed administration was set up
in a charitable institution. The governing body was composed of seventeen
persons, all of whom, with the exception of the archbishop, were to remain in
office for one year only. The direction of the hospital was headed by five
chairmen: in addition to the archbishop, there were to be two members of the
court, nominated by the Duke (one to be an ecclesiastic, the other a layman), one
representative elected by the state juridical organs of the Senate and the *Camera
dei Conti* (in alternate years), and the first mayor of the city.[48] Then there were
twelve rectors: four to be nominated by the City Council, two by the Compagnia
di San Paolo, and six by the guilds of merchants and trades. Of the latter, two had
to be bankers, cloth or silk merchants or wholesalers, the other four had to be
members of other trades. It is clear enough that this broad representation broke
with the rigid bi-polar pattern that had dominated the organisation of charity up
until that time and for the first time presented an image of the town as articulated
in a series of bodies – the City Council and the court, certainly, but also the
clergy, the magistrates, and a range of trade organisations. Ducal power and

---

[46] D., T.XII, p. 257, *Supplica della Compagnia di S. Paolo*, 30.8.1649.
[47] Ibid., p. 260, *Patenti d'erezione dell'Ospedale della Carità*, 30.8.1649.
[48] The Senate of Turin, together with those of Chambery and Nice, constituted the supreme judicial
authority, with jurisdiction over civil and criminal cases, whereas the *Camera dei Conti* of Turin
and the *Chambre des Comptes* of Chambery (which survived only up to 1720) were courts with
jurisdiction over fiscal and economic matters. The Senates and Chambers of Accounts also
had the task of registering the orders issued by the sovereign and enjoyed a theoretical right of
remonstrance, i.e. could oppose them if these appeared to clash with the existing laws.

municipal power were no longer antagonists, but were seated side-by-side in the governance of the new institution. An image of concord and of cooperation in the running of a common enterprise replaced the conflictual image of the preceding period. And above all, the power of the two older blocs seems reduced – the Council and the Duke were not the only forces in play.

The period of open competition for control over charity did not end, therefore, with the victory of one of the two parties, and certainly not with the establishing of a centralised, absolutist direction, but rather with the emergence of a broad new configuration of power. A period started in which a corporate pattern of control of charity prevailed – a pattern which lasted up until the earlier decades of the eighteenth century. During this time, there were shifts in the internal balance of power, which reflected changes outside the institution. For example, in 1685, following a request made by the hospital's governing body, a royal decree increased the number of governors elected by the Senate and by the *Camera dei Conti* to four – thus quadrupling their representation.[49] However, while this provision reflected the increased prestige of the magistracy, it did not affect the corporate logic of the hospital's administrative arrangements.

We find further evidence of this pattern of control over charity if we examine the emergency provisions which supplemented the hospital's normal activities in times of crisis. Although from 1650 on the Ospedale di Carità was the body officially responsible for dealing with the problem of the poor, its opening did not involve the winding down of 'outdoor' forms of aid, of the type which had traditionally been provided by the City Council. Periods of deprivation and dearth were still dealt with by large-scale distributions of bread, expulsions of unwanted outsiders and by aid to the homeless in the street. These provisions are interesting because they reveal the shifts which were occurring in the balance of power between the various groups which had a part in the administration of charity. Over the second half of the seventeenth century emergency measures of this kind were taken by committees chaired by the archbishop and formed by representatives of the hospitals and the Compagnia di San Paolo, the City Council and the other most prominent corporate bodies of the town. In other words, a corporate pattern similar to that found in the administration of the Ospedale di Carità emerges. A committee of this kind in 1670, for example, faced with the enormous number of poor in the city, decided on special distributions of bread. This was to be entrusted to the Ospedale di Carità, but paid for by the various bodies represented on the committee. During the shortage, deserving poor people were in addition to receive an eight-day licence from their parish priest allowing them to beg.[50] In 1676, 'the survey of the poor, their name, surname and their place of origin' carried out with the aim of

---

'sending them to their own places if foreigners and to the hospitals if citizens' was entrusted to a mixed delegation, made up, for each parish, of a governor of the Ospedale di Carità, a brother of the Compagnia di San Paolo, the parish priest and a *Cantoniere* of the City.[51] Similar action, managed by similar committees, was taken again during the crisis of the 1690s, and sporadically in the first years of the new century.[52]

The first thing which is striking here is the drastically reduced role of the City Council. By this time, even in forms of aid which had been those most typical of its own system, the Council was evidently taking part as just one of several bodies responsible for welfare measures. It is true that the Council still kept control of large islands of responsibility – for example, outdoor medical relief (which expanded to its fullest extent precisely in these years) – but it had undoubtedly lost its dominant hold over the system as a whole.

The influence of representatives of the court and the sovereign also seems to have been reduced. There are no longer traces of a direct role exercised by the knights of San Maurizio e San Lazzaro who, in the early seventeenth century, had been the body which led the Duke's attack on the Council's charity system. In fact, it was not until the middle decades of the eighteenth century that the central power took over a central part in the determining of policies towards the poor. At first glance, the role of the sovereign may seem greater than before due to the fact that orders prohibiting begging now took the form of ducal edicts. But this should not be interpreted as a sign of real independent authority. The minute books of the Ospedale di Carità in 1683 provide us with an example of what was probably the normal sequence of events leading up to an edict on begging. In March, the board of governors of the hospital decided that it was necessary 'to obtain an edict ensuring that all the beggars of the town are forced to come to the Vigna [the hospital's building]'. In a meeting held a few days later 'the minute of the edict which has to be presented to His Royal Highness in order that he may be pleased to sign it, for the consignment of all the beggars that are in this town' was read and approved.[53]

Among the powers on the rise, on the other hand, the ecclesiastical authorities stand out. The archbishop was not only the head of the governing body of the Ospedale di Carità but a key figure organising and mediating between the various groups involved in the administration of charity. It was he who was the coordinator of the emergency measures for the poor, it was to him that complaints about the malfunctioning of the relief system were presented and

---

[51] AOC, Ordinati, 9.2.1676. Other expulsions of outsiders were carried out in 1678 and 1679. Ord., 26.5.1678, c.248 and 29.9.1679.

[52] See for example AOC, Ordinati, 7.11.1691 and AST, s.r., Confraternite e Congregazioni, m.1, fasc.2, 'Congregazioni per provedere all'emergenza dello Spedale di Carità, 23.12.1709'.

[53] AOC, Ordinati 14 and 21.3.1683. The edict in question is published in D., T.XII, p. 268, and bears the date 13.4.1683.

to him that pleas for new forms of intervention were made.[54] He was also consulted when there was discussion over criteria determining which categories of the poor should be given aid and which turned away.[55] Important decisions such as the one to set up a hospital for incurables (in reality a ward within the existing hospital of S. Giovanni) were taken in his presence, after long discussions between the usual range of delegates of various corporate groups.[56]

It is interesting to note that it was only in the mid-seventeenth century that ecclesiastical authorities became involved in the management of the charity system in Turin. This is much later than one would expect if we accept the usual idea that the Church regained a central role in the field of charity as a result of new policies decided on at the Council of Trent. In Turin the Church had very little impact during the long period in which the City Council dominated the organisation of welfare, and only emerged as a force when this control broke up and responsibility for charity began to be divided between various different groups.

Some reassessment of the nature of ecclesiastical power and influence over charity is also needed. The archbishop's role was essentially that of an arbitrator and intermediary between the various groups involved in the administration of charity; there is no evidence of an attempt to expand the Church's direct control over the running of institutions, nor of any marked desire to promote independent policies or projects of its own. On the very few occasions when the Church acted independently, it aroused opposition. One of these rare instances occurred in the 1660s, when the archbishop's office issued permits to beg which it evidently had not previously agreed with the other authorities. The Ospedale di Carità immediately condemned the measure as unacceptable, and it was not repeated.[57] It does not seem appropriate, therefore, to talk of a 'desecularisation' of charity brought about by the more aggressive stand taken by the Church at the Council of Trent. Indeed, the Church failed to gain that direct supervisory role over charitable institutions which had been advocated by the Council;[58] though in the long run it did succeed in extending its control over the distribution of charity, thanks to the rise of the parish.

The Church was much more successful, in fact, in achieving this other goal of Tridentine policy, gradually managing to turn the parish into the focus of local devotion. As a consequence, the authority of the local clergy – above all, at the lower levels of the hierarchy, that of parish priests – grew considerably. In Turin, it was above all the lower clergy's control over access to the sources of charity

---

[54] AOC, Ordinati, 11.5.1664; Ord., 26.11.1663.
[55] Ibid., 21.5.1673.
[56] Ibid., 15.7.1665; AOSG, Ordinati, 26.6.1667, 9.3.1668.
[57] AOC, Ordinati, 9.7.1664.
[58] This seems to be true of Italy in general. See Pastore, 'Strutture assistenziali', p. 439.

that was increased. Parish priests took over responsibility for inspecting the poor and assessing the extent of their neediness, a task which had previously been in the hands of City Councillors. They were, in other words, entrusted with the crucial responsibility of deciding who was poor and who was not. These changes did not, however, occur until the second half of the seventeenth century. It was probably the emergency measures taken to deal with dearth in 1670 which established for the first time that temporary licences to beg were no longer to be issued by Councillors, but by parish priests. Two years later, even the municipal medical service, though still firmly in the hands of the City Council, transferred responsibility for assessing the financial condition of applicants to priests (this task, too, had previously been carried out by delegates of the Council).[59] The image of the parish priest who knew the poor of his territory, and who had a crucial pastoral role over them, steadily gained general recognition. In 1700, the rules of the Ospedale di Carità also assigned the parish priest the part of reliable informant capable of making a first assessment of need for those who applied for admission or for bread.[60] By the late seventeenth century, therefore, the parish priest had won a new role as welfare broker or intermediary for obtaining charity; but he did not (yet) manage or dispense aid directly. As we shall see, that step came only in the eighteenth century when the influx of donations to the parish churches provided them with their own funds to use for charity. But the territorial importance of the parish was already well established by the end of the previous century – as is confirmed by the fact that when a census of the poor was carried out in 1676 (managed by the usual collection of representatives of the various corporate bodies), the parish took the place of the *cantone* as the territorial unit adopted.

The internment of the poor

From 1650 the Ospedale di Carità was officially the body which was responsible for the repression of begging. From this date on, the orders which prohibited begging in the town instructed mendicants to go to the hospital where they would be interviewed by the governors, then kept in the hospital if truly needy, otherwise dismissed, after having sworn not to beg any more. In the meantime, 'collectors of the poor' paid by the hospital combed the city and arrested those breaking the prohibition on begging. When they were brought to the hospital, they were then supposed to be punished at the discretion of the governors – with a period of incarceration on a diet of bread and water, with cropping of the hair, or with whipping in the case of persistent offenders.[61] It is

[59] Ord., 10.9.1672.
[60] D., T.XII, p. 274, 1.6.1700.
[61] The 1650 orders prohibiting begging are given in Borelli, *Editti*, pp. 236 ff.

clear, however, that the Ospedale had difficulty in asserting full control over begging. Especially in periods of deprivation and famine the city continued to be overrun by beggars and the indigent.

The governors of the hospital put their failure to control the problem down to an unwillingness on the part of the citizens to provide them with adequate financing. In the early decades of its existence, this complaint had some substance, for the hospital was beset by continual financial problems. It attracted few benefactors and was supported almost exclusively by donations from a few of the governors themselves, who obstinately persisted in shoring up their own institution. Often there was no money for the most basic necessities and on several occasions the governors themselves had to fill this gap by making loans without interest to the hospital, or simply by donating the money. In the calamitous year 1677, for example, there was not even wood to cook the soup for the poor, and ten or so governors were obliged to give either bundles of wood or money to get over the emergency.[62] The governors' disappointment over the cool reception which the town gave to the hospital is occasionally evident even in the routine language of the anti-begging orders. The citizens – so the governors complained – refused to give 'on the mere pretext that the hospital did not abolish the unbearable nuisance of vagabonds and beggars, and saying that they cannot give alms to everyone'.[63] The controversy was taken up vehemently by the City Council, which – having itself been the object of continual requests to support the hospital and contribute to the special measures against beggars – bitterly criticised the archbishop and His Highness over the problem of beggars and the deficiencies and inadequacy of the institution.[64] In 1679, after it had been invited to impose a small tax for the support of the poor, the City Council indignantly replied that the citizens would give *voluntarily* 'when they were sure that the town would be purged of the poor, and they [the citizens] be freed from the continual nuisance and from the infestation of churches, streets, and their very own doorsteps'.[65] The dispute was obviously a vicious circle, with the hospital maintaining that it was insufficiently funded and that it 'could not aid such a large number of people without the help they had hoped for, and in part been promised by the citizens', and the latter justifying themselves by replying that the hospital had failed in its function of eliminating beggars.

To what extent were these last accusations justified? It is certainly true that the Ospedale di Carità only functioned very partially as a place for interning and punishing beggars. It was far, however, from being inactive. In the 1660s (which is the earliest date from which the minute books survive) it housed several

---

[62] AOC, Ordinati, 7.11.1677; for cases of loans made at zero interest, see ibid., 27.8.1679, 21.1.1685, 1.4.1685; for wine for the poor, see ibid., 30.11.1683.

[63] Borelli, *Editti*, p. 241, 1.4.1664. See also ibid., pp. 240–5, 30.3.1661, 8.1.1670, 4.12.1676.

[64] Ord, 26.11.1663, 13.8.1679.

[65] Ibid., 25.8.1679.

hundred poor persons.[66] This made it by far the largest charitable institution in the town, for the hospital of S. Giovanni contained no more than fifty or so patients at this time. In addition, the Ospedale di Carità seemed to take seriously the plan of finding the poor places in the world of work, an idea which had been mentioned only very briefly at the time of the institution's foundation. Thus many boys and girls were placed as apprentices with outside masters.[67] Moreover, contracts were made with a series of masters who transferred their workshops inside the institution and were supposed to teach their trade to young inmates entrusted to them. By the 1660s, at least, there were several silk-spinning machines working in the hospital, together with a silk winder at which more than forty boys and girls were employed.[68] In addition there was a ribbon manufactory, which employed thirty or so apprentices.[69] In the 1680s, a shoe-maker's workshop, where twelve young people were trained, and also a milliner's workshop were set up.[70] Later on, various other types of productive activity were tried out – among them the manufacture of woollen hosiery and silk and gold cloth.[71] From 1689, however, it was cloth production that became the main activity of the poor in the hospital. It was originally set up as a govern-ment manufactory, but after a few years (in 1704) was ceded to the hospital which ran it in partnership with a company of merchants.[72] Assured of a steady demand for its output in the shape of clothing for the ducal troops, the wool manufactory in the Ospedale di Carità grew to become one of the largest in the state. In 1713, 170 poor persons were employed there – see table 5 – and this grew to reach a peak of 500 in the decades which followed. The hospital obtained almost a fifth of its annual income from this enterprise.[73]

The Ospedale di Carità did, then, fulfill its aim of giving a trade to the young people it interned, but it only tackled the problem of begging partially. Only some of the poor were brought in by the 'collectors of beggars'- the majority

---

[66] In 1665, the figure of 400 inmates is mentioned. AOC, Ordinati 15.7.1665. The minute books have survived only for 1664–65; there is then a gap until 1674, when a complete series starts.

[67] Ibid., 26.9.1683.

[68] Ibid., 11.5.1664 and 20.8.1664; 17.5.1665; 7.8.1675.

[69] Ibid., 31.7.1664, 30.6.1666. In this case, the apprenticeship was supposed to last three years, after which the sons or daughters could be dismissed from the hospital. The master paid the hospital a fixed amount a day in return for their work.

[70] Ibid., 6.7., 3.7. and 24.8.1687. The agreement with the cobbler ceased after just two years 'as it was scarcely useful'. Ibid., 26.6.89.

[71] Ibid., 20.6.1701, 29.12.1702.

[72] Ibid., 24.6 and 23.11.1698; 21.9.1704. See, for example, the partnership agreements drawn up in 1707 between the hospital and Signori Giò Clemente and Co. and Giuseppe Fogliano for ten years. Ibid., 6.3.1707.

[73] In 1715 the hospital earned 8,714 *lire* income from the work of inmates (who at the time numbered 837). Of this total, 7,235 *lire* came from the wool manufactory. The hospital's total income amounted to 42,456 *lire*. See ibid., Cat.VI, Parte I, 1, 'Ricoverati e poveri 1715–1864'.

Table 5. *Inmates of the Ospedale di Carità, by age, sex and occupation (1713)*

Male

	0–7	7–10	10–15	15–20	20–25	25–30	30–35	35–40	40–45	45–50	50–60	60	Total
Staff[1]			35	16	19		2	1	6	1	1		81
Male nurses					2					3			5
Apothecary boys			2			2							4
Infirmary													
Sick		8							2		10	2	22
Disabled		1				3	5			4			13
Helpless	27												27
Fallen sick							3					11	14
Tailors			13				2					1	16
Shoemakers				29					1		2		32
Cabinet-makers					1								1
Hosiers			1										1
Silk spinners									2				2
Cloth weavers					3							3	6
At the farms					2						3		5
Royal silk mill			11										11
Woollen mill		60	43	1	6						2		112
Total	27	69	105	46	30	8	12	4	11		22	15	349

Female

	0–7	7–10	10–15	15–20	20–25	25–30	30–35	35–40	40–45	45–50	50–60	60	Total
Staff[1]				3	5	10	15	13			3		49
Nurses				5				1			6		12
Infirmary													
Sick	2		16				9					2	29
Incurables						10							10
Contagious						7							7
Disabled												41	41
Almost always ill							12						12
Blind				2							3		5
Fallen sick			7	6			6	7				27	53
Helpless	72												72
'Piazzate'[2]											5		5
Wool spinners					23		2				10		35
Cotton workers									2				2
Cloth workers							4						4
Seamstresses				9									9
Glovers			6										10
Hosiers			10				12						22
At the farms				1								1	2
Silk workers		45	26	8	2		3						84
Woollen mill		28	21	6	1		2						58
Total	74	73	86	40	31	10	82	23			27	71	517
Total m/f	101	142	191	86	61	18	94	27	11		49	86	866

[1] Includes door-keepers, bakers, cleaners, those assigned to the refectory, herdsmen, porters, cooks etc. (often ex-inmates).

[2] They have the benefit of one 'piazza', that is a fund sufficient for the maintenance of one inmate, which had been donated by a benefactor. The latter usually kept the right to nominate the beneficiaries.

Source LPqM, M.18, fasc.5, *Tabella de' poveri esistenti all'Hospedale della Carità, luoro età, professione e impiego*, 2.4.1713. NB In the document age groups overlap.

were admitted on their own application.[74] Indeed, at certain times, the hospital complained that the number of applications was too high, and admission was restricted to cases 'which cannot be postponed'.[75] In practice, the hospital was used for many purposes other than forcible confinement. First of all, there seem to have been a continual influx of children and adolescents left 'in trust' at the institution. This practice is first described in the first rules of the hospital to have survived – dating from 1700;[76] but it seems probable that it had existed since the hospital was set up, given the high number of girls and boys who appear among the inmates, and for whom various forms of manufacture and apprenticeship were organised. These young people usually remained in the hospital until they had acquired a trade and could find a place in work outside. In 1713 (the earliest year for which we have details by age, sex and occupation of the inmates) there were as many as 461 young people (or over half the total) under the age of twenty (see table 5).[77]

The 'incurables' also accounted for a substantial proportion of the total in the Ospedale di Carità. This was a general term which was usually applied to all those who, due to age or disability, were incapable of working or looking after themselves. The numbers of incurables – unproductive, and by definition long-stay inmates – particularly worried the hospital governors. In theory, access to the Ospedale di Carità was forbidden to inmates of this kind; but the frequency with which the minutes complain about their numbers and the expense they cause shows that the regulations on this point were far from successful.[78] The report of 1713 shows 206 persons (the great majority women) who were categorised as infirm, incurable or invalid; this amounted to nearly a quarter of the total inmate population.

To a lesser extent, other categories of poor – poor people who succeeded in getting admitted for an agreed, short period and a few of the insane – took up hospital resources and left even less for beggars.[79] A large number of people ill with syphilis – especially women – also sought to be cured of their illness in the hospital. They were probably attracted by the fact that the hospital had always, since its foundation, had a permanent doctor and surgeon (who, at least since 1679, were resident in the institution).[80] We have already noted that the demand

---

[74] Ibid., Cat.VIII, Opera Bogetti, busta 1, 22.5.1657.
[75] Ibid., Ordinati, 26.12.1678, 9.9.1685.
[76] D., T.XII, p. 272, 1.6.1700.
[77] Note the absence of any children between the age of seven and ten; this is due to the fact that children were sent out to nurses until the age of ten. The high numbers of inmates under seven are probably children who have not yet been sent to wet-nurses.
[78] AOC, Ordinati, 9.7.1664, 15.7.1665, 24.5.1682, 20.2.1684.
[79] Ibid., 9.7.1691; 2.7.1665, 2.3.1687.
[80] Ibid., Cat.VIII, Opera Bogetti, busta 1, 22.5.1657. The doctor's and surgeon's apartments in the hospital are mentioned in the minutes of 3.12.1679. There was also a pharmacy, which was open to the public as well.

for treatment for syphilis was very high, and that there existed no specific facilities for dealing with it. Thus the Ospedale di Carità, like the two other main hospitals, ended up taking on cases of syphilis, even though this was against the rules.[81]

Right from the time of its foundation, therefore, it is clear that the Ospedale di Carità had an eminently charitable function rather than a punitive one. All this does not mean that the hospital had no effect on the problem of begging – it did alleviate it; but at the same time, it was a long way from eliminating it. On at least one occasion, it was even necessary for the Duke to send an order to the hospital to get rid of the twenty-five or thirty most notorious beggars who pestered Turin's good citizens in the churches.[82] A considerable gap between the original intentions of the hospital and the actual results was somehow inevitable (and seems to have been the normal fate of similar plans for internment elsewhere). As soon as the hospital came into existence, it was besieged by the needy, overcome by the pressure of demand from the poor who saw in it a place where their old, their children, or their difficult cases, might be placed. Nor were benefactors immune from this logic. There is no lack of agreements made with well-off individuals, who, in exchange for payment, sought admission for impecunious members of their families, or for poor people under their protection. In 1692, for example, signor Griotero committed himself to donating a farm on condition that the hospital took in several female relatives (*alcune sue nipoti*) and, when the moment came, arranged for their marriages and provided them with dowries. In 1695 another man offered to pay the hospital if six infirm poor persons he knew were received by the hospital and kept until they died or recovered.[83]

So, those who complained about the ineffectiveness of the hospital in repressing begging and made this an excuse for evading the insistent demands of the governors for donations, actually shared with the poor the perception of the hospital as a charitable institution and one which could relieve them of their obligations towards the needy who were dependent on them. Moreover, attitudes toward confinement seem to have been highly ambivalent. Forcible arrest of beggars was by no means a policy which commanded universal consensus – indeed, it tended to provoke widespread opposition. A ducal order issued one year after the founding of the Ospedale di Carità made it illegal to obstruct the collectors of beggars in their duty by 'taking the poor from their hands, insulting them, and throwing water and other dirt at them'.[84] Episodes of this kind, and

---

[81] It seems that, at least in the early years, the Ospedale di Carità was not equipped to give those with syphilis the specific treatment they needed; but they kept them until – on intercession from the Ospedale di Carità – they were admitted for treatment at the S. Giovanni or the San Maurizio and Lazzaro hospitals. Ibid., 17.5.1665.

[82] Ibid., 14.1.1698.

[83] Ibid., 20.4.1692, 5.9.1695.   [84] Borelli, *Editti*, p. 237, 11.1.1651.

complaints about them, continued for a long time. In the two decades after the hospital's foundation, 'continual incidents and obstruction' which prevented the arrest of the poor were referred to, and the governors asked the Duke to provide the collectors with an escort of twenty-five guards. In spite of repeated petitions for an escort, this request, evidently considered too dangerous politically, was never granted. However, penalties were established for anyone who prevented beggars from being taken, and the collectors were supplied with 'pointed truncheons'. In addition, His Highness gave them the right to carry his insignia, so that they would command more respect.[85] We do not know who it was who was involved in resisting the collectors, but it is difficult to believe that a society so criss-crossed by links of vertical solidarity (based on bonds of kinship, community of origin, trade, neighbourhood, etc.) could be so sharply divided in its attitude to forcible internment, with the poor defending beggars and the rich trying to incarcerate them. It seems more probable that internment was seen by many as right in theory, but unjust every time it affected someone they knew.

It is unlikely, therefore, that the failure to apply the policy for incarcerating beggars strictly was what lay behind the reluctance of benefactors. The financial difficulties of the Ospedale di Carità in the first decades of its life are only partly attributable to its lack of rigour over internment. There is good reason to be sceptical about the justifications given by the citizens since donations did eventually start to arrive despite the fact that neither the policy over incarceration nor the balance of different types of inmates in the hospital had changed. From the 1670s onwards, and then more markedly from the 1700s, donations started to flow in (see figure 3). The small-scale gifts from governors desperately trying to shore up the institution's finances gave way to numerous substantial legacies from outside. Yet the precise records we have for the eighteenth century make it clear that the hospital's inmate population continued to be made up in large part of voluntary admissions, and, in particular, of children placed 'in trust' by their families, of old people living on their own and of the disabled.[86]

In explaining the difficulties of the hospital's early decades, we should not underestimate the importance of the fact that at that time the total amount of income derived from private donations to charitable institutions of all kinds was still very limited. Institutions which aimed to house hundreds of inmates (and thus needed large and regular flows of funds) were at that time a novelty for Turin. Not only the Ospedale di Carità but also older institutions (like the hospital of S. Giovanni), if they wanted to expand, were faced with a need to find

---

[85] AOC, Ordinati, 11.5.1664; also 15.7.1665, 24.9.1666, 8.1.1668; Borelli, *Editti*, p. 224, 4.12.1676.
[86] On the composition of inmates in the eighteenth century, see S. Cavallo, 'Conceptions of poverty and poor relief in Turin in the second half of the eighteenth century', in S. J. Woolf (ed.), *Domestic Strategies: Work and Family in France and Italy, 1600–1800*, Cambridge 1991.

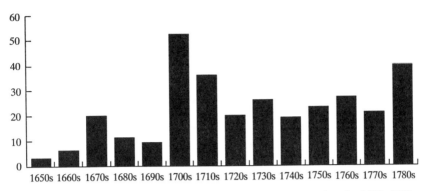

Fig. 3. Ospedale di Carità. Number of bequests and donations by decade, 1650–1789.

new means of financing themselves. If they were to be able to extend the scale of their activity, they stood in need of a new pattern of charity. And this is exactly what developed. Charitable giving to institutions took off with the emergence of forms of social reward which indissolubly linked the charitable act with the acquisition of prestige, and of resources for the bestowing of patronage and influence.

Charity and prestige

One of the ways in which the Ospedale di Carità eventually succeeded in exciting the benevolent interest of the local citizenry was to set itself up as a financial institution. One of the means of attracting money thought up by the governors was in fact to seek out individuals who had unused capital and convince them to invest with the hospital, at a reasonable rate of interest (usually 5 per cent). Since disinterested aid was not forthcoming, the governors were now offering something in exchange; and from the 1670s on, the number of loans to the hospital grew steadily. The attraction of this arrangement to lenders can be partly explained by the fact that there was a chronic lack of places where savings could be invested due to the absence of a banking system in Piedmont.[87] Opportunities for secure investment were therefore very scarce. Nonetheless, especially in the first decades, loans to the Ospedale di Carità may also be seen as a form of charity, for at that time the hospital was hardly a safe investment. The offer of a loan to the hospital at a time when it was in financial difficulties

---

[87] The private banks were only involved in loans to merchants to finance trade, and did not deal with private individuals. In 1711 John Law approached the government with various banking projects, but by the time the Duke and his ministers got round to becoming interested in the idea, Law had moved on to Paris and to more ambitious projects. G. Prato, *Problemi Monetari e Bancari nei Secoli XVII e XVIII*, Turin 1916.

is often presented in the minutes as an act of charity: 'he benevolently offered a loan of 3,000 *lire* at 5 per cent', 'he is prepared to help the hospital with a loan'. Obviously, the character of the transaction was inherently ambiguous. Apart from anything else, it might be that what started out by being a form of earning money from the institution's difficulties turned out in the end to be a charitable act; for especially in the early years, the hospital was often unable to return the money when the loan expired, and on a few occasions the lenders had to negotiate a return of part of the sum and leave the rest as a donation. In most cases, however, these difficulties were resolved by the governors managing to cobble together another loan which made it possible to repay the earlier one. There are even cases of the governors themselves lending the sum necessary to return a loan at the expiry date. It seems probable that the governors were, in some sense, considered responsible for the hospital's solvency, especially in those cases where particular governors had acted as guarantors for the loan; indeed, it is likely that it was precisely their personal mediation between the lender and the institution which made the loan appear relatively safe.

The ambiguity inherent in the real nature of monetary transactions with the hospital was even greater in the case of the annuity contracts (*vitalizi*) which also became numerous from the 1670s on. The balance of advantage to the hospital of these contracts is much more obvious: elderly people entrusted a sum of money to the hospital in return for a rate of interest higher than that normally paid (perhaps as high as 8 or 10 per cent, whereas the legally permitted rate was 3 or 4 per cent), on the condition, however, that on their death the capital sum was kept by the hospital. The arrangement contained an element of risk for the Ospedale since a lender who lived longer than expected could use up most of the capital; but in most cases, it came out clearly the gainer. We may note that this type of arrangement too is often presented as a charitable act '*Donates* a capital sum of . . . at his death, in the meantime to be paid the annuity of . . . ' [my emphasis]. And indeed it was a kind of charity. It seems quite plausible that it may not have been difficult to find private individuals willing to accept a contract of this kind; the decision to let the Ospedale di Carità have this opportunity may thus be considered a deliberate choice by donors to benefit it.

The financial activities of the charitable institutions constituted an important source of income which does not however appear in my reckonings. Contracts to provide annuities, for instance, were very common, but it is difficult to arrive at an exact estimate of their value. The minutes record the date when a contract was made, but only rarely do we know when the hospital inherited the capital, and thus we cannot know how much the hospital had to pay out and how much – if anything – the effective 'donation' amounted to. It must thus be taken into account in the discussion which follows that the sums actually received by the institutions were greater than those we can calculate with certainty.

Later on, when it was in a healthier financial state, the Ospedale di Carità was also able to make loans itself. The prevalence of usurious lending at exorbitant rates of interest made a loan from the hospital at the legal rate of interest, or just slightly above it, very attractive to borrowers. However, it was mainly the prosperous S. Giovanni which became heavily involved in lending. Its financial activity became so successful that in a few decades the hospital was able to compete with Turin's largest lending fund. So in 1729, when the interest rate paid to holders of *Luoghi dei Monti* (credits in the city's public debt) was sharply reduced, the S. Giovanni hospital was able to declare its willingness to offer a higher rate, and thus obtain a large influx of capital.[88]

The charitable institutions need, therefore, to be taken into consideration also for the crucial part they played in the city's financial scene. The change of fortunes that they underwent in the late seventeenth century was certainly linked to some extent to the growth of these financial activities, which allowed them to attract citizens' interest. But the main reason was that they managed to transform themselves into a forum for exhibiting prestige in the city. In the closing decades of the century, to be one of the benefactors of Turin's charitable institutions became one of the main forms of social recognition sought after by the rising number of families who were entering into the local elite. Involvement in charities became a symbolic statement of the social success and mobility which one had achieved – a vehicle for social competition between families and between individuals.

In the case of the Ospedale di Carità, this development was greatly assisted by the acquisition of a more dignified building and a move to the centre of the city. The attempt to move to a better location was a constant feature in the strategies adopted by the governors. When it was founded in 1650 the Ospedale was set up in modest rented premises a long way outside the city boundaries. Then in 1661 it moved to a former Capuchin monastery just outside the city walls. Since this was situated within an area ear-marked for urban expansion, the move was an important first step towards full integration into the fabric of the city.[89] The edict which announced the opening of the new premises explicitly stated that the purpose of the move was to encourage citizens to donate more liberally by shifting the hospital nearer the town.[90] This first move does seem to have had some effect in the desired direction, for it was in the 1660s that the first substantial legacies began to arrive from 'outside' (i.e. not from members of the governing board). In the first ten years after the move (1661–70), the total value of legacies and donations to the institution rose to around 58,000 *lire* (see table 6). This was a marked improvement, but still not sufficient for the hospital's

---

[88] AOSG, Ordinati, 11 and 28.1.1729.
[89] This move was made possible by the gift of a member of the ruling house of Savoy, Prince Maurizio, who donated almost two-thirds of the sum needed. AOC, Cat.I, Documenti di fondazione, vol. 1, 1649–1700, fasc.1, 'Origine del Regio Spedale generale della Carità'.
[90] Borelli, *Editti*, p. 240, 30.3.1661.

Table 6. *Known amounts of charity to the Ospedale di Carità by decade*
1650–1789

	Amount	No. of legacies and donations	Known	Unknown	Partly known	Subject to condition
1650s	1,680	3	2	1	—	—
1660s	57,880	6	5	1	—	1
1670s	161,985	20	13	3	4	2
1680s	56,864	11	7	3	1	—
1690s	30,212	9	6	2	1	1
1700s	105,457	52	33	16	5	—
1710s	113,800	36	27	8	1	—
1720s	154,217	20	17	2	1	—
1730s	445,600	26	24	2	—	—
1740s	141,093	19	17	2	—	—
1750s	342,365	23	21	1	2	—
1760s	343,466	27	20	6	1	—
1770s	280,490	21	16	3	2	1
1780s	181,353	40	38	2	—	1

Note: Amounts considered in tables 6 and 7 are those which were actually paid to the hospital after various deductions. The discrepancy between amounts figuring in wills and those eventually paid can be substantial especially in cases where the hospital was made 'universal heir' and in the case of funds for masses for the dead. In both cases, I have included only what was the clear profit for the hospital (if any), once the payment of debts and bequests to legatees, and expenses for the chaplain saying masses, for candles, etc. had been subtracted.

needs, given that the annual cost of simply maintaining the inmates amounted to around 40,000 *lire*,[91] not to mention the cost of refurbishing the building, which was also planned. Moreover, the great bulk (55,000 *lire*) of legacies and donations was contributed by just two benefactors – Giò Antonio Arnulfo and Giorgio Turinetti.[92] In the ten years which followed there was a sharp increase in donations, to over 162,000 *lire*. But once again, although the total number of legacies was considerably higher than before, this figure was reached mainly due to just four large donations, which accounted for 140,000 of the total.[93]

It is not particularly surprising, therefore, that this increase was not maintained. In the 1680s and 1690s there was a fall both in the number of legacies and in the total sum given. It was only from 1700, after the hospital had finally achieved its long-standing ambition to move into the centre of the town, and had begun to construct the monumental premises in which it was to remain

[91] AOC, Ordinati, 15.7.1665.
[92] AOC, Cat.XV, Donazioni, parte I, Eredità, vol. 1; and ibid, Cat. IX, Chiesa.
[93] The donations in question came from a merchant, Marchisio (approx. 28,000 *lire*), the abbot S. Martino d'Aglié (65,500 *lire*), the merchant Rochati (16,500 *lire*), and one of the ladies of Regent Cristina's chamber, the heirless widow of Baron Servan (over 25,000 *lire*). AOC, Cat.XV, Donazioni, parte I, Eredità, vol. 2. For Marchisio's will, see Ins., 1685, l.3, vol. I, 22.6.1673; for S. Martino's legacy, AOSML, m.3, fasc. 8; for Rochati's, AOC, Ordinati, 23.5.1683; for Baron Servan's widow, ibid., 27.11.1677.

Table 7. *Ospedale di Carità. Distribution of bequests and donations by amount
1660–1789*

Lire	500 to 1,000	<3,000	<5,000	<10,000	<20,000	<50,000	<100,000	100,000 and over
1660–1699	24,3	32,5	5,4	2,7	21,6	10,8	2,7	—
1700–1749	34,4	34,4	11,5	10,7	6,7	4,9	—	2,5
1750–1789	27,3	23,2	8,1	15,2	13,1	8,1	3,0	2,0

See footnote to table 6 for the criteria used to calculate amounts of charitable giving.

for two centuries, that there was a real change in the pattern. Not only did the
number of legacies increase by a factor of five in the first ten years of the new
century, but donations – which previously had been divided between a few very
large gifts and many very small ones – now tended to be in the middle range (see
table 7). A third of the donations now fell into the 5,000 to 10,000 *lire* bracket,
and 60 per cent were between 1,000 and 10,000 *lire*. By contrast, there were
fewer really large donations – just one over 10,000 *lire* in this decade.

The hospital thus became more reliant on a flow of 'normal' funds, rather than
on exceptional gifts; giving to the Ospedale di Carità had become a generalised
practice for a broad section of the Turin elite. By this time, in other words, the
hospital had succeeded in involving the middling ranks of society, and no longer
had to rely on enormously rich individuals at the top of the social scale, such as
banker Turinetti and Abbot D'Aglié, on those who had no heirs, like the widow
of Baron Servan, or on those who wished to spite their relatives.[94] The fifty-two
donors of the decade 1700–10 include people from a wide variety of social
groups – the baker Collino, who left the hospital all his property, and instructed
that a plaque be put up in his honour, the doctor Capellis, who donated 5,000 *lire*
and the master of the royal stables, Dumaré, who left 1,500 *lire* on condition that
the poor prayed for him every evening.[95]

The type of pattern which emerged in these first years of the eighteenth
century persisted up until the middle of the century, when the average value of a
legacy to the Ospedale di Carità began to shift upwards. This was not because
the social composition of the benefactors changed; indeed, we might say that the
'middle classes', in particular the mercantile groups, were even more thoroughly
involved. But the same groups which had previously given a couple of thousand
lire now gave 10,000 or 15,000. This might partly be the result of inflation in the

---

[94] The legacy left by Arnulfo seems a case of this kind. Arnulfo's will provides evidence of his bad
relationship with his son-in-law, Count Pietro Bartolomeo Dalmazzone, husband of Arnulfo's
only daughter and father of the only heir. Ins., 1690, 1.9, 10.10.1661. It is not surprising that, after
Arnulfo's death, Count Dalmazzone contested the donation to the hospital.

[95] For Collino, ibid., 1752, 1.5, 30.4.1752; for Capellis, AOC, Cat.IX, Chiesa, 30.9.1704; for
Dumaré, ibid., Ordinati, 24.2.1703.

second half of the century, but it might also suggest that a widespread increase in available wealth had taken place.[96]

The tenacity with which the governors fought to bring about a move of the hospital's premises into the centre of the city demonstrates the influence which locality and physical appearance were considered to have on the way an institution was looked upon and on charitable attitudes. The hospital eventually made it into the city in 1685, after a brief period of confinement on the hill outside Turin. This hillside location had been the result of financial difficulties which had obliged the governors to put themselves in the hands of the ducal authorities. For the hospital had found itself in trouble at a time when the regent, Giovanna Battista, was trying to sell the land to the east of the city and to encourage building on it. The presence of the hospital in that area clashed with these plans, which aimed at making this an imposing official entrance to the city and to the ducal palace. It was therefore thought that removal of the hospital would significantly increase the value of the area. Recourse was made to rhetoric about the danger of infection; the hospital was accused of putting public health at risk, as it caused 'most serious damage to nearby buildings by its unbearable fetid smells, and the citizens fear infection from the excrements of such a multitude of poor and sick'.[97] If the hospital was prepared to move out of the way of the new development, the regent was prepared to donate it the spacious building of the Vigna on the hill outside Turin. This offer was too financially attractive to be turned down, for not only did the arrangement provide the hospital with premises large enough for its needs (after twenty years in the ex-monastery, which it had never had the money to finish refurbishing);[98] but it also provided it with a significant income from the rent to be derived from the old building.[99] The other side of the coin, however, was that the agreement relegated the hospital to a location outside and distant from the town, and this went against the strategy of trying to integrate the hospital into the urban fabric, which had long been pursued by the governors.

However, the exile (which took place in 1679) did not last long. A campaign

---

[96] There are no comprehensive studies either on spending power in this period or on the distribution of wealth. The only indication in support of my argument is found in Prato's claim (based on very partial data) that there was an increase in wealth in the first three decades of the eighteenth century, and then a larger increase after 1750. G. Prato, 'Risparmio e credito in Piemonte all'avvento dell'economia moderna', in *La Cassa di Risparmio di Torino nel suo Primo Centenario*, Turin 1927, pp. 36ff.

[97] LPqM, m.18, fasc.1, 'Donazione fatta da Madama Reale . . . , 30.1.1679'.

[98] Rebuilding had gone ahead in dribs and drabs throughout the almost twenty years that the hospital was in the old priory. Work could only proceed when there were funds available or promised.

[99] This old building became a ghetto for Jews. In 1739 the rents for this ghetto totalled about 30,000 *lire*, thus making up over half what the hospital made from its property (58,745 *lire*). AST, sez.I, OPCB, m.237, fasc.16, 'Stato dimostrativo de' redditi e delle spese de Regio spedale di carità di Torino, 9.3.1739'.

was immediately launched against the move, a campaign which did not balk at using underhand methods such as the anonymous publication of a pamphlet which claimed that the transfer was seriously 'prejudicial to the poor' – and hence, indirectly, held the regent responsible for the damage. After a protest by the regent, the governors were forced to deny the veracity of this pamphlet publicly and to dissociate themselves from it.[100] However, their manoeuvre proved effective. After some hard bargaining, an agreement was reached which seemed to contain substantial risks for the hospital, but which eventually turned out well: it was decided that the governors should build, at their own expense, new premises for the Albergo di Virtù (for which the regent wanted a more dignified building), and that the Ospedale would then become the owner of the Albergo's old premises.[101] As a consequence of the expansion of the city into that area, these now faced onto the smart new street which led down to the river Po which connected the Doranea gate, built by Guarini, to the ducal palace. The Ospedale di Carità thus acquired a prestige location and established itself a few hundred metres from the nerve centres of the court and the state administration (plate 7).

Already in March 1683, even before the inmates were transferred from the Vigna, the governors had approved the plan to rebuild the new premises in a way which would give them an appearance fitting to the status of the new site.[102] Work was started at once, but subsequently came to a halt due to the serious economic difficulties in which the whole state found itself in the late 1680s and in the 1690s, as a result of the war with France, fought on the Duchy's soil. Building got properly under way again only at the end of the century, and it was only in 1700, when the facade of the building, with its arcades, and its church giving on to the fashionable Contrada di Po, were completed, that the Ospedale began to assume its finished appearance.[103] It is at this point that, as we have seen, donations began to pour in. In the early years, many of these were given specifically to finance building work, and seem to show the citizens' approval of the new premises.[104] In addition, in June 1700 the contribution of 9,000 *lire* per year and 200 sacks of corn – which had been granted by the Duke when the hospital was founded, but had been suspended for ten years due to the

---

[100] AOC, Ordinati, 18.4.1679.

[101] This agreement was made in August 1682. So officially, the stay in the Vigna, on the hill outside Turin, only lasted three and a half years; but it was only in June 1685 that the Ospedale di Carità was actually able to transfer the inmates to the new building, after some building work had been done. Ibid., 20.5.1685, 24.6.1685.

[102] Ibid., 28.2.1683, 14.3.1683, 21.3.1683.

[103] Ibid., 28.5.1697, 2.6.1697, 13.6.1700, 28.12.1700, 16.1.1701. It seems that the cross-like plan of the building was finished only around 1715.

[104] As examples of donations for building, see, for the church ibid., 12.9.1700 (Spada's donation), 11.7.1700 (Grondana and Miglyna); for the women's section, see T.P. vol. XXI, c.90–98, 20.4.1704 (Quaglia).

war – was renewed.[105] From this time on, the financial state of the institution improved notably; it left behind it the instability which had characterised it in the early decades and was capable of supporting the very heavy expenses which its ambitious building plans involved.[106] It was able to rely on a relatively regular inflow of donations, and on the substantial property it had accumulated through its acquisition of buildings and, above all, through its financial activity.

Apart from achieving a high profile within the urban fabric of Turin, the Ospedale di Carità also took on new functions at the turn of the century. These had began to emerge with the first move towards the town. The first sizeable legacies, which date from the 1660s and 1670s, merit attention in this context, because they were the first examples of the custom of linking the donation to a series of conditions which had the evident aim of celebrating the donor and his or her charitable act. In the course of these years, a number of practices and rituals were established which later became habitual. To this period belong the first examples of instructions to have busts of the benefactor made, bearing the family arms, and similarly the first memorial tablets, to be placed at strategic points in the hospital, giving details of the donation. In 1661, the year of the hospital's first move closer to the city, Giò Antonio Arnulfo left instructions for what seems to have been the first bust. He gave the hospital a series of donations, in the form of income rights over land or capital (*censi*) and houses, for a total value of 37,000 *lire*. Arnulfo belonged to a family of wholesalers which repeatedly appears, from the 1620s on, in government registers of contracts for supplying corn, for farming of the salt tax, and other enterprises, and for loans to the Duke.[107]

Busts and statues soon became a usual means of celebrating the most prominent benefactors. The Ospedale di Carità (as also the hospital of S. Giovanni) transformed itself into a gallery of urban prestige. Busts and memorial tablets continued to accumulate until well into the nineteenth century, gradually invading the corridors, refectories, dormitories and even courtyards of the two hospitals (see plates 8, 9 and 10). In the end, this form of homage became a kind of cliché, and so was devalued. But there is little doubt that for many decades after the introduction of the practice, it made a strong impression – which encouraged others to compete to ensure a place in this gallery of faces and family coats of arms.

---

[105] D., T.XII, p. 268, 13.6.1700.

[106] Apart from the cost of its own building, and that for the Albergo di Virtù, the Ospedale also had to pay for the refurbishing of the ex-monastery it had formerly inhabited, and which was now its own property, to turn it into a ghetto for the Jews.

[107] On Arnulfo's donation to the hospital, see note 90 above. The instructions to set up a bust are in AOC, Ordinati, 25.6.1665. On the Arnulfo family, PCF, reg. 1623 f.15, 1627 f.63, 1643–44 f.300, 1649 f.249, 1653 f.79 and 89.

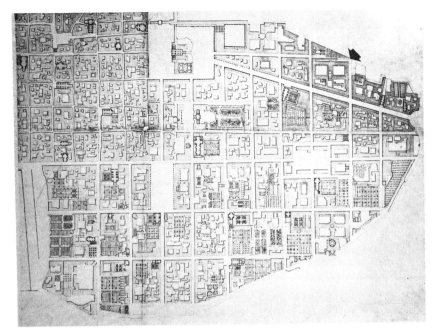

Plate 7. Plan of Turin showing the internal structure of buildings, *c.* 1765 (detail). The sign indicates the Ospedale di Carità in the porticoed Contrada di Po. (AST, p.s., Carte Topografiche per A e per B, Torino 16.)

Among the conditions which Arnulfo specified, apart from the bust, was that a hundred of the hospital's inmates – fifty men and fifty women – should attend his funeral wearing 'as a veil or hood 4 lengths of silver coloured woollen cloth each', to be provided at the testator's expense, and each bearing a two ounce candle.[108] Such use of inmates in funeral choreography was another fashion subsequently imitated by others; in 1688, Arnulfo's funeral was taken as a model for that of another prominent benefactor, Cavalier Michel Angelo Golzio, secretary of state for finance, who also ordered a marble bust.[109]

Apart from instructions specifying the attendance of the poor at the funeral, another clause which started to become common in this period was that which required inmates to say prayers at fixed times of day in memory of the donor and his generosity to the institution. In 1671, for example, Michele Rochati, a furrier who had been a governor of the hospital for many years, left a house worth 16,500 *lire* on the condition that the inmates said a *Salve Regina* for his soul,

[108] AOC, Ordinati, 25.6.1665. Arnulfo also specified that he should be buried in the hospital's church.
[109] Ibid., 8.1.1668.

Plate 8. Ospedale di Carità, bust of baker Collino, 1718
(Regione Piemonte, Assessorato all'Istruzione e Cultura).

Plate 9. Ospedale di Carità, bust of Countess Berga
Caissotti, 1742 (Regione Piemonte, Assessorato
all'Istruzione e Cultura).

Plate 10. Hospital of S. Giovanni, busts in the courtyard (Archivio Museo Civico, Turin).

Plate 11. Ospedale di Carità, memorial tablet of Michele Rochati, a furrier, 1677 (Archivio Museo Civico, Turin).

before lunch and dinner, *in perpetuum*. In addition, the governors were required to put up two stone tablets (one in each refectory) stating this duty, in Italian (see plate 11).[110]

Alongside the introduction of a genre of sculpture, then, the closing decades of the seventeenth century saw the development of a repertoire of imposing baroque rituals. The use of the poor to add to the scenography of these had precedents in many of the rituals of penitence and piety which had become common, in court circles, in the first half of the century. During Easter week, for example, thirteen poor men and thirteen poor women had their feet washed by the Dukes, and were then served a meal by the *gentiluomini di bocca* (gentlemen of the royal table).[111] Similar rituals took place on St Joseph's day, or on the anniversary of the death of the Blessed Amedeo di Savoia.[112] With the growth of rituals in the hospitals, however, this symbolic use of the poor was extended to wider social circles. The same sort of ceremony of serving the poor at table was now introduced at the Ospedale di Carità, thus making it a pious ritual in which all the urban elites could take part.[113] The celebratory practices which grew up at

[110] T.P., vol. XII, 8.7.1671.
[111] An example of this ceremony is mentioned by De Gaudenzi, 'Torino e la corte', for 1644.
[112] Alessio, *Vita della Serenissima*.
[113] AST, sez.I, OPCB, m.237, fasc.16, 'Avvertimento per le Signore invitate a servire a tavola Gesù Cristo riconosciuto ne' poveri dell'Ospedale di Carità', late seventeenth century.

this time around charity and charitable institutions formed a way in which wider social circles could appropriate rituals after decades in which they had been used mainly by the court. It is true that the requirement for small numbers of poor people to attend funerals had a long tradition; a few wills leaving property to the hospital of S. Giovanni even in the second half of the sixteenth century specified that four or six (at the most, twelve) poor, dressed in white or black cloth, should be present.[114] But these were certainly modest rituals compared with the grandiose choreography centred around the poor which emerged in the later seventeenth century. The proliferation of busts and statues also constituted a democratisation of a previously more exclusive form. In the first half of the century, busts and statues were used mainly (in combination with painted portraits) in the celebration of the ruling dynasty or of the families of the high court aristocracy – and, in any case, only in ducal residences.[115] This genre of portraiture received a crucial boost from the customs which were becoming widespread in the charitable institutions, where it fulfilled the desire for symbolic tributes to members of much more modest elites – like the merchant Arnulfo or the secretary of state Golzio.

Charity and patronage

The hospital of S. Giovanni also experienced a marked upsurge of donations in the closing decades of the seventeenth century, and here too, it seems to have been inextricably entwined with the celebration of the prestige of benefactors and of their lineages. The pattern was very similar to that which I have described for the Ospedale di Carità, and the chronology was almost identical. As with the Ospedale, grandiose rebuilding projects (agreed in 1676 and begun in 1680) gave new impetus to the influx of funds.[116] Here too, it became increasingly common for benefactors to ask for busts (or, in this case, also statues), to be set up to commemorate their donation (see plates 12–13). Some of these were fine works sculpted by well-known artists. The first in the series seems to have been the statue of Abbot Amoretti, in 1682. The Abbott had made his 24,000 *lire* gift conditional on the construction of this statue, which he specified should be

---

[114] For example AOSG, Cat.4, Cl.1, vol. 2, fasc. 1; vol. 24, fasc. 2; vol. 63, fasc. 2; vol. 2, fasc. 4 and 6.

[115] L. Mallé, 'Appunti e revisioni per la scultura del '600 e '700 in Piemonte', in *Arte in Europa. Scritti di Storia dell'Arte in Onore di Edoardo Arslan*, vol. I, Milan 1966. On genealogical portraiture, see A. Griseri, 'Il cantiere per una capitale', in *I Rami Incisi dell'Archivio di Corte: Sovrani, Battaglie, Architetture, Topografia*, Turin 1981.

[116] Like the Ospedale di Carità, the new hospital of S. Giovanni was built in the new extension of the town. The regent donated half of the land (10.8.1678). The other half was bought by the hospital in February 1680, and in March the plans of the architect Castellamonte were approved. Regione Piemonte, Assessorato all'Istruzione e Cultura, *L'Ospedale Maggiore di San Giovanni Battista e della Città di Torino*, Turin 1980, pp. 15–19.

placed above the entrance, no less. In addition, he required that the poor should recite prayers in his honour, three times a day.[117]

The upsurge in the flow of funds to the hospital of S. Giovanni was also linked to the opening (in 1668) of a section for incurables.[118] The decision to open this new ward was partly the consequence of a desire to separate the hospital's functions as a refuge from its functions as a centre of medical treatment. For in the course of the century, the hospital moved significantly away from the form I described in the previous chapter, and medical concerns acquired much greater importance. This change had been made possible partly by the considerable enlargement of the premises in 1651,[119] and also by the extension of the hospital's role as a place where young surgeons could practise (see chapter 5).

However, the decision to open a ward for incurables was not only the result of internal administrative reorganisation, but also a response to strong pressure from below. For years representatives of the various corporate bodies in the town had been talking about the urgent need to set up an institution specifically for the elderly, crippled or otherwise non-able-bodied who were continually being sent to existing institutions because there was nowhere else for them to go.[120]

The opening of the new section also brought with it a new form of charitable giving; on payment of a given sum (fixed at 5,200 *lire*), the benefactor secured the acquisition of a bed and of the right *in perpetuum* to nominate who was to occupy it. During the donor's lifetime, the right was of course his personally, after his death it passed to whoever he had named in the agreement (usually firstborn descendants in the male line). Inmates nominated by these benefactors had the right to remain in the hospital until their death. This new procedure linked the gift indissolubly to the name of the family which directly controlled who could use it. Possession of rights over a bed was thus a sort of status symbol, and many benefactors set up more than one (the highest number recorded is nine). For the number of beds which the family disposed of was a measure of its power and its ability to exercise patronage on behalf of its clients.

It was probably the ability of this new form of charity to provide tangible proof of a family's prestige and influence which accounted for the very marked increase in legacies and donations which occurred after the opening of the section for incurables. Between 1660 and 1667 the hospital received only six smallish legacies (total value a few thousand *lire*); whereas between 1668 and 1677 it had over 40,000 *lire* left to it. And in the following decade over twenty-three beds were established (see table 8).

---

[117] AOSG, Ordinati, 31.1.1680.
[118] AOSG, ibid., 9.3.1668.
[119] A first, modest enlargement had taken place in 1598. Caffaratto, *L'Ospedale*, p. 23, p. 30.
[120] AOSG, Ord. 26.6.1667. See also the Ospedale di Carità's repeated petitions to the archbishop (note 54).

Plate 12. Hospital of S. Giovanni, statue of Abbot Amoretti, 1682
(Archivio Museo Civico, Turin).

Much of the hospital of S. Giovanni's growth was due to this new system; the
number of beds rose from thirty-six beds in the mid seventeenth century to about
220 (including beds for both curables and incurables) in 1730, and 450 in 1792.
More than 177 beds for incurables were founded by private benefactors between
1668 (when the new ward was opened) and 1754 – the year in which the
hospital started to place restrictions on this kind of donation in an attempt to
encourage the founding of beds for curable patients instead. By this time, the

Plate 13. Hospital of S. Giovanni, statue of Count Scaglia
di Verrua, 1722 (Archivio Museo Civico, Turin).

governors had realised that the system had perverse effects. For benefactors had
a clear preference for donations specifically to the ward for incurables rather
than for general donations to the hospital (figure 4). The new section at the
hospital of S. Giovanni became much larger than expected and this threatened to
distract it from what was by this time seen as its principal work – that of treating
the ill. The hospital filled up with the elderly and those incapable of working
who, as a report on the state of the institution complained, had no need for

Table 8. *Hospital of S. Giovanni. Endowments of beds for incurables and curables, 1668–1790*

Year	Inc.	Cur.	Year	Inc.	Cur.	Year	Inc.	Cur.	Year	Inc.	Cur.
1668	2	—	1700	2	—	1732	4	—	1764	1	—
1669	—	—	1701	3	—	1733	—	—	1765	1	2
1670	2	—	1702	—	—	1734	4	—	1766	—	—
1671	1	—	1703	2	—	1735	8	2*u	1767	—	—
1672	—	—	1704	1	1	1736	2	—	1768	1	—
1673	—	—	1705	1	1	1737	1	—	1769	—	—
1674	—	—	1706	—	—	1738	2	—	1770	—	—
1675	—	—	1707	—	—	1739	5	—	1771	3	—
1676	1	—	1708	—	1	1740	4	—	1772	—	—
1677	2	—	1709	3	2	1741	4	—	1773	2	—
1678	7	—	1710	1	—	1742	—	—	1774	1*	—
1679	1	—	1711	12	—	1742	3*u	—	1775	1	—
1680	4	—	1712	9	—	1744	1	—	1776	—	14
1681	u	—	1713	4	—	1745	1	—	1777	1	—
1682	3	20	1714	4	1	1746	3	—	1778	—	—
1683	2	—	1715	2	—	1747	5	—	1779	—	—
1684	2	—	1716	1	—	1748	2	—	1780	—	3
1685	2	—	1717	2	1	1749	1	—	1781	—	—
1686	—	—	1718	1	2	1750	4	—	1782	—	1
1687	2	—	1719	2	—	1751	1	—	1783	1	—
1688	2	—	1720	2	1	1752	3	40	1784	2	2
1689	1	—	1721	1	—	1753	—	—	1785	—	1
1690	—	2	1722	—	—	1754	1	1	1786	—	1*u
1691	3	—	1723	1	—	1755	7	—	1787	—	7
1692	—	—	1724	—	—	1756	2	1	1788	—	—
1693	2	—	1725	2	—	1757	3	—	1789	—	2*u
1694	1	—	1726	—	—	1758	4	—	1790	—	1
1695	3	—	1727	—	—	1759	2	—			
1696	—	—	1728	2	—	1760	21*	—			
1697	1	—	1729	1	—	1761	—	—			
1698	1	—	1730	5	—	1762	1	2			
1699	—	—	1731	6	1	1763	2*	—			

Inc. = Incurables; Cur. = Curables.
Note: The dates are those of the disposition and they do not always coincide with those of the setting up of beds. Sometimes the testator did not indicate the exact number of beds but stated that as many as the estate permitted be established. In this case the letter u (undetermined) appears in the table. The asterisk indicates the acquisitions of rights of nomination for beds existing already.

treatment, 'but only food for their hunger'.[121] Those who benefited from the beds provided by donators were in fact mostly old people living on their own, and the system of beds for incurables gave them a kind of insurance for their old age; often, they were old servants who had passed their lives in the service of the family which owned the rights to the bed. Meanwhile, the places available for the sick grew much more slowly. Between 1668 and 1754, seventy-eight beds

[121] LPqM, m.19, fasc.7, 'Sentimenti sugeriti dal Principe di Francavilla . . . , 1734'.

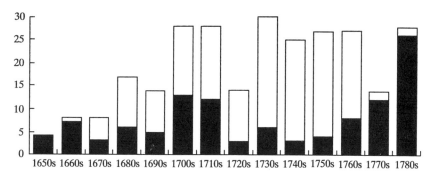

beds for incurables

Fig. 4. Hospital of S. Giovanni. Number of bequests and donations by decade, 1650–1789.

were donated for the curable (as against 177 for incurables), and even this figure was only reached due to the existence of two large gifts from the Marquess Villa and from Costeis, the banker, who gave money for twenty and forty beds respectively.[122] In over eighty years, just seventeen benefactors opted for this kind of donation, as against 114 who founded one or more beds for incurables, with their nomination rights.

For much of the century, the board of governors did not feel able to stop or regulate a practice which attracted most of the donations and bequests received by the hospital. Measures were taken in 1754 and 1773, to limit at least the period in which a family had control over the nomination of inmates, and in 1762 the governing board went as far as to prohibit the acceptance of further endowments.[123] But the attitude of the governors was contradictory since, when money was needed, they resorted to this means which they knew would easily procure funds from the public. In 1760, for example, to face the extra expenditure for building, the governors put twenty-three entitlements to the nomination of beds for incurables up for sale at 3,000 *lire* each. The only modification was that these new beds should revert to the hospital on the death of the testator's immediate descendant. Some twenty-one of these beds were sold within a year.[124]

Finally, in 1780, it was decided to grant the right of nomination for beds for curables as well.[125] Benefactors thus apparently gained control over access to the hospital on the part of patients needing treatment – in rather the same way as in

[122] AOSG, Cat.4, cl.1, vol.7, fasc.16, (Costeis), ibid., vol.2, fasc.16, (Villa).
[123] The measures are mentioned in AOSG, Ordinati, 21.1.1754, 27.5.1775.
[124] Ibid., 16.1.1760.
[125] Ibid., 20.4.1780.

the English voluntary hospitals, where patients were admitted on the basis of a letter of recommendation supplied by one of the subscribers.[126] Fourteen out of the twenty-eight bequests received by the hospital in the next ten years were for the founding of beds for curables and this enthusiasm might lead us to think that, if the system had been introduced earlier, the large flow of funds which for decades had been going to beds for incurables might have gone instead to the sick. However, there are reasons to doubt this. The measure adopted in 1780 was never fully applied in practice and therefore never provided the same kind of control as did the beds for incurables. Only the first nomination made by the family was actually accepted; subsequently, the bed passed under the control of the hospital. It is curious, moreover, that these new beds were used the first time for incurables – even if they were designated as being for the sick. So it appears as if the medical staff did not want to give up their control over access to treatment at the hospital (a right which had been theirs since the seventeenth century), not even temporarily. I have no direct evidence that it was medical personnel who were responsible for preventing the 1780 provision from being carried out. But, unlike the English hospitals, where the letter of recommendation system had been incorporated at the time of foundation, in Turin the change was alien to the way in which access of the curable sick to the hospital had been regulated for over a hundred years.

The support for the incurables section, and the dysfunctions this caused the hospital, clearly show that the expansion in charitable giving in the late seventeenth century was motivated much more by the desire of benefactors to increase their prestige and influence than by consideration of the needs of the poor. Up until the middle decades of the eighteenth century, this search for symbols of social recognition remained a powerful motive behind charity.

The management of charity

I wish now to discuss the social background and motivations of those who were most actively involved in managing and directing institutions, for they have a number of traits which distinguish them from benefactors.

First of all, it should be noted that being a governor might imply very different levels of commitment. For some, it meant no more than occasional attendance of the governing body's weekly meetings, and the willingness every so often to carry out some charge for the hospital or to intercede on its behalf. For others, it constituted a regular daily activity. At the Ospedale di Carità the most active governors were 'governors of the week' chosen on a rotation basis, and this sub-committee oversaw the normal running of the institution, discipline,

---

[126] See R. Porter, 'The gift relation: philanthropy and provincial hospitals in eighteenth-century England', in Granshaw and Porter (eds.), *The Hospital*.

Table 9. *Governors at the Ospedale di Carità. Number of years in office
(from 1672 onwards)*

No. Years	1	2	3	4	5	6	7	8	9	10 or more	Total
	88	28	14	10	5	1	2	4	3	15	170

Note: The governors in this table are those elected between 1672 and 1700.

and the admission of new inmates. Apart from this, certain governors specialised in the management of one particular field of activity. So the task of obtaining the hospital's food supply, or the raw material needed for the inmates' work, the supervision of that work itself, and the supervision of building work were all tasks entrusted to individual 'directors' who had wide powers and discretion. For example, in the 1670s and after, Count Giovanni Michele Vergnano was responsible for the reconstruction of the building the hospital was to move into, as well as for the building works carried out at the ghetto for Jews, and at the Albergo di Virtù. For over a decade, Vergnano had a free hand in deciding who should be employed on these three sites, where materials should be bought, even which architects and engineers should plan the buildings. Domenico Ubertino Romero, a lawyer, had similarly wide powers at this time in dealing with the Jews who rented apartments in the ghetto, as did the governors Vittone and Carlo, who were responsible for making indentures of apprenticeship for the 'sons and daughters of the hospital' and for seeing that they were trained properly.

The hospital was thus in reality run mostly by a small number of individuals who managed to keep the post of governor for long periods of many years. The rule requiring a quarter of the members of the governing body to be re-elected every year did create considerable turnover among part of the governing body but the governors most involved in managing the hospital were continually re-elected and might remain on the board for ten or even fifteen years (see table 9).

At the hospital of S. Giovanni, long length of service was necessarily even more common and up until well into the eighteenth century, governorships were life posts. Thus it was not uncommon for governors to remain in crucial positions within the institution for twenty years or more.

It is evident that the power of the governors was not only a power over the form that aid to the poor should take, or over which particular poor individuals should be selected for admission or outdoor relief, but was also a control over the various types of contracts and work relationships which the hospital was involved in; given the size of the big hospitals, the ability to decide who should benefit from the allocation of its resources was no mean economic power. To give concrete examples, we may note that the governors had control over the recruitment of the workmen employed in various capacities by the hospital and of the artisans who set up their workshops in the hospital, or who worked outside but used the labour of the inmates. They also controlled the choice of suppliers of corn, beef, wine, hemp, silk, shoes, bricks, lime, and so on. It is clear that a governor could use this discretion to favour those under his protection, and to offer patronage which could be invoked at some later date.

A particularly obvious case of the intertwining of management of the hospital and the pursuit of personal interests was the hospital's practice of sending children and babies out to wet-nurses by the hospital of S. Giovanni. Nurses had originally been chosen from various areas in Piedmont, but in the late seventeenth century they were taken exclusively from one fairly small region (part of the Canavese). This was obviously the consequence of favouritism, since the area in question was the feudal domain of the Carroccio family, and for three generations it was precisely this family which held the post of chairman of the board of governors. Carroccio's patronage allowed the population of this poor area to establish a real monopoly over the hospital's 'nurslings', and thus to secure for themselves a significant source of income. This case shows how control over the administration of an institution could be used to pursue strategies for creating support and personal influence in social contexts outside.[127]

Nor should we forget the influence which control over the hospital offered its governors *vis-à-vis* other elites in the town. As I have already mentioned, the governors employed hospital funds in financial dealings with private individuals – lending money at reasonable rates of interest to those who had urgent need of cash, and providing an opportunity (often in the form of an annuity) for those looking for a safe investment for their capital. It was not always easy to obtain these privileges which the hospitals had to offer and in many periods the governors maintained wide discretion over whether or not to take on a given commitment. We should remember in this context that there was a major shortage of safe places where savings could be employed – and, of course, a shortage of opportunities for obtaining credit at non-usurious rates of interest – so control over access to one of these constituted a most significant power.

It seems likely, in fact, that, to some extent, the hospitals reserved these financial opportunities for their 'clients', people who had already had dealings with them. There is no doubt, for instance, that having been a benefactor of an institution in the past at least improved the terms of the agreement. Thus in 1731 the Compagnia di San Paolo loaned 5,000 *lire* to Substitute Procurator General

---

[127] For a broader discussion of this case see my article 'Strategie politiche e strategie familiari intorno al baliatico. Il monopolio dei bambini abbandonati nel Canavese, tra Sei e Settecento', *QS*, 52 (1983).

Brucco (money he needed to pay for a farmhouse) 'in memory of the generosity of the late Senator Giò Paolo' (his father) who had given the company donations while he was alive, and, on his death, had left 1,000 *lire* and silverware to fund spiritual exercises.[128] A few years later, during a time of economic crisis and very high prices, the governors of the hospital of S. Giovanni gave the Prince of Francavilla a loan at the very favourable rate of 4 per cent – noting in the minutes that this was due to the substantial donations which the Prince, and especially his mother, had given the hospital:

> Although, given the money shortage and the circumstances of the present war, the hospital could obtain 5 or even 6 per cent interest from a sum of 24,500 *lire*, given that the matter concerns a family so beneficent towards the hospital, and that the undertaking is so completely safe, the board has agreed to the request.[129]

We might almost say, therefore, that there was a kind of exchange between charity to an institution and access to the financial resources the latter could offer. Often, a charitable donation should not be seen in isolation, but rather as part of a chain of exchanges which might go back to the previous generation or beyond. This kind of cycle-of-exchange perspective obviously leads us to modify the way we normally think of charity. Charity was not always a completely spontaneous gift, but might also contain an element of obligation, a repayment for a favour granted in the past, or at any rate a way of confirming one's bond with a particular institution. And even in those cases where a donation was given without any thought or intention of personal interest, a social link was in any case established which might, in the future, be used to advantage.

What kind of people actually occupied the position of governor of a charitable institution? Among governors who had the longest tenure on the board of the Ospedale di Carità, we find a marked prevalence of men from the mercantile and financial strata – 'merchants', 'bankers', 'wholesalers', or state officials with posts in the organs of administration and control of finance and commerce. The dividing line between these two categories was blurred in this period. As historians have noted,[130] and as the careers of these governors confirm, commercial entrepreneurship and speculation in state finances were intimately intertwined; the roles of private entrepreneur and financial officer of the state frequently converged in the same individual persons. The governors of the Ospedale di Carità had made their fortunes through activities which range from commercial deals (mainly with foreign states) to dealings in foreign exchange, to loans to the state, to tax-farming, to victualling and contracting out state services. At the same time these same men often held posts in the financial

---

[128] ASSP, Rep.Lasc.160, 12.8.1731.
[129] AOSG, Cat.10, cl.3, vol.2. The Princess had founded seven beds for incurables in 1711, and her son had added another two in 1731.
[130] Bulferetti, *Assolutismo*; Stumpo, *Finanza*.

apparatus of the state, and sat in the special forum which judged disputes between workers, masters and merchants (the *Consolato*) which had been set up in 1676. Giò Michele Vergnano, whom I have already had cause to mention, supplied salt to the government salt-tax offices in the 1650s and wheat and luxury goods to the court in the 1660s, and loaned money to the Duke during the war with Genoa. He acquired a title of nobility and was granted feudal land and rights to community taxes.[131] The Vernonis, a family of booksellers who also lent money to the Duke, figure among the governors for over twenty years – first with Giuseppe, who was on the board from 1674 to 1686, then with Giovanni Battista (from 1691 on). The Marchisios were present on the board of governors first with Matteo (up until 1665), then (from 1676 to 1686) with his son Michel Angelo, who was an official at the *Consolato*, and with Carlo Antonio (up until 1688). This family was at the same time engaged in banking (in partnership with the state auditor Garagno, who was himself a governor from 1691 on) and in providing contracts for the military reserve in the 1660s and 1670s. These seem to be cases of genuine family dynasties maintaining control over an institution. Other cases of family succession are not hard to find: for example, the lawyer Domenico Ubertino Romero who became a governor in 1688 on the retirement of Carlo Romero, a goldsmith who had been a governor from 1681 to 1687; or Gabriele Grondana, master auditor, who took the place of his father Giò Matteo, a tax-farmer. Members of these same families also met, in these years, on the smaller governing board of the hospital of S. Giovanni, in spite of the fact that there turnover was limited by the tendency for governors to remain in office for life. Thus Giovanni Andrea Marchisio, brother of Michel Angelo, was a S. Giovanni governor from 1681 to 1683, and Ludovico Vernoni was on the board for over thirty years (1685–1719).

It is clear that the careers of these individuals and families bear many analogies with those of the financiers who only a few decades before had reached the top of the social scale through their involvement with state finances and had had a prominent role in the formation of the court. Historians of the Piedmontese state usually draw a clear-cut distinction between the rapid upward mobility experienced by this latter group and the opportunities open to subsequent generations. They see social advancement and enrichment through exploitation of the state's financial needs, and through the combining of private entrepreneurship with public office, as one which was restricted to the early seventeenth century, and later declined.[132] However, this seems unlikely if we remember that management of a large part of the services which the state

---

[131] All the biographical data on these individuals was taken from wills and from the files of the Patenti Controllo Finanze (PCF) and from *Patenti e Concessioni sovrane e camerali* (in AST, s.r., art.687).

[132] Stumpo, *Finanza*.

offered, and of much of its tax and customs and excise income, remained in private hands via the farming-out system. In the early eighteenth century, tax collecting, contracting for supplies and provisions to the army and the making of loans to pay for wars were still all methods of making fortunes for many individuals; two of the most spectacular cases were Baron Marcello Gamba and Count Olivero, both of whom were auditors of the *Camera dei Conti* (the state organ which had jurisdiction over fiscal matters), and very active governors at the Ospedale di Carità. Men like these managed to accumulate large amounts of wealth in a short time partly through taking advantage of the urgency of the state's needs in time of war, but also as a result of more permanent features of state organisation. For the shift toward a situation where the state managed its own finances directly came very late. It was only during the Spanish war of succession at the beginning of the eighteenth century that, for example, an attempt was made to collect the general excise duty directly, without the help of intermediaries.[133] And it was not until the end of the reign of Vittorio Amedeo II (1684–1730), and the beginning of the reign of his successor, that a network of salaried officials began to be built up and a gradual centralisation of state finances thus became possible.[134] The shift towards direct management of public services also took a considerable time. One of the very earliest steps in this direction came in 1697 with the transfer of responsibility to public functionaries of the postal dispatch system – which up until that time had been farmed out to the Gonteri family (an arrangement which had brought in very little income to the state).[135]

Cases of enrichment and social advancement were still therefore very frequent in the late seventeenth century; it is true, however, that they appear less spectacular than a few decades earlier. The growth of a more rigid pattern of social barriers now blocked access to the highest honours and entry into the ranks of the court aristocracy, and this may have led historians to underestimate the persistence of processes of social mobility. As we shall see, it was precisely the isolation of court families, and in particular their separation from careers in the state rather than in the Dukes' personal service, which a few decades later led them to go down in the social scale as rapidly as they had risen. From the 1720s onwards, in fact, they became the principal victims of measures taken to restore to the royal demesne fiefs which had been acquired through the system of favours and rewards, and to restore the state's rights to taxes. In symbolic terms, too, their pre-eminence in the hierarchy of status came under attack. However, in the decades at the end of the seventeenth century and the very beginning of

---

[133] L. Einaudi, *La Finanza Sabauda all'Aprirsi del Secolo XVIII e Durante la Guerra di Successione Spagnola*, Turin 1908, pp. 1–43.

[134] Quazza, *Le Riforme*, vol. I, pp. 127 and 133–4. Quazza's comments are, however, all too brief and it would be very valuable to know more about this important transformation.

[135] Einaudi, *La Finanza*, p. 38.

the eighteenth, this fall from grace was yet to come, and the pattern of a closed court society at the top of the social hierarchy meant that there were many individuals and families who experienced dissonance between their notable economic rise and the fact that they were denied full recognition in social and status terms. This is a crucial element if we wish to explain the search for prestige which led certain social strata to invest a great deal of energy and money in charitable institutions, and to construct them as arenas for the celebration of prestige which were open to all the elites of the city.

4

Charity and gender

Women and convents

I wish now to consider whether there is any gender specificity in the patterns of donations to charity. Did women and men support charity financially to different degrees, and did they favour some forms of initiative rather than others? Did patterns of male and female involvement in charity change over the period considered?

The first point to note is that, overall, the contribution made by women was much smaller than that of men; if we take the period from 1670 (when private charity began to flourish) to the late eighteenth century as a whole, only 22 per cent of bequests came from women. However, if we divide the period into thirty-year blocks, the picture becomes somewhat less uniform, and we can see that women's contribution reached its peak in the period 1671–1700. In these decades the number of bequests left by women made up 28 per cent of the total (and if we consider the 1690s alone, over 30 per cent). It then went down to 20 per cent in the first thirty years of the eighteenth century, and subsequently remained stable in 1731–60 (despite the high-point of 30 per cent in the 1750s); it finally fell to an average of 16 per cent in 1761–90 (see table 10). These figures for legacies confirm the impression given by the other sources examined in this chapter, that there was considerable variation over time in women's involvement in charity. Women, and in particular aristocratic women, appear much more active in charity in the later seventeenth century and the earlier decades of the eighteenth, after which they rather sink into the background.

The general picture which historians have offered us of women's contribution to charitable initiatives is a somewhat paradoxical one. On the one hand, female involvement in charity is said to have been given particular impetus by Counter-Reformation preaching, while on the other, these same teachings were crucial in encouraging the exclusion of women from the public sphere and the curtailment of their financial independence and economic activities. Both the Catholic and the Protestant Reformation played a key part in fostering principles of female inferiority, subordination and obedience, and thus in the rise of an ideal which saw women's roles as lying primarily in the family and the domestic sphere.[1] In the context of these changes, charity remained one of the few public activities that women were encouraged to pursue, in as much as it was consistent with the motherly and caring qualities held to be especially feminine. However, even in the fields of charity and of religion, women were expected to behave rather differently from the way they had in earlier periods. For, after the 'Indian summer' that the late Middle Ages had represented for female spirituality, individual initiative and charismatic attitudes in female religious and pious behaviour were now discouraged and were to be replaced by a model of plainer virtue to be achieved through prayer, obedience and humility. Moreover, the Church engaged in determined repression of exactly those types of religious expression which had hitherto featured prominently among women – such as prophecy and mysticism.[2] The official model of what female saintliness consisted of changed in this period along the same lines: the identification of the holy life with the active witnessing of Christian values within the community (an ideal which could be pursued by the laity as well) gave way to the idealisation of the contemplative and secluded life as the highest form of perfection that women could reach on earth.[3] It is this repression of non-orthodox forms of religious expression that has usually been seen as the background to the transformation of convents – in particular the fact that Tridentine rules forced them to become strictly secluded, cloistered institutions, and led to the more informal female communities being made to take solemn vows.[4]

A rather gloomy picture of the increasing involvement of women in charity and religion thus emerges from studies whose approach relies perhaps too heavily on ecclesiastical prescriptions. They portray the impact of the Counter-Reformation essentially in terms of an imposition from above of attitudes and ideals which were somewhat foreign to women. Other scholars have instead presented the models of pious and religious behaviour fostered by the Church as, in part, an adaptation of forms of expression which were already gaining an

---

[1] S. Marshall (ed.), *Women in Reformation and Counter-Reformation Europe. Private and Public Worlds*, Bloomington and Indianapolis, Ind. 1989; J. R. Farr, 'The pure and disciplined body: hierarchy, morality and symbolism in France during the Catholic Reformation', *JIH*, 21 (1991). For discussion of the parallels between the effects the Reformation and the Counter-Reformation had on women, see N. Z. Davis, *Society and Culture in Early Modern France*, Stanford 1965 (especially chapter 3); L. Roper, *The Holy Household. Women and Morals in Reformation Augsburg*, Oxford 1989.

[2] Vauchez, *Les Laics*; O. Niccoli, *Profeti e Popolo nell'Italia del Rinascimento*, Bari 1987.

[3] G. Zarri, 'Le sante vive. Per una tipologia della santità femminile nel primo Cinquecento', *Annali dell'Istituto Storico Italo-Germanico di Trento*, 1980, reprinted in Zarri, *Le Sante Vive. Profezie di Corte e Devozione Femminile tra '400 e '500*, Turin 1990.

[4] Zarri, 'Monasteri'.

Table 10. *Bequests and donations by women 1671–1790*

	Excluding those to asylums for penitents	% of all donations	Including those to asylums for penitents	% of all donations
1671–1680	13	26.5	16	32.7
1681–1690	14	25.5	19	34.5
1691–1690	12	31.6	14	34.2
1701–1710	21	18.9	22	19.8
1711–1720	19	21.8	21	23.0
1721–1730	14	26.9		
1731–1740	14	16.3		
1741–1750	15	21.1		
1751–1760	21	30.0		
1761–1770	13	18.3		
1771–1780	9	16.4		
1781–1790	11	14.1		

irresistible hold on women.[5] According to this view, 'devotion became the style' among higher status women,[6] large numbers of whom were giving themselves over to religious fervour to an extent which was unexpected and not entirely welcomed by the ecclesiastical hierarchy. The Church thus found itself in the position of having to cope with this new pattern. The rapid rise in the numbers of convents, and in the numbers of women taking holy vows in the post-Tridentine period, needs also to be seen as to some extent a movement from below. It would be wrong to see this 'feminisation' of religious orders as solely a question of forcible confinement and exclusion. The flood of entries into the convents got out of hand and the ecclesiastical authorities were even driven to change tack in their preachings and moral tracts, and to re-evaluate the dignity of marriage (traditionally looked down upon by comparison with the religious state), in order to counterbalance the appeal exercised by the convent.[7]

In Turin, as in other parts of Europe, there was a major expansion of women's activity in charitable and pious works in the seventeenth century, at least among aristocratic women. Part of this activity took place within formal organisations of pious lay women, the most important of which was the Compagnia di Santa Elisabetta (later renamed Compagnia delle Umiliate, or Company of the Humbled). This had ceased activity after the plague of 1598, but took on new life under the Jesuits, who assumed responsibility for its spiritual guidance from 1605 on.[8] In the early decades of the Company's existence, members visited

[5] L. Chatelier, *L'Europe des Dévots*, Paris 1987; E. Rapley, *The Dévotes. Women and Church in Seventeenth Century France*, Montreal and Kingston 1990, and the references Rapley cites.
[6] Rapley, *The Dévotes*, p. 17.
[7] Ibid., p. 18.
[8] Tesauro, *Istoria*; A. Monti, *La Compagnia di Gesù nel Territorio della Provincia Torinese*, Chieri, 1914–20, vol. 1, p. 183.

patients and guests at the Ospizio dei Pellegrini (Hospice for the Pilgrims), but this duty was soon transferred to those at the hospital of S. Giovanni. In groups of friends, relatives or neighbours, the 'sisters' of the Company went every week to the women's infirmary where they 'visited, consoled and served' the inmates, handed over the alms they had collected in the town and those obtained from the 'most comfortable and most pious' among the sisters, and gave back the linen they had washed. They also kept lists of names and addresses of the infirm poor in the city and went to visit them in their homes, informed themselves as to their needs and helped them with a little money.[9] At least if we go by the numbers of prominent women on its membership lists, the Compagnia delle Umiliate seems to have involved most of the female representatives of the elite groups of Turin.[10]

Other organisations of pious women were created in this period which, however, had a more transitory existence, and have left only fragmentary traces of their activities.[11] It is likely that a study of these companies would reveal a trend similar to that already noted by scholars working on similar associations elsewhere – namely, a flowering of devotional and charitable organisations in the most dynamic phase of the Counter-Reformation, which was subsequently squashed, or at least regimented, by the ecclesiastical authorities.[12] Women's energies, however, also went into charitable and religious activities outside the companies, although these have so far been largely under-investigated.

In Turin, this less formalised area of female commitment seems to have become particularly widespread from the 1620s on. It was aristocratic women who were behind the setting up of three new nunneries at this time – that of the Capuchins in 1624, of the Carmelites in 1623, and the convent of the Visitation in 1638. It was women, in fact, who arranged for the orders in question to come to Turin, and they who financed the buildings to house them.[13] Women were also crucial in the establishment and maintenance of two institutions for penitents – that of Santa Maria Maddalena and that of Santa Pelagia – which were later also converted into convents (in 1671 and 1692 respectively). The asylum of Santa Maria Maddalena was set up by pious court ladies in 1634; the daughters of the Duke were especially important since they donated the building and its land.[14] We know less about the details of who founded the house of Santa Pelagia in

---

[9] AAT, 17.8.4, c.413, 'Avisi per il Padre che succederà nella direzione della Compagnia dell'Umiltà', no date.

[10] Membership lists are held in ibid., 17.8.2, 'Libro della Tesoreria della Compagnia dell'Umiltà 1646–1658' and 17.8.3 'Libro della Tesoreria 1669–1768'.

[11] An example is the Company of the Seven Sisters. Ibid., 17.8.16, 'Libro dell'entrata e spesa, 1634'.

[12] Jones, *The Charitable Imperative*, part II; Rapley, *The Dévotes*.

[13] Cibrario, *Storia*, vol. II p. 58; Claretta, *Storia della Reggenza*, vol. II, pp. 553, 558–60.

[14] AST, n.s., Conventi Soppressi, m.658, Monastero di Santa M. Maddalena in Torino, 'Memorie della Fondazione'.

1659,[15] but we do know that it was primarily women who were responsible for its financial upkeep – twelve out of the sixteen legacies received between 1659 and 1714 came from women. Some of these were also very sizeable, enough to set up a pharmacy or to add an extension to the building.[16]

The fact that religious institutions were the preferred beneficiaries, at least in selected periods, of donations and bequests from women, would justify the impression that the female charitable impulse is under-represented by the figures for overall trends in giving which have provided the basis for the discussion so far (see figure 1). These figures, focusing as they do on those secular forms of charity, omit donations which were directed towards religious houses, such as convents and, for the sake of consistency, do not register bequests to asylums for penitents, given the hybrid nature of these institutions at the time. If however we include at least asylums for penitents in table 10, the proportion of charitable legacies coming from women in the period 1671–1700 increases from 27 to 34 per cent.

Another important feature of women's charitable activity before 1730 is the fact that it is aimed at women. Overall, 35 per cent of the donations and bequests made by female benefactors in the period 1671–1730 were destined for women. If we take the 1680s and 1690s on their own, over half were so directed.[17] Apart from bequests and donations to convents and institutions for penitents, many other charitable functions performed by women were intended to help fellow members of their sex. The setting up of funds for dowries is an important example. These funds (the administration of which was usually entrusted to the Compagnia di San Paolo) provided young women with the sum necessary to marry or, more commonly, to enter a convent. Many women also left bequests for unmarried and 'endangered' young women at the Soccorso and the Deposito, the institutions I described briefly in the previous chapter. Others set up funds to distribute alms to widows and, in one case, even to found a community of poor widows 'in which they can maintain themselves and live a holy life'.[18] Finally, a large legacy was left for the founding of an institution for the *malmaritate*, women with marriages which were recognised to have failed.

[15] Ibid., m.654, 'Breve relatione de' successi del Monastero di Santa Pelagia, 1722'. This account contains little information on the institution's foundation, which is simply attributed to 'the piety of certain pious persons'.

[16] See, for example, the bequests of Giovanna Solara di Govone (T.P. vol. XIV, c.5, 15.4.1680) and of Cristina Villecardet S. Giorgio (Ins. l.5, c.363, 18.6.1705) for gifts to be used for additions to the building, and that of Angela Truchi Gromo di Ternengo for the pharmacy (T.P., vol. XX, c.147, 15.2.1713).

[17] Male legacies for women were also common but such bequests constitute only 13 per cent of the male total in the period up to 1730.

[18] Legacy of M. Margherita Dal Pozzo di Voghera (ASSP, 146, 16.5.1658 for the will, and 25.1.1674 for the codicil). The first women admitted were all Marchioness Dal Pozzo's servants.

One feature is common to these various charitable initiatives: they are largely concerned with the vulnerability inherent in a single woman's position – not only financial vulnerability but also in terms of honour. Thus the typical recipients include widows, women who albeit married are unable to live with their husbands, and women not yet married and unable to be so because they do not have a sufficient dowry. We can see that women's charitable activity shows distinctive features in relation to its male counterpart in this period. I will return to this shortly, but first I wish to discuss another striking characteristic of female charity.

There is little doubt that the largest slice of women's charity, particularly in the decades of the seventeenth century and the beginning of the eighteenth, went towards the financing of what we might call the 'cloistering of women'. Bequests left directly for the maintenance of the convent, together with those left to provide individual women with dowries to enter a convent, represent a feature of the wills of upper class women in this period. This leads us to question the image of forced segregation from the world which we usually associate with taking vows in this period and to ask what the convent really represented for women.

Recent studies of religious life have shown very clearly how – in accordance with the prescriptions issued by the Council – the doors of convents closed on nuns in the post-Tridentine period, and how excursions to, and activities in, the secular world came to be forbidden.[19] We should note, however, that although – from the early seventeenth century on – convents were sealed with regard to *exits* from their walls, they did not prohibit *entry*. Indeed, precisely in the decades when Counter-Reformation propaganda was at its height, they seem to have developed into centres of a female social life focused on religious and mystical practices which involved both secular and religious women. Convents were visited daily by ladies of the aristocracy and even provided the latter with periods of temporary retreat from the world. Even Duchess Cristina herself kept apartments at the Carmelite convent,[20] and other ladies of her court had similar arrangements. Thus for example we discover from her will (dated 1705) that Cristina Villecardet S. Giorgio kept 'silver, provisions and other effects' in the convent of Santa Pelagia (previously an institution for penitents). It is likely that she kept for her own use an apartment in the wing of the convent whose construction she had paid for. It is significant that she considered these parts of the convent as in some sense hers: there, as her will specified, the nuns were expected to allow her son 'to store harvest and forage during the present war'.[21]

---

[19] For the by now large bibliography on the subject see M. L. King, *Women of the Renaissance*, Chicago, Ill. 1991; Zarri, 'Monasteri'.

[20] On the religious habits of Cristina, see *Harangue Funèbre*, and S. Guichenon, *Le Soleil et son Apogée ou l'Histoire de Christine de France*, Turin no date.

[21] For Cristina Villecardet's will, see above, note 16.

Convents at this time were to some extent private spaces; the nuns themselves had their 'own' apartments, built by their families when they entered the convent.[22] It seems likely that these rooms may have been used to put up temporarily other women friends or family.

The architectural structure of convents thus encouraged contacts between outside and inside, and gave related lay and religious women – sisters, aunts and nieces, mothers and daughters – the chance to maintain selected elements of a shared life. When we are interpreting women's enthusiasm for financing the cloistering of women, we should bear in mind that convents and institutes for penitents in this period were not distant and foreign institutions for female donors but familiar places, part of their daily social life.

We should also note that it was quite common for upper class women – either widowed or older unmarried women – to go into a convent permanently for the last part of their lives.[23] So although it is usually the involuntary and coercive aspects of segregation in convents which have been emphasised, we should remember that, in this period, at least in certain social ambiences, the cloistered life could also be a choice, and one which was idealised by many women.[24] In this context it is interesting that signs of an emotional bond with the convent often show through in the wills of women leaving property to religious institutions where they had been brought up, or where they often went as adults. Many women broke with the usual and expected practice of having themselves buried in the family vault in some church, and ordered instead that they should be buried within the walls of the convent to which they were affectively linked, often wearing a nun's habit. This wish recurs frequently in wills up until the early eighteenth century. Perhaps one of the last women to ask for this was Ludovica Ponte Villecardet who, in 1727, arranged to be buried alongside the 'beloved and revered nuns of Santa Clara, in the habit which is already prepared in the house'.[25] Some of those who still wanted to maintain the custom of family burial nonetheless asked to have a part of their body sent to a convent.

---

[22] The custom of providing nuns with their own apartments seems to have lasted much longer in Turin than in other Italian cities, where it seems to have disappeared with Tridentine policy (Zarri, 'Monasteri'). An example is to be found in the dowry contract of Cristina Piosasca which laid down, apart from the dowry, payment of a sum for 'the building of two rooms for the use of the said Cristina' in the nunnery of the Crocifisso (Ins. 1667, l.11, 5.9.1667).

[23] See for example the cases of the Marchioness of Pancalieri, cited in the will of her daughter, Maria Valperga di Masino (T.P. vol. XIV, c.7, 12.10.1675); Francesca Germonio, widow without issue, who withdrew into the convent of the Visitation in 1689 (Ins. 1689 l.10, c.55, 26.9.1689); and Francesca S. Giorgio, who entered the convent of Santissima Annunziata in 1670. (This last case is cited in the financial agreement drawn up between Francesca's son, Guido Aldobrandino and his wife Cristina Villecardet, ibid., 1682, l.3 c.1399, 27.2.1681.)

[24] This more positive view of the convent is increasingly emphasised in recent studies. King, *Women*, pp. 81 ff.

[25] AOSG, cat.4, cl.1, vol.24, fasc.9, 20.3.1727. Many wills also prescribe burial in the vault of the Company of the Humbled.

Thus Margherita Falcombella Perachina wanted her heart to be sent to the nuns of the Visitation at Pinerolo, the convent where she had been 'one of the first young pensioners' and where her daughter had taken vows. She also prescribed that a plaque should be affixed to commemorate the bond of affection which linked her to the convent.[26]

The use of convents by lay women did not therefore disappear during the Counter-Reformation decades; indeed it tended to increase, not least because of a rise, in the early seventeenth century, of the number of women living in their own homes as members of third orders – partly as a reaction to the Council of Trent's decision that all women's religious houses should be enclosed.[27] In Turin as elsewhere it became widespread practice among many single and widowed women of the upper classes to join a religious order on the basis of simple vows, and for these female secular tertiaries the convent was the focus of devotional activity. The example was set by the Duke's daughters, the Infanti Maria and Francesca Caterina, who became members of the third order of the Franciscans in 1629. Together with their ladies in waiting, they rejected worldly dress and clothed themselves only in 'woollen cloth of a colour similar to that worn by the friars', under which they wore 'girdles with little sharp objects sewn into them'. The life of this female court centred around collective confessions and prayers, flagellation and fasting – practices for which the convent provided the principal arena. The Duke's daughters went every day to the convent of the Capuchins (an order which they themselves had brought to Turin) and every two weeks they led a ritual of 'public self-accusation' there. The institution for penitents of Santa Maria Maddalena, which had been founded by the Duke's daughters and remained under their protection, was another stage for the female court's religious life. Here aristocratic ladies would take part in prayers and in rituals of self-mortification such as serving the converted women at table.[28]

The rituals which took place in convents thus extended to institutions for penitents. Further evidence of the analogies existing between the two types of institutions comes from linguistic usage: although they were not officially convents, the two institutions supposedly for penitents were, right from their foundation, normally referred to as such, and documents of the time refer to their inmates as 'nuns' or 'sisters'. Was there a real basis for this linguistic usage? What was the nature of these institutions?

Asylums for penitents

If we are to believe the hagiographic literature, it seems that the conversion of prostitutes – 'insatiable beasts sucking the blood and the wealth of men' – was

---

[26] Ins. 1686, 1.7, 10.7.1686.
[27] Zarri, 'Monasteri', pp. 402–6.   [28] Alessio, *Vita della Serenissima*.

the activity in which the institutions for penitents were initially engaged.[29] All the other documents which have survived, however, suggest that the women in the asylums were far removed from being ordinary prostitutes. Some interesting evidence is provided by the deeds made by women when they granted their dowry to one of the two institutions. My search for these contracts, registered in the notarial records in Turin, revealed a small number of dowry deeds – ten over a period of twenty years.[30] Data from this small sample of contracts, plus information on two other inmates gathered from other sources,[31] give us some idea of the type of women who were resident in the institutions for penitents in the period before their official conversion into convents.

Three of these twelve women about whom we have information were widows, three are described as unsatisfactorily married, and five were unmarried (in the case of one, there is no data on marital status). It is, however, difficult to see which, if any, might be identified as 'penitents'. There is just one case where sin and penitence are referred to. Anna Marchetta from Saluzzo did decide to enter the convent of Santa Maria Maddalena in 1646 'given the vanity of the world', to 'do penance for her sins'.[32] Should we take this as an allusion to concrete facts in this woman's past life, or simply as a highly generic formula, a general allusion to the temptations or risks which might potentially beset a young widow or unmarried woman? It is possible that these women may have been involved in some scandal; but it is equally likely that it was merely their isolation and the absence of marital control over them that made their reputation extremely vulnerable and retreat into the institution desirable.

The social ambiguity intrinsic in being a woman who was not under the protection of a man seems at any rate to have been the reason why the *malmaritate* were in the institutions. It seems significant that both Orsola Maria Castelli and Vittoria Oddonina requested admission to the House of Santa Maria Maddalena immediately after the sentence of the archiepiscopal court which formalised their separations from their husbands. In other words, they

---

[29] Ibid. for an account of Santa Maria Maddalena's inauguration.

[30] I examined twenty years of notarial records in the case of Santa Maria Maddalena (twenty years in the period between 1636 and 1671, chosen on the basis of the availability of an index) and seventeen years (1659–75) in the case of Santa Pelagia. The figure of ten contracts officially registered is low, given that the institutions housed between forty and fifty 'sisters'. This might suggest that most of the women entered the institution without a dowry. It seems more likely however, that registering contracts of this type with the state register was still by no means universally adhered to. I checked the reliability of the notarial records by searching for dowry contracts for an officially recognised convent – i.e. for an institution which it was impossible to enter without a dowry – of similar size (the convent of the Crocifisso), and found only eight contracts over twenty years.

[31] One of these women is cited in the will of Carlotta Baron Servan (AOC, Cat.XV, Parte 1a, Eredità, vol. 2, 1676–92, 14.1.1678), the other in the documents regarding the institution of Santa Maria Maddalena (AST, n.s., Conventi soppressi, m.658).

[32] Ins. 1646, l.7, 22.6.1646. Anna Marchetta is also the woman whose marital status is not specified.

applied for admittance precisely at the moment at which they would otherwise have had to enter into the difficult situation of women who were both 'single' and 'married' – women for whom society could propose no safe matrimonial solution.[33] The third 'unhappily married' woman, Teresa Bene, had been married for fourteen years but had been abandoned eleven years previously by her husband who had gone to live outside the territory of the state of Savoy. As was the case with the other women, as soon as she succeeded in reclaiming her dowry from her husband in 1661, she used this to pay the dowry required for admittance to the convent of Santa Pelagia, putting an end to her long and ambiguous sojourn in the secular world.[34]

We do not know the reasons why these women came to be partially 'freed' from the bonds of marriage. Only in the case of Vittoria Oddonina do we have an interesting piece of information: a few days after the signing of the contract, the convent returned the dowry on the grounds that 'having taken her vows, the said Vittoria was discovered to be possessed and so haunted that she cannot continue to wear the habit'.[35] Probably the husband too had rejected her on the ground of her insanity.

Vittoria Oddonina represents an extreme case of the range of inconvenient women of one kind or another which the institutions for penitents seem to have catered for. Their main function seems to have been to defend personal and family honour, accepting women whose position was such that their reputation was open to insinuation if not open attack. But their protective role extended more generally to women with life-histories which for some reason did not run along the expected tracks.

For some women entry into one of the institutions for penitents seems to have been determined less by direct social pressures than by a genuine desire for retreat. Angela Gariglio seems to have entered the House of Santa Maria Maddalena simply because, after the death of her husband and of the daughter who was her only child, she felt no reason to remain out in the world.[36] We should not forget that even women whose very high social status made their sexual honour almost invulnerable to attack – such as ladies of the court – were often tempted by the idea of retreat. The two institutions for penitents also made this ideal accessible also to women who were not sufficiently well-off to enter a real convent. The latter all required much higher dowries than the institutions for penitents. Even the poorest, the convent of the Crocifisso, whose rates were lowest, asked for between 2,000 and 4,000 *lire*.[37] This can be compared with the 600 to 1,500 *lire* paid to enter the institution of Santa Maria Maddalena.

---

[33] Ibid., 1670, 1.5, 19.5.1670 and 1671, 1.12, 3.8.1671.   [34] Ibid., 1662, 1.7, 7.10.1661.

[35] Ibid., 1671, 1.12, 8.8.1671.

[36] AST, n.s., Conventi soppressi, m.658, 1.2.1635.

[37] See, for example, Ins. 1663, 1.6, 1.6.1663 (dowry of Orsola M. Benedicti) and 5.6.1663 (dowry of M. Clara Ruschis).

Considerations of cost probably also explain why younger women of good families 'became nuns' in institutions for penitents. The Alpe sisters, who entered the asylum of Santa Pelagia in 1666, seem to be a good example. The death of their father, who had been a tax-farmer, threw the family into financial straits. The mother was under pressure from her husband's creditors and in dispute with her son, who was the heir; she was thus forced to withdraw her daughters from the more costly convent of the Annunziata at Pancalieri, where they had taken vows, and place them in the institution of Santa Pelagia, where they were admitted for a dowry of about 1,300 *lire* (as compared with the 2,000 *lire* given to the nuns at the Annunziata).[38] In the institution, the two girls found themselves in the company of women of very different age and experience. But this mixture of conditions and moral states does not seem to have represented a problem. Were the sisters on a par with other inmates at least in terms of social background? We do have some information on the social origin of seven of the twelve women I have been able to identify. The widows Vasar and Gariglio came from families of merchants, the widow Galla from a family of artisans who owned their own workshop. As we have seen, the Alpe sisters were daughters of a failed financier, and the young women Lucia Rolandi and Passerona came from the minor nobility.[39] So the institutions seem to have taken in women who were not poor but came from the middling strata, or women of good social status whose families had fallen on hard times. The idea that the asylums for penitents represented an alternative to the much more elitist city convents, crowded with daughters of the aristocracy and upper classes, thus seems to be confirmed: these institutions gave women of respectable and yet more modest social origin, who could not afford to pay a large monastic dowry, the opportunity to pursue the ideal of retreat and contemplative life which was widespread at the time among women.

In Turin we do not find evidence to substantiate the claim that in Italian institutions for penitents 'most inmates came from the working classes, although the asylums occasionally sheltered women from the upper levels of society'.[40] The situation was quite the reverse: if there were any women of the labouring classes (and I have not found any examples), they were the exception. The profile of inmates in Turin also casts doubt on the assumption that, as proclaimed by the documents of foundation, these institutions aimed at redeeming common

---

[38] Ibid., 1666, 1.11, 4.11.1666 (dowries of the Alpe sisters), 1665, 1.10, 31.7.1665 (for the will of their father Gioanetto Alpe), and ibid., 8.8.1665 (for the inventory of possessions, debts and credits drawn up after the death of Gioanetto).

[39] For Caterina Vasar see ibid., 1665, 1.10, 30.8.1665; for Caterina Galla, ibid., 1662, 1.7, 27.6.1662; for Lucia Rolandi, ibid., 1670 1.9, 6.9.1670; for the Passerona girl see the will of her godmother, Carlotta Baron Servan, cited in note 31.

[40] S. Cohen, 'Asylums for women in Counter-Reformation Italy', in Marshall, *Women in Reformation*, p. 169.

prostitutes. Although it is not impossible that the sexual behaviour of some in the institutions had evoked disapproval or scandal, the term 'streetwise ex-prostitutes' seems totally inappropriate.[41] As I already mentioned when discussing the asylums for women 'in danger of losing their honour' run by the Compagnia di San Paolo, institutional protection of sexual honour was provided only when social honour was also at stake.[42] A similar pattern seems to be observable in the institutions for penitents, with the difference that these were places of permanent retreat, while the Soccorso and Deposito aimed at restoring the damaged reputation of a young woman and at returning her to the outside world in a socially safer condition.

Other sources confirm the fact that penitent women, with a history of moral corruption behind them, were in a minority among the residents in the asylums. In 1671, the constitution which admitted the asylum of Santa Maria Maddalena into the order of the Franciscans was mainly concerned with justifying the deviation from the institution's supposed original functions.[43] The articles of the constitution tried to play down the numbers of 'pious women and virgins' among the inmates, arguing that this category of woman was essential instead for the good government of the institution. Thirty years later, in 1700, new articles of constitution expressed the same concern for the lack of adherence to the wishes of the founders.[44] The articles invited the convent to 'admit virgins and widows in limited numbers only, so as to remedy the disorders resulting – as experience has shown – from an excessive number of pious women and virgins' and encouraged it to accept also women not capable of bringing a dowry, at least at times 'when the income of the nuns was sufficient'. Clearly, the entry of women without a dowry was not expected to be very frequent.

The case of the Santa Pelagia refuge was no different. As an account of the institution's history records, here too the inmates were made up of 'three classes of persons'. Apart from the penitents, there were 'the unsatisfactorily married' and the 'young women in danger'; all categories were 'governed by young women or widows of impeccable honour and repute'.[45]

The fact that women of different age, marital status, sexual experience and social background shared the same domestic space and life for the remainder of their years certainly represents the most striking feature of institutions for

---

[41] Ibid., p. 175.

[42] On female honour more generally and on the connection between sexual honour and social honour, see S. Cavallo and S. Cerutti, 'Onore femminile e controllo sociale della riproduzione in Piemonte tra Sei e Settecento', *QS*, 44 (1980), reprinted in E. Muir and G. Ruggiero, *Sex and Gender in Historical Perspective*, Baltimore, Md. and London 1990.

[43] *Regole e costitutioni delle Reverende Monache del Terz'Ordine di S. Francesco, dette Convertite del Monastero dei sta. M. Maddalena nella città di Torino . . . confermate da Monsignor Illustrissimo e Reverendissimo Arcivescovo Michele Beggiamo . . .*, Turin 1671.

[44] *Costituzioni per le Molto Reverende Monache del Monastero di Sta. M. Maddalena Eretto in Torino . . .*, Turin 1700.   [45] 'Breve relatione' (cited note 15).

penitents. Moreover, as we have seen, these asylums attracted women of even higher social status, as regular visitors from outside. The account of Santa Pelagia's history also mentions the habit of 'certain ladies of the first rank' coming in and staying for a period in the institution at certain times of the year. The unifying feature among these women was of course the vulnerability of female honour common to the widowed and unmarried women and the deserted wives who made up both the inmates and the visitors. It is hard to understand, however, how a society which attached such paramount importance to social boundaries and distances could have allowed this degree of intermingling. We can assume that criteria for stratification were different for men and women: while male society was highly segregated according to age, marital status (which, for men, was primarily a question of dependence on, or independence of, the father), and above all social status, women's stratification was shaped by a hierarchy defined by their position in terms of sexual honour.

The social composition of inmates in institutions for women retained its heterogeneous character up until the eighteenth century. By the 1720s, however, the notion of honour as an overriding principle gave way to a clear segregation on the basis of differing moral, social and marital states. The new institutions for women created in this century, such as the Forzate and the Provvidenza, now catered for precise categories of women, either girls or adult women, either married or virgins, etc. But even within existing institutions, changes were taking place which aimed at eliminating the promiscuity of earlier decades.

The timing of this change is well documented by the fate of a bequest left to Santa Pelagia by Enrichetta Ponte di Scarnafigi. In 1695 the Countess Ponte laid down in her will that the handsome sum of 50,000 *lire* should be left for the construction of a refuge for *malmaritate* within the walls of the convent, to be under the direction of the nuns. By 1695 the institution had officially been a convent for three years – yet it was evidently still entirely conceivable that a convent could run the kind of establishment envisaged by the donor.[46] Twelve years later, in 1707, the countess already felt sufficiently uncertain about the project to add a codicil to her will, to the effect that 'if the nuns say they are unable to comply' the legacy should pass to the Compagnia di San Paolo, which was to set up a fund for dowries instead.[47] When Enrichetta eventually died, in 1720, the legacy had become totally incompatible with the new identity of the convent. It was refused indignantly by the nuns 'because it would be of no profit, and indeed of considerable prejudice to the convent and its decorum, liable to disturb their tranquillity, and the label of *malmaritate* most odious to the relatives of the nuns and their young pupils'.[48]

---

[46] T.P. vol. XX, 17.12.1695.   [47] Ins., 1720, l.8, 2.4.1707.

[48] 'Breve relatione'. The reference to pupils reflects the fact that at this time, convents provided education for young aristocratic girls.

Within the space of a few decades both the presence of lay women and the presence of women with a somewhat ambiguous past had become something embarrassing and even to be ashamed of. Perhaps it is no accident that it was soon after the rejection of the Ponte di Scarnafigi legacy (in 1722) that an account of the convent's history came to be written. This record of the institution looks back on the years when it was an asylum for various ambiguous categories of women with a certain amount of disdain, and as something belonging definitely to the past. The main intention of the account seems to have been to construct a new and completely respectable image for the convent, laying to rest as part of an obsolete history former practices which, in reality, were integral to its all too recent past.

It was not just the asylums for penitents which changed their character, for convents in the full sense underwent transformations along similar lines. A whole series of features which had previously been common more or less disappeared by the end of the 1720s. After this date examples of the use of the convent by lay women, either for pious, devotional practices, or as a retreat or refuge, or for female company, and of the custom of being buried within the convent, are extremely rare.

How do these institutional changes relate to ecclesiastical prescriptions? As we have seen, the prohibitions on nuns passing beyond the convent walls can certainly be attributed to instructions emanating from the Council of Trent; but the other kind of closure, to entry *from* the outside, occurred much later and does not seem to have been directly linked to explicit Church policy. The transformation which took place in asylums for penitents was similarly independent of ecclesiastical intervention: the mixed composition of their inmates was not affected by the assumption of the monastic rule. Only some decades after the official adoption of their new status as convents did former asylums for penitents change their intake of inmates and became a more homogeneous entity. Furthermore, this was not in any sense encouraged or foreseen by the statutes governing the new convents.

The reshaping of the nature of convents that I have briefly outlined should be analysed in the more general context of changes at the level of the way social hierarchy was defined. It has recently been suggested that a new concern for boundary making in society at large emerged during the Counter-Reformation century, drawing heavily on concepts of honour and social purity.[49] It could well be that the process of differentiation which we see emerging in the convents represented an aspect of this tendency towards greater hierarchisation in the body social more generally. It would also appear that criteria for stratification were deeply gendered. If this is the case the convent would be not just an example of

[49] Farr, 'The pure'.

a general trend but an ideal vantage point for the analysis of the relationship between gender and the creation of social boundaries.

Women and property

The chronology of changes affecting the convent closely corresponds to that of the previously noted decline of female initiative in charity. As I suggested at the beginning of this chapter, women became much less prominent as benefactors from the 1720s onwards. However, it was not so much that the numerical importance of their charitable donations declined (table 10), but that the nature of their involvement in charity changed after this date. How can we explain these developments in the female contribution to charity?

I have already mentioned that the introduction of the new Counter-Reformation religious orders to Turin, as also the growth of female religious rituals, was partly encouraged by the need of the ducal authorities to strengthen the court and the court's image in the city. In the 1620s and 1630s, a whole series of public religious events sponsored by the ladies of the ducal court – such as the founding of the Capuchin convent, the taking of vows by the Duke's daughters themselves, or the crowning of the statue of the Madonna in the Capuchin church – can be seen as occasions for celebrating the court. We should be aware of the impression that these kinds of ceremonies must have made: the opening of the asylum of Santa Maria Maddalena, for example, was marked by a procession of the first penitents to be received, wearing crowns of thorns on their heads, and carrying a large wooden cross. Each penitent was flanked by two ladies of the court and followed by their royal highnesses, by male and female courtiers and by ecclesiastical dignitaries – all singing and chanting prayers and litanies, accompanied by trumpets and the firing of muskets and artillery.[50] This kind of baroque theatrical event displayed the link between privilege and piety, between court and religion, and legitimised the social distinction of this elite.

It is true that some did criticise these forms of religious expression as excessive and considered them unseemly for women. Thus the account of the life of Infanta Maria of Savoy mentions people at court who disapproved of the practices of flagellation and mortification of the flesh practised by ladies of the court. Others remarked that 'the redemption of prostitutes is no business of princesses'.[51] On the whole, however, at least at first, the explosion of new forms of religious expression among women met with official approval – both from the secular and the ecclesiastical authorities. The fact that a hagiographic literature developed describing the saintly lives of several of the ladies of

---

[50] Alessio, *Vita della Serenissima.*   [51] Ibid.

the court who were most involved in these activities is itself evidence of this approval.[52]

We might surmise, therefore, that the peak in women's initiative in charity and religion was simply the female contribution to a Counter-Reformation fervour which to some extent characterised the male court as well. But it would be quite wrong to reduce this kind of activity among women *solely* to the strategy of reinforcing the legitimacy of the court. Apart from anything else, this motive was strongest in the first decades of the seventeenth century but died out later on; in later years, the persistence of female religious and charitable activism can only be explained by reference to women's subjective motivations. Why did they respond so enthusiastically to the appeal of the Counter-Reformation? What needs did the activities centred around convents and institutions fulfil?

Let us look in detail at the decline in women's charitable giving after 1720. First of all, no new initiatives were launched specifically by women after this date and whereas in the earlier period they had founded convents and asylums for penitents, from the early eighteenth century on they contented themselves with giving to existing institutions. When they did assume a prominent initiating role, it seems only to have been when they were acting together with their husbands, or at any rate as representatives of the family group. An obvious case of this pattern is to be found in the asylum for girls of the Provvidenza. Right from its foundation, this institution seems to have been very much a family affair (see figure 5). The asylum was started in the 1730s by the husband and wife Ignazio and Elena Graneri, by Elena's brother, Renato Birago, and by Renato's sister-in-law, Angelica Ponte di Casalgrasso. When Angelica died, it was Renato's wife, Vittoria, who took over her place as superintendent of the institution.[53] Three lines of individuals related by marriage thus directed the asylum in the first two decades of its existence. Two of them were also major donors. In the decades which followed, management of the institution passed into the hands of families (the Carrons, the Saluzzo di Garessios and the Turinettis di Priero) who were closely related to the Graneris and Biragos, as well as to each other.[54] The distance between this kind of pattern in which wives and husbands, and women and men of a kinship group, founded and managed an

---

[52] See the works cited in note 17 of chapter 3 and especially *La Virtù Educata in Corte*, the account of Donna Margherita Forni, who was a lady in waiting to Infanta Maria until the latter's death, when Margherita was thirty-eight. At this point Margherita entered the Carmelite convent, where she died at fifty-six, having acquired a considerable reputation for saintliness and for healing powers.

[53] The list of the directors of the asylum of the Provvidenza is in P. Gribaudi, *Il Regio Educatorio della Provvidenza nei suoi Due Secoli di Vita (1735–1935). Notizie Storiche*, Turin 1935. For the donations of Renato Birago, his wife Vittoria Scarampi and that of Vittoria's son's mother-in-law, Vittoria Saluzzo di Valgrana, see T.P. vol.XXIV, 16.4.1746, Ins., 1743, 1.10, c.117, 18.9.1743, and T.P. vol.XXIII, p. 408, 11.12.1742.

[54] For the donations of Teresa Delfina Simiane Solaro (later Cacherano) and Vittoria Provana Turinetti, see Ins., 1764, 1.6, 23.5.1764 and 1752, 1.7, c.175, 17.6.1752.

institution, and the essentially autonomous activity of women in the organisation of convents and asylums for penitents a few decades earlier, is very clear. It must be emphasised, however, that women were often instrumental in creating new bonds with the institution: sibling and in-law ties are in fact as strong as marital ties among the governors and benefactors of the Provvidenza (figure 5). Although women had lost the prominent independent role in charity which they enjoyed a few decades earlier, it would be simplistic to say that, in the more family-based pattern of charity of the mid eighteenth century, they simply adhered to a policy set out by their husbands. Women continued to take initiatives in charity, although their contribution now appears more hidden and difficult to detect.

A similar kind of tendency seems to have been at work in legacies to existing institutions. Here too, women's bequests seem to have become subject to the logic of a wider family strategy. Thus it became frequent for a wife's will to favour the same charitable institution as that favoured by her husband. An example of this kind of case is the widow Peyrone Martin, who founded a bed for incurables at the hospital of S. Giovanni, just as her husband had done two years previously. Similarly, Anna Teresa Agili Ricca made the Ospedale di Carità her main heir in 1758, leaving it approximately 26,000 *lire*. Five years later, her husband did the same, leaving around 103,000 *lire*.[55] The Ospedale was also the principal heir of the Murenas, husband and wife, who (like the Riccas) had no direct descendants.[56] In these latter two cases the woman's will actually pre-dates that of her husband, but nonetheless one has the impression that both wills were products of a common family strategy. The wills contain evidence, for example, that both the city treasurer Ricca and Giovan Battista Murena had long-standing business relationships with the Ospedale di Carità, where they had kept capital invested for many years. We might see their wives, therefore, as using their own wealth to reinforce the policies pursued by their husbands. A significant number of wills were even signed by husband and wife jointly.[57]

This tendency to share a strategy with the husband was sometimes made explicit in eighteenth-century wills; especially in the later decades of the century, phrases like 'according to the will of my husband' or 'wishing to obey the will of my husband' became quite common in wills leaving bequests to charity.[58] It is true that the women concerned were widows who enjoyed usufruct of their husband's money until their death, and who therefore, in a sense, were

[55] Ins. 1758, l.10, vol.2, 14.9.1758; 1763, l.8, 30.6.1763.
[56] Rosa Rivolat Murena drew up her will on 22.9.1767 (OC, Cat.IX), her husband Giovan Battista on 9.6.1771 (Ins. 1771, l.6).
[57] See, e.g. the will of Anna Gioanna and Pietro Baldassare Boggio, Ins. 1751, l.6 vol. II, 4.6.1751.
[58] See, e.g. the wills of Clara Lucia Capella Valfré, Ins. 1731, l.4, vol.2, 20.3.1731; of Paola Racchia Campana, AOC, cat.IX, 4.5.1771; and of Teresa Scapuj Bussano, AOSG, cat.4 cl.1 vol.64, fasc.18, 10.4.1786.

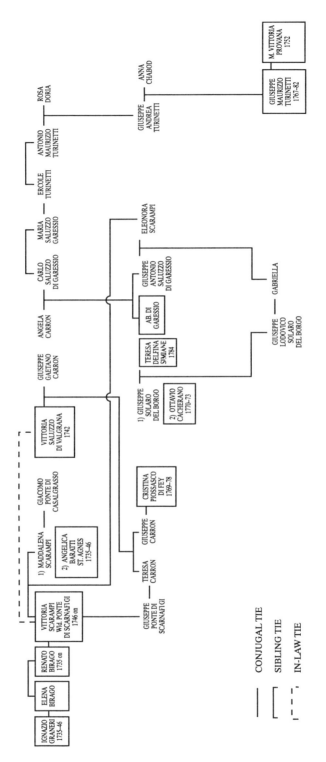

Fig. 5. The House of Providenza: kinship relations among governors and benefactors

Names in boxes are benefactors or governors of the Institution.
Dates refer to the year of the donation or to the period during which they were
administrators, when this is known precisely.

————— CONJUGAL TIE

⎵ SIBLING TIE

- - - - IN-LAW TIE

disposing of money which was not their own. Widows, however, not only followed these guidelines faithfully, but frequently left a part of their own independent wealth to the same institution chosen by their husband.[59]

Another frequent destination of female charity in the eighteenth century was the creation of resources for patronage for future use by the marital family. The purchase of rights of nomination of beds for incurables to be transmitted along the inheriting line within the family was a typical expression of this type of charity. Indeed the peak in charitable legacies from women in the decade 1751–60 is to be attributed almost entirely to legacies with such bequests. In 1760 a large number of rights of nomination to beds for incurables (founded by families which had died out) were put onto the market at lower prices than usual by the hospital of S. Giovanni and women in particular took advantage of this opportunity.[60]

The fact that a significant number of women used their own property to back up a policy benefiting the family of their husbands seems a phenomenon particularly worth noting. Up until the beginning of the eighteenth century, the normal pattern was for women who had no direct heirs, or only step-children, to leave their wealth to someone in their family of origin. During the following decades, by contrast, the tendency to identify with the family of marriage grew. Even charitable bequests which might benefit the family line followed this pattern. Whereas previously women without issue had generally left nomination rights over beds for incurables to a brother or a sister and their descendants, there was an increasing tendency to leave them to someone in the husband's family. Even step-children or heirs designated by the husband might benefit. Thus Caterina Quaglia, the widow of a well-off merchant, founded a bed in 1704, to add to that donated in 1687 by her husband, and she left the nomination rights to his brother's son, who was also her husband's heir. Similarly, in 1731 the Countess Maria Vittoria Trotti Valperga di Masino, who also had no children of her own, left rights over two beds to her step-son.[61] These two cases also illustrate another feature of the transformation – the fact that the new pattern tended to emerge earlier in families engaged in merchant or administrative activities than it did among the court nobility.

These changes seem to testify to a growing sense of obligation and loyalty towards the family of marriage. Previously, a wife's links with her family of origin – in the broad sense, including not only her relatives in the patrilineal line but also those in the lines springing from her brothers and sisters or her parents' brothers and sisters – seem to have been given more importance than links

---

[59] For example Delfina Cavoretto Leone did not just conform to the wishes of her husband who had drawn his will four years earlier but in addition left 1,000 ducats of her own for the same purpose. Ins. 1749, 1.3, 17.3.1749 (for Delfina's will); ASSP 161, 28.4.1745 (Pietro Paolo's will).

[60] See above, chapter 3, note 124.

[61] AOSG, Cat.10, cl.3, 11.4.1704; ibid., Cat.IV, cl.1, vol.65, fasc.6, 22.3.1731.

with her husband's family, especially among the aristocracy. Of course wills favouring the family of origin continued to be common, especially among widows without children. But it came to be quite normal for women to distribute their property between the lines springing from the family of origin and those deriving from the family of marriage. To cite a couple of examples: in 1725 Ludovica Roncha Lionne founded two beds for incurables and left nomination rights of one of them to her sister, those over the other to her husband and subsequently to his brother (who was again her husband's heir); in 1755, Giacinta Brunetta, widow of Davico, founded three beds and left rights over two of them to her husband's brother, over the other one to her brother's sons.[62]

Another major change which needs to be taken into account is that by the mid eighteenth century women no longer tended to have large sums of their own to give away to charitable institutions. In the 1760s, 1770s and 1780s, 38 per cent of the legacies left by women are very small sums left for the saying of masses for the donor's soul. Legacies which took the form of life annuities or pensions were also very numerous in these years. The hospital or institution was required to pay the income from the sum donated to the benefactor or to the persons designated by her, as long as they were alive. Only after the death of the beneficiaries (who were often young and numerous) could the institution fully dispose of the sum as it wished. In 1771 for instance, Caterina Ferri, widow of Carbonelli, left the hospital of S. Giovanni a certain sum to be used to establish a bed for incurables – but on condition that the income from this money should go to Caterina's mother and sister as long as they were alive. In 1783 Teresa Margherita Ghersi Finasso made the Ospedale di Carità her main heir, but on the condition that they paid 100 *lire* per year to each of her sister's sons and daughters.[63]

Entrusting charitable institutions with the task of paying pensions and annuities seems to have been a way of defending what little wealth many women had from the pressures of heirs – a way of asserting a socially unorthodox desire to favour one particular relative over another who might be the expected beneficiary or even to favour people outside the family. These arrangements involving small annuities or pensions were generally agreed with the institution in question in the form of a contract which was made before the will, and they seem to have rather taken the place of legacies to the institutions in wills themselves. We have to remember that, compared to this kind of contract, the making of a will was a much more public and controlled affair, given that wills were often made in front of members of the family, or its delegates. Thus Caterina Viglietti, widow of the banker Casabianca, drew up a contract in 1778 with the hospital of S. Giovanni, in which she designated the hospital as her main

---

[62] Ibid., Cat.10, cl.3, 19.1.1730 and 17.12.1755.
[63] Ibid., 3.9.1771; Ins., 1783, l.12, 11.11.1783.

heir, on condition that it paid a pension every year to persons nominated by
her. When she came to make her will, two years later, she could refer to the
agreement with the hospital as a past commitment by which she was already
bound. In this way, charity became a means of circumventing prescribed norms
and expected behaviour as to who should benefit from women's property, and
of transcending in particular the growing obligations towards the family of
marriage.

This is an extreme example of how charity could be shaped to respond
principally to the needs of benefactors. The institutions involved in such
arrangements were often saddled with a long list of duties to perform. The case
of widow Casabianca – who obliged the hospital to pay nine annuities and a
number of other payments – is not exceptional.[64] For many years the hospital
derived no benefit from the money it had been donated since the cost of paying
these annuities and providing Caterina's nominees with beds more than
absorbed all the interest they could obtain by lending it out.[65]

Overall, then, there seems to be a considerable amount of evidence to suggest
that women's ability to exercise their own discretion in the way they disposed of
their property tended to become significantly more restricted in the eighteenth
century. Does this tendency reflect major transformations in the legislation
concerning female inheritance and control over property? Until the mid
seventeenth century no system had been developed which excluded women from
becoming the main heir to the family property. Piedmont was in fact one of the
areas in which Lombard law – which prescribed equal division between all
the children – persisted longest. Then, under Spanish influence, the first
restrictions appeared on making women the heir, and on women's share of
inheritance.[66] In 1648 an edict was introduced which consented to, and
encouraged, primogeniture, but only in highly general terms.[67] This edict in fact

---

[64] The hospital had to pay 100 *lire* per year to Father Carlo Cerruti, 250 a year to the widow Rosa
Grognardi, 150 to the lawyer Giuseppe Gioanni Calcino, 150 to the daughter of Sig. Franco
Scotto (Caterina's goddaughter), 100 to master mason Franco Pagano, 100 to Sga. Domenica
Vietti, 500 to the servant Caterina De Marchi (plus providing the latter with a bed for incurables
and a mattress and blankets), 150 to Maria Teresa Garola, 100 to the tailor, Giuseppe Mayner. It
also had to give another bed for incurables to one of Caterina's nieces who was unwell. AOSG,
Cat.IV, cl.1, vol.65, fasc.9 – 16.4.1779 for the agreement with the hospital; 12.9.1780 for the
will.

[65] The annuities on their own amounted to 1,600 *lire*, i.e. to 5 per cent of the capital donated
(32,031 *lire*), whereas the interest obtainable was normally calculated as being 4 per cent.

[66] S. J. Woolf, *Studi Sulla Nobiltà Piemontese All'Epoca Dell'Assolutismo*, Turin 1963, p. 151.
This process occurred much earlier in the south of Italy – which was under Spanish rule. M. A.
Visceglia, *Il Bisogno di Eternità. I Comportamenti Caritativi a Napoli in Età Moderna*, Naples
1988, chapter 1. For a comparison of various different systems of inheritance, see J. P. Cooper,
'Patterns of inheritance and settlement by great landowners from the fifteenth to the eighteenth
centuries', in J. Goody, J. Thirsk and E. Thompson, *Family and Inheritance. Rural Society in
Western Europe 1200–1800*, Cambridge 1976.

[67] Borelli, *Editti*, pp. 849–50, 16.7.1648.

does not seem to have altered practice very fundamentally. It was only in 1680 that a need was felt for an edict which laid down the rules for defining primogeniture more precisely.[68] In the closing decades of the seventeenth century, primogeniture was well on the way to becoming established. According to Bulferetti's calculations, the number of cases in which inheritance by primogeniture was followed remained very small in the two decades following the 1648 edict (just eight cases in the 1650s and eleven in the 1660s), but doubled (to twenty-two) in the 1670s,[69] and it seems likely that this trend continued in the following decades (for which, however, no calculations are available). It is true that many families never opted for primogeniture – which not only created a hierarchy between the various children, but also made part of the family property inalienable.[70] However, there is no doubt that from the late seventeenth century onwards, the tendency came to be to concentrate inheritance in the hands of one (male) heir – whether or not this was formalised as primogeniture. The rules on primogeniture did not explicitly exclude a woman from becoming the principal heir. In legislative terms, it was only in the eighteenth century – with the Royal Constitutions of 1723 and 1729 – that women came to be actually barred from becoming general heirs to the family property.[71] But in practice this occurrence had become very unlikely much earlier. With the consolidation of primogeniture, increasing emphasis was placed, at the ideological level, on the male line and its dominant role in keeping the family name and estate, while women appeared more and more linked to their family of marriage.

Inheritance of fiefs was regulated by separate legislation, but here too we encounter a trend toward a restriction of women's rights, as in the regulation of inheritance to ordinary property. Whereas an edict of 1648 concerning 'dowries to daughters of vassals and other provisions for the conservation of fiefs' could still declare that women should inherit when there were no direct male heirs, the 1729 constitutions made female succession to fiefs virtually impossible by laying down that a male 'even if of another line' took precedence over a woman.[72]

Another consequence of the establishment of primogeniture was that it tended to reduce the slice of the family property women did receive. Laws did exist to ensure that women were not forced to give up all their remaining rights to the family inheritance when they received the dowry. However, in these same years

[68] Ibid., pp. 850–1, 3.4.1680.

[69] Bulferetti, 'La feudalità e il patriziato nel Piemonte di Carlo Emanuele II', *Annali della Facoltà di Lettere, Filosofia e Magistero dell'Università di Cagliari*, 21 (1953), p. 427.

[70] Woolf, *Studi*, pp. 152–3.

[71] On the Royal Constitutions, see M. Viora, *Le Costituzioni Piemontesi 1723, 1729, 1772*, Turin 1928.

[72] Borelli, *Editti*, pp. 843–6, 2.6.1648; D., T.VII, p. 577, section I, clause 4.

the proportion of the family property women could be deprived of increased. In 1679 it was prescribed that women should surrender no more than half of the *legittima* (the proportion to which they were entitled by right); by 1723, on the other hand, it had become acceptable to surrender up to two-thirds.[73]

Severe limitations were introduced by the Royal Constitutions of the 1720s not just on women's rights to inherit but also on their freedom to dispose of their own property afterwards. Women were made subject to the same restrictions binding minors and the feeble-minded, and they could only leave their property to others in the presence of a judge or prefect and five other witnesses, of whom two had to be members of the family.[74]

What seems clear, however, is that the 1720s constitutions set their seal on a transition towards a new system governing women's access to and control over property, which had been going on for some time. The decades at the turn of the century in which women were so active in religious and charitable activities in the convents and elsewhere also seem to have been the years in which their financial power was under attack. By the middle of the eighteenth century women's financial position had been significantly eroded: the impression that they had less money for charity and less scope for independent charitable initiatives appears to be justified. Ideological changes were taking place at the same time: for women, the conjugal link was becoming dominant, and replacing a wider configuration of kin relationships based more on the family of origin. This new perception of the family was also reflected in the joint charitable ventures of husband and wife and in the tendency for female charity to be part of the policy of the family of marriage.

Charity as an expression of conflict within the family

A number of wills of female benefactors provide us with a key source in our attempt to link the changes affecting women's relationship with property and the family to the changing patterns of female involvement in charity. Wills provide evidence of fierce conflicts with husbands and elder sons – conflicts which seem to reflect growing tension in women's relationships with the family of marriage, and with the principles of patrilineality and primogeniture. The conflict was a conflict over property, but it is interesting that this did not focus on the dowry, as we might have expected. When disputes arose over the dowry, these took place between a wife's father and his son-in-law. In contrast, those conflicts which placed wives directly in contraposition to their husbands or sons centred on what were termed 'extra-dowry assets' (*stradotali*).

Historians have largely ignored this component of women's property,

---

[73] D., T. VII, p. 279, *Regie Costituzioni*, Lib.V, Tit.XII, capo 2, 20.11.1723.
[74] Ibid., clause 9, p. 322.

concentrating all their attention instead on the dowry as if this was the only economic resource at women's disposal.[75] Even legal historians have devoted little attention to the matter, and when they do, they display considerable uncertainty as to what the rules regulating the use of *stradotali* were. The initial basis of extra-dowry property was a gift made to a daughter by her father at marriage – which did not, however, form part of the dowry, and was not subject to the same rules of inheritance. Unlike the dowry, extra-dowry items were fully the property of the woman herself; it seems that any interest on this property was usually recognised as being due to the husband, but a wife had full rights of transmission, and could leave the property to whomsoever she wished. However, the question of who had rights over interest was unclear and controversial legally; some judgements implied that income from extra-dowry property was due to the husband only if such interest was employed for the benefit of both husband and wife, others that a husband had unconditional rights, and some even that the interest belonged to the wife.[76] The presence of various, incompatible interpretations in the jurisprudence on the subject may be an indication that there was a change over time in attitudes towards extra-dowry property – a change which, however, left no trace in actual legislation.

My comments therefore, will be based mainly on the evidence provided by the wills. It seems that fathers' gifts to their daughters – the gifts which formed the initial kernel of extra-dowry property – were common for much of the seventeenth century. Substantial sums could be involved, but there also seems to have been a tendency for the size of these gifts to diminish later on in the century. It was also common for other relatives (mothers, sisters, brothers, uncles) to give gifts at the time of marriage. However, extra-dowry property might also be added to substantially after marriage as the result of gifts and legacies from relatives and friends. Once again, it was mainly relatives of a woman's mother – uncles and aunts on the mother's side – or a woman's own brothers and sisters, who were involved; but sometimes relatives from the family of marriage, especially brothers-in-law and sisters-in-law, might be involved. The existence of extra-dowry property therefore seems to show a kind of alternative circulation of property, parallel to the official circulation which sent wealth down the lines prescribed by the principles of patrilineality and primogeniture. Some part of family wealth seems to have been transmitted, through collateral relatives or down the matrilineal line, to women and younger sons – those who were excluded by the normal form of transmission.

---

[75] The few exceptions concern the medieval and late medieval period. See in particular J. Kirshner, 'Materials for a gilded cage: non-dotal assets in Florence, 1300–1500', in D. I. Kertzer and R. P. Saller, *The Family in Italy from Antiquity to the Present*, New Haven, Conn. and London 1991.

[76] F. Arro, *Del Diritto Dotale Secondo i Principi del Gius Romano e della Giurisprudenza dei Magistrati*, Asti 1834, vol. II, p. 447; M. A. Benedetto, *Ricerche sui Rapporti Patrimoniali tra Coniugi nello Stato Sabaudo*, Turin 1957, p. 84.

The first reason why extra-dowry property is interesting is that it seems to reflect the way in which social and emotional bonds really worked within a woman's family of origin and family of marriage. In this sense, the circulation of *stradotali* may be seen as providing us with a sketch of the family as it was experienced emotionally by women as opposed to the image of the family derived from the formally prescribed transmission of wealth.[77] We might, therefore, see the size and the circulation of extra-dowry property as an indication of the vitality of loyalties which lay outside the official ones laid down in the rules of inheritance. Second, extra-dowry property brings out the fact that the economic resources which women possessed were often much more significant than is normally assumed, and, above all, that they were more complex – and not limited exclusively to the dowry, nor totally controlled by their husbands. Finally, the most intriguing aspect of extra-dowry property is that – unlike dowries, or the shares allotted by law to younger sons, or to a mother – it was not rigidly defined by the automatic and ascriptive criteria of gender and birth-order within the family. Extra-dowry property grew in size in accordance with the relationships women had with various members of their families of origin and of marriage. Rather unexpectedly, we can see that women had an active – if circumscribed – role in building up part of their personal wealth.

The misleading notion that a woman's dowry was her only property seems to have gone unchallenged – partly because historians have made use of a very limited number of sources. Dowry contracts, in fact, have been virtually the only documents used by most attempts to estimate the extent of women's independent wealth. Wills like those I have used are more complete documents than dowry contracts since they often contain information which gives us some idea of the extra-dowry property accumulated by the end of a woman's life. The wills I have examined show that, among aristocratic women, *stradotali* could be worth a considerable amount, sometimes even more than the dowry. Countess Gazzelli left 14,000 *lire* in extra-dowry property – a sum which compares well with an average of roughly 10,000 *lire*, which was what women of the new nobility *de robe* (the stratum to which the countess belonged) normally received as a dowry. Delfina Solara, a woman of the court aristocracy, left extra-dowry property amounting to over 40,000 *lire* – which again is more than the largest dowries given even within this elite in the late seventeenth century (30–40,000 *lire*).[78]

---

[77] S. T. Strocchia has an interesting discussion of gender-based experiences of kinship in 'Remembering the family: women, kin and commemorative masses in Renaissance Florence', *RQ*, 42 (1989).

[78] Ins., 1717, 1.1, 11.9.1716 (Gazzelli's will). The reference to Delfina Solara's extra-dowry property is in the will of her sister, Irene Simiane (see below, note 80). Sizes of average dowries in the various elite strata are given by Woolf, *Studi sulla Nobiltà*, p. 156.

Wills therefore demonstrate the quantitative significance of extra-dowry property. To obtain a clearer idea of what a woman's real economic position was, however, we would need to have details of all the property she received in her lifetime, and what she did with it.

It was precisely over this variable part of female property, the part which could be actively managed, that conflict became increasingly frequent in the late seventeenth century. It is at this time that husbands started to claim rights over *stradotali*, arguing that they constituted part of household property rather than a wife's personal wealth. Wills provide retrospective evidence of these disputes, some of which had been going on for decades. We may take the case of Cristina San Giorgio – whom we have already encountered as a generous benefactress of the Santa Pelagia institution, to which she liked to retreat and to which she donated a new wing. Her will, which was drawn up in 1705, refers to various incidents in a long conflict with her husband (covering the whole of their married life) over rights to her property. Cristina married the Marquis Aldobrandino in 1657, but in 1664 she had already asked for a formal 'recognition of her extra-dowry property', allegedly partly usurped by her husband. Further incursions on this wealth which Cristina considered her own continued, and indeed increased, in subsequent years. In 1681, she succeeded in obtaining a second public agreement, in which the Marquis was obliged to acknowledge an impressive list of seventeen loans which Cristina had made 'from her own property' at various times from 1662 onwards. This long document gives us an idea of the form that conjugal relationships within this class took on an everyday basis when it came to questions of property. For sixteen of the loans in the list written documents existed, each one drawn up in the presence of a notary; some of these loans were for quite modest sums, but Cristina had faithfully preserved all of the documents and was able to produce them. Item 17 consisted of a series of other 'transactions' which Cristina also claimed back, but 'for which there is no documentation or obligation at all'. As witnesses verifying the truth of her claims, Cristina was able to call on four prestigious men, including the Rector of the College of the Jesuits and the first President of the Senate. With the help of their mediation, the couple succeeded in reaching an agreement by which Aldobrandino agreed he owed his wife 20,000 *lire*. The Marquis handed over 2,500 *lire* and promised to pay the rest later.[79] However, in 1705, when Cristina drew up her will, he still owed the remaining 17,500 *lire*. It will come as no surprise to learn that the will left nothing to the Marquis, except for the interest (which belonged to him by law) on her dowry and on his debt to her. One more detail of the will indicates how she still felt threatened by her husband: mistrust of him had led her to deposit a box containing the precious deeds documenting the long

---

[79] Ins., 1682, 1.3, 7.2.1681.

struggle with the Compagnia di San Paolo, which she also designated as her executor.[80]

The use of public deeds drawn up by notaries for every transfer of money from wife to husband, added to the involvement of noted dignitaries to act as arbitrators, seems to indicate that the keeping of separate accounts and an independent management of a wife's property were commonly accepted principles in the late seventeenth century, at least among the aristocracy. In theory at any rate, attempts on the part of husbands to appropriate extra-dowry property seem still to have been considered illegitimate at this time. In later years, by contrast, women's rights over personal property were less and less likely to be recognised. Evidence from wills seems to suggest that the appropriation of *stradotali* by the family of marriage became increasingly common, and that in the end it came to be taken for granted that gifts and legacies of this kind formed part of the general property of the family of marriage, and that they should be managed by the husband.

As we have seen, no legislation was passed during this period explicitly regarding extra-dowry property; however, I believe we can find at least indirect evidence of a shift in attitudes which is also reflected at the judicial level. As I have already mentioned, the Royal Constitutions of 1729 imposed restrictions on women's rights to donate property and it may well be that this constituted an attempt to give the patrilineal family firmer control over extra-dowry property and thereby reduce this particular form of property circulation which deviated from the principles of primogeniture. The 1723 Royal Constitutions laid down that 'women and persons of unsound mind' could not make donations (outside wills), unless a judge or prefect was present, plus five witnesses, two of whom had to be members of the family.[81] It is not specified who the two relatives had to be nor from which side of the family they had to come; but the mere fact of making a simple transfer of property such a highly public act reflects the extent to which the idea of a woman having the right to dispose of a portion of her own property autonomously had come to seem abnormal.

It seems that the erosion of women's control over extra-dowry property took place first on the grounds of domestic expenditure; husbands and husbands' families started to claim that household expenditure was a wife's responsibility. This attack on their property seems to have been resisted at first by some women. At the end of the seventeenth century and the first years of the eighteenth, Vittoria Teresa Zuchetti-Caissotti was involved in a long legal action against her father-in-law, whom she accused of not having ever paid her the annual pension, victuals and clothing which he had promised in the dowry contract of 1692; this had obliged her to dig into her own resources (which in this case were very

---

[80] Ibid., l.5, 1705/1706, 18.6.1705; and l.5, 1706, 24.5.1706 for the codicil.
[81] D., T.VII, pp. 322–32, *Delle donazioni*, 1723, clause 9, and 1770, clause 14.

substantial, since she was her father's main heir) in order to keep herself, her husband and her children. When making her will in 1715, Vittoria reaffirmed the claim that her father-in-law was obliged to pay her heirs the money she had been forced to spend, but she also had to admit that she had given up the long lawsuit. She justified this on the grounds of 'the age of over seventy years' of her father-in-law; but her withdrawal was probably more to do with her inability to win, the willingness of the courts to decide in favour of a wife in this kind of case having decreased.[82]

Irene Francavilla was involved in a similar claim – though this time on behalf of her non-inheriting son and against her husband. Her husband had failed to keep to the commitments he had made in his second son's marriage contract to furnish food and clothing to this son, his wife and servants, and Irene had thus been forced to use up some of her own property for this purpose. In the will she drew up in 1724, Irene denied her husband any right to use her extra-dowry property, and laid down that all her goods, including the money that she claimed her husband owed her, should go to the person she had always intended it should, her second son.[83]

As we can see, then, women stubbornly continued to claim back money they saw themselves as having been forced to spend unjustly out of their own funds; however, by this time, these claims seem to have been mainly assertions of principle, without much hope of actually regaining the money owed them. The situation is very different from that in which we saw Cristina San Giorgio obtain her husband's signature to a punctilious reckoning of his debts to her under the approving eye of local dignitaries. And it seems that any attempt to take action through the courts was no longer conceivable, as it had been for Vittoria Zuchetti.

Cases like those I have described may, in fact, be seen as the last flickering of an older system of property rights. By the end of the 1720s, wives' wills normally show substantial identification with the new lineage of marriage. Ludovica Spatis, for example, in 1727, agreed to her husband paying for 'expenses incurred in his house with her extra-dowry property'. These were expenses incurred in repairing houses at Turin and at Villareggia (where her husband's fiefs were) and a country residence outside Turin.[84] The wording shows that Ludovica did not consider use of extra-dowry funds for the benefit of her family of marriage as a legal obligation, but rather as a favour, and it is clear that she was anxious to point out that the expenses had been met from her own money; nonetheless, she seems to have basically accepted that it formed a legitimate part of her role as a good wife to use her own property to refurbish the family homes.

[82] Ins., 1715, l.10, 7.9.1715.
[83] Ibid., 1725, l.2, 16.12.1725.   [84] AOSG, cat.4, cl.1, vol.24, fasc.9, 20.3.1727.

Similarly, in 1728, Gioanna Amabilia Isnardi Simiane willingly exonerated her husband from any repayment of the 2,000 ducats which she had received at the time of her marriage from her family, along with her dowry and trousseau.[85] The family of marriage seems to have been successful by this time in asserting itself as the unit to which women owed their first loyalty. At the same time, the idea that there was a part of a wife's property which was not subject to a husband's control seems to have weakened; often, indeed, the very concept of extra-dowry property ceased to appear in the documents.

These changes in property relationships between spouses seem to run parallel to the changes I described earlier in the pattern of women's charitable donations: in both cases, we can observe a growing tendency for women to consent to using their own property in pursuit of strategies benefiting the lineage they had married into. There would seem, therefore, to be a strong relationship between changing patterns in the form taken by female charity and changes in relationships within the family.

It also seems legitimate to see women's enthusiasm for religion and charity in the late seventeenth century as one aspect of the conflict arising within the aristocratic family, for the period in which such enthusiasm was strongest was also the period in which husbands and elder sons were putting pressure on women over their right to dispose of extra-dowry property. In some cases, such as that of Cristina San Giorgio, the link existing between large donations and conflict with husbands and sons seems clear. But in general, a decision to donate large sums to convents and other institutions often seems to have been connected with a desire to challenge the claims husbands and/or sons were making. In her will of 1713, Angela Truchi-Gromo – who had inherited her father's estate – left large bequests to the convent of Santa Pelagia and most of her remaining wealth to the hospital of San Giovanni. To her son she left only the minimum she was obliged to leave by law (the *legittima*); and she conceded this only on condition that he quit the hemp factory and land which her parents had bequeathed to her and which he had 'unjustly occupied', and that he returned the property which her brother-in-law had left her for the duration of her lifetime, as well as compensating her for the expense to which she had been forced to go in order to regain possession of her dowry.[86] In this case, too, it seems clear that Angela was using charitable donation as a socially and morally acceptable way of preventing her son (with whom she had been in conflict for years) from obtaining a substantial part of the property which normally, under the conventions of primogeniture, would have been due to him.

The particular form taken by female charity in this period seems also to be connected to women's personal experience within the family. The preference for convents and female asylums, especially, becomes explicable in this context –

[85] Ins., 1728, l.5, vol.1, 30.4.1728.   [86] T.P. vol.XX, 15.22.1713.

for it may be seen as one aspect of the anti-matrimonial rhetoric which was widespread in benefactresses and in general in women of this social class. Retreat from the world was idealised as a refuge against men and the difficulties of married life. We should be clear that this had paradoxical effects – for women were, in fact, making themselves the principal patrons of an institution which had a crucial role in securing the working of the primogeniture system (since it provided the way for the elimination of undesired female heirs). Subjectively, however, the financing of convents and female asylums, or the setting up of funds for widows or women with broken marriages, was evidently a way of expressing conflict in the family of marriage, through a rhetoric of women's vulnerability and isolation.

In the late seventeenth century women with broken marriages became the deserving poor *par excellence* in the eyes of aristocratic women through, it would seem, a kind of projection of their own personal experiences. Concern for the risks to which a widow was exposed and for the plight of women separated from or deserted by their husbands was thus a way of giving expression to women's concerns and to the conflict rife in the aristocratic family. Once again, we can see that the setting up of particular types of charitable initiative was the product of discourses which reflected the conflicts in which benefactors were involved as well as the needs of the poor. The emergence of new definitions of poverty was not only due to a new way of perceiving the poor, but also the result of a metaphorical transposition of conflicts existing within the world of the elites.

5

Hospitals and poor relief in the age of absolutism

Attacking the independence of charitable institutions

The early decades of the eighteenth century are generally considered to be the period in which the Piedmontese state set about the reorganisation of poor relief and medical assistance. In the field of poor relief, King Vittorio Amedeo II issued edicts in 1716 and 1717 which launched his plan for establishing a network of *ospedali di carità* in the larger towns and *congregazioni di carità* in the smaller ones. These institutions, which were supposed to reform poor relief throughout the state in accordance with a uniform model, clearly resemble the French *hôpitaux généraux* and *bureaux de charité*: at least on paper, the policy adopted in Piedmont appears to be the only Italian initiative of ambition and magnitude comparable to that carried out by Louis XIV a few decades earlier. As far as medical assistance was concerned, the reform of the Turin Faculty of Medicine was drawn up in the 1730s, and it is claimed that this transformed the city's principal hospital, S. Giovanni, turning it into an institution for medical training as well as patient care.[1]

These measures have been seen as showing the leading role which the absolute state was taking on in the field of welfare organisation. Control over the provision of relief and medical care is thus portrayed as an example of the absolute state extending its functions.[2] In spite of their reputation, however, these provisions have not really been the object of careful research, and very little is known about their real impact. The positive assessment of Piedmontese welfare policy is mainly the corollary of a glorification of the Savoyard state as a particularly successful example of absolutism. With regard to the edicts of 1716 and 1717 interpretation has been considerably coloured by the general acclamation afforded to King Vittorio Amedeo II, under whose government they

---

[1] D. Carpanetto, 'La facoltà di medicina a Torino nel XVIII secolo', *Giorn. Acc. Med.*, 140 (1977); D. Balani, D. Carpanetto and F. Turletti, 'La popolazione studentesca dell'Università', *BSBS*, 76 (1978), pp. 129–75.

[2] Quazza, *Le Riforme*, vol. II, pp. 385–98.

were adopted. This sovereign, who is often depicted as the Italian equivalent of the Sun King, has been given the credit for reorganising almost every aspect of the state administration.[3]

The reputation of these edicts also owes much to the influence exercised on subsequent chroniclers and historians by the pamphlet *La Mendicità Sbandita*, written by the Jesuit André Guevarre to coincide with the issuing of the edict.[4] Later accounts have unquestioningly accepted Guevarre's rhetorical presentation of these measures both as novel and as a product of King Vittorio Amedeo's fertile mind.[5] In the following pages, I will attempt to show that Guevarre's pamphlet must be read as a work of propaganda on behalf of the absolutist monarchy. If it is analysed in the context of how poor relief in Turin developed, the 1716 reform in the capital hardly seems innovative in relation to existing policy. And if we take the most ambitious part of the plan – the creation of a centralised structure of *congregazioni di carità* (which would complement the activity of hospitals in larger centres, providing outdoor relief in smaller localities) covering the entire territory of the state – it was not until the 1760s that there was any real attempt to translate this idea into practice. The revolution in the welfare system that the edicts proclaimed never materialised. Their real consequences lay elsewhere, in their ideological and symbolic contribution to the image of power and efficiency which the newly constituted Savoy monarchy sought to foster in this period. In spite of its centralist rhetoric, Vittorio Amedeo's policy seems to have been not to offend local sensitivities and the corporate system of government, at least as far as poor relief policy was concerned.

It was only in the 1730s, during the reign of Vittorio Amedeo's successor, that the government started to interfere significantly in the management of charitable institutions in Turin, with the result that the hospitals, particularly the medical hospital, were for several decades subject to confrontations between state officials and governors. However, this is not necessarily a clash between conservative and modernising forces, as we might be induced to believe by analogy with the French situation – or rather the interpretation which has been given of the similar conflict in French hospitals. According to the established

---

[3] Ibid.; G. Symcox, *Victor Amadeus II. Absolutism in the Savoyard State 1675–1730*, London 1983.

[4] A. Guevarre, *La Mendicità Sbandita Col Sovvenimento Dei Poveri*, Turin 1717. The work is part of the tradition of pamphlets printed in this period in various Italian and French cities to mark the inauguration of similar projects for the poor, beginning with the publication of *La Mendicité Abolie par un Bureau de Charité a Toulouse*, Toulouse 1692. On the activities of Father Guevarre, see C. Joret, 'Le père Guevarre et les Bureaux de Charité au XVII et XVIII siècle', *Annales du Midi*, I (1889).

[5] This interpretation can be found in A. Carutti, *Storia del Regno di Vittorio Amedeo II*, Turin, 1897, p. 460. It is taken up by G. Prato, *La Vita*, p. 332; Quazza, *Le Riforme*, vol. II, pp. 313 ff; and more recently G. Symcox, *Victor Amadeus II*, pp. 199–201.

view, the traditional administrations put up a strenuous resistance to the medical reform of hospitals, advocated by the more progressive medical profession and more enlightened representatives of the state.[6] Study of the situation in Turin, however, gives a much more peaceful example of relations between the medical profession and traditional hospital management, and shows a pattern of transformation of the medical institution which developed, from the mid seventeenth century, within the framework of the existing administration and not in conflict with it.

The clash which did occur was that between state officials and hospital governors in the mid eighteenth century; but this was not centred on an attempt by the former to impose reform, rather it was a struggle for control of the hospital, related to the rise of a social group, i.e. state functionaries, within the city's power structure. The significance of this attack on the autonomy of institutions was not lost on the benefactors themselves, for they immediately adopted counter-measures to challenge the exclusion of private citizens from the management of charitable resources. It became increasingly common in this period for benefactors to place rigid conditions on the use of their donations. The outcome of this social conflict over the handling of poor relief was thus far from positive. On the one hand, this dispute over authority paralysed the hospital's activities for years, making it chaotic and ungovernable, and on the other, the hoarding of charitable resources, as donators reacted by restricting their donations to particular categories of recipient, did not help the poor, but made access to welfare more complex and laborious.

The era of so-called reform should therefore be seen as a period of conflict between elites arising from the emergence of a bureaucratic class which was claiming a monopoly of control over city institutions, and eliminating direct lay participation in government responsibilities. Up to the 1720s and 1730s, it is difficult to draw a clear distinction between bureaucratic duties and professional and entrepreneurial activities. Public appointments were common amongst the richer members of society, and the duties of civil servants were taken on alongside the tasks of merchant, entrepreneur, lawyer and landowner. The political identity of a particular individual was defined by his membership of the cliques and bodies which made up the city's elites (the Municipality, the Compagnia di San Paolo, the guilds, the *Camera dei Conti*, the Senate and the court), rather than by any position he might hold in the state apparatus. Thus those who were entrusted with the management of charitable institutions acted

---

6 See in particular L. S. Greenbaum, '"Measure of civilization": The hospital thought of Jaques Tenon on the eve of the French Revolution', in *BHM*, 49 (1975); 'Nurses and doctors in conflict. Piety and medicine in the Paris Hotel-Dieu on the eve of the Revolution', *Clio Medica* (1979). Also T. Gelfand, *Professionalizing Modern Medicine. Paris Surgeons and Medical Science and Institutions in the Eighteenth Century*, Westport, Conn. and London 1980. For a critical view C. Jones, '"Professionalizing modern medicine" in French hospitals', *MH*, 26 (1982).

as representatives of the political, devotional and professional bodies which had nominated them, more than as state officials. Even representatives of consultative and judicial bodies which to our eyes would seem to be ramifications of the state, such as the *Camera dei Conti* and the Senate, should be seen in the context of this corporate structure as the expression of a social milieu – namely the magistrature – rather than as spokesmen for a central authority.

A departure from this corporate model only emerges in the late 1720s, when the role of state representatives in civic institutions begins to expand. This process occurs partly through turnover in the individuals involved in the management of the hospitals and partly through changing attitudes. We can observe how members of the judiciary, who were already sitting alongside the governors as representatives of the Senate or the *Camera*, now became advocates of central government directives and wished to take on a supervisory role over and above the administrative boards. In other words, their identity as government officials became more important than any other corporate loyalty; being an administrator increasingly became a specialised and professional task. This caused a gradual separation of activities and roles which had previously been blurred; the various social groups came to be more clearly defined. This process of specialisation in administrative duties did not simply arise from a central design of absolutism, but should be seen as part of a social group's strategy for advancement. The ideology of the superiority of professional administration had started to take hold particularly in the legal profession and amongst the officials of the judiciary, who were coming to dominate positions as state functionaries. From the 1720s, these groups launched an open attack on the existing system of privilege, in an attempt to achieve greater status for the bureaucratic office. The clearest expression of this tendency was the attack on the privileges of the court aristocracy, which, as we have seen, had reached a position of supremacy amongst the elite by the mid seventeenth century. In 1720, the very families which only a few decades earlier had been the beneficiaries of extremely rapid social mobility, and had monopolised the most important court appointments, were now the victims of expropriation of the land and income which they had acquired through ducal favours in the previous century – a development which was orchestrated by the bureaucratic elite. The decree which authorised this expropriation (known as *avocazione dei feudi*) was an attack on the dominant position of the court families, not just on their wealth.[7]

The assault on the previous social order also occurred at an ideological level. One example is the attempt by jurists to justify the primacy of bureaucratic duties in doctrinal terms. In 1738, on the basis of lengthy juridical arguments, it was proposed that a new definition of the concept of nobility should be

[7] The decree was issued on 7 January 1720, Quazza, *Le Riforme*, vol. I, p. 164.

introduced, which would include a broad swathe of officials. It was in fact claimed that those deserving the title of noble included:

> amongst the magistrates [. . .] not only the presidents [of the *Camera* and the Senate], senators and *referendari* [presidents of the provinces], but also assistant magistrates, lawyers from various judicial bodies, procurators, down to the master auditors, while amongst those with political and administrative duties not only secretaries in the cabinet and offices of the state, but also the court archivist, higher officials, the general treasurer, the general auditor for war expenditure, and general and provincial intendants. Amongst the military, not only governors and fortress commanders, but also colonels, lieutenant-colonels, regimental majors and captains with more than ten years in that rank. And that is not all: even the local officials are to be considered nobles – judges, prefects and provincial intendants. Finally the assistants of the general attorneys and procurator-fiscals . . . [8]

Service to the state was now emerging as a new basis on which to achieve status. Public office was becoming just as prestigious as noble blood or nobility bestowed by the sovereign.

It is interesting to note that indications of this revolution in social hierarchy are already to be found, some years earlier, in a decision taken by the Compagnia di San Paolo to redefine the social categories which could benefit from the special assistance for *poveri vergognosi* (by now this had come to refer to those of some social standing who had fallen on hard times and were assisted in secret in order to avoid damaging their reputation). An entry in the 1734 minute-book lays down four categories of *poveri vergognosi*: to the traditional ones for 'nobles by birth' and 'nobles nominated and created by sovereign kings', they added a third category embracing all 'those who have been made noble by their profession'. These were 'military officers down to and including ensigns, . . . graduate officials, . . . officials of the Royal Court, . . . lawyers, petitioning professors and doctors, . . . city councillors and the brothers of this Company'. The fourth category consisted of 'the rich who had fallen on hard times', with the proviso however that 'greater regard must be given to the said second and third categories [i.e. recently created nobles and those ennobled by their profession] than to the impoverished rich'.[9] We thus encounter in this document of 1734 parameters for defining status which were similar to those used shortly afterwards to reformulate the entire concept of nobility. In this case, however, it was not purely an ideological matter, but also a provision which would actually affect decisions as to who benefited from the Company's charitable activities. Evidently, the enhanced prestige of the state official was already by the early 1730s such as to have some impact on social practices. It is particularly striking that the 'profession' had achieved greater status than wealth.

[8] Ibid., p. 345.   [9] ASSP, Rep. Lasc. 161, Elemosine, 21.2.1734.

In other words, failed merchants who together with impoverished nobles had once been the typical candidates for the condition of *povero vergognoso* now found themselves marginalised as beneficiaries of charitable assistance. It was no coincidence that the merchant class, which still wielded considerable economic power, was the group that reacted most strongly to its ejection from public office and to the affront to its prestige, and invested significant energy and resources in creating areas of charitable activity under its own exclusive control.

The 1717 *congregazioni di carità*

The state takeover of welfare is usually considered to start with Vittorio Amedeo's edicts of 1716 and 1717 concerning the 'suppression of begging'. The new measures were primarily introduced in the capital, where in August 1716 a first edict outlawed begging and alms-giving within the city's territory, and assigned the role of chief relief agency to the Ospedale di Carità. All beggars were ordered to report to the hospital within three days. Here they were to be examined and given relief if they deserved it, or expelled from the city if they were foreigners or undeserving. Anyone caught begging after the three days had elapsed was liable to arrest and punishment by the hospital guards.[10] Similar measures were extended to the rest of the kingdom ten months later with the edict of May 1717.[11] Hospitals for the poor (based on the existing model in the capital) were to be established in all towns, and *congregazioni di carità* in all those centres not large enough to justify a hospital. The whole system was supposed to be a pyramidal organisation made up of a number of *congregazioni generali* which superintended the *congregazioni di carità* and hospitals within their area, and these supervising bodies in turn would be subordinated to the *congregazione generalissima* based in the capital.[12] The objective of the edicts was to establish a uniform system of poor relief across the kingdom, which would be capable of responding to the needs of the poor at local level, while being subordinated to central control. But to what extent were these proposals put into practice?

In Turin, the reform is supposed to have been fully implemented at an early stage. It is usually maintained that the new provisions radically reformed poor relief in the capital, and placed it under the control of the Ospedale di Carità. The volume and scope of the hospital's activities were expanded, and it was given a new repressive function, which led to a policy of confinement on a massive scale. Historians even talk of a 'reopening' or rebirth of the hospital, which is

---

[10] D., T. XII, p. 280, 'Regio editto col quale si proibisce di mendicare nella città e nel territorio di Torino', 6.8.1716.

[11] Ibid., p. 34, 'Regio editto per lo stabilimento di ospedali generali o di congregazioni di carità in tutti i Comuni dello Stato', 19.5.1717.

[12] All the provisions are published in D., T. XIII, pp. 31–92, and partly in Guevarre, *La Mendicità*.

said to have fallen into decline shortly after its foundation, dating supposedly to 1627.[13] This account clearly conflates two different stories. As mentioned in chapter 2, a hospital for the poor (named Annunziata) was actually set up by the Duke in 1626, but it had a very troubled existence, and closed down only a few years later. This brief episode has no connection with the creation of the Ospedale di Carità which, as we have seen, was set up in 1649, not by the Duke but by the various representative bodies of the city's elites.[14] After early difficulties, this new hospital was able, by 1683, to win enough financial support from the citizens of Turin to commence the construction of a large building, which was completed in 1715, shortly before the edict banning begging was issued.

The Ospedale di Carità was thus in very good shape when Vittorio Amedeo introduced his measures. Far from being re-established or revived by the 1716 edict, it had been operating continuously since its foundation. Equally, the number of inmates does not point to an expansion in the practice of confinement. Annual reports, available from 1715, show that this did not rise as a consequence of the 1716 edict (figure 6). If anything, there was a decline in the hospital population between 1715 and the mid 1720s, when the numbers started to rise again.[15] It was not until the late 1730s, however, that the numbers of poor in the hospital exceeded the figures for the crisis years at the beginning of the century, such as 1709 when the number of inmates had reached 1,359.[16] The volume of relief provided was therefore already considerable several years before the edict; evidently numbers fluctuated as a result of war, epidemics and the economic situation in general.

The minute books and a detailed report on the hospital's activities written in 1700 reveal, rather than a rupture, a striking continuity in the measures adopted towards the poor. The hospital was already giving shelter to children, the old and the disabled, and organising weekly distributions of bread to poor families in the community – exactly as in the guidelines contained in the 1717 edict. The hospital was also arresting, punishing and expelling able-bodied and foreign beggars.[17]

---

[13] Prato, *La Vita*, p. 337; Symcox, *Victor Amadeus*, p. 200.

[14] The separate identity of the two hospitals is also proved by the fact that the Ospedale di Carità did not benefit from the income of the 1627 hospital when it closed; this income was in fact incorporated into the patrimony of the hospital for the sick of San Maurizio e Lazzaro, which was also a product of the Duke's patronage.

[15] ACT, Collezione XII, 'Statistica della Popolazione 1714–1832'. The series is incomplete, as can be seen in figure 6.

[16] AST., s.r., Confraternite e Congregazioni, m.1, fasc. 2, 'Congregazioni per provvedere all'emergenza dello Spedale di Carità di Torino', 1709.

[17] Compare the 'Deliberazione della congregazione dell'ospedale della carità di Torino', 1.6.1700 (D., T. XII, p. 272) with the regulation contained in the 'Regio editto col quale Sua Maestà conferma l'erezione e le prerogative dell'ospedale della carità di Torino', 17.4.1717 (ibid., p. 286).

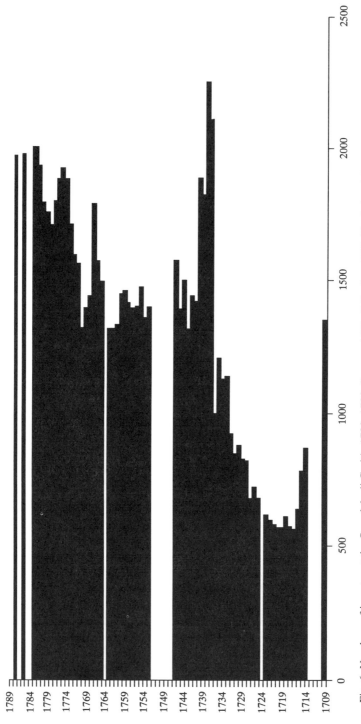

Fig. 6. Numbers of inmates at the Ospedale di Carità, 1709–1788. Source: ACT, Collezione XII, 'Statistica della Popolazione 1714–1832'. The series is incomplete but I was able to supplement data (drawn from the records of the Ospedale di Carità) for 1768, 1776 and 1779.

The changes introduced by Vittorio Amedeo were thus marginal when viewed in the context of the history of poor relief in Turin. They amounted to instructions to exclude children aged under seven from admittance ('so that the hospital does not fill up with useless persons') and to make the traditional ban on admittance of those infected with contagious diseases more effective. The new measures did not redefine the nature of hospital administration, and far from marking a shift towards state control, they confirmed the existing corporate management structure. A minor amendment increased the number of governors from thirty-one to thirty-five, but this did not involve an alteration in the balance of power in the governing board. In fact the number and distribution of the eleven 'nominated' governors (i.e. those elected by various representative bodies) remained unchanged. It was only the number of governors co-opted by this core body which increased from twenty to twenty-four. It was not until the 1730s that central government started to lay claim to the management of the hospital and other charitable institutions, with the introduction of a royal official (*Regio Protettore*) to supervise administration. Up to this date, however, the hospital retained a mixed and uncentralised form of administration, remaining dependent on the corporate bodies which had founded it in 1649. This corporate structure was by no means nominal or merely formal; it clearly shaped the decision-making process not just in the day-to-day administration, but also in important matters of policy. The decision in 1683 to build a new hospital is a significant example. It is generally suggested that institutional building in Turin formed part of an urban architectural programme whose aim was to convey the unity and strength of the dynastic power.[18] The grandiose aspect of the Ospedale di Carità, however, was not the result of royal planning. The minutes record that the governors examined the plans on several occasions and sent them to the different bodies they represented. The last mention of these negotiations is to be found in March, when the order was given to show the final drawings 'to the magistrates [of the Senate and the *Camera dei Conti*], the City of Turin [City Council], the Archbishop, the Marquis Pallavicino [the court representative] and others, so that, after careful consideration, they could be presented to His Highness for approval'.[19] The sovereign appears only at the end of the decision-making process, as the one whose signature is required to finalise an agreement which has already been reached.

Let us now consider the most ambitious part of Vittorio Amedeo's project – that which concerned the provinces. There is no argument about the fact that the royal plan to unify the poor relief system was a failure. The report on the number and condition of the *congregazioni di carità* which was ordered in 1725 and completed a year later, leaves little doubt: only 76 of the 399 *congregazioni*

[18] See for instance Comoli Mandracci, *Torino*; Pollak, *Turin*.
[19] AOC, Ordinati, 21.3.1683.

which had been planned were actually able to give any relief to the poor. The other 323 were classified in the report as either 'very poor' or 'extremely poor' and as inactive for this reason the lack of funds in turn was attributed to a lack of local initiative.[20] Historians have accepted this explanation without question, thus reinforcing the established view of the relationship between central government and localities as one of initiative versus resistance to change. The failure of the project is imputed to local inertia in the face of central directives, not to any inherent weakness in the plan itself.[21] However, we should note that the 1717 measures were extremely vague and deficient. First, the definitions of the territorial units in which the *congregazioni di carità* were to be set up were far from unambiguous. The lengthy regulations sometimes refer vaguely to 'all the lands and places' of the state where these organisations were supposed to be set up, and at other times refer to 'communities' or even 'parishes'. The same lack of clarity is to be found in the territorial definitions of the supervisory bodies, the *congregazioni generali*. It is unclear whether these were to be based on the diocesan seat or the provincial capital. Finally, no attempt was made to define the tasks of the *congregazione generalissima* (or *congregazione primaria*), the apex of the pyramidal structure based in Turin: 'the Congregazione Primaria will supervise the good management of the various *congregazioni* in its province and also deal with the petitions and requirements of the *congregazioni generali*'.[22] However it would appear that for about ten years the only activity carried out by the *congregazione generalissima* was to arbitrate in disputes between the various *congregazioni*.[23] The need to define the duties of the *congregazione generalissima* more precisely was not expressed until 1744 and 1745. For the first time, it was underlined that it should keep regular contacts with the provincial congregations, and require a report from them at least once a year. The provincial congregations were described as having fallen completely into disuse, and most of them only existed on paper; they had not met for years and had not observed the rule obliging them to obtain a report from their local *congregazioni* every six months.[24]

One has the impression that the edict was more effective at projecting an ideal image of the bureaucratic state than at putting into action a system of supervision

---

[20] AST, s.r., Confraternite e Congregazioni di Carità, m.l., fasc. 3, 'Stato delle Congregazioni di Carità date per insufficienti al soccorso quotidiano de' poveri', 1726.
[21] Prato, *La Vita*, pp. 332–6; Quazza, *Le Riforme* p. 316.
[22] Although a hierarchical structure had been discussed from the outset, it was not until 1719 that a royal edict ordered the foundation of the *congregazioni generali* and the *congregazione generalissima* in the capital. See *Editto regio per lo stabilimento di una congregazione primaria e generalissima sopra gli ospizi e congregazioni di carità*, 20.7.1719, in D., T. XII, p. 92.
[23] LPqM, m.18, Fasc. 9, 'Lettere e memorie concernanti l'erezione, interessi e maneggio degli Ospedali di Carità ne' stati di S.M., 1718–1728'.
[24] Ibid., m.19, Fasc. 23, 'Memoria in risposta alla lettera del Sig. Conte di S. Laurent delli 23 febbraio 1745', 10.3.1745.

capable of functioning. Nor did the edict create direct administration by state functionaries at the local level. In fact it demonstrated complete respect for local power structures in the formation of governing bodies for hospitals and *congregazioni*, stating that their composition should depend on 'the custom of the locality'.[25] It gave very few guidelines on how the *congregazioni* should be managed (how often the governors should meet, etc.), but it allowed even these few directions to be altered 'according to the necessities of time and place'. Finally the edict did not attempt to introduce standard criteria for the distribution of poor relief throughout the country. It only supplied very general guidance on the age groups and categories to be preferred (the old, children, women living alone, etc.), acknowledging that more precise criteria had to be established by local administrators 'according to the needs of the poor, the customs of the locality and its forms of government'.[26]

However the edict was not completely without effect, and 399 *congregazioni* nominally existed by 1726, although the majority had already ceased to function, or perhaps had never functioned. The figures show that the edict did stimulate local initiatives, but not of the kind that its rhetoric would have us believe. Poor relief agencies (some of which were totally new, some revivals of defunct organisations, and some mergers of existing ones) sprang up in this period, out of the local conflict over influence and prestige.[27] But these initiatives occurred independently from each other and had various meanings and characteristics. In terms of setting up a single coherent poor relief system across the country, the 1717 plan proved to be a failure.

As I have already mentioned, it was in 1745 that the issue of centralisation was finally raised. In particular, an attempt was made to transform the *congregazione generalissima* into a body with real functions. It certainly had very little authority at the time: when its secretary wrote to the *congregazioni* in the province of Turin, requesting them to answer a number of questions for the compilation of a general report, only fourteen out of a hundred replied.[28] Records of the consultations which took place in 1745 also confirm the impression that the *congregazione generalissima* never operated effectively and had hardly any knowledge on the state of the local *congregazioni*. In fact most of the discussion revolves around the necessity of getting a map of the state showing where the various *congregazioni* were located, and a blank book for each province in which to register the local and provincial congregations.[29] For some reason, however,

---

[25] 'Istruzioni degli Ospizi Generali dei Poveri', part I, paragraph I, clause 3, and paragraph III, clauses 3 and 6, in Guevarre, *La Mendicità*.
[26] Ibid., part I, paragraph III, clause 9, and paragraph IV, clause 3.
[27] A. Torre, 'Il consumo di devozioni: rituali e potere nelle campagne piemontesi nella prima metà del Settecento', *QS*, 58 (1985).
[28] LPqM, m.19, Fasc. 23, 'Lettera dell'abate di Rodi al Conte di S. Laurent', 11.6.1744.
[29] Ibid., 'Memorie in risposta . . . '.

the attempt to resume Vittorio Amedeo's plan did not lead to concrete action. We have to wait another two decades before seeing any substantial achievement in the direction indicated in 1717. In the 1760s, steps were taken which involved more serious central government involvement in the organisation of poor relief in the kingdom.[30] On this occasion, an inquiry into the conditions of the poor and their specific needs in the different regions was ordered, and the task was assigned to the *intendenti*, the royal representatives in the provinces. The results of this inquiry formed the basis for the plan which was submitted in 1767 for the establishment of a network of hospitals for the poor (now called *ospizi*) throughout the country. More informal structures of the type envisaged in the original plan for the *congregazioni* were definitively dropped, but at least this less ambitious project was partly implemented, and many of the planned hospitals were in fact built in the last decades of the century.[31]

More extensive study of the provincial archives would reveal a more detailed picture of the result of the plan at local level and its various stages of development. This initial examination of the documents kept in Turin suggests that different dynamics underpinned government poor relief policy between 1717 and the 1760s. The rationale which led to the 1717 edict was quite different from the one which stimulated its revision in 1745 or the achievements of the 1760s. Historians have tended to perceive these events as episodes in the same story, whilst in fact they were largely unrelated.

The 1717 plan was not a piece of legislation designed to be acted upon, but rather an exercise in propaganda, a manifesto on behalf of the absolute monarchy proclaiming its centralising aspirations. The plan itself was a paper tiger, and it did not envisage real reform, nor did it expect any to take place, as analysis of the text of the edicts has revealed. Further support for this view can be found in Father Guevarre's account in his pamphlet of the ceremony which accompanied the announcement of the measures. A huge publicity campaign surrounded the event, and the Jesuits, led by Father Guevarre, broadcast it in a series of sermons in the city churches and alms collections around the houses. The high point of the celebration was the procession which took place on Wednesday 7 April 1717, with the participation of all the inmates of the Ospedale di Carità, the poor to whom the hospital distributed bread at home every Sunday, the hospital governors, the confraternities, religious orders and canons of the chapter. They assembled at the cathedral in the morning, and then paraded through the city, until they reached the hospital door where Father Guevarre delivered a sermon. So far there was nothing new. A procession with the involvement of the assisted poor, the clergy and the city authorities recalls

---

[30] D., T. XII, 'R. P. con cui S.M. istituisce una giunta . . . ', 22.9.1766, pp. 139 and 141.
[31] P. Chierici and L. Palmucci, 'Gli Ospizi di Carità in Piemonte. Appunti per la lettura del fenomeno insediativo', in E. Sori (ed.), *Città e Controllo Sociale*, Milan 1982.

the earlier ceremonies which had accompanied the launch of the city's first poor relief plan in 1541, and the opening of the first and second hospitals for the poor in 1627 and 1650. In addition, similar displays of the assisted poor in a place noted for its symbolic or sacred character had been re-enacted every time orders had been re-issued for the prohibition of begging and the census, examination and selection of those in need. But while the ceremony was not in itself new, important symbolic innovations were introduced to the well-established ritual.

Traditionally, the gathering of all the poor would take place at the cathedral, the hospital or the town hall. In 1717, Piazza Castello by the royal palace was used for the first time. Guevarre describes how, after the sermon at the hospital door, the procession departed again and in the same order reached Piazza Castello in which six long lines of tables were waiting, three for the men and, some distance away, three for the women. All the tables faced the windows of the palace from which the royal family would have watched the spectacle. The poor were served a meal by court pages and maids of honour, to the sound of trumpets and under the direction of courtiers and ladies in waiting. A line of 200 soldiers enclosed the square (which Guevarre described as the 'theatre') and held the crowd back. The meal concluded with a ritual thanksgiving and the poor sang choral orations to the health of the King.

Piazza Castello and the royal palace had thus acquired a crucial importance in the proceedings, and the royal family had become the focal point of the celebration, an exalted role which had never been enjoyed by any previous sovereign. In the past, royalty had held a place of honour in the processions, ahead of the clergy, but now they came to occupy a distant and superior position which was exclusive to them. More than that, the ceremony gave the appearance of being arranged in homage to the royal family: the thanksgiving was exclusively directed to them, and the employment of courtiers to serve the meal to the poor made the monarch and his entourage the primary dispenser of charity.

There can be little doubt then that the novelty of the 1717 edicts has been overemphasised. They were a version of old measures, but their originality lay in their use of traditional ritual in the search for identity and consensus for the recently established monarchy. It should be recalled that this period was a turning-point in the history of the Savoy dynasty. In 1713, the House of Savoy had emerged from the Treaty of Utrecht with its position considerably enhanced not only in terms of territory and power, but also in status.[32] It

---

[32] The two treaties secured the restoration of the territories of Nice and Savoy (which had been occupied by the French), the recognition of Vittorio Amedeo's rule over the Monferrato area (which had been contested for a long time), and the acquisition of territory in Lombardy and the Kingdom of Sicily.

represented the only Italian state acknowledged as an interlocutor and courted as an ally by the great powers. The attribution of the title of king, granted for the first time to a sovereign of the House of Savoy, amounted to recognition of the new respect in which the state was held on the international scene. Thus these measures towards the poor were taken in the crucial period in which Vittorio Amedeo was forging his prestige as an absolute sovereign. The way in which such initiatives were presented undoubtedly contributed to building the image of an efficient and strongly centralised state, which is still shared by many historians. Guevarre's work betrays such a purpose by its constant glorification of the 'supreme monarch', Vittorio Amedeo, and his reforms, as do the edicts which lay great stress on the rhetoric of renewal. The publication and circulation of this work contributed considerably to the survival of the myth.

The first lying-in ward and school for midwives

The first episode involving encroachment by state officials into the administration of charitable institutions in Turin occurred in 1730, with the appointment of a *Regio Protettore* (Royal Protector) to all boards of governors. This was a supervisory office and holders of it were responsible for relations between the hospital administration and central government. The First President of the Chamber was appointed to the Compagnia di San Paolo, the Grand Chancellor to the Ospedale di Carità, the First President of the Senate to the hospital of S. Giovanni.[33] The establishment of these posts represented the first case of direct state interference in the administration of what were then autonomous institutions, and it was greeted with great resentment. For years to come the *Regio Protettore* was to remain the object of controversy, and was continually accused of exceeding his authority. In 1739, the request for limitations to be put on interference from the *Regio Protettore* was the major item in a long document protesting over the state of their hospital submitted to the King by the board of governors of the hospital of S. Giovanni. The various complaints and requests included:

> that the First President continues to be protector for the hospital [. . .] by giving the hospital advice, favours and assistance, when so requested by the governors and administrators, without interfering in the business and management of the hospital. That said administration be entirely in the hands of the Hospital Governors without the *Riformatori* [government officials placed in charge of the University] or any other person interfering, as Your Majesty can rest assured that it will continue to be administered with due care and charity [. . .] and Your Majesty can in all confidence hope for greater advantage to the

---

[33] All these appointments were dated 10.8.1730. D., T.XII, pp. 73, 363, 647, 891.

Hospital under the sole administration of the governors from the Cathedral Chapter and the City Council than from any other addition or new intendance that you are about to confer upon it.[34]

We will return to this document of 1739 on further occasions, as it represents the most explicit expression of the violent conflict which for some years had been afflicting welfare institutions. In it the governors denounced what appeared to them to be unacceptable interference by central government in the running of the hospital. It had all begun in January 1728 when it was proposed that the board of governors should set up a new maternity ward and school for midwives: the project was presented as the King's personal wish but it was to be funded by the hospital. The institution was requested to make three rooms available for the initiative in the recently constructed wing. One room with eight beds was for expectant mothers, one small room was for delivery, and one was to provide living quarters for the chief midwife, a French woman called Chevassus, whom the King had had trained in Paris. The governors attempted to oppose the King's project on the grounds of shortage of space and the bad example to the foundling girls, especially the older ones, constituted by the presence of the kind of women who were more likely to require this service. The protest fell on deaf ears, and the sovereign refused even to hear the governors' envoy's arguments through to their end. Faced, however, with the intransigence of the governors who then resorted to sending their protest in written form, the King finally requested documentary proof that the hospital had been founded as an ecclesiastical institution, arguing that only in this case could it be free from temporal control. It proved a clever move, which forced the governors to reject the secular and civic identity of the hospital which they had proudly displayed for two centuries and to claim that this was indeed a religious institution. However, research into the hospital archives could not substantiate this claim: the hospital's origins were obscure, and all the governors could prove was that it had been administered by the clergy from 1300 to 1541, when the City had become part of the board of governors (see chapter 1). The dispute was finally entrusted for arbitration to the Senate, whose verdict was predictable: the hospital of S. Giovanni was a 'lay institution' and therefore subject in every sense to the King's authority.

The governors managed to delay the implementation of the royal plan for a couple of years, but finally in 1730 the maternity ward was established in the hospital building and entirely at its expense. The hospital was made responsible not only for maintaining the patients, but also for paying the chief midwife's salary, which the King had fixed at the far from negligible

---

[34] ACT, C.S.666, *Rappresentanza del venerando spedale maggiore di San Giovanni Battista e della città di Torino*, 1739.

figure of 300 *lire* a month. The hospital was also obliged to provide her with the rich food reserved for hospital officials, as well as with candles, firewood and coal.[35]

Interference by government officials in the management of welfare institutions continued in the following years, and not only at the hospital of S. Giovanni. Their attitude became particularly aggressive during the crisis in the early 1730s (caused by involvement in the Polish war of succession in nearby Lombardy, serious drought and epidemics among livestock), which saw royal appointees decisively taking control of the emergency measures to deal with the sick and destitute. In spite of resistance from the boards of governors, the three principal welfare agencies, the hospital of S. Giovanni, the Ospedale di Carità and the Compagnia di San Paolo, were obliged to expand to maximum capacity both in terms of hospital patients and outdoor relief 'without any distinction between persons', whatever their place of origin, and 'without concern over whether the income of the institution is sufficient, it being our precise intention that debts should be made in order to deal with the situation'.[36] These provisions, which were greeted with hostility by the governing bodies, presented the *Regi Protettori* with the opportunity of asserting greater authority within the institutions. At the hospital of S. Giovanni, for example, the *Regio Protettore* (who was also the President of the Senate) personally gave out the instructions for dealing with the emergency and ensuring that the sovereign's directives were acted upon. The extraordinary measures he ordered all aimed to increase the number of patients the hospital was able to treat: these included converting some rooms which were now to be used as an infirmary, delaying the return of foundlings from the towns of their wet-nurses (which had traditionally occurred at seven years and was now temporarily changed to ten), and appointing an additional doctor whom he chose himself.[37] The total relief package imposed by central government had important ideological implications, because the institutions which until then had also played a role in relation to the elites (from the supply of credit to the celebration of prestige) were now being changed into a purely welfare structure. In fact, insistence on the full extent to which the needs of the poor had to be met and financed, even to the point of disinvestment and sale of property to meet the demand, had the effect of significantly changing the economic policy and character of these institutions: there was a drastic curtailment in the investment of profits in financial operations and in expenditure with a symbolic aim (rituals, buildings,

[35] The disputes over the maternity ward can be found in the hospital minutes for 20.1.1728, 30.1.1728, 8.2.1728, 22.2.1729, and 13.3.1730, and in the *Rappresentanza* of 1739, which was referred to above.
[36] ASSP, Rep. Lasc.161, Elemosine, 8.7.1734; a similar order was issued to S. Giovanni on 7.1.1734 (D. Vol. XII, p. 652).
[37] AOSG, Ordinati, 20.6.1734.

etc.); hospitals were increasingly restricted to the primary role of assisting the poor.[38]

It is arguable, however, as to whether these royal initiatives in the field of poor relief increased efficiency and were therefore to the public advantage, as they were proclaimed to be. Equally, the degree to which they extended medical practice and brought about innovations within it is questionable. The maternity ward is an ideal example for examining the issue. The idea of a ward to deal with a category of patient which had traditionally been excluded from early modern hospitals, and the plan to set up a school of midwifery, may at first appear an extremely progressive initiative, not only in Italy but in the European context as well. With the notable exception of the Hôtel Dieu in Paris, and a few others, the introduction of maternity facilities into hospitals was very much a late eighteenth-century phenomenon.[39] In Italy there were already refuges where unmarried mothers could go to give birth (e.g. in Ferrara from 1580, Rome from 1600 and Florence from 1679), but these should be seen as expressions of policies typical of the Counter-Reformation climate and designed above all to protect a woman's honour. They were, it would seem, very different from the maternity wards set up, from the mid eighteenth century on, in response to medical arguments strongly influenced by demographic theories and therefore by concern for the well-being of the mother and child.[40] Yet the links between the old refuges for unwed mothers and the eighteenth-century institutions should not be underestimated, given that the early maternity wards were principally for unmarried mothers.[41]

The setting up of the maternity ward in Turin was motivated by social rather than medical reasons. It was not connected to demographic concerns, and, if anything, reflected the paternalism which the government, or rather the King in person, wished to show to subjects suffering from the breakdown in the protection afforded by the community to female honour. Early documents

[38] On the serious financial problems of the hospital of S. Giovanni, which was obliged to consume some donations intended for expanding the number of beds, and to contract debts in order to deal with far-reaching welfare responsibilities, see ibid., 21.5.1744, 21.3.1746, and 28.8.1747.

[39] The early initiatives emerged in Strasburg (1728), Berlin (1751), Vienna (1752) and Copenhagen (1762). In London a separate lying-in hospital was set up in 1739. See N. M. Filippini, 'Gli ospizi per partorienti e i reparti di maternità tra il Sette e l'Ottocento', in Sanità, Scienza e Storia, 2 (1990)–1 (1991), Gli Ospedali in Area Padana fra Sette e Novecento, edited by M. L. Betri and E. Bressan. On the English case, M. C. Versluysen, 'Midwives, medical men and "poor women labouring of child"', in H. Roberts (ed.), Women, Health and Reproduction, London 1981; D. Andrew, 'Two medical charities in eighteenth century London', in Barry and Jones (eds.), Charity and Medicine; A. Wilson, 'The politics of medical improvement in early Hanoverian London', in A. Cunningham and R. French (eds.), The Medical Enlightenment of the Eighteenth Century, Cambridge 1990. On the Parisian Hôtel Dieu, J. Gélis, La Sage-Femme ou le Médecin. Une Nouvelle Conception de la Vie, Paris 1988, pp. 56–61.

[40] Filippini, 'Gli ospizi'; Gélis, La Sage-Femme; Andrew, Philanthropy.

[41] On the Italian case, Filippini, 'Gli ospizi'; on the English case, Wilson, 'The politics'.

concerning this institution concentrated on the need to offer unmarried women somewhere to give birth in secret and abandon the child, while there was no reference to greater safety in childbirth.[42] It was not until the last two decades of the century that concern over the health of the mother and child began to motivate welfare policy on maternity.[43] But in earlier years, even the desire to eliminate infanticide is not mentioned as a reason for establishing the maternity ward, and this only features some ten years after its foundation in the previously mentioned 'Rappresentanza' of 1739, where the prevention of 'frequent infanticides' is included in a list of the benefits brought about by the institution.

There would appear to be two principal motivations in the foundation documents: 'to give a safe refuge to those young women who incautiously lose their greatest gift' and the charitable desire to assist 'married women without a permanent dwelling and who because of their poverty do not have the opportunity or the means to give birth in their own homes'.[44] However, the former reason was the more important in practice: unmarried women were certainly preferred. While the former were admitted directly by the midwife without having to supply any document, the admission procedure for the latter was considerably more complicated. Married women had to obtain a declaration from the parish priest attesting to their state of poverty, and then an authorisation from the director of the institution. Records show that over 80 per cent of the women who were admitted to the ward for childbirth were, in fact, unmarried or at least declared themselves to be so. They nearly all left their babies at the hospital, while nearly all the married women took theirs away.[45] It is striking that there were not more stringent checks to prevent married women passing for unmarried in order to abandon the child. The regulations do mention this possibility, and dictate that 'where this deception is discovered, it shall be the husband rather than the wife who will incur the punishments prescribed by Royal Constitutions', but there does not seem to have been any way that these abuses could have been discovered, given that the concealment of the pregnant woman's identity seems to have been the major concern of the institution. Provisions to protect the woman's anonymity, in fact, take up the greater part of the regulations:

[42] 'Memoriale per lo stabilimento di una sala per le donne gravide . . . ', 6.5.1728, in AOSG, Cat. 10, Cl. 1, Fasc. 3, and *Regolamento per l'opera stabilita a benefizio delle partorienti . . .*, 9.7.1732, in D., T. XII, pp. 649–51.
[43] See for example the new municipal provisions later in this chapter (note 57).
[44] See also *Manifesto del Vicario di Torino*, 19.6.1728, in D., T. XII, pp. 644–6.
[45] AST, p.s., IPIM, 'Libro degli esposti' 1 and 2 (1736–45, 1760–66); ibid., LPqM, m.16 d'add., Fasc. 6 (1780–89). For the characteristics of the abandoning mothers see my article 'Bambini abbandonati e bambini "in deposito" a Torino nel Settecento', in *Enfance Abandonnée et Société en Europe XVIe–XXe Siècle*, Rome, Collection de l'Ecole Française de Rome, 1991.

The above-mentioned maids shall open and close the door of the ward without allowing any persons to enter unless they have the midwife's consent, and shall accompany said persons to the bed of the woman with whom they wish to speak, and shall not allow the said persons to go to any other bed, so as not to inconvenience the women who do not want to be seen. [. . .] Each woman admitted shall give her name to the midwife who shall enter it in the register, and any of them who do not wish to be known, they shall inform the midwife so that, if she were asked,she shall not say it. [. . .] All those who shall serve in the above-said ward, in whatever capacity, shall be required and obliged to keep silent on and conceal the things which cannot be divulged without offending other people's honour. [. . .] In the event that a woman with labour pains should present herself with a mask in order not to be known, she shall be served by the midwife without the latter ascertaining who she is. [. . .] The midwife may not show the woman even to a good friend, without her consent.[46]

This institution thus offered to both married and unmarried women the possibility of disposing of unwanted children and to the unmarried it offered, in addition, that of keeping the pregnancy secret. It is significant in this respect that unmarried women were admitted in the seventh month of their pregnancy, when this was reaching the most visible stage, while married women only in the ninth. This considerable degree of concern for the preservation of the woman's honour would appear to be a response to the decline in the community's control over sexual behaviour which traditionally had protected unmarried mothers by identifying the father and forcing him to take responsibility for the child, thus re-establishing the woman's reputation.[47] Institutions like the maternity ward took over the role which the community was no longer able to carry out. Even though it did not undertake to search out the father, as occurred in France and in some Italian states (such as Lombardy), the institution maintained the traditionally protective attitude towards the mothers; it did not punish them, nor did it hold them responsible for their behaviour, but rather it considered them unfortunate victims and justified in abandoning the symbol of their dishonour.

The second objective in establishing the lying-in ward was that of opening a school for training midwives. Immediately after the foundation, a notice was issued by the police authority, the *Vicario*, which ordered all the midwives in the city and boroughs to report to his office within fifteen days, and state their name, age, address and the period of time in which they had continuously exercised the art, 'so that they can demonstrate their sufficient experience for approval and permission to continue the said exercise, and those who are not qualified can be

---

[46] 'Memoriale per lo stabilimento di una sala per le donne gravide . . . ', 6.5.1728.
[47] S. Cavallo and S. Cerutti, 'Onore femminile e controllo sociale della riproduzione in Piemonte tra Sei e Settecento', *Quaderni Storici*, 44 (1980), reprinted in E. Muir and G. Ruggiero, *Sex and Gender in Historical Perspective*, Baltimore, Md. and London 1990.

placed [at the hospital] where they can be trained'.[48] The establishment of the
maternity ward was therefore an opportunity to introduce a licensing system for
midwives, and from that time, midwives were obliged to follow a six-month
course at the maternity ward if they wished to practise in the Turin area. During
the course, the chief midwife was to make them 'closely observe the nature of
the disturbances both before and after delivery, and lead them by the hand
through the various phases under her supervision and direction'. The hospital
surgeon was to give a lecture on anatomy twice a year to the student midwives,
which would also be open to those who were already practising. At the end of
the course, the students obtained a certificate of good conduct from the governor
and a certificate of competence and obedience from the instructress. With these
documents, they could then apply to sit the exam and finally obtain the licence
from the College of Surgeons which would allow them to carry out their trade
and display their sign. The examiners were the Professor of Surgery at the
Faculty of Medicine and another college surgeon 'experienced in the obstetric
profession'.[49]

However, the training at S. Giovanni did not become the only route by which
to enter the profession. It had little effect, especially as far as the provincial
midwives were concerned, as it would have been extremely difficult to attend
a course in the capital. Course attendance required residence or at least an
undertaking to work full-time in the hospital, and it was certainly not free. The
students had to pay the chief midwife one golden *scudo* (about 7 *lire*) as a
one-off charge, and the hospital's treasurer 15 *lire* per month for their board.
Admission to the course was also limited to married women who were literate
and possessed a certificate of good behaviour issued by the parish priest, and an
authorisation from the husband.

Even in Turin, the school for midwives co-existed for a long time with
traditional forms of training. It is notable, moreover, that the merits of the new
institution were not used to launch an attack on those women whose knowledge
was based on practice. The latter indeed were still treated with a certain
benevolence: as late as 1772, a royal ordinance recognised that not just in the
provinces but in the capital too, many unauthorised midwives were practising
this profession who were genuinely skilled and prescribed that they should be
allowed a licence.[50]

In spite of its limited impact, the 1728 project is of substantial interest as it
shows the kind of instruction and practice of obstetrics which at that time was
considered most progressive. It reveals the division of labour considered

[48] *Manifesto del Vicario di Torino*, 19.6.1728, in D., T. XII, pp. 644–6.
[49] Ibid.; *Regolamento per l'opera stabilita a benefizio delle partorienti*, 9.7.1732, in D., T. XII,
pp. 649–51; *Regolamento per l'Università di Torino*, 20.9.1729, Capo 12, Par. 14, in D., T. XIV,
p. 734.
[50] D., T. X, p. 232, *Regio Biglietto al Magistrato della Riforma*, 16.11.1772.

appropriate for male and female practitioners, which tasks were to be carried out by the midwife and which by the doctor and surgeon.

Undoubtedly the key role in training was assigned to the instructress-midwife who had been trained at the Hôtel Dieu of Paris, the temple of European obstetrics, and was herself French. The male medical profession would appear to have been able to give only a very limited contribution to the training of midwives through twice-yearly lectures on anatomy. In the 1760s, doctors were assigned a somewhat wider role in education: a course in obstetrics was introduced at the university and attendance at this became obligatory for prospective midwives wishing to obtain a licence.[51] It was, however, a purely theoretical course held with the aid of a 'machine', and of a 'small book' which was supplied to the students. All practical understanding of obstetrics was still handed on by women to women. Not surprisingly, the course was mainly attended by female pupils, and by only a small number of student surgeons, who saw little need to learn about a profession which was almost entirely exercised by women.[52]

The surgeon's role within the maternity ward was also extremely restricted. The regulations restate the traditional prohibition on the use of surgical instruments by a midwife 'in the case of a dead foetus in the womb, if it is impossible for her to extract it with her hands', and her duty to call the surgeon should delivery prove to be 'extremely difficult'. It is interesting on the other hand that with regard to another field that the medical profession had tried to monopolise – i.e. the prescribing of medicines and therapies – the regulations were somewhat contradictory. The first regulation, which was drawn up in 1728 by the Royal Surgeon Rouhault (another French import by King Vittorio Amedeo II), permitted the midwife to 'bleed patients and give enemas during delivery without notifying the doctor, and she can also do it during the period of pregnancy, except in the case of illness when she shall leave the treatment to the doctor'.[53] But four years later, in the officially approved regulation of 1732, the midwife was prohibited from 'ordering and giving internal medicines to women in labour, and also bleeding without a doctor's authorisation'. Thus the monopoly over therapeutic operations had not yet been unambiguously established in the early eighteenth century. However, both regulations agreed on another point: the midwife was given absolute dominion over attendance at

[51] *Regio Biglietto*, 17.3.1761, in D., T. XIV, p. 625.
[52] T. M. Caffaratto, 'I primordi dell'insegnamento universitario dell'ostetricia a Torino e la figura di Michele Aliprandi', *Minerva Ginecologica*, 20 (1963).
[53] Pietro Simone Rouhault was a surgeon in Paris and a member of that college, when he was called to Turin by the King in 1718. He was initially appointed the King's Surgeon and Surgeon General of the Royal Armed Forces, and then Professor of Anatomy at the University. In his *Osservazioni Anatomico-Fisiche*, Turin 1724, he wrote on the anatomy of the placenta, foetal circulation and alimentation and the factors which precipitated the birth. G. G. Bonino, *Biografia Medica Piemontese*, Turin 1825, vol. II, p. 63.

the delivery, this being justified for reasons of decency. The surgeon could be admitted only in exceptional circumstances and after considerable precautions:

> the surgeon responsible for bleeding shall immediately withdraw on completion of his operation and shall not go to any bed other than the one where the woman lies whose blood is to be let; if the said surgeon is called upon to let blood during the delivery, he shall leave after letting the blood and shall not wait to see the birth.

Even the surgeon called to deal with difficult deliveries 'may not bring another surgeon under the pretext of requiring assistance, and shall not be permitted to enter the room until requested'.[54]

The limitations on the male practice of obstetrics continued at least until the end of the century, and not only in the maternity ward at S. Giovanni. There would appear to have been a certain conflict between the government and the medical profession over this question, and the former seems to have resisted pressure from the latter. In fact, restrictions which had previously only been imposed by tradition were now put down on paper: the Royal Constitutions of 1771 introduced a prohibition on the profession being practised by surgeons unless they had obtained a special licence from the King.[55] This measure aroused protest from the College of Surgeons who pointed out the discrepancy in requesting them to examine and license the midwives, while they could not exercise the profession. A few months after the publication of this decree, they sought to obtain authorisation to practise at least for those who were appointed to examine the midwives. But the request was not conceded, and only the six most renowned surgeons of the city obtained the licence as a personal concession.[56]

The restrictions on practising midwifery probably explain the lack of interest amongst young surgeons in the university course in obstetrics. It is only in 1789 that we find any notion that obstetrics could constitute a desirable part of a surgeon's curriculum. An order concerning the establishment of a council service using salaried midwives to assist poor women giving birth at home declared that all new appointments of surgeons for the poor should give preference to those who had attended a course of obstetrics, so that they could be of assistance to the council midwives. The same document, however, reasserted the purely supplementary role of the surgeon who 'although not normally admitted to the practice of obstetrics', could assist the midwife in an emergency, should she request him to do so.[57]

---

[54] 'Memoriale per lo stabilimento di una sala per donne gravide', 6.5.1728, in AOSG, Cat. 10, Cl. 1, Fasc. 3; 'Regolamento per l'opera stabilita a benefizio delle partorienti', 9.7.1732, in D., T. XII, pp. 649–51.
[55] *Regie Costituzioni*, Tit. IX, Capo I, Par. 17, in D., T. XVI, p. 742.
[56] *Lettera della Segreteria Interna al Magistrato della Riforma*, 2.11.1772, in D., T. XIV, p. 749.
[57] *Manifesto della città di Torino per la destinazione di alcune levatrici in soccorso alle povere partorienti*, 1789, in AST, C.S.4793, Capo XVII.

So it appears that at the end of the century the 'profession' of midwife, as it had by then become defined, had lost none of its status and had suffered no erosion of its authority. Although, in Piedmont as elsewhere, there were attacks by enlightened thinkers such as Muratori and Giovan Battista Vasco on untrained midwives and on unqualified medical practitioners more generally, it appears that these opinions were far from universal;[58] certainly, the discrediting of female control over childbirth was not as violent and effective as in other parts of Europe, and did not lead to a takeover by the male medical profession.[59] On the contrary, the responsibilities of the authorised midwife were extended in the late eighteenth century. The duties of the six midwives employed by the City now included registering the women who called them out, monitoring the condition of mother and baby for fifteen days after the birth, and, if death should occur during this period, recording the probable causes in the register.[60] Midwives were therefore being given administrative tasks which involved an element of control over maternity, aimed at protecting the health of mother and child, but also at preventing desertion of the baby, infanticide or simple neglect. The transformation of the midwife's function into that of custodian of women's good conduct in matters relating to their sexuality and to the reproductive process has generally been seen as a negative development. It is said to have led to a break-down of the traditional bond of trust and solidarity between herself and the women in her care, and introduced an element of suspicion and hostility.[61] However, any assessment of the new measures as an attack on women should perhaps be tempered by the consideration that they also showed confidence in professional women and a recognition of their abilities. The midwife was promoted to the status of health official, and her medical and diagnostic abilities were acknowledged, as can be seen from the instruction to record the cause of death. It should not be forgotten that the 'profession' (and this definition was in

---

58 On eighteenth-century writings against midwives, T. M. Caffaratto, 'Mammane, levatrici, ostetriche', *Minerva Ginecologica*, 14 (1957); C. Pancino, *Il Bambino e l'Acqua Sporca. Storia dell'Assistenza al Parto dalle Mammane alle Ostetriche (Secoli XVI–XIX)*, Milan 1984.

59 On the late chronology of this process in Venice, N. M. Filippini, 'Levatrici e ostetricanti a Venezia tra Sette e Ottocento', *QS*, 58 (1985). On France, M. Laget, 'Childbirth in seventeenth and eighteenth century France: obstetrical practices and collective attitudes', in R. Forster and O. Ranum (eds.), *Medicine and Society in France*, Baltimore, Md. 1980, pp. 158–60; on the English case, J. Donnison, *Midwives and Medical Men: a History of Interprofessional and Women's Rights*, London 1977. For a comparative overview, Gélis, *La Sage-Femme*, p. 291.

60 The city was divided into three areas, and each was assigned a midwife (with a salary of 72 *lire*) and an assistant (with a salary of 24 *lire*). They were required to have attended the course at the maternity ward, and had to reside in the area and never leave without notification.

61 Pancino, *Il Bambino*, pp. 28–31. In some countries (particularly Germany), this supervisory role already appeared in municipal instructions in the late sixteenth century. M. Green, 'Women's Medical Practice and Health Care in Medieval Europe', *Signs*, 2 (1989); R. Blumenfeld-Kosinski, *Not of Woman Born: Representations of Caesarean Birth in Medieval and Renaissance Culture*, Ithaca, N.Y. and London 1990 (chapter 3); Gélis, *La Sage-Femme*, pp. 45–9.

itself an act of recognition) of midwife was perhaps the only female occupation which underwent an increase in status during the eighteenth century.

The esteem in which a qualified midwife was held can already be seen in 1728 in the economic and social status of the midwife appointed to the maternity ward at S. Giovanni. Her salary was identical to that of the four hospital doctors in 1732 – lavish treatment, even if we consider that she had to be available twenty-four hours a day, to assist at a birth at any time of the day or night. In addition, she enjoyed other privileges such as the requirement for the hospital to supply her with a personal maid and the food reserved for officials. The innovative thrust of the 1728 project thus lies in having given enhanced status to midwifery and to a midwife trained in a hospital under the guidance of an educated and expert instructress. This project certainly did not imply any theoretical or practical superiority of the man–midwife, but it did introduce an element of differentiation between midwives.

How then are we to explain the fierce conflict over the establishment of the maternity ward between central government and the hospital governors which continued for about a decade? It might be argued that the governors were guilty of traditionalism in resisting a reform from above. In fact, however, the opposition of the governors never concerned the nature of the initiative; they never questioned the usefulness of 'a safe place for daughters who go astray' or the 'instruction of Piedmontese women in the profession of midwife', nor were they sparing in their praise of these intentions. The reasons for their opposition were primarily the financial burden and the possible effects on the morals of the abandoned girls in their care. Once the institution had been established, the conflict continued on apparently trivial grounds whose significance is at first difficult to grasp. The governors' grievances were directed against the chief midwife appointed by the King, whom they accused of being negligent, dishonest, avaricious, and only interested in grabbing all she could, whether it was money or food. Food took on a particular symbolic importance, and the insinuations relating to the midwife's gluttony became the main pretext for their hostility towards her. According to a rumour which the governors attributed to the cook, the main courses served to the midwife were 'of such abundance that they would have sufficed three people'. Her husband, also French, ate 'continuously' with her in the hospital. Finally they doubted whether all the food prepared for the patients ever reached its intended destination. The governors had other examples of how she was supposed to have exploited her office: one maid had not been sufficient for her needs and she had brought in another two 'outsiders' paid by the hospital and it was suspected that it also paid for their board. She took money from the patients and demanded 33 *soldi* for swaddling, even if they had brought their own. She made the patients work for her and pocketed the proceeds.[62] In

---

[62] Document quoted in Caffaratto, *L'Ospedale*, p. 66.

the end, as is clear from the 'Rappresentanza' of 1739, the governors requested the dismissal of Chevassus and her replacement by a local midwife:

> the above-said midwife believes that she is not responsible to the hospital administrators, but only to the *riformatori*. She has not fulfilled and continues not to fulfil her duties as prescribed by the Regulations. There have been serious disorders, and she has been absent from work for more than three months, having returned to her own country with the intention of staying until next spring. She has substituted another Frenchwoman during her absence, and she has left with only the permission of those whom she believes to have authority over her.

The document perhaps gives some hints which allow us to clarify the real nature of the conflict: the controversy concerned not the purpose of the maternity ward, but who controlled it. It was the alleged flouting of their authority that rankled with the governors. Even their xenophobia, which was reflected in continuous references to the 'French woman' and her 'foreign' relatives and servants, demonstrated their sense of impotence: she appeared uncontrollable not only because she came under the authority of the university rather than the hospital, but also for the more subtle reason that she was not appointed by the governors and therefore did not come from the network of personal contacts and common interests which had traditionally affected the recruitment of hospital personnel. She was a 'foreigner' in terms of the 'family' which made up the hospital, and in the eyes of the governors this was tantamount to unreliability and an absence of loyalty to the institution.

After ten years of sterile argument with the university officials who had authority over the maternity ward, the governors adopted a different strategy which aimed at the gradual absorption of the new institution into their control. They wrong-footed the government representatives by competing with them on their own ground, i.e. by using the rhetoric of innovation and the myth of French progressiveness which until then had been the justification for undermining the hospital's independence. They criticised the inadequacy of the anatomy lessons in the training programme, and offered to organise themselves a course of regular twice-weekly lessons for midwives to be given by Verna, a surgeon who enjoyed their confidence. They even added that women should be uncovered during delivery, according to 'the practice in Paris'(!).

The proposal to reorganise the teaching of anatomy was a clever move which showed them not to be traditionalists or incapable of change. The important thing for them was that it was under their control and carried out by their men, such as the surgeon Verna, a member of the family that for generations had monopolised the greater part of the medical posts in the hospital.[63] Thus they

---

[63] From 1689 until the end of the eighteenth century, the family held posts as surgeons and doctors at San Giovanni. See Bonino, *Biografia Medica*, vol. II, pp. 59–60; 219–21, for the more famous of them, Alberto, Andrea (Alberto's nephew) and Giovan Battista (Andrea's cousin).

managed to place one of their men in the maternity ward, which until then had been a kind of autonomous body within the hospital. The governors finally took full control of the institution in 1740, when they succeeded in sacking Chevassus and appointing Anna Libonis in her place. The latter was in every sense the perfect candidate for the governors: not only was she 'from our country', married and a qualified midwife, but she was also a 'daughter of the hospital', a foundling who had been brought up by the hospital, and who had continued to live and work there after she had grown up and married. She came from the traditional pool of labour that the hospital used for recruitment. She had been trained by Chevassus for several years and had taken over during her absences in Paris. She had never been out of the governors' sphere of authority, and she had the respect of the Verna uncle and nephew team of surgeons, who in fact supported her nomination and vouched for her ability.[64] From that time the conflict over the maternity ward ceased as it had now been brought under the control of the old administration and its protégés.

The hospital reforms of the 1730s

The conflict between royal officials and hospital administrators which started with the maternity ward proposal in 1728, and was then rekindled in 1734 by the appointment of the *Regio Protettore*, erupted violently towards the end of the 1730s when the government reforms of the Faculty of Medicine, carried out between 1720 and 1738 as part of the more general reform of the university, finally caught up with the hospital. The new medical curriculum attached particular importance to practical medicine, which took up three of the five years of study, and assigned a key role to the hospital in training students. The latter were required to regularly attend demonstrations on cadavers in the hospital during the last two years of study. This period would involve lessons at the patients' bedside, and they would discuss the illnesses observed at weekly meetings. Only those who had been awarded a university degree could practise medicine, and then only after a further two years of training in a hospital or with an accredited physician. Practical hospital experience also became essential for students of surgery. As a result of probably the most innovative of the reforms, surgery became a university faculty from 1721. The period of study was originally set at three years, but was lengthened to five years in 1738, in line with the courses in other faculties. The first three years were dedicated to the study of theoretical issues while the last two were entirely given over to hospital practice.[65]

[64] AOSG, Ordinati, 5.12.1740.
[65] On the university reforms, see T. Vallauri, *Storia delle Università degli Studi*, 3 vols, Turin 1816; Quazza, *Le Riforme*, pp. 385–98. The text of these provisions is in D., T. XIV, Capo IV,

The reforms clearly assigned a pivotal role to the hospital in medical training and research. They increased the number of medical and surgical students training in the institution, and boosted the number of doctors employed from one to four, in order to meet the growth in teaching duties. A final provision linked the hospital even more closely to the university by stipulating that its chief physician and surgeon were to be chosen from among the university professors.[66]

However, the claim that these reforms 'medicalised' the hospital is not correct.[67] When these provisions were put into effect, the hospital of S. Giovanni did not conform to the model of *rifugio indifferenziato* (non-discriminating refuge) which Italian medical scholars consider to be typical of hospitals in this period.[68] It is true that, as we know, it contained a large section for incurables, and another for foundlings, but at least from the sixteenth century, the section dealing with the sick had a pronounced medical function. Witness to this fact is the 1541 regulation stipulating that the hospital physician and surgeon had to do rounds of the sick patients twice a day.[69] In the following decades, as we have seen in the second chapter, the hospital of S. Giovanni had become increasingly specialised in the treatment of syphilis sufferers. Then, in the seventeenth century, it gradually abandoned its hitherto characteristic role – that of providing a combination of care and medical treatment. Indeed we find in fact less and less evidence of the caring arrangements stipulated with some of the patients, which were numerous in the previous century (the last, isolated case is mentioned in a will dated 1667). Moreover, there is no longer any sign of an involvement of governors in the admission procedure, which would suggest that this task had by now been taken up by the medical staff, possibly by the young training surgeons who lived day and night in the hospital. In Turin too, as in France during the same period, there was a rapid expansion of medical personnel practising and training in the hospital, especially surgeons, from the mid seventeenth century on.[70] As a consequence, the hospital served increasingly as a place for the practice of medicine, and its organisation was more and more dominated by purely medical concerns. These developments are usually heralded as decidedly positive but it should be pointed out that they also led to a breakdown of that complementary system of hospital care and assistance in the community which we looked at in chapter 2.

'Dell'insegnamento della medicina', pp. 643–9; Capo V, 'Dell'insegnamento della chirurgia', pp. 655–66; Art. IV, p. 723; Art. V, p. 733.

[66] 'Regio Biglietto', 29.7.1739, in AOSG, Ordinati, 2.8.1739.
[67] Cf. D. Carpanetto, 'Gli studenti di chirurgia', in Balani, Carpanetto and Turletti, 'La popolazione studentesca', p. 168.
[68] A. Scotti, 'Malati e strutture', pp. 250 ff.; G. Cosmacini, *Storia della Medicina e della Sanità in Italia*, Bari 1987, pp. 234 ff.
[69] ACT, C.S. 657.   [70] Gelfand, *Professionalizing*.

Whatever the judgement on these transformations, there can be little doubt that, at the time of the eighteenth-century reforms, the hospital of S. Giovanni was already carrying out the functions of training and maintaining the medical profession, albeit on a fairly minor scale. From the second half of the seventeenth century, if not earlier, young surgeons resident in the hospital carried out the duties of dresser, in accordance with the chief surgeon's instructions.[71] Originally there were just three of them, but their number increased to four in 1680, to five in 1702, to six in 1716, and finally to thirteen in 1738 to keep pace with the increase in beds.[72] These surgeons were assisted with simple duties by a group of nurses who were drawn from the ranks of the ex-foundlings taken back by the hospital. Moreover in the late seventeenth century, a private benefactor donated funds to create the post of assistant hospital physician, which was reserved for a young doctor to work full time in residence in the hospital, 'to observe the progress of diseases and report on them to the chief physician, and take action in cases of emergency'.[73]

Both the position of dresser and assistant hospital physician were occupied by young practitioners who wanted to enter the profession. Judging from the number of applications for this kind of practical experience, the posts must have been considered prestigious and useful additions to a *curriculum vitae*. They were initially employed by the board of governors, with the chance of having their periods of service extended if they proved suitable. Some young surgeons and physicians, after a long stint in the hospital, obtained important appointments, like that of chief regimental surgeon, court surgeon or even *protomedico* (i.e. chief royal physician and supreme medical authority in the kingdom). Many acquired more modest positions in the army medical service, and a great number went on to practise in the provinces.[74]

Although the information available on careers is limited, the governors' statement in 1739 that 'nearly all the surgeons in his Majesty's cities and states

---

[71] Their existence is occasionally recorded in the Minute Books since 1639. At this date, for instance, a Spirito Ponsio was helping the barber surgeon of the hospital (AOSG, Ordinati 2.1.1639), and the presence of the 'young barber and surgeon' Ludovico Paysio is mentioned three times since 1641 (ibid., 26.5.1641, 25.10.1643 and 17.5.1648). Since the 1670s, both the beginning and end of their period of service are recorded in the Minute Books.
[72] AOSG, Ordinati, 24.3.1680, 24.7.1702 and 10.12.1716. For the 1738 figure, see the *Rappresentanza* referred to above.
[73] The donation was probably in the last twenty-five years of the century, but in any case before 1690 (as can be inferred from the minute of 3.2.1690). The benefactor, Canon Giordano, reserved the right to nominate the doctor for the post during his lifetime.
[74] This information can be found in the minutes, which sometimes mentioned the future position of a surgeon or doctor leaving the hospital. Among the more successful careers, there was that of Antonio Maria Reyna, assistant doctor in 1700, qualified doctor at the hospital of S. Giovanni in 1708 and finally *protomedico* in 1739, also that of the surgeon Schina, hospital dresser until 1708, then Surgeon-Major in the Artillery Regiment of Carignano, and finally that of Giovan Battista Balbis, hospital dresser from 1710, and then member of the Turin College and Surgeon to the Prince of Carignano.

have been trained in the hospital' does not appear to be without foundation.[75] There is no doubt that when the reforms were introduced, the hospital of S. Giovanni had for many decades been an important centre for medical training. Moreover, informal but solid links already existed between medical staff employed in the hospital and the university. The chief physician in the hospital often held a chair in the medical faculty, while the chief surgeon held the office of anatomist. In any event, both of them were usually very prominent figures in medical circles.

The reforms did not therefore completely redefine the hospital's identity. Apart from the increase in the number of students and doctors, the real changes occurred in the political life of the hospital. The language of reform supplied an ideological justification in terms of innovation for the expansion of university control over the hospital. By attaching greater importance to teaching than patient care, the reforms subordinated the management of the hospital to the Faculty of Medicine, or rather to the authority of the *Magistrati della Riforma* (or *Riformatori*, the civil servants to whom the administration of the university had been assigned).

Before the reform, it had been the board of governors who had appointed the dressers and doctors, and made sure that they fulfilled their duties as required. It also took disciplinary measures in cases of negligence and breaches of the regulations.[76] Certainly the opinion of the chief physician and surgeon had a significant bearing on the choice of dressers and medical assistants, who were often the doctors' pupils or even their relatives. For instance, Alberto Verna, who held the post of chief surgeon at the hospital of S. Giovanni for over forty years (having served seven as a dresser), established a veritable medical dynasty in the institution. Two of his nephews succeeded him, after serving long periods as his assistants, while a third nephew became an assistant physician. However, on paper, every decision on the various aspects of hospital life remained in the governors' hands until the 1730s, when their authority became the object of fierce attacks.

It should be emphasised that these attacks did not come from the medical profession, but essentially from the King and his reformers, government officials who were pressing for bureaucratic control. Central government gradually deprived the governors of all their authority. On the pretext of wishing to avoid straining the hospital's finances, it was established that the hospital would pay only a fraction of the salaries for the four physicians (whose numbers had been increased to meet the growth in teaching duties), and the rest would be paid by the university.[77] This measure weakened the authority of the governors, as the

[75] 'Rappresentanza'.
[76] For example AOSG, Ordinati, 8.2.1689 and 3.4.1731.
[77] *Regio Biglietto* dated 29 July published in D., T. XII, p. 653.

doctors were no longer financially dependent on them. Then two weeks later, the board was suddenly stripped of its traditional prerogative of selecting doctors, on the pretext that its recent selection had been disappointing and the new appointees were unable to meet the standards required of the post.[78] In the same period, it was decided that the dressers would also be appointed by the *Riformatori*, and chosen from among the surgical students at the Collegio delle Provincie, an institution created to promote university education by providing a royal scholarship to over 200 young men from the provinces (another example of the development of royal patronage in the eighteenth century).[79] All these measures, and more generally the emphasis on the teaching role of doctors rather than their obligations to the sick, had the effect of reducing the governors' authority over the medical staff. Although the hospital's administrative structure had not formally changed, in reality two powers were daily disputing its control within its walls. The governors give the impression in the *Rappresentanza* of 1739 that they were less and less in control of the management of the hospital:

> The Royal Constitutions concerning the University have stipulated that the doctor and surgeon in the Hospital must always be professors in the said University. The poor have been adversely affected by these provisions, for as the doctor and surgeon are not seen to be under the authority of the hospital administrators, the latter can no longer correct the former if they do not carry out their duties, much less dismiss them. The hospital doctor is currently advanced in years, with infirmities which prevent him from visiting the sick twice a day. Thus he instead visits only some of his patients during his rounds, or sometimes none at all, and then sends the assistant physician on the rounds, and the chief physician comes in the evening when he can. The surgeon is deemed to have great theoretical knowledge but insufficient practical experience, and although it is his duty to carry out the difficult operations of removing gall stones, cleansing cataracts, suturing arteries or performing surgery on what is called the 'king's evil' [scrofula] and similar things, these duties are actually being performed by former surgeons of this hospital, the Verna uncle and nephew who continue their charitable work in the women's ward [. . .]. The Hospital is full of praise for the royal decree that physicians and surgeons also be university professors. However, conscience requires it be reported that it is not advantageous to the Hospital, because neither the physician nor the surgeon have any real dependence on it, and it is harmful to the sick because they are no longer treated with the punctuality and charitable feeling that previously existed [. . .] and the said abuses which were introduced a few years ago have probably cost the lives of many who could have been cured.

Further on, the *Rappresentanza* broadened its complaints to include the young students of the Collegio delle Provincie who had replaced the thirteen

---

[78] AOSG, Ordinati, 9.8.1739.
[79] *Regolamento de' Giovani studenti di Cirurgia nel Collegio delle provincie che serviranno all'ospedale S. Giovanni*, in D., T. XIV, p. 658, 18.8.1738.

young surgeons previously employed as dressers by the hospital, and who worked five at a time on twenty-four-hour shifts. They were not only accused of not treating the sick properly, but also of having committed several 'instances of insubordination' which even the *Riformatori* were unable to stamp out although they took action on two occasions.

The document is obviously a biased source and the portrayal of the hospital as slipping into chaos is perhaps an exaggeration. It is however quite believable that the dispute over its control was creating serious disciplinary problems. It is also plausible that the underlying ideology of the reforms, which shifted the emphasis to the training of medical staff, was reducing the treatment of the sick to a secondary role. Hence the persistent references by the governors to the discrepancy between theoretical and practical ability.

The situation had not changed a few decades later, when an anonymous report complained that 'the university professors only do one round a day, and some go months, others years without setting foot in the Hospital. [. . .] The result is that the sick get inexpert and inappropriate treatment from the two young physicians.'[80] It is also significant that the most serious failures in hospital organisation, such as the disproportion in beds for curable and incurable diseases, were not addressed in the reforms. Indeed the rate of growth of beds for incurable diseases was increasing in this very period of conflict (in the thirty-year period from 1728 to 1757, about ninety new beds were created, while 104 had been created in the previous sixty years).

The reforms were not part of a conflict between 'progressive' and 'conservative' forces, but merely promoted the changes in the power structure which were occurring at the same time in other charitable institutions. The most acute conflict with the representatives of central government occurred in the following decade. In spite of the apparent victory over the maternity ward, which was brought back under the control of the board of governors, the traditional administration was losing in the long term. By the 1750s, state control appears to be consolidated, and we find that the *Riformatori* are now on the administrative board. This was partly due to the bureaucratisation of the City Council, which supplied four of the eight governors. In the second half of the eighteenth century, the Council was no longer an independent power base, but simply an extension of the King's administration. The councillors and the *Vicario* had become government officials in charge of management of the city's affairs.[81] Another expression of this development can be observed in changes to the

[80] 'Relazione anonima' (written towards the end of the century, but before 1793), quoted in Caffaratto, *L'Ospedale Maggiore*, p. 143.
[81] The *Vicario* was by now one of the posts with the closest links to the sovereign, through weekly consultations. D., T.III, p. 1461 (note). For the transformation of the post of *Vicario* and the bureaucratisation of the City Council, see also D. Balani, *Il Vicario tra Città e Stato. L'Ordine Pubblico e l'Annona nella Torino del Settecento*, Turin 1987, pp. 33–79.

municipal medical outdoor relief system which had been operating for nearly two centuries. Its original responsibilities were abandoned, and it became essentially a medical service for inmates in the prisons and the new houses of correction founded by the state.[82]

The change which the hospitals and charitable institutions underwent in the middle of the century concerned the exercise of power rather than the organisation of poor relief. However, the attack on institutional autonomy did eventually affect the recipients, because it caused the threatened elites to take action to defend their usurped power, thus altering the opportunities for assistance open to the poor. The fact that the institutions were still entirely dependent on private charity for their survival meant that benefactors could maintain their control by placing restrictions and conditions on the use of their donations.

The privatisation of charitable resources

The conflict over charitable institutions in this period had a considerable impact on charitable donations. One might expect the expulsion of private citizens from the control of charitable resources to have a paralysing effect on private charity, by removing the incentive for benefactors. However, the opposite occurred and legacies and donations reached consistently high levels in the period from 1730 to 1770, after the decrease in the 1720s – albeit without ever reaching the peak which occurred in the first decade of the century (figure 1). If we now shift our attention from the quantity to the quality of charitable initiatives, we realise that they also have some new features. Firstly they have pronounced social connotations. During this period new institutions appear which are managed and financed by restricted and homogeneous social groups, unlike previous initiatives which were virtually open to all civic elites. In the context of that more fragmented elite structure described at the beginning of this chapter, investment in charities became a means by which to reassert the dignity and prestige of one's own social group, and consolidate separate spheres of influence.

Charitable activity appears to have been particularly marked amongst the groups most affected by the campaign of centralisation carried out by state officials: the court aristocracy which suffered a substantial decrease in privilege and status, and the merchants who were being ousted from those (mainly financial) positions in the state which they had previously occupied. The House of the Provvidenza was founded in the 1720s by the court aristocracy, and very soon was accommodating about a hundred girls aged between ten and twenty-

---

[82] ACT, C.S.4793. By contrast, the service to the sick and destitute of the City was frozen (see chapter 2).

five.[83] From 1731, with the sole exception of the treasurer (responsible for the accounts and organising work for the girls) who was usually a merchant, the five directors and the lady directress were all drawn from the most exclusive court milieu, where they held the highest offices. In some periods, the institution appears indeed to be run solely by restricted kin groups within the court.[84] Another example of this trend is the Bogetti Institution for infectious diseases, established with the huge donation which the banker Ludovico Bogetti made available to the Ospedale di Carità in 1733 (it was the largest recorded donation in the 200-year period under examination). For the rest of the century, this institution was entirely financed by members of the mercantile and banking elite, who thus upheld the founder's desire to provide a form of display of the munificence and prestige of this social group.[85]

Bogetti's wishes are particularly worthy of attention, because they illustrate very well how the exclusion of certain social groups from public life affected charitable activity in this period. His donation would appear to be an attempt at radical reform which aimed at breaking down all the barriers which had traditionally barred access to the early modern hospital. In fact, he left his gift on the condition that the Ospedale di Carità, from that time on, admitted all people in need without distinction, 'not only the healthy, but also the sick, and among these, sufferers of any disease, whether contagious or not contagious, curable or incurable, and coming from this city or any other of his Majesty's territories'.[86] The inspiration for the donation appears therefore to have been the ideal of an all-inclusive charity, which would transcend all types of preference and privilege. However, if the whole will is taken into account, the polemic against the exclusions which, at least in theory, had typified the hospital, appears to be a metaphor for the exclusions that were occurring amongst the elite groups, for all the other instructions in the will were concerned to uphold exclusive and corporative forms in the allocation of charity. Its only innovative feature was that it supported social groups other than the ones which were being favoured at that time. Thus Bogetti entrusted the Compagnia di San Paolo with a fund to

[83] The exact year of its foundation is unclear, but in 1735 the institution obtained royal recognition. The identity of the governors and benefactors can be found in LPqM, m. 228. See also Gribaudi, *Il Regio Educatorio.*

[84] Renato Birago, his brother-in-law Ignazio Graneri and his sister-in-law Agnese Ponte di Casalgrasso were involved in the administration in the 1730s and 1740s, and later his wife, Vittoria Birago, took over from the sister-in-law. The other families who appear in the lists of governors and benefactors (the Saluzzos, the Carrons and the Turinettis) were also closely related. See chapter 4.

[85] AOC, Cat. VIII, Busta 1, Fasc.11, 'Stato e riparto delle piazze nell'opera Bogetti eretta nel Regio Spedale di Carità'.

[86] For the will of Ludovico Bogetti, see Ins., 1.9.1733, 26.8.1733. After some discussion over the admissibility of accepting a donation which challenged the hospital's regulations over admission, his instructions were enacted by the creation of a separate institution named after the benefactor for the treatment of infectious illnesses and venereal diseases in particular.

supply alms regularly to *poveri vergognosi* on the condition that distribution started with 'bankers and merchants, and then worked down' and was 'to the exclusion of the nobility'. Bogetti therefore favoured those social groups which had been marginalised by the new definitions of hierarchy and privilege, while he excluded the nobility which was by then largely made up of state officials.[87] The corporative character of his instructions is also explicitly stated in the donation which funded the merchants and bankers to take part in the annual spiritual exercise organised by the Jesuits. This was an important symbolic occasion which brought together the male elites of the city, and to which the merchant class was evidently having difficulty in gaining admittance.

Bogetti's instructions should therefore not be read simply as an attack on the discriminatory aspects of charitable organisations; they have a powerful symbolic value, and this becomes even more evident if the 'exclusions' blamed in the will are seen in the context of Bogetti's personal experience. Gabriele, Ludovico Bogetti's brother and business partner, was one of the last representatives of independent administration in welfare institutions. He had been a governor of the Ospedale di Carità for more than ten years, and had died shortly before this institution came under the control of the *Regio Protettore*, and before the introduction of other antidemocratic measures which lowered the quorums for voting and decision making.[88] Ludovico himself was the last representative of a trade organisation to hold the highest office of *Primo Console* within the Consulate – the body which had jurisdiction over legal cases concerning industry and craft organisations, and a consultative role in economic matters. It was in 1733 (the very year that Bogetti made his will) that the three members of the Consulate, who until then had been members of the Merchants' Guild chosen by the king from a short-list presented by the guild itself, had to be state-employed lawyers, while merely advisory responsibilities were left to the two leading bankers in the city.[89] We cannot know how much these events impinged on Ludovico's last wishes, but there can be little doubt that these experiences, this exclusion from the local centres of power, must have considerably embittered the non-bureaucratic elites and influenced the nature of their charitable donations.

However, the correspondence between charitable initiatives and specific social milieux did not only affect groups which were losing out but it reflected more generally the social fragmentation occurring at this time amongst urban elites. As we will see in the next chapter, even the state was to establish its

---

[87] Another fund for the same purpose was given to the testator's occupational confraternity, the Congregazione dei Mercanti.
[88] Gabriele's last testament (which he made with Ludovico) was in 1730 (Ins., 1730, l.4, vol. 2, 29.4.1730). The introduction of the *Regio Protettore* occurred in 1734 and that of the regulations which changed the voting rules in 1737 and 1738 (D., T.XII, pp. 306 and 313).
[89] *Regio Editto pel nuovo stabilimento de' Consolati*, 15.3.1733, in D., T.III, p. 781.

own institutions, whose foundation was also clearly intended to reinforce the bureaucracy's identity and form an area of government patronage.

Another aspect of the changes which affected existing and newly founded institutions in the mid eighteenth century is the 'privatisation' of welfare resources: there was a growth in the number of those donations which restricted their use either by specifying the beneficiaries or by preserving nomination rights, thus allowing benefactors to continue to influence welfare policy in spite of government interference. The ratio between restrictive testamentary dispositions and open ones in the period 1730–1789 was three times the ratio for the previous sixty years (1670–1729). The hospital of S. Giovanni, for instance, recorded a considerable increase in the endowments of beds for incurable diseases (over which the donating family maintained the right to nominate the occupant): in the forty-year period 1728–67 there were 112 new beds of this kind, while there had only been 104 in the previous sixty years (figure 4). As I have already mentioned, administrators endeavoured to obstruct this tendency in the 1750s (although they were only partially successful in their attempts), by restricting the endowments for beds for incurable diseases. But prospective benefactors did not give up, and indeed attempted to extend nomination rights to beds for curable diseases as well. This condition was occasionally accepted: in 1765, for example, Michel Antonio Giacobino, an apothecary, ordered the foundation of two beds for curable diseases while stipulating that patients had to be chosen from amongst his relations and servants from his household.[90] An even more significant reaction to the new restrictions was that the practice of nominating beds for incurables, which had hitherto been limited to the hospital of S. Giovanni, was now extended to the Ospedale di Carità, which had never accepted this type of qualified endowment: sixteen new beds controlled by benefactors were created between 1740 and 1789.[91]

The nomination of the beneficiary of a charitable donation became increasingly common even for the smaller institutions, especially those for women. Benefactors started to found *piazze* or 'places', donations of capital which yielded sufficient income to maintain facilities for one or more patients in perpetuity, and these would be nominated by the benefactor, or by persons chosen by him or her. This practice became normal in the institutions founded in this period (such as the Provvidenza and the Bogetti Institution), but was also introduced into existing establishments. The House of the Soccorso, a small institution which had previously held no more than about twenty young girls, grew between 1734 and 1789 through the gift of at least twenty-six places reserved for relations or young women chosen by benefactors'

---

[90] Ins., 1765, l.12., 4.12.1765.
[91] AOC, Cat. XV, 43, 'Fondazioni letti per Incurabili, 1724–1839'. Before 1740 there was just one nominated bed for incurable diseases, founded in 1724.

families.[92] During the 1770s, as many as forty-one of the girls at the Provvidenza, out of a total varying between eighty and one hundred, were 'placed'.[93] Even the ruling dynasty entered into this contest over influential resources. Members of the royal family were responsible for nineteen of the forty-one places, and these were used to reward groups of civil servants. They were in fact allocated to 'the daughters of well-deserving persons in the state or royal service, and employment in the court, judiciary or treasury'.[94]

Attitudes to the funding of charity had therefore changed again: in the latter part of the seventeenth century (which had witnessed the sharp increase in private contributions), charity had turned from a civic duty into an expression of status, whereas now it became an instrument of protection and self-defence. Previously, a donation had essentially been a way of displaying one's prestige, a search for honour and ritual acknowledgment. The influence over the allocation of charitable resources was not clearly held by individual persons, nor was it precisely delimited, as it was always possible to exercise influence by becoming a member of administrative boards, which were relatively open, or through personal contact with their members. But in the new climate of the mid-century people demanded from their involvement in charity a more immediate and tangible 'return'. The exact amount of patronage to which a donation entitled the benefactor now had to be negotiated in advance and written down. For the non-bureaucratic elites, removed from the administration of institutions, charity became a vehicle for preserving some of their influence. Indeed donations were increasingly used to constitute their own areas of group protection. It should be observed that funds were often reserved for very restricted groups, specific occupational categories, the poor in a given locality, or even the benefactor's own kinship group.

One group of donations, for example, were for the poor in localities where the benefactor had influence. On the one hand there were donations restricted to the poor of certain parishes, which gave the parish priest the role of arbiter and executor of the testator's wishes. This was probably a sign of the new importance the parish had taken on in marking identity and defining social relations. In passing it should be remarked that for the first time, thanks to these kinds of funds, the clergy were being directly involved in the distribution of charity, whereas until then their role had been restricted to issuing the declarations of

---

[92] Two places were created by the Maid of Honour Francesca Gabuti (ASSP Rep. Lasc. 161, 8.7.1734), another two by Giuseppe Gianinetti (ibid., 30.4.1752), fifteen by Tomaso Crosa (T.P., vol. XXIV, p. 368, 22.10.1751), two by Domenico Borbonese (T.P., vol. XXIX, p. 93, 31.1.1776), an unspecified number by Giuseppe Bernocco (ASSP, Rep. Lasc. 160, 31.1.1774) and by Rosa Teresa Foassa Arpino (ibid., 161, 15.1.1786).

[93] This can be inferred from the accounts of the Opera della Provvidenza in LPqM, m.20, Fasc. 1, m.18 d'add., Fasc. 3.

[94] OPCB, m.228.

poverty required by charitable institutions (and thus assessing who was poor and who was not).[95] On the other hand, there were numerous provisions for the poor living on the donator's feudal lands. These were generally funds for the sick and the weakest sections of the community (often widows), and for one or more annual dowry for daughters of the poorest families in the lands controlled by the testator's family.[96] But there was no shortage of donations which sought to create privileged access to institutions in Turin for the poor of an estate. For example Ottavio Nicolò Provana di Leynì left 1,500 *lire* in 1736 to the hospital of S. Giovanni with the proviso that requests from the sick of Leynì should always be given preferential treatment.[97] Finally, there were also 'moral' legacies which intended to save (or discipline) the souls of the poor rather than their bodies; these were used for financing 'missions' – series of sermons and religious initiatives organised by Jesuits and Capuchin monks in the villages where the benefactor was lord.[98]

Another example of restricted legacies were those in favour of the testator's trade or social group. In the middle of the eighteenth century, Turin witnessed the development of forms of corporative welfare which are generally associated with a much earlier period.[99] While only seventeen donations and legacies were left to assist members of respected social groups who had fallen on hard times in over half a century from 1677 to 1729, there were twelve in just a decade from 1730 to 1739. Donations of this type also changed in their nature: in the early period, the great majority of legacies are in favour of those who have fallen on hard times, without further specifications. The few exceptions around the turn of the century concerned funds especially reserved for 'nobles in the strict sense of the word', and these were clearly an attempt to reassert the privileges and exclusiveness of the court aristocracy when it was being subjected to the first attacks on its supremacy.[100] From the 1730s onwards the purpose of the legacy becomes increasingly specific and the social category which was beneficiary more clearly defined: for some benefactors *poveri vergognosi* are only 'first class, feudal landowners having been installed for ten years'; for others 'merchants having lived in Turin for at least three years before becoming

---

[95] See for example the legacy left by Michel Antonio Defontaine to the parish of Carmine, ASSP, Rep. Lasc. 161, 12.9.1754.
[96] For example Count Giuseppe Bonaventura Orsini di Rivalta made the Compagnia di S. Paolo his sole heir in 1761 with the obligation to use the profits to give alms to the sick and widows on his feudal lands and to provide two dowries per year to daughters of needy families living in one of the villages within those lands, Rivalta. ASSP, Rep. Lasc. 162, 5.4.1761.
[97] AOSG, Cat. 4, Cl. 1, Vol. 38, Fasc. 11, 11.5.1736.
[98] ASSP, Rep. Lasc. 160, 31.1.1762.
[99] Ricci, 'Povertà'.
[100] See for example the wills by marchioness Francesca Maria Crivelli Scarampi Germonio di Sale (Ins. 1689, 1.10, 26.9.1689), by marchioness Giovanna Maria Grimaldi Simiane di Pianezza (ASSP, scat.107, fasc.147, 15.12.1692), and by marchioness Maria Margherita Provana Tana d'Entraque (Ins. 1714, l.12, vol.1, 15.11.1714).

impoverished', etc.[101] In particular a distinction between 'first' and 'second class' *poveri vergognosi* appears repeatedly after the previously mentioned will by Ludovico Bogetti in 1733. Bogetti left several legacies in his will to assist 'the categories which are excluded from the alms given by the Compagnia di San Paolo to *poveri vergognosi*, that is to say starting with the merchants, bankers and those of similar condition, and carrying on down'. The members of these groups, which in other wills expressly included also doctors and notaries, came to be defined as 'second class *poveri vergognosi*'.[102] Such directives as Bogetti's were clearly a response to the exclusion of these non-noble impoverished rich from the Company's new provisions for deciding who was to be defined as shamefaced poor. Although the regulation which put nobility acquired through office on a par with established noble families as preferred beneficiaries was only formally laid down in 1734, a year after Bogetti's will, there are several reasons for believing that the changed definition of *povero vergognoso* had already been applied for several years. In 1730 Ignazio Gabuto, a representative of the ennobled bureaucrats, had in fact already mentioned in his will the 'regulations which have been introduced or are to be introduced' by the Company concerning 'who shall be truly considered such' (i.e. *povero vergognoso*).[103] Moreover, in 1719, the distinction between first and second class shamefaced poor was already being applied in 1719 to applicants to the House of the Soccorso, the institution for girls and young women run by the Company.[104]

Over the coming years with the boom in donations to *poveri vergognosi*, Bogetti's clear wording became a model for many other benefactors from the same merchant and professional background. Bogetti's instructions were also imitated in wills which provided funds for spiritual exercises, which increased considerably during this period. The beneficiaries were sometimes occupational groups, elites in the area of the benefactor's feudal lands, or even kinship groups.[105] The late development of assistance to *poveri vergognosi* in Turin is a further indication that large sections of the elites were now increasingly anxious to set up forms of group-defence in order to counter-balance their loss of power and prestige.

[101] The wills of Count Pietro Paolo Leone di Leynì, 28.4.1745 (ASSP, Rep. Lasc. 161) and Gio Francesco Bossone, 27.11.1756 (ibid., 160).
[102] See for example the first will of the doctor Carlo Amedeo Alberito, 13.12.1730 (Ins. 1730, l.3), and the donation by Pietro Francesco Bosso, 13.2.1781 (ASSP, Rep. Lasc. 160).
[103] ASSP, Rep. Lasc. 161, 5.9.1730. See also Alberito's will mentioned in previous note.
[104] Ibid., Soccorso.
[105] Gio Francesco Spatis, Count of Casalgrasso, Lombriasco, Corveglia and Moriondo, and Baron of Villareggia, left the Compagnia di San Paolo his sole heir on condition that they organised every year two series of religious ceremonies lasting eight days for the people born in the villages on his feudal estates or resident there for at least ten years (ASSP, Rep. Lasc. 162, 2.8.1773). Paola Racchia, widow of Campana, instructed the Padri della Missione (who had taken over the Jesuits on their suppression) to accept four family members every year for religious ceremonies (AOC, Cat. IX, Chiesa e Camposanto 1665–1882, 4.5.1771).

This widespread sense of impotence had another important consequence: the family and kinship group acquired particular significance in this period as beneficiaries of legacies reserved for particular groups. This is without doubt a new phenomenon. Until a few years earlier it would have been unthinkable to mention explicitly that the benefactor's relations might need to use the legacy themselves. Now, however, richer relations, or those without direct descendants, increasingly felt the need to provide for the poorer branches of their families by creating permanent trusts for a whole variety of purposes. Reserved places multiply in institutions assisting women and girls, but there are also funds for the education and training of boys, or for their religious careers, and funds for matrimonial or conventual dowries. The new importance of the family may in part have been caused by a democratisation of participation in charity, which brought in benefactors who were from social groups who were themselves at risk. However, this narrowing of the gap between benefactor and beneficiary seems to have been mainly an effect of the general climate of insecurity. With the diminished opportunity to exercise patronage and, conversely, receive protection, the family identity acquired greater emphasis, and even distant and perhaps forgotten links were revived. Kinship became the guarantee against destitution, adversity and changes in fortune. The centralisation of charitable resources caused a return to more restricted forms of solidarity: not only dependent on occupation, the community and the immediate locality, but also and above all on the family.

But what is meant here by 'the family'? It is striking that the kinship group seen as relevant encompasses several lines of descent, as the following examples illustrate. In 1752 the apothecary Giuseppe Gianinetto left 20,000 *lire* to the Soccorso, on condition that it accommodated two daughters of his 'relations or descendants' in perpetuity: one had to be a descendant of Signor Vachiere, the benefactor's nephew through his sister, and the other had to be a descendant through either the male or female line from his deceased father-in-law, Giacomo Filippo Fiando. The merchant Giuseppe Bernocco left 21,000 *lire* in 1774 to the same institution for the maintenance of daughters between twelve and twenty years of age, giving preference to any descendants of his married sister, and his wife's brother and sister (i.e. the Mattieu, Vay and Demode families). The Boggios, husband and wife, founded a dowry fund in favour of their kinship group: they left 20,000 *lire* in 1751 to the Compagnia di San Paolo in order to pay every two years for a dowry of 1,200 *lire* (a far from modest figure) for the temporal or spiritual marriage of descendants of the husband's father, the wife's grandmother and the husband's paternal uncle, in that order. Daughters between twelve and forty years could be accepted but priority had to be given to the older applicants and the dowry could also be allocated to a daughter whose marriage had not yet been arranged – all instructions which attempted to avoid giving the dowry to anybody outside the family. Prior Beffa made the Ospedale di Carità his sole heir in 1763 on condition that for three years the income was to be set aside for the exclusive benefit of his relations whether through consanguinity or marriage, and not only by helping the destitute, but also by supplying clothes, dowries and money for a religious career or professional training. In subsequent years, his relations were still to be given priority.[106]

It is clear that the idea of 'family' now included female as well as male lines of descent. Whereas previously provisions in favour of the family were restricted to members of the patrilinear descent group, i.e. to all those bearing the same name, now all relations emanating from the household nucleus and the married couple were included (see for instance in the examples above the numerous provisions in favour of the descendants of sisters and in-laws). We find in this kind of charitable initiative a confirmation of the increased importance of the marital bond over patrilinear ideology that was observed when we analysed changes in female charitable behaviour during the eighteenth century (chapter 4). However, shifts in the destination of charity in this period also highlight a consequence of this re-definition of the family which has so far gone largely unnoticed: the new importance of the marital link brought about an expansion, and not, as one would be tempted to assume, a contraction of the kinship group. Whereas the system of patrilineage allowed the exclusion of all female relations who entered a different lineage and of the lines they contributed to perpetuate, the new situation in which kinship ties were defined in relation to the marital couple gave rise to a less selective and non-hierarchical perception of kinship. For there was parity within this new family pattern between the relations of each spouse in each marriage throughout the family history, and they were all eligible for equal treatment. Paradoxically, therefore, the growing focus on the marital couple, usually associated with the rise of the nuclear family and thus with a reduced role of kinship, multiplied kinship ties and obligations.

The tendency to found trusts for the benefit of kin became pronounced and began to be a source of concern to some. This is evident from the criticism it inspired in the Senate as early as 1730 and from the restrictive legislation included in the Royal Constitutions of 1770. These declared illegal all bequests or contracts establishing perpetual or temporary annuities to the benefit of descendants, relatives or others, and stated that legacies should be restricted to relatives within the first degree of kinship; moreover, these kinds of legacies should not exceed the sixth part of the estate when there was only one beneficiary, and the fourth part in case of several beneficiaries.[107] Apparently,

---

[106] Giuseppe Gianinetti's will of 30.4.1752 (ASSP Rep. Lasc. 161); Giuseppe Bernocco's will of 31.1.1774 (ibid., 160); agreement between the Boggios, husband and wife, and the Company of St Paul, of 4.6.1751 (Ins., 1751, l.6, vol. II); Prior Gio Antonio Beffa's will of 12.12.1763 (AOC, Cat. XV, Lasciti dotali, 33).

[107] *Ordinanza del Senato di Piemonte* of 5.7.1730 and Capo 3 of the *Regie Costituzioni* of 1770, clauses 3–4, in D., T. VII, pp. 165 ff.

provisions for the kin were attacked in as much as they were seen to constitute a 'new form of entailment', and an obstacle to the free circulation of property. It is reasonable to assume, however, that hostility towards these practices also reflected the state's anxiety over the increased role of kinship and the growth of interest groups. Indeed, the fact that the state and the royal family extended their role as patron in the second half of the century, setting up charitable funds and disciplinary institutions (discussed in the next chapter) to be used for the exclusive benefit of their protégés, can be seen as a reaction to this threatening phenomenon. Practices such as *lettres de cachet* and more generally the dispensing of 'favours' by which royalty intervened in the private troubles of respectable families, saving them from the dishonour of poverty and scandal, have usually been interpreted as attempts at creating a sort of 'fusion' between the subjects and their King, and at turning royal power into true paternal authority.[108] If considered in the context of the new importance acquired by informal systems of protection, however, the growth of these personalistic forms of royal patronage seems to point to the vulnerability of the monarchy rather than its strength: far from consecrating the undisputed authority of the King, it revealed the need for the monarchy and the state to engage in a kind of competition with kinship groups and other kinds of solidarity groups.

The nature of the systems of protection had changed dramatically from the 1730s on. The concentration of control over welfare resources and urban policies in the hands of state officials closed off the many vertical channels through which the poor had been able to obtain protection when a wider range of elites had access to control over institutions. This created a powerful sense of impotence and frustration amongst the non-bureaucratic elites, and widespread insecurity throughout the social fabric. The response was to create new forms of protection, and society fragmented into a myriad different identities, usually horizontal (linked to a profession, a trade or more especially a family or group of kin), which constituted a basis for tiny systems of mutual aid functioning through the direct control of limited resources. Patronage, which for a long time had been a widely accessible resource and therefore used flexibly, now became rigid and restricted, and directed above all through kinship ties. The rich increasingly confined themselves to looking after those who were close to them. Private charity had by this time created a more elitist welfare system, and resources were mainly channelled towards the *poveri vergognosi*. In this changed situation, the opportunities for the poor to obtain assistance were considerably diminished, and restricted to membership of a solidarity group. It is no accident that the urban working classes started in this context to set up their

---

[108] A. Farge, 'The honour and secrecy of families', in *A History of Private Life* (general editors P. Ariès and G. Duby), vol. III, *Passions of the Renaissance*, edited by R. Chartier, Cambridge, Mass. and London 1989.

own associations separate from their masters, with a clear intention of creating adequate funds to insure against adversity. More generally, this weakening of the ties of inter-dependence between the rich and the poor was to have repercussions on the stability of the entire social system and on public order, and was to lead to the emergence of direct class confrontation.

6

The state system of relief

Ambiguities in the government's poor relief policy

The second half of the eighteenth century witnessed a new development in the form of direct intervention by central government in poor relief administration. After 1750, several institutions (whose chief purpose was the repression of unruly and idle youth) were established as part of a government initiative, and for the first time were placed under the immediate control of state administrative bodies. Some of them, such as the Casa di Correzione (1757), the Ritiro del Martinetto (1776) and the Ritiro degli Oziosi e Vagabondi (1786), were placed under the jurisdiction of the Ministry of the Interior for crucial matters such as the admission and release of the inmates and their length of stay, while the day-to-day running of the institutions was entrusted to one or more governors appointed by the king.[1] The Casa delle Forzate (1750), for women who were considered to have exposed their families to scandal, was placed under the authority of the *Vicariato* (the office responsible for policing the city), the Ritiro di S. Gio' di Dio (1755), the workhouse for girls, under the supervision of the *Consiglio di Commercio* and the Istituto delle Figlie dei Militari (1774), for daughters of the military, under the Ministry of War.[2]

It was not only the administrative arrangements of these new institutions which constituted a departure from tradition, but also their aims and intentions, and the manner in which they were financed. Firstly there was an inversion of the traditional policy of poor relief which had given priority to those conventionally regarded as deserving poor (the old, the very young, the infirm and single women). The new institutions now directed their energies towards

---

[1] AST, p.s., Segreteria Interni, 'Corrispondenza relativa OO.PP.', reg. 244, 245, 273; ACT, c.s. 6067, 'Copia de' Regolamenti . . . per la casa di correzione', 1786; D., T. XIII, p. 833, 'Piano di Regolamento pel ritiro delle donne di mala vita', September 1787.

[2] D., T.III, pp. 1534–5, 'Regie Patenti colle quali S.M. commette al Vicario . . . ', 29.10.1751; ibid., T.XVI, p. 352, 'Regie Patenti colle quali S.M. approva . . . ', 7.9.1758; ibid., T.XIII, 'Regolamento pel ritiro delle figlie de' militari', 6.7.1779, pp. 285 ff.

young people and able-bodied adults, sections of the community previously ignored by welfare policy. So the composite community of the old hospital for the poor was replaced by a homogeneous, youthful and mainly male population. Secondly, these state-run establishments were genuine workhouses centred around the institution's workshop. While it is certainly the case that the inmates of relief institutions had always been involved in some form of productive activity, there can be little doubt that these government initiatives now formed part of a comprehensive economic policy. The declared objective was to counter the devastating effects of unemployment and proletarianisation which was affecting both urban and rural workers in the last decades of the eighteenth century. The new institutions were to spread a knowledge of simple productive processes among the poor. Typically these would involve all members of the family, were easy to learn, and required small amounts of capital for equipment and raw materials, such as wool, hemp and *moresca* (a by-product of silk manufacture). It was hoped that this vocational training would extend the range of job opportunities open to the young and unemployed in the towns and that the new skills would also spread throughout the countryside, thus supplying the peasant family with another source of income over and above its meagre earnings from the land, and stemming the flood of rural poor into the cities. There was, in addition, a mercantilist side to the policy, for incentives were given to the industries concerned in the hope of keeping raw materials such as hemp and *moresca* – which had hitherto been exported – in the country. This raw material could be used to produce low-quality cloth and manufactured goods which would find an easy outlet amongst the poor themselves and could also be used for military and government orders (e.g. in the manufacture of uniforms etc.).[3]

Finally it should be emphasised that the poor relief policies developed in the second half of the eighteenth century by central government were not restricted to Turin itself; they were in fact seen as models that could be repeated in the various localities administered by the state. Within a few years of their establishment, some of the workhouses in the capital (such as the Ritiro di S. Gio' di Dio and the Ritiro degli Oziosi e Vagabondi) set up branches in other parts of the kingdom. Moreover, as has already been pointed out, the project for *congregazioni di carità* which was originally drawn up in 1717, but had remained largely on the drawing board, was taken up again in this period. This led to the foundation of hospices for the poor in the principal towns of the kingdom.[4]

---

[3] These government projects and experiments are documented in some detail by Ghiliossi, the head of the *Consolato*, in his account: 'Mezzi per provvedere ai mendici volontari e necessari ed agli operai i quali si ritrovano disoccupati . . . ', 1788 (B.R., St. Pat. 879).

[4] Chierici and Palmucci, 'Gli Ospizi'.

The government's attempt to introduce the necessary structures to deal with poverty within each locality also signalled its determination to combat the increasing problem of wandering beggars, and the disorders associated with vagrancy. Government policy in the second half of the eighteenth century was in fact largely inspired by anxiety about public order. Poor relief was not only organised to meet the increased demand for assistance caused by changes in the labour market, but to cope with the need to control a population which was now being commonly referred to as turbulent and dangerous. As far as women were concerned, the new focus on public order meant that for the first time, institutions were established with the aim of eliminating street prostitution; their inmates were therefore the most destitute women, and no longer just daughters of good family who had happened to fall on hard times.

The growing feeling that the poor were becoming ungovernable was also responsible for the increasingly repressive character of the internal life of charitable institutions in this period, for these were now required to teach discipline as well as a skill. For the first time, even the institutions to which admission was voluntary became places of confinement where the inmates were segregated from the outside world and subjected to a prison regime. As we shall see, the message of control and intimidation was also expressed in the architecture of these institutions in the last decades of the century.

State intervention therefore brought about a complete change in the perception of the aims of welfare. The new institutions were understood as providing training for the discipline of labour, rather than assistance. Their purpose was to attack the roots of the material and moral conditions that created poverty, and not merely to mitigate some of poverty's consequences. While it is true that this policy was innovative in its systematic approach to social problems such as unemployment, public order, juvenile delinquency and prostitution, it also had the effect of destroying the benevolent attitudes traditionally shown by charitable institutions to the poor, and transformed them from places of voluntary refuge into places of coercion and confinement.

This shift also affected the way in which the new institutions were financed; for they never made any of the traditional appeals to private charity. Indeed they took great pride in the fact that they were totally independent from this insidious type of funding. As enterprises devoted to the public good, they were seen as meriting the support of the state, which had in fact supplied all the funds required for their foundation. It was thought rather naively (especially in the early period of these experiments) that they would be able to maintain themselves entirely from the proceeds from the sale of goods produced by the inmates.

This elimination of private funding and interference completed the process (which had been under way for some decades) whereby poor relief was removed from the control of the laity. What was the impact of these developments on the poor? It is too often assumed that the transfer of welfare to the state was advantageous to the destitute since central control of resources signified a policy which responded more to the needs of the poor rather than to the needs of one's soul or one's social standing. Consequently it tends to be implied that there was a more impartial distribution of poor relief, and that the inconsistencies inherent in a privately funded system were overcome.[5] However, the situation in Turin shows the need to reconsider this somewhat simplistic optimism. Careful analysis shows that of the various new institutions created by the government towards the end of the century many were in fact concerned with privileged sectors of the community and attempted to reinforce the state's role as patron and provider of protection. Indeed, together with the increase in provisions for dealing with idle youths and prostitutes (part of wider-ranging economic and public order policies), this period also witnessed an increase in the use of charitable resources to maintain the status of specific social groups and families, and to fund the government's strategy of rewarding loyalty and service in public office and the army. Admission to these forms of aid was still highly personalised, but now it was monopolised by central government; privilege did not disappear but became more selective, favouring those employed by the state. At the same time, the treatment of the destitute poor was itself extremely ambivalent. Welfare institutions were in fact pursuing policies which contributed in the ongoing process of concentration of industrial activity – a key factor in the impoverishment of the labouring classes.

Finally, it should not be forgotten that during this period welfare policy was considerably influenced by social and cultural changes within the elites. The new view of poverty as inseparable from its social and economic causes, and the method employed to fight it – based as it was on the collection and analysis of data and long-term schemes – served to justify claims to scientific management of public welfare and thus to endorse the new role acquired by government officials. In other words innovations in policy also contributed to the aggrandisement of this increasingly influential class, whose identity was now founded solely on service to the state. The advantages of the new policy for the needy, on the other hand, were at the very least ambivalent, for the concentration of power in the hands of a group of professional administrators was also responsible for undermining the ties of obligation which had existed between the elites and labouring people; and this created a particularly critical situation for the poor.

---

[5] This Weberian tendency to consider public and state control as superior to private and local has pervaded much of the most influential literature on charity. See for instance Webbs, *English Poor Law History*, part I, *The Old Poor Law*, pp. 425–6. For a discussion of this literature, J. Barry and C. Jones (eds.), *Charity and Medicine Before the Welfare State*, London 1991, introduction.

From charities to workhouses

The first institution that typified state intervention in the second half of the eighteenth century was the Ritiro di S. Gio' di Dio, usually referred to as 'delle Rosine' after the name of the first superintendent. It was founded in 1755 under the direction of Rosa Govona (an expert in several forms of manufacturing who was already managing a similar poorhouse in her Piedmontese hometown of Mondovì), and admitted young girls between thirteen and twenty-five, who were then employed in spinning and weaving wool, and producing cloth, gloves, socks and silk ribbons.[6] The originality of Rosa Govona's manufactory consisted in its being the first institution for girls from the lower classes modelled on existing establishments for girls of better social position. Unfortunately we do not know what induced the young girls to enter the institution or to be sent there by their families. It is quite possible that they were socially isolated and destitute, as the institute's second name would suggest ('Ritiro delle Povere Figlie Raminghe e Abbandonate' – 'shelter for wandering and abandoned young women'). Further evidence of the humble social backgrounds of the inmates is the fact that on admittance they were only asked to pay 35 *lire* for their clothes and linen, for this was only a quarter of the sum required as the minimum dowry among the poorer classes.

The idea of providing destitute girls with a skill which they could continue to practise elsewhere immediately caught the attention of the governors of the hospital of S. Giovanni – who perceived this initiative as the means of getting the foundlings for whom they were responsible back into the community. As a result of population growth and the increased incidence of infant abandonment, the hospital of S. Giovanni was having problems in placing all its foundlings. The traditional system had been apprenticeship for the boys and marriage for the girls, or alternatively employment of both girls and boys as nursing staff in the hospital's medical wards. But this had become woefully inadequate and the hospital was overcrowded with adolescents who had been returned from the villages to which they had been sent for wet-nursing (where they stayed until the age of ten) and for whom no employment was to be found. In 1755 the hospital and Rosa Govona's institution concluded a mutually advantageous agreement which guaranteed the latter a substantial contingent of inmates with which it could commence its manufacturing activity. The hospital contracted to send a first consignment of fifty girls to the Ritiro and to send more as they were returned from their wet-nurses, up to a maximum of 200. The male foundlings were housed in a separate building called the Opera di Pietà which could take up

6 On the Rosine institutions, see C. Danna, *L'Istituto Creato da Rosa Govona*, Turin 1876; P. Matta, *Breve Monografia del Regio Istituto delle Rosine*, Turin 1889; C. Turletti, *Vita di Rosa Govona, Fondatrice del Regio Istituto delle Rosine*, Turin 1896.

to a hundred.[7] The boys were employed in the manufacture of hats and scarves as well as in the same activities carried out by the girls. The fact that there were twice as many girls as boys partly reflected the relative numbers among abandoned children, given the preference for abandoning girls and the higher death rate among infant boys.[8] Another factor was the greater difficulty experienced by the hospital in placing the girls.[9]

In the event, however, the agreement with the hospital of S. Giovanni only remained in force for five years. By 1760, arguments over selection had led to its breakdown, since Rosa Govona wished to reject all children returning from their wet-nurses who were sick or unfit. The hospital took back all the girls and shortly afterwards all the boys.[10] From that time on Rosa Govona's institution only recruited girls and exclusively from outside the hospital. The episode highlights the extent to which concern with productive efficiency was central to the new institution, and how this clashed with values upheld by more traditional hospitals like S. Giovanni.

In spite of the failure of this original arrangement, the Ritiro expanded very quickly. Two years after its foundation, it had 170 inmates, and this figure increased to 230 in the 1780s.[11] After the institution had been in operation for only two years it started to set up a network of subordinate institutions in various towns around Piedmont. Apart from Rosa Govona's original establishment in Mondovì, houses were founded in Fossano (1757), Savigliano (1758), Saluzzo (1760), Novara (1766), Chieri (1770), S. Damiano (1770) and Iglesias (1771).

If we are to believe the workhouse's own rhetoric, its success was due to the originality of its system of funding. For the first time in Piedmont, an institution claimed to be able to maintain itself simply with the proceeds of its inmates' work. It made no appeal to the generosity of benefactors, nor did it require a fee to be paid for the inmates, and from its foundation rejected all dependence on traditional forms of funding institutions. It adopted the rule that it could not accept 'any fixed fund or capital that came on the instructions of final wishes or any other order or endowment'.[12] In fact, however, the insistence on the

---

[7] D., T. XIII, pp. 662 ff, 'Ordinato della congregazione dell'Ospedale S. Giovanni col quale approva . . . ', 16.12.1755.

[8] The three two-year periods examined (1718–19, 1730–31 and 1752–53) show that the number of abandoned girls was higher by between 16 per cent and 18 per cent. S. Cavallo, 'Assistenza femminile e tutela dell'onore nella Torino del XVIII secolo', *Annali della Fondazione Luigi Einaudi*, vol. 14, 1980.

[9] Applications for adoption, for example (usually submitted by the family of the wet-nurse or at least by a family resident in the same community or area), occurred for about 30 per cent of the boys and only 10 per cent of the girls. Ibid., p. 135.

[10] D., T.XII, pp. 667–70, 'Ordinato della congregazione dell'ospedale di S. Giovanni in Torino, col quale determina . . . ', 17.5.1760.

[11] ACT, Collezione XII, 'Statistiche della Popolazione 1714–1832'.

[12] AST, p.s., LPqM, m.19 d'add., Fasc. 2, 'Testamento della signora Rosa Govona', 17.4.1768, and the *ordinato* of the hospital of S. Giovanni 16.12.1755, in D., T. XII, p. 662.

institution's self-sufficiency was mainly ideological, and was part of an attempt to take issue with the supposedly perverse nature of private charity and traditional models of welfare management, and to advocate the expansion of state control over institutions. This polemic against the kind of interference in institutional policy that private charity could bring was particularly appropriate at a time when, as we have seen, restrictive conditions increasingly accompanied charitable acts (in the attempt to stem further incursions by the state). The success of S. Gio' di Dio was, in reality, due to the significant privileges assigned to its manufacturing activities. The Ritiro was favoured with regular work from government commissions,[13] and benefited above all from exemption from the usual inspection by the guilds. These inspections aimed at limiting competition between producers and at making sure that standards of quality were observed. The Ritiro was released from these traditional controls and placed under the direct supervision of the *Consolato*, the central supervisory body for manufacturing and commerce, which adopted a much laxer attitude.[14] This made it possible to contravene guild regulations which, especially in periods of low demand, imposed a redistribution of orders amongst the various workshops in the city and fixed the maximum number of looms for each manufacturer in order to avoid the creation of large manufacturing units. The institution was also able to place on the market lower quality products than those permitted by the guilds and to ignore regulations concerning pay and treatment of the workforce.[15]

There can be little doubt that the activities of the Ritiro and its subsidiaries contributed to the process of industrial concentration and to the break with corporatism which were responsible for the violent disputes that were unleashed between artisans at the time. While it was true that the new welfare initiatives were intended to deal with the problems of poverty and unemployment, they also represented an important instrument in the reorganisation of manufacturing industry, which was one of the principal causes of the hardships afflicting urban society.

Not surprisingly, the privileges and freedom from guild controls that were granted in this period to state institutions provoked considerable hostility amongst the citizenry. The Ritiro was at the centre of a great deal of controversy, and indeed surrounded by such 'regrettable slander' that it was threatened with closure. The protests came from 'traders and artisans' as well as the 'bodies that possessed or lived by alms' – the older charitable institutions – for whom

---

13 An example of this favouritism in the granting of contracts for military supplies can be found in 'Stato della quantità di Panni e Ratine assegnata ai sottonominati fabbricatori . . . ', 21.4.1781, in AST, sez.I, Commercio, Categ. IV, m.12.

14 OPCB, m.239, 'Regolamento per le manifatture nell'Opera del raccoglimento e ricovero delle povere figlie . . . ', 9.7.1756.

15 Complaints about the quality of products manufactured by the Ritiro were very common. For example, ibid., LPqM, m.20, 'Stato dei beni ed effetti . . . e delle rendite e negozi delle figlie'.

the Ritiro's claims to self-sufficiency appeared to constitute a provocation.[16] The citizens were also shaken by the betrayal of the institution's original intentions. At the beginning the initiative had been presented as a means of providing work and a place where poor girls in the city could go, even on a daily basis, to earn some money for themselves and their families, while learning a trade that they could then exercise elsewhere. In practice, however, it appeared to many as a place of exploitation rather than training for a trade. The young women were in fact subjected to a life of hard work and total confinement and were not allowed to quit and find another situation. The institution's rules even stipulated that permission to leave was entirely the supervisor's decision, and that she would only grant it when she was sure that the girl requesting it was 'free from all risk of danger'.[17] The indignant protests of the time prove that a long and in practice coercive confinement was the general rule. In the 1770s, the Bishop of Saluzzo complained that 'the girls are kept in total subjection and discomfort, they are never allowed to express their own feelings, and are unable to marry, enter into service in a private house, or to take up a trade or art other than the one they are carrying out'.[18] The evidence of Margarita Doy suggests that the only way to leave the institution was to run away, since she justified her escape by saying that: 'she feared that the same would happen to her as to the other girls who had either died under the burden of hard work and harsh treatment, or had left the institution having spent their best and most vigorous years without earning a penny'.[19]

Confinement, exploitation and coercion were, in short, the real reasons for the Ritiro's success. Even the growth of subsidiary institutions in other towns took place at the expense of the workforce since, once the girls were trained and able, their release into society was endlessly postponed if they were considered suitably qualified to help in the setting up of new establishments. At the same time, however, the policies adopted at the Ritiro clearly show that marriage as the obligatory destiny for women was by now no longer the rule in the way that it had once been and that new career opportunities as instructors and teachers were opening up for them. It was no accident that, unlike previous institutions for young girls, the Ritiro did not contemplate any provision for dowries which would have enabled its inmates to marry. The local parish registers record only two marriages of girls from the institution over a ten-year period.[20] The break

---

[16] Ibid., Fasc. 6, Plico 2, 'Nuovo, sorprendente e vivamente contraddetto è stato l'impegno in cui si è messa Rosa Govona . . . ', 26.2.1760.

[17] D., T. XIII, p. 309.

[18] LPqM, m.15 d'add.

[19] Ibid., m.16, Fasc. n.n., 'Lettere del Prefetto e Vescovo di Saluzzo riguardanti la condotta di Margarita Doy', 1771.

[20] Parrocchia della Gran Madre di Dio, 'Libro dei matrimoni della parrocchia di S. Marco e Leonardo', II and IV (decade 1755–65).

with tradition represented by the Ritiro and its aims related not only to its abandonment of the paternalism and tolerance which, up to that time, had typified the attitudes of institutions towards their inmates. An important aspect of this 'revolution' was also the scarce concern which the institution showed for the future of its charges, or at least the very different destiny it envisaged for them.

The institutions change their architectural form

In the middle of the century, the state-run institutions were still in an experimental stage and, because of their unpopularity, their future was also uncertain. This was reflected in their buildings. Initially the new institutions did not make substantial investments in construction, and they rented modest buildings which had often been designed for other purposes. They would only be capable of buying a small house after a few years, and then would expand slowly, constantly adapting the building to new requirements and to the growing number of inmates. For example, the Ritiro di S. Giò di Dio was initially housed in the small convent which originally housed the order of friars of the same name. The Istituto delle Figlie dei Militari was established in 1774 with two, and then four, rented rooms. It was not until 1783 that the institution was able to purchase the house on two floors with fourteen rooms that they had rented since 1778. In the case of the House of the Forzate, hostility towards the royal initiative actually made it impossible to find rented accommodation. In the end the King donated a building originally used as a dye-works, but it was another ten years before the administrators started restructuring it.[21]

For a long time, therefore, the new institutions maintained a modest and anonymous appearance which reflected the difficulties encountered by the state in attempting to impose a policy which broke completely with the values that had guided poor relief for centuries. After the grandiose period of the Ospedale di Carità and the hospital of S. Giovanni, which were built in the previous century, welfare architecture did not produce any single work of any importance until the last decades of the eighteenth century. It was only then that the break with paternalistic and charitable traditions was expressed visually in the Ritiro del Martinetto, an institution for prostitutes (1776), and in the Ritiro per gli Oziosi e Vagabondi (Retreat for the Idle and Vagabonds) (1786).

The first thing that strikes us about these two institutions is that for the first time they were housed in isolated buildings outside the city. The Ritiro per gli Oziosi was established in the house which had been used for spiritual retreats

---

[21] OPCB, m.219, Fasc. 12, 'Informativa del primo Presidente della Camera al Primo Segretario degli Interni', 13.10.1747; D., T. XIII, p. 85, 'Lettere Patenti con le quali S.M. cede un sito con fabbrica . . . ', 9.10.1750.

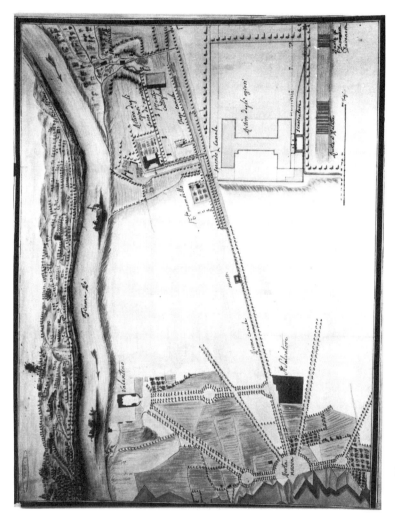

Plate 14. Ritiro degli Oziosi e Vagabondi, location (on the right hand-side the city walls) (ACT, Cart.39, Fasc.1, Dis.21).

organised by the Jesuits (which fell vacant when the order was suppressed), and which had been constructed away from built-up areas in order to foster the contemplative life (plate 14). The institution for prostitutes was housed in a proto-industrial complex originally used for the production of cheese, in the region of Martinetto outside the city. As with other government institutions, these two retreats both used existing premises, but for the first time they were completely restructured for their new function before any of the inmates were allowed to enter. The amount of expenditure which the government decided to invest in these ventures demonstrates its new-found commitment to tackling the problem of the poor. It also shows the importance attached to the physical appearance of the buildings and their symbolism. The Martinetto project set aside 14,150 *lire* for restructuring a house that had cost 12,000 *lire*.[22] In the case of the ex-Jesuit retreat, the predicted cost even exceeded 100,000 *lire*.[23] The latter had only been constructed in 1713 and refurbished some seven years previously, in 1779; the extensive nature of the alterations was not therefore due to deterioration of the building, but demonstrated the desire to carefully organise the available space and give the institution a definite image.

The external appearance of the new institutions, as well as the location, radically differed from the seventeenth-century palace-like hospitals. Typically the new building was humble and free from the slightest decoration, the bare and linear facade immediately conveying its message of intimidation. As occurred elsewhere in Europe, this welfare architecture was charged with moral connotations.[24]

Measures were also taken to isolate the inmates completely. The building was entirely surrounded by a wall, and provided with a large courtyard and enclosed garden to allow the taking of fresh air in controlled conditions. The chapel now became an internal structure for the exclusive use of the Ritiro, and was no longer open to members of the public. This represented a break with the baroque hospital's chapel which was one of the most popular places in town for offering prayers for the dead.[25] The new institutions had no links with life in the city. They were no longer places of worship, and no longer contained artisans' workshops or rented rooms. The sole purpose of the buildings was to provide shelter (or more precisely, imprisonment) to the poor. As contacts with the outside world were explicitly banned, the traditional tolerance of the comings and goings of both inmates and visitors disappeared and the gates stayed firmly

---

[22] ACT, C.S. 6066.
[23] Ibid., C.S. 6067.
[24] R. Evans, *The Fabrication of Virtue. English Prison Architecture, 1750–1840*, Cambridge 1982.
[25] The fact that the Ospedale di Carità was obliged by legacies to celebrate over 11,000 masses for the dead every year shows how widely used its chapel must have been. AOC, Cat.IX, Parte I, Chiesa dell'Ospizio, busta 1, fasc.19, 'Stato delle messe a carico del Regio Spedale della Carità di Torino'.

closed. Guards stood sentry over the Ritiro degli Oziosi. Originally plans had
even been drawn up for a cavalry company which would patrol the institution
in order 'to avoid any disturbances that could arise due to the great number of
people being confined', and provision had been made for a stable to house thirty-
two horses.[26]

The fifty or so women 'of ill-repute' held in the Martinetto were sent there
after having been arrested during the night and having had their heads shaved in
the courtyard of the city's prison.[27] They were kept at the Martinetto for a year
for the first offence, and for longer periods for successive offences. Like the
inmates at the Ritiro degli Oziosi, they were employed full-time in working
hemp and *moresca*. The manufacturer Carlo Ghiglione directed work at both
institutions. The Martinetto provided treatment for syphilis as well as trying to
correct the women's scandalous life-styles. A surgeon and his assistant resided
permanently at the institution, and divided the infected, who were given the
mercury-based salivation treatment, from the healthy ('who will probably be
very few').[28] The prospect of receiving free treatment, a diet rich in protein and
a period of convalescence may have made confinement less abhorrent. The rules
even provided for the voluntary admission of women wanting to be cured,
but we do not know how many found this offer attractive enough to make use of
it.

At the Ritiro degli Oziosi, the element of coercion was also predominant. The
institution included a section for detainees (for up to 350 inmates) in which
young people between the ages of twelve and twenty-five years who 'were
shown by definite proof to be layabouts and vagabonds' were detained for a
period of at least five years, and another section (in light in plates 15 and 16) for
young people of respectable social origins arrested on the request of their
families 'should these have reason to fear that a child or relative of theirs was by
stubborn licentiousness about to bring a respectable family into disrepute'.[29]
According to the original plans, there was to be another section, next to these
two, for voluntary admission. The Ritiro had been conceived as a long-term
project for combating unemployment and an institution which would also
attract the poor outside. In the periods of greatest economic hardship,
unemployed workers were invited to engage in manufacturing work in the hemp

[26] ACT, C.S. 6067, 'Indice generale per le Quattro Tavole esprimente il Progetto per la Riduzione
della Fabbrica di Esercizi Spirituali . . . ', 12.1.1786, table II, c.20.
[27] LPqM, m.19 d'add., Fasc. 1, 'Non è necessario credo di far lungo ragionamento . . . '. On the
Martinetto or 'Ospizio Celtico' in general, ACT, C.S.6067, 'Copia dei Regolamenti . . . per la
Casa di Correzione', 1786, pp. 129–30.
[28] 'Progetto del marchese Pallavicino Vicario di Torino per un Ritiro delle Donne di mala vita'
(LPqM, m.19 d'add., Fasc 1). The surgeon was paid a fixed sum for each woman under
treatment.
[29] 'Copia de' Regolamenti . . . ; per la Casa di Correzione'; D., T.XIII, pp. 840 ff., 'Regolamenti
della casa di correzione per gli oziosi e vagabondi', 1792.

and *moresca* workshops at the Ritiro, in exchange for which they were to receive food, a bed for the night and a modest payment.[30]

According to optimistic government reports, the initiative was effective in containing unemployment. For example it was claimed that in 1787 the institution gave work to 1,200 unemployed workers each month, enabling them to maintain their families.[31] Moreover, about 800 women were engaged in spinning *moresca* at the farmhouse near the Ritiro and received 8 *soldi* for each pound of yarn.[32] We must, however, be cautious about such one-sided accounts; it would appear from a letter of protest drawn up by workers that very few wished to join in the initiative, discouraged as they were by the miserable living conditions at the Ritiro. The inmates claimed that they only received two bowls of rice soup and a pound of bread a day, and no payment, 'not even enough to buy a flask of wine and tobacco, visit the barber's, or get a shirt washed'.[33] In spite of the official claims, it is very probable that voluntary admission to the Ritiro was extremely limited, and that it was principally a place of detention. The great majority of the inmates came under one of the categories targeted by public order measures taken in the late 1760s – measures which reinforced the association between indolence and criminality. The patrols charged with policing the city four times a day were now also expected to arrest young idlers found playing certain games, probably linked to gambling (billiards, *laschine* and *carrozzino*), who were presumed 'petty thieves', and anybody in possession of a knife or any other prohibited arm, as well as able-bodied beggars.[34]

The discipline imposed on the inmates throws further doubt on the claims that the institution assisted the unemployed on a temporary basis. According to the regulations introduced in 1786, 'a metal legging with a ring' had to be attached to the detainees in the Ritiro, so that when they were working and when they were in bed, they could be chained to a ring secured to the wall.[35]

The discipline and control over the organisation of institutional life appears to have been extremely harsh compared with institutions in the mid century. The organisation of internal space is worthy of particular attention, because it seems to have been mainly concerned with preventing large gatherings of inmates both by day and by night. Plans exist for the three floors of the Ritiro degli Oziosi; and for the basements we have a description of rooms although no plans.[36] It is

[30] AST, p.s., Commercio, Cat. 4, m.21 da ord., 'Regole per l'esecuzione del progetto di somministrare le moresche ai filatoglieri disoccupati della città', no date (but 1788 or 1789).
[31] B.R., Storia Patria 879, 'Mezzi per provvedere ai mendici volontari . . . ', 1788.
[32] AST, p.s., Commercio, Cat. 4, m.21 da ord., Fasc. 32, 'Filatoieri disoccupati . . . '.
[33] Ibid., 'Memoria rimessa il 1.12.1787 al Conte Corte . . . '.
[34] Ibid., LPqM, m.19, Fasc. 30, 'Memoria con un piano circa l'arresto di mendicanti validi e invalidi, oziosi e vagabondi . . . ', 20.5.1766; ibid., Fasc. 3, 'Il Marchese Pallavicino Vicario ordina . . . ', 14.5.1776.
[35] 'Copia de' Regolamenti . . . per la Casa di Correzione'.
[36] ACT, Cart. 63, Fasc. 3, Drawings 1–4.

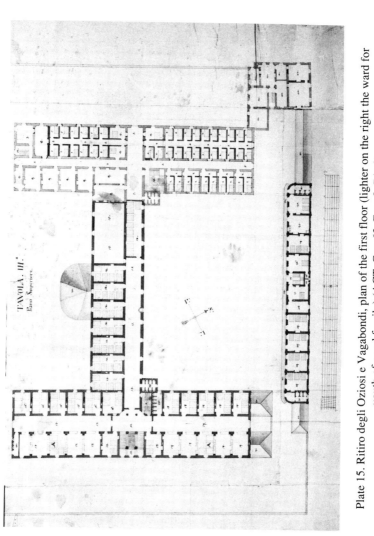

TAVOLA. III.ª
Piano Superiore.

Plate 15. Ritiro degli Oziosi e Vagabondi; plan of the first floor (lighter on the right the ward for youth of good family) (ACT, Cart.63, Fasc.3, Dis.3).

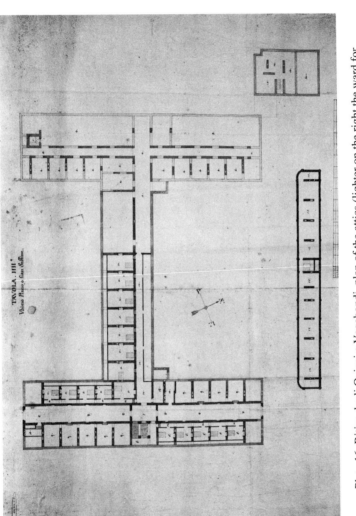

TAVOLA. IIII.ª
Ritiro Ozioso e Vagabond.

Plate 16. Ritiro degli Oziosi e Vagabondi, plan of the attics (lighter on the right the ward for youth of good family) (ACT, Cart.63, Fasc.3, Dis.4).

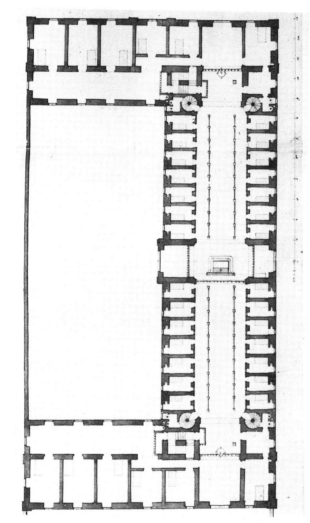

Plate 17. 'Plan for a house of correction to be built outside the city', plan of the first floor (ACT, Coll.SI, s.D. 1573).

possible, therefore, to reconstruct the purposes to which rooms were put on all four floors. The rooms were relatively small: they were able to accommodate between eight and twenty people, but in the larger rooms there were partitions that divided them into cubicles (plates 15–16). It is interesting that a cellular structure was by then typical of this kind of institution; in fact we find the same pattern in the rival project for the Ritiro which was not carried out (plate 17).[37] Even access to the chapel was designed to prevent gatherings of inmates in the vestibule: separate access was provided from all floors, dormitories and wards. It seems possible that the fragmentation that characterises the workshops was motivated by a concern to prevent rioting, and not just by the requirements of the organisation of work. Only the small section for inmates 'of good family' (which could take up to fifty young men) had a large workshop on the ground floor. The main part of the Ritiro could hold 350 inmates, and contained small workshops on both the ground floor and the top floor which were used by those in particular dormitories. The only exception to this pattern was the workshop for the production of canvas in the basement. So whereas in previous hospitals for the poor, different functions were divided according to floor (in the Ospedale di Carità for example the canteens, dormitories and manufactory were on three separate floors), this was now replaced by a division into small rooms for work and for rest situated near each other. The absence of any reference to canteens in the registers and plans would lead us to believe that gatherings were not even allowed at mealtimes, and that the food was distributed to each floor.

The gulf between institutions for the poor planned in the late eighteenth century and the model which had prevailed up until the early decades of the same century can clearly be seen in the sobriety of the buildings, the isolation from city life, the organisation of living space and the internal regime. The institutions lost even the outward appearance of benevolence so typical of the baroque hospital; they were no longer the voluntary domicile of the poor nor were they magnificent meeting-grounds for different classes, where the rich celebrated their own munificence as they ritually dispensed patronage and protection to the poor. The new buildings were reduced to the function of controlling and intimidating a populace which was now perceived as dangerous and alien.

New definitions of poverty in the second half of the eighteenth century

Tendencies similar to those discussed above are to be found in the wider framework of the urban welfare system. The existing hospitals show an increasing concern for the behaviour of their residents – who come to be perceived as a threat. This leads to a change from the paternalism and tolerance of the previous

---

[37] ACT, Coll. Simeon, s.D, Disegni 1572–3, 'Ergastolo progettato farsi fuori Porta Nuova', Architect Mario Ludovico Quarini.

period to a more repressive policy. In the 1770s, new regulations were introduced into the Ospedale di Carità, which made it more difficult for residents to maintain contacts with the outside world and, in general, imposed a more rigid discipline. The inmates were subject at all times of the day to surprise inspections, and were controlled by a network of overseers and their assistants and by what are explicitly referred to as 'spies'.[38] In the same period, the hospital of S. Giovanni introduced rules which for the first time laid down explicitly how ex-foundlings living in the hospital – carrying out duties in the infirmary, kitchen, laundry or looking after the younger children – should behave (in reality most of the rules applied to girls) when they became the responsibility of the hospital and were employed in maintaining its services. The new rules sought above all to restrict the possibility of leaving the building: the girls could only do so as part of a group of at least twelve, and under the supervision of an assistant governess. Girls were also supervised when they went to the river to wash clothes, and they were prohibited from choosing a confessor from outside the hospital 'in order to remove the pretext for going out'.[39]

Accompanying these changes in the regime of institutions, there was a shift in the categories of the poor singled out for attention: by now, even traditional welfare agencies concentrated more on young able-bodied adults. From the 1760s, the largest hospital, the Ospedale di Carità, progressively changed the nature and pattern of its work. First of all, there was an extension of the duration of assistance; the hospital now provided for families over longer periods and not just in emergencies, as had been the case a few decades earlier. Relief to families remained linked mainly to difficult moments in their lives or to incidental factors (such as illness, death or the absence of one of its members) which upset the delicate balance between consumers and producers inside the family. The hospital's clientele had mainly consisted of single people, widowed heads of households and wives in charge of families due to the absence of their husbands. From the 1760s onwards, however, the number of 'normal' families (i.e. a male head with wife and numerous offspring) among the recipients started to increase. The reasons for dispensing relief also changed, and references to sickness became less frequent compared to references to a 'larger family' or shortage of work. Up until the 1740s and 1750s, the poor rarely received charity for more than two years, while it now became a permanent source of support for many households. Particularly in the 1770s and 1780s, it became common for families to receive bread for over ten or even twenty years. Furthermore, outdoor relief (the distribution of bread and payment to wet-nurses to feed and look after babies in numerous families) took on massive proportions; outdoor aid was increasingly granted to poor families, in addition to the more traditional

---

[38] AOC, Cat. III, Ordinati, 28.7.1774.
[39] AOSG, Cat.1, Cl. 3, 'Regolamenti e istruzioni 1602–1896', Fasc. 2, 1772.

policy of admitting some of the children, or old or disabled members of the family, into the hospital itself.[40] The families receiving bread from the hospital every week totalled 1,287 in 1785, whereas there had been only 187 of them in 1758, 379 in 1766 and 874 in 1782.[41] In the same period the number of children for whom the hospital paid a wet-nurse increased enormously. According to the regulations, the institution was obliged to provide a wet-nurse only when the mother had a declaration by a doctor or surgeon that she was producing no milk of her own. But this condition does not appear to have been binding. From the 1770s, even three or four children from the same family were often wet-nursed at the cost of the institution, and this practice confirms the long-term relationship which had developed between poor families and the hospital. It is also interesting that it became increasingly widespread for a mother to be paid a sum in cash for the cost of wet-nursing her children, rather than having them sent to wet-nurses hired by the hospital, as had been the custom for many centuries. This development may have been simply due to the practical difficulties caused by organising the wet-nursing of what was by now an enormous number of new-born babies, but it could also represent the spread of the idea that families had a right to financial assistance for each child born – which could then be used either to pay a wet-nurse or to subsidise the family budget if the mother was breast-feeding.[42]

These developments represented a significant shift in policy. They replaced a definition of poverty as triggered by natural causes only (sickness, social isolation, the death or absence of a family member) with one that took into account social factors (unemployment, low wages, shortage of work). In some ways, therefore, the typical beneficiary of the poor relief dispensed by the Ospedale di Carità was becoming more and more similar to the young unemployed who attracted the less benevolent interest of the new workhouses.

The social and economic changes taking place in both the country and the towns in the second half of the eighteenth century are essential to a full under-standing of the new policy on poor relief. In the countryside, the introduction of new forms of farm management caused a reduction in the number of small-holders and tenants, forcing them to become wage labourers and to abandon the land.[43] Emigration ceased to be seasonal and limited to certain areas, as in the past, and became a mass phenomenon: beggars and vagrants no longer necessarily came solely from the weaker sections of society (old people and children), but also came to include a great number of able-bodied young

40 Cavallo, 'Conceptions of poverty', pp. 189–93.
41 AOC, Cat. IV, Part I, 1, 'Ricoverati e poveri: 1715–1864'; LPqM. m. 16 d'add., Fasc. 5, 14, 27; OPCB, m. 237, Fasc. 16.
42 AOC, Cat. VI, 'Libri dei Baliaggi: 1760–1801', vol. 654 and 658.
43 Cf. G. Prato, 'L'evoluzione agricola nel secolo XVIII e le cause economiche dei moti del 1792–98 in Piemonte', in Mem. Acc. Sc. Tor., Series II, vol. LX, 1909.

men.[44] But the urban working classes were also suffering from impoverishment; a long period of depression hit the artisans in the 1770s and 1780s (particularly in the silk industry, where a large section of the city's workforce was concentrated), and the plight of urban labourers was worsened by serious inflation in the 1770s.[45]

However, the difficulties faced by the urban workforce were not solely determined by short-term factors, but also arose from permanent structural change that had been taking place for several decades in the organisation of traditional craft industries, causing considerable social conflict. Since the 1730s trade had become increasingly concentrated in the hands of an oligarchy of merchant-manufacturers, and an attack had been launched against the guild constraints which attempted to enforce the sharing out of work amongst the various masters so as to ensure the survival of small workshops.[46] From that time on, there was bitter conflict between the smaller masters and the merchants, which should be seen as a clash between strong and weak producers, with the latter trying to avoid the separation of sales from production, but gradually being reduced to the status of dependent producers in the service of a handful of powerful merchants.[47]

The following decades saw the breakdown of the traditional organisation of labour and of the hierarchy regulating who could perform a particular task. Many journeymen were reduced to the condition of casual worker or day-labourer, masters were employed as wage-earners, and mere apprentices carried out work previously the domain of journeymen.[48] It is clear that these changes worsened the economic position of the artisan and undermined his status. Young men, in particular, were affected by the growing instability and turnover in the labour market, and they found it increasingly difficult to enter a higher rank (many apprentices often being sacked before they had completed their time). Nor were the poorer masters above resorting to improper practices in an attempt to bolster their weakening position. Consequently, disputes multiplied in the second half of the eighteenth century not just between richer and poorer producers, but also between masters and journeymen, and between journeymen and apprentices.

These transformations had their effects on the guilds and on craft associations.

[44] On the nature of emigration in the early decades of the eighteenth century, see Levi, *Centro*. For the harsher measures taken against vagrancy, see Balani, *Il Vicario*, pp. 157 ff.

[45] Prato, *La Vita Economica*; Woolf, 'Sviluppo economico'.

[46] For a summary of these defensive measures, see AST, p.s., Commercio, Cat. IV, m.10, Fasc. 4, 'Parere sopra le provvidenze . . . ', 1773.

[47] An outline of these conflicts can be found in E. de Fort, 'Mastri e lavoranti nelle università di mestiere tra Settecento e Ottocento', in A. Agosti and G. M. Bravo (eds.), *Storia del Movimento Operaio, del Socialismo, delle Lotte Sociali in Piemonte*, Bari 1979, vol. I; for the silk industry, see AST, p.s. 'Commercio', Cat. IV, m. 7, 8 and 9.

[48] See for instance 'Ricorso di trecento circa giovani lavoranti di stoffe d'oro . . . ', 1741 (ibid., m. 8, Fasc. 21).

From the late 1730s, the guilds began to fragment, creating a variety of distinct groupings expressing particular sectoral interests within the craft. Especially striking is the tendency of the journeymen to set up separate horizontal organisations in an attempt to create a separate identity for themselves and to provide funds for mutual aid. Early examples of this trend are to be found in the granting of authorisations to raise funds to assist sick and out-of-work waged members of a particular craft. In 1736–37, the stocking weavers, cobblers, hatters and printers were all authorised to have their own patron saint independent from the masters.[49] At this time, there was still a benevolent attitude towards initiatives of this kind, a benevolence which was subsequently eroded; a few decades later, the goldsmiths were refused permission to set up their own company, as were the silk weavers in 1771. Even when presented as associations confined to religious and charitable purposes these initiatives met with opposition. In the second half of the century, tailors, locksmiths, wigmakers and silk workers were prohibited on several occasions from celebrating their saint's day and from making a collection on behalf of needy members. Such gatherings were now described as occasions for 'disorder and incitement', for 'encouraging one another to change masters' and for instigating 'a factious and independent spirit'.[50]

The measures against journeymen's gatherings testify to a now consolidated identity that set them apart from and in conflict with other levels of the craft. Journeymen were able, in this period, to impose rights such as 'Saint Monday' and the payment of *fricasse* – a sum which every apprentice had to pay to the journeymen on commencing his apprenticeship, a custom which can be interpreted as a symbolic attempt to re-establish control over the labour market and reaffirm boundaries between journeymen and unqualified apprentices.[51]

Urban society in the second half of the eighteenth century was characterised not only by a situation of economic deprivation but also by an unprecedented climate of insecurity and social conflict. Quite apart from the economic crisis of the 1770s and 1780s and the unemployment that this caused, and apart from the new emigration from the countryside, more complex changes were also taking place which undermined established relations between elites and labouring classes, and created new antagonisms between social groups. Economic developments, combined with restrictions on the traditional spheres of patronage (due to the centralisation of power and prestige in the hands of state officials), helped to erode the web of interdependence which held together the different

[49] D., T. XVI, pp. 875, 995 and 1164. De Fort, 'Mastri e lavoranti', p. 105.
[50] Ibid., p. 119; AST, p.s., Commercio, Cat. IV, m. 10, Fasc. 3, 'Sentimenti dell'avvocato Graneri sulla supplica dell'Università dei mastri', 27.11.1771.
[51] The royal edict which laid down penalties for holding 'Saint Monday' was issued on 24 March 1783. On the *fricasse*, see 'Relazione dell'Illustrissimo Conte di Pralormo per levar l'abuso delle Fricasse . . . ', 1771 (BR, Storia Patria 907).

levels of the social hierarchy. In this alarming situation of social conflict, the change in poor relief policy would appear to be more of an emergency package than a coherent plan to combat unemployment. The exponential increase in the assistance given by the Ospedale di Carità to the able-bodied poor on the one hand, and the criminalisation of idle youth on the other, were two aspects of a policy which aimed to maintain control over a population which was increasingly perceived as dangerous and unfettered by the ties of patronage.

Another consequence of this unravelling of the social fabric was, as previously mentioned, the fragmentation of the welfare system into a series of micro-systems for protection of one's own group. So the same fragmentation of identity and solidarity found within the crafts was also evident in the way in which charity was distributed. Although, after decades of acute conflict, the management of charitable institutions had passed into the hands of government officials, private benefactors had managed to retain substantial control over how funds were spent.

It should be stressed that the state did not resist this concession to corporatism, but took part in the practice just like any other interest group or powerful family. We have already observed this behaviour in relation to the places controlled by the government at the Provvidenza. This particularistic management of 'public' resources became more pronounced in the closing decades of the century: many of the new institutions created by central government in this period were exclusively for their own employees.

The clearest examples of state-sponsored particularism are the institute for the Figlie dei Militari and the Convitto per Vedove e Nubili di Civil Condizione which were set up in the 1770s and 1780s expressly for the daughters and widows of the military and civil servants. The former accommodated eighty daughters, aged between eight and eighteen, of soldiers who were either in service or had died in war. The founding of this institution was part of a moral campaign which the government was carrying out to change the barracks into a purely male preserve by eliminating the presence of families and female partners.[52] The intention was to provide the daughters with moral, religious and vocational education (they were employed in working *moresche* and embroidering in both wool and gold for the troops) far removed from the risks inherent in a military environment. If the possibility of marriage arose, the daughters could hope to obtain one of the four dowries which the institution made available each year.[53] It should be stressed that in order to be admitted to the institution, the girls had to obtain a letter of recommendation from the

[52] OPCB, m. 221 ult. add., 'Piano dell'ospizio delle Figlie dei Militari che convivono nei quartieri', *c*.1775. For living conditions in the army, see S. Loriga, *Soldati. L'istituzione militare nel Piemonte del Settecento*, Venice 1992.
[53] LPqM, m.18 d'add., Fasc. 4.

commander of the regiment in which the father had enrolled – testifying to his merits as a soldier. Girls who had lost their mothers were also preferred.[54]

As its full name suggests, the Convitto provided shelter both for widows of noble or distinguished families, who 'wished to live there (paying a small rent), in order to defend their status, in order to economise or because of economic strictures or in search of solitude', and for 'daughters [unmarried women] of mature age whose position the public perceives to be like that of a widow'.[55] A modest payment (250 *lire* per year) was in theory required for admission to the institution, but a list of residents after 1788 shows that in the majority of cases the fee was paid by a state body or a member of the royal family. Moreover, the great majority of the residents were widows and daughters of state officials or army officers.[56]

The government used these two institutions to satisfy material needs arising from old age and solitude and protect the honour of social groups favoured by the state. This policy created areas of consensus and dependence, while enhancing the image of a morally honourable ruling class. The state had started to take on the role of patron and defender of the reputation and decorum of distinguished families somewhat earlier. In the 1750s, several houses of correction had been established specifically for members of respectable families. The Opera delle Forzate had existed since 1750, and this institution held young women 'distinguished by birth' whose scandalous and undisciplined behaviour endangered both their and their family's reputations. About a dozen women (they were all adult women aged between twenty-eight and sixty) were detained there, of whom we know nothing except their Christian name and age.[57] The internment of these women was in fact surrounded by mystery; arrests were carried out in great secret and with little respect for the due process of law. The decision was taken directly by the *Vicario* (the chief of police) in person on the basis of a private petition, and was exempted from the requirement for a full investigation, in order to avoid publicising the event and causing public scandal.[58] The concern over keeping the identity of the internees hidden explains why they were always referred to by their Christian name in the institution's records, and why their files were actually burnt when they left.[59]

The abuses to which such practices could give rise were evident to

54 'Regolamento pel ritiro delle figlie de' militari'.
55 OPCB, m. 228, Convitto di vedove nobili e di civil condizione, 'Regolamento provisionale', 1786. The institute also admitted a small number of daughters for their education (for an annual fee of 185 *lire*) 'in order to give the residents the satisfaction of seeing a young relation being educated in their company, or even educating them themselves'.
56 OPCB, m.228, Convitto di vedove nobili e di civil condizione, 'Convittrici ammesse sotto il Regio Governo'.
57 LPqM, m.18, Fasc. 5, 1761.
58 D., T. XIII, pp. 1534–5, 'Regie Patenti colle quali SM commette al Vicario . . . ', 29.10.1751.
59 ASSP, 252, Ordinati del Deposito, 9.5.1780 and 1.12.1783.

contemporaries and disapproved of by some. One of the King's councillors made an unsuccessful proposal to review the arrest procedure, arguing strongly for the need to compile 'very convincing proof, because it might be that a husband who has become bored of his wife, or a parent-in-law who had tired of the daughter-in-law, could easily imply terrible calumnies in order to be rid of her'.[60] By authorising these arbitrary arrests, the government was clearly conniving in some murky business in order to marginalise women who, for whatever reason, represented a threat or a nuisance to a respectable family.[61]

The male equivalent of the Istituto delle Forzate was the Casa di Correzione, founded in 1757, where about twenty 'unruly' youths of good family were detained secretly on request from their relations.[62] (Its role was taken over in 1786 by the Ritiro degli Oziosi where, as we have seen, a separate section was set up for young men 'of good family'.) As in the case of the Forzate, the families paid an annual fee (in this case 180 *lire*) for the inmates' food, clothing, medicine and medical expenses in case of serious illness.

A description of the institution's inmates in 1771 allows us to draw the profile of the internees.[63] They were mainly between fifteen and twenty-one years of age, with only the occasional thirty-year-old or even forty-year-old recidivist. The most frequent justifications for confinement were an idle life-style spent in gambling and frequenting hostelries, squandering the family fortune, and abandoning the paternal home, school or the profession chosen by the father. Despite the lack of information on the inmates' social origins, there can be no doubt over their respectable background: they were trained for professions such as surveyor, and their fathers (master wig-makers and cheese-mongers, shop-keepers, etc.) belonged to the craft or trade elite. The more detailed information we have on at least one of the internees confirms the impression that some of them came from families connected with the royal household, and that their private affairs were a matter for concern, being perceived as potentially damaging to the image of the court milieu itself. Giovan Battista Ugo, the son of the Financial Officer of the Royal Park, was said to have been admitted because his family 'which enjoys his Majesty's protection' would suffer particularly from the son's 'grave excesses'.

The register also records the length of detention, which ranges from six months to three years, with an average stay of about a year and a half. The period of detention was not decided at the beginning, but depended on the behaviour of the detainee. The family, however, had a crucial role in determining the length

[60] OPCB, m.221, 'Sentimento del Signor Conte Benzo', 22.10.1751.
[61] There is a clear analogy between these practices and the French *lettres de cachet*. See A. Farge and M. Foucault, *Le Désordre des Familles. Lettres de Cachet des Archives de la Bastille*, Paris 1982; Farge, 'The honour'.
[62] 'Saggio de' Regolamenti per la casa detta Scuola di Correzione', 1757 (OPCB, m.223).
[63] AST, p.s., Segreteria Interni, 'Corrispondenza relativa OOPP', reg. 273, 1771–1816.

of stay. Not only was the release to be decided upon by agreement with parents or relatives on the basis of observable 'signs of repentance', but often it was delayed because of the difficulty allegedly encountered by the family in finding a suitable arrangement or occupation for the detainee. Clearly, in many cases families were in no hurry to resume responsibility for their difficult relation and the fact that the institution offered no resistance to keeping them demonstrates the extent to which it served the interests of family dynamics.

The organisation of charity undoubtedly underwent profound change during the second half of the eighteenth century. New measures were taken to assist the able-bodied poor but it would be wrong to think that these constituted the only face of state intervention and that they represented a victory for a concept of poverty based on need. Privilege still played a crucial role in the definition of poverty. Many central government initiatives in this interventionist period were a means of reinforcing the resources of state patronage. There has been a pervasive tendency, in historical studies as well as in the literature on social policy, to accept unquestioningly the claims of professionalism, impartiality and rationalism associated with the assertion of central control over welfare. This study has suggested that centralisation did not bring with it more equitable forms of protection, nor did it eradicate the sectoral interests and favouritism found in traditional or private administrations. Government control simply signified a shift in the nature of privilege in favour of state 'clients', in particular state employees – thus confirming the mantle of dignity that was by then associated with bureaucratic service. Far from being a non-patron, the state can be said to have assumed the role of super-patron in this period.

Conclusion

In this concluding section I would like to draw together some of the main themes and arguments which have emerged from my study of Turin, focusing in particular on those which might most fruitfully be pursued in relation to other urban contexts. In addition, I would like to move beyond the immediate scope of this book and briefly consider ways in which some of the implications of my findings could be explored in related fields.

The discovery that organised and well-established policies towards the poor existed in Turin well before the Savoyard restoration suggests that there is less of a gulf than has perhaps been assumed between the sophisticated organisation of charity in the Italian cities with a strong tradition of self-government and the provision for the poor available in cities such as Turin, whose local governments have often been portrayed as mere reflections of feudal relations. Turin's City Council and the urban elite which ran it in the fifteenth and sixteenth centuries were much less passive and subordinate actors than this traditional interpretation might lead one to suppose. It is clear, in fact, that measures for the relief of the poor which were adopted by the municipality in this period placed Turin firmly within the mainstream of European social policy. While unsuspected similarities thus exist between the kind of provision made in cities such as Venice, Milan or Florence and those made in Turin, it also becomes evident that in a number of crucial ways the Turinese experience should be seen as quite distinct from that which characterises the other cities.

We may point to the fact first of all that in Turin, a thriving system of charity controlled by the municipal government lasted well beyond the Renaissance. Indeed, civic provision for the poor became more extensive and more sophisticated in the later sixteenth century, precisely when similar municipal systems were supposed to have died out as a consequence of the decline of autonomous local governments and the expansion of central control. This suggests that the authority and jurisdiction of the City were consolidated rather than eroded in the early phase of the rise of central government and we have seen, in fact, that the conflict between the two powers left the municipal government in a strong position, with its role in important areas of life considerably enhanced.[1]

Turin seems to challenge the pattern found in other Italian cities not only in terms of the chronology of these developments but also in terms of the forms of assistance which were typical. In Turin, with the exception of the Compagnia di San Paolo, the confraternities – usually seen as one of the main agencies of charity in the Italian system of assistance to the poor – are notable for their absence from the charitable scene. There were a dozen confraternities in the city, but they mainly concerned themselves with devotional activities and only acquired modest charitable functions in the eighteenth century, when a few of them were endowed with funds providing one or two dowries a year. However, these dowries mostly went to members of the benefactor's family, or to members of his trade or profession.[2] It is true that the Compagnia di San Paolo does not conform to this pattern, and played a very significant part on Turin's charitable scene, but it was an organisation which differed considerably, both in terms of its size and financial resources, from all other confraternities in the city. I doubt that this large and influential body can be adequately described as a mere association of devout laymen; it seems, rather, to have provided a principal arena for the exercise of power in the capital. The label 'confraternities' clearly embraces religious associations which were very diverse in nature, and the undeniable role that these played in Italian religious and, at times, political life does not always imply that they also had a significant impact as dispensers of charity.

Another phenomenon which figures prominently in accounts of Italian measures towards the poor – the early development of policies of confinement of beggars and institutionalisation of the sick – also seems to be absent from Turin. Up until the mid seventeenth century, in fact, both custodial and medical institutions in the city were establishments of very modest size; residential care represented only a minor part of overall provision whereas outdoor relief was the prevalent form of assistance. My findings thus cast doubt on the view expressed by Geremek, and endorsed by others, according to which the system of *renfermement* as a solution to the problem of begging first developed and

---

[1] These findings are in keeping with those of some recent studies which have looked afresh at the relationship between urban and central governments in this period. For example P. Benedict (ed.), *Cities and Social Change in Early Modern France*, London 1989, in particular the article by R. A. Schneider. For an Italian case, F. Benigno, 'La questione della capitale: lotta politica e rappresentanza degli interessi nella Sicilia del Seicento', *SS*, 47 (1990).

[2] These provisions can thus be seen as an expression of that 'privatised' form of charity which, as described in chapter 5, was widespread precisely in the eighteenth century. A list of confraternities and of the charitable funds some had at their disposal is given by Cibrario, *Storia di Torino*, vol. II and by Martini, *Storia delle Confraternite*. There were fourteen funds in all, administered by five confraternities and providing around twenty dowries a year. Ten of these fourteen were set up in the eighteenth century.

became widespread in Italy from the fifteenth century on – that is, almost two centuries before it did in France. Certainly, in the case of Turin, not only do hospitals for beggars not appear before the mid seventeenth century but an analysis of their function demonstrates how reductive it is to see them as simply the expression of a policy of *renfermement*. Such institutions did not eliminate but became, in part, instruments of the system of outdoor relief that was to remain an important form of welfare provision throughout the period examined. Furthermore, entry into them remained predominantly voluntary until the middle of the eighteenth century. Rather than being organised according to some centralised attempt at social engineering, these institutions appear to have been governed far more by the pressures placed on their resources by the community (from the requirements of the poor for welfare to those of the rich for opportunities to enhance their status and influence). Only in the second half of the eighteenth century did Turinese institutions for the needy come to resemble more closely the image so often ascribed to them, as places for the confinement and disciplining of the poor. Even at this point, however, the increased element of coercion was not indiscriminate but aimed at a particular group, namely the idle and criminal young who were perceived as a threat both by the family and by society at large. In the case of the old, children and family units on the other hand, more traditional outdoor relief and a greater proportion of welfare resources were made available precisely during this period. In other words, not even with the growth of central control over institutions did these become purely a means of social control; rather, they continued to interact with the needs and fears of the community.

I do not believe that the features described so far are specific to Turin. In many other Italian cities, too, the importance of institutional care was very modest in the fifteenth and sixteenth centuries, and even in part of the seventeenth century. This is true also with regard to the sick poor. Even in a city like Venice, which was notable for its initiatives towards the poor and for its dense network of institutions, residential care for the sick poor was for long negligible; in the mid sixteenth century only two hospitals accepted medical patients and only one of these took non-contagious patients (about twenty in 1556, in a city of 150,000), the other being devoted to syphilis sufferers and patients with skin diseases.[3] It is possible, then, that historians have extrapolated unjustifiably from the cases of Florence and Milan, and that 'the great hospital of the Renaissance' was an exception rather than the rule. The scale of residential care available in Italy may have been exaggerated, and other forms of relief neglected, as a result of the tendency to view hospital records as the obvious source for a history of poor relief and medical care. This institutionally based approach has been reinforced

---

[3] R. Palmer, 'L'assistenza medica nella Venezia cinquecentesca', in B. Aikema and D. Meijers (eds.), *Nel Regno dei Poveri*, Venice 1989.

in recent decades under the influence of Foucault's work which has turned all attention away from forms of assistance in the community. In the case of Turin, the creation of a system of medical outdoor relief in the later sixteenth century – which continued to expand until as late as the 1670s – has received scant attention in the historiography of the city, although many accounts discuss the activity of the city hospitals extensively. Even less attention has been paid to the compelling sense of civic identity and community that made non-institutional aid to the poor and sick appear as a civic duty well into the seventeenth century. It is possible that a similar bias has operated elsewhere, and that this has led to similar forms of provision being overlooked.

Analysis of Turin thus suggests the importance of paying more attention to sources of medical and poor relief outside the institutions; it also indicates a chronology for the development of the hospital as principal resort for the sick poor which needs to be tested against evidence from other cities. For a long time, Turin's medical hospitals seem to have been small establishments serving a relatively elite clientele (able to pay in order to gain admittance), rather than providers of free care. In addition, except in the case of syphilis patients, the hospitals were long-stay institutions, furnishing a response to social isolation rather than merely treatment for medical complaints. It may then be fruitful to shift the focus of attention from the Renaissance hospital to the Baroque hospital, and examine that great wave of hospital building which occurred in various parts of Europe from the mid seventeenth century on as the expression of a major transformation in the provision of medical care. What factors lay behind these new developments? In this book I have linked the appearance of large Baroque establishments for the poor and sick to an expansion of the composition of the elite and suggested that the newly emerging social groups, given their exclusion from existing avenues for the celebration of prestige, needed new opportunities for the public display of their status. I believe that this correlation between upward mobility and the explosion of a celebratory architecture, both residential and institutional, in the Baroque age is not specific to Turin. Certainly, the transformation of hospitals into the principal providers of medical relief also needs to be related to the wider use that members of the medical profession came to make of these institutions. In Turin, as elsewhere, there was from the second half of the seventeenth century on a major increase in the number of medical personnel (especially surgeons), and in their involvement in hospital life. However, an analysis of the process which brought medical practitioners into the hospitals would require an investigation into the changing characteristics of the medical profession and could not be undertaken here.

Another area on which my material from Turin can perhaps shed new light concerns policies aiming to preserve or restore women's honour. Refuges for fallen women or women in danger of falling have often been described in rather unchanging and ahistorical terms as attempts to control female sexuality. Important differences between such institutions have therefore been neglected in favour of a view which tends to present too uniform a picture of them. In Turin, institutions specifically for women continued to be set up throughout a period of over a century but it is clear that there were major changes in their nature and functions and in the kind of women they catered for. For a long time the women in these establishments continued to come from socially elite groups. Thus the declared aim of saving the honour of fallen women was applied almost exclusively to women from privileged social groups. Refuges do not seem to have accepted the kind of women who made up the majority of prostitutes – adult, unmarried and unprotected women of low social status. For the behaviour of such women damaged no one but themselves; it did not harm the name of distinguished family ancestors, nor the still vulnerable reputation of a late husband and his family. This close link between concern for women's sexual honour and concern for social honour implies that these institutions need to be seen (much more than has hitherto occurred) within the context of the rise and decline of elite groups and, accordingly, within the context of changing definitions of *povero vergognoso*. With few notable exceptions, assistance to those who were regarded as shamefaced poor is an area which has been neglected by research on charity, because it has been thought of as a limited phenomenon belonging only to a much earlier period. My research on Turin, however, has revealed the continuing importance of aid to the shamefaced poor throughout the period examined, and indeed has shown it to be particularly significant precisely in the eighteenth century, the period when a rationalisation of poor relief was supposed to have been introduced by the enlightened state.

Not until the late eighteenth century did the social groups targeted by institutions for women become differentiated, and society deem it necessary to set up institutions for the rehabilitation of ordinary prostitutes. It may be that prostitution at this time assumed such proportions that it appeared to represent a major problem of public order. It is also possible however that the emergence of disciplinary institutions for women of low social status reflected a shift in the meaning of honour or even a decline in the significance of this concept. A shift of this kind seems, in fact, to have been an underlying factor in another type of change which affected institutions for women. For a long time establishments for the social elite accepted women of very different moral, economic, marital status and age – a promiscuity which can only have been justified on the basis of the overriding importance of the fact that they were all in situations which put their honour at risk. At the beginning of the eighteenth century the institutions lost this promiscuous character and women inmates came to be classified and segregated along the same lines as men. This seems to suggest that for a certain period the notion of honour did function as a specific classificatory principle in organising women and it thus opens the way to a gendered analysis of stratification. Naturally, these hypotheses need refining and testing: nonetheless, they promise new possibilities for tackling the meaning of the association between women and honour. Although it is usually taken for granted that such a connection exists, the precise nature of the link has not been explored and tends to be treated as atemporal.

The need for an approach which takes more account of gender also becomes clear in the study of attitudes towards charity. The evidence from Turin shows that women's charitable activity differed significantly from men's, in particular in one of the periods examined, and that women undertook independent initiatives and shared a language specific to themselves. This contrasts with more usual interpretations of female charitable activity, which see it as a controlled exercise in autonomy within agreed limits, or even as a mere reflection of strategies decided on within the family.[4] These interpretations effectively portray female charity as an area where consensus was constructed, whereas my work on Turin suggests that it was a site of conflict, an arena in which women expressed the tensions they were subject to in the family, and one where they often went against what was expected of them.

The family conflicts in which women benefactors found themselves involved also provide interesting evidence regarding family patterns. In Turin, as elsewhere, there is evidence that, as the eighteenth century progressed, the nuclear family was gaining ground at the expense of the preceding ideology of the lineage, and there are signs of greater companionship between husband and wife. This confirms what many historians have written regarding the emergence of a more 'modern' family with values somewhat closer to our own. However, it should be pointed out that for women this change also involved both a loss of control over a share of property which had been clearly their own and a contraction of specifically female forms of self-expression, not least in the field of charity. This suggests that we should perhaps qualify the positive judgement which usually greets the emergence of the 'affectionate' family. In particular, we should desist from talking of 'the family' as though it was one undifferentiated object, and from considering changes in family patterns as having the same consequences for its various members.[5] At the same time, however, the full consolidation of the domestic family eventually brought about a shift in the

---

[4] Marshall, *Women in Reformation*. For the latter interpretation see the articles by L. Ferrante and by I. Fazio in L. Ferrante, M. Palazzi and G. Pomata, *Ragnatele di Rapporti. Patronage e Reti di Relazione nella Storia delle Donne*, Turin 1988.

[5] Only recently for instance a more gendered analysis has started to emerge of effects of changes in systems of inheritance and property. S. M. Okin, 'Patriarchy and married women's property: questions on some current views', *Eighteenth Century Studies*, 2 (1983–84); A. L. Erickson, 'Common law versus common practice: the use of marriage settlements in early modern England', *EcHR* 73 (1990); S. Staves, *Married Women's Separate Property*, Boston, Mass. 1990.

destination of property away from primogeniture and kinship ties defined by the male line. Instead there emerged a more equitable system of obligations within which members of the female as well as of the male line were considered as full kin. In this study we have observed a definite trend in this direction at least in wills drawn up by childless couples: in the second half of the eighteenth century they disposed of their property according to an idea of kinship which was comprehensive of all ties emanating from the marriage. Contrary to current assumptions, these findings also reveal an unexpected correlation between the rise of the companionate marriage and of a language of domesticity on the one hand and the expansion (rather than the attenuation) of a language of kinship on the other.

Finally, I would like to say a word about the general methodological approach which I have adopted in this book. In trying to find out what motivated a person to become involved in charitable activity, I have given particular importance to social dynamics and in particular to dynamics of conflict and to the effect that these had on the personal experiences of donors and other dispensers of charitable resources. I have indeed seen these dynamics as the chief determinant of different attitudes towards the poor and as a crucial stimulus to charitable activity. This approach would seem to be justified in so far as it has enabled me to establish a set of correlations – between what donors sought to gain from their charitable acts at different times and the different forms that their charity took – which might well apply elsewhere. To summarise, a link seems to have existed between the persistence of civic ideals and the prevalence of an impersonal type of charity; between the emergence of more 'personalised' forms of giving and patterns of intense social mobility; and, finally, between the prevalence of a 'privatised' type of charity and the restrictions placed on lay access to the control of institutions which resulted from the bureaucratisation of the exercise of power. I hope also to have convincingly explored a more differentiated notion of patronage and of the value that charity had for its dispensers than the one which frequently underlies discussions of the subject. The tendency so far has been to see personal motives for investing in charity and strictly 'humanitarian' impulses as mutually exclusive, and to take it that the latter account for the majority of charitable acts. Moreover, it is often assumed that one can talk of the personal interest of donors only if there is evidence of an obvious and concrete 'reward' for their benevolence. In this book I have suggested instead that an individual's personal circumstances *always* played a part in his or her motivations for charitable activity and that, even in the absence of more direct relationships of patronage, acts of charity could still have considerable symbolic or metaphorical importance. We have seen, therefore, how the meanings that charity embodied for benefactors and governors could shift, how giving could represent at different times an endorsement of civic identity mainly aimed at the rival power of the Duke; evidence of rank and status intended primarily as a message to a donor's peers and, finally, a means to preserve a share of institutional power from the attack of state functionaries.

The focus of this study has undoubtedly been on the donors and their motives for giving, and on changing definitions of poverty rather than on the actual recipients themselves. I hope, however, that on the way I have also succeeded in highlighting the shifts which took place in the nature of the resources which the poor could draw on. I am conscious of the gap that existed between the emergence of definitions of deserving poor at the level of official discourses of charity and the way in which the organisation of assistance changed in practice; similarly I am aware of the part played by the poor in determining the relationship between the two. Here, perhaps, we may at least have learned something about the changing nature of the 'languages' with which the poor had to engage in order to gain access to assistance – from the language of citizenship to that of the vulnerability of the female sex; from the language required to flatter the aspirations of the new rich, to that defining membership of one of those solidarity groups through which charity came to be distributed in the last period examined by this study.

Bibliography

Printed primary sources

Alessio B., *Vita della Serenissima Infanta Maria di Savoia*, Turin 1663

Arpaud M., *Vita dell'Infanta Caterina di Savoia religiosa del Terz'Ordine di S. Francesco*, Annecy 1670

Avvertimenti per la Cura de' Poverelli Infermi, nella Città di Torino, Turin 1680

Baldesano G., *La Sacra Historia di S. Mauritio Arciduca della Legione Thebea . . .*, Turin 1604 (second edition)

Borelli G. B., *Editti Antichi e Nuovi dei Sovrani Principi della Real Casa di Savoia*, Turin 1681

Cellario C., *Oratio Contra Mendicitatem Pro Nova Pauperum Subventione*, Louvain 1531

Codreto A. A., *La Fragranza dell'Amaranto. Istoria Panegirica della Serenissima Infanta S. Maria Figlia del Gran Carlo Emanuele*, Turin 1657

Codreto P., *Spreggio del Mondo. Vita e Morte della Serenissima Infanta D. Francesca Caterina Figlia del Gran Carlo Emanuele*, Mondovì 1654

Memorie di Alcune Opere Pie Fatte da Madama Reale Christina di Francia, Duchessa di Savoia, Regina di Cipro, Turin no date

Costituzioni per le Molto Reverende Monache del Monastero di Santa M. Maddalena Eretto in Torino . . ., Turin 1700

De Medina J., *De la Orden qu en Alqunos Pueblos de Espana se ha Puesto en la Limosina: Para Rimedio de los Verdadores Pobres*, Salamanca 1545

De Soto D., *Deliberación en la Causa de los Pobres*, Salamanca 1545

De Villavincencio L., *De Oeconomia Sacra circa Pauperum Curam*, Anvers 1564

Duboin F. A., *Raccolta per Ordine di Materia delle Leggi, Editti, Manifesti . . . Emanate dai Sovrani della Real Casa di Savoia sino all'8-12-1798*, 23 Toms, Turin 1818–69

Ferrero di Lavriano F. M., *Istoria di Torino*, Turin 1679

Fiocchetto G. F., *Trattato della Peste et Pestifero Contagio di Torino dell'Anno 1630*, Turin 1631

Guevarre A., *La Mendicità Sbandita Col Sovvenimento Dei Poveri*, Turin 1717

Guichenon S., *Le Soleil et Son Apogée ou l'Histoire de Christine de France*, Turin no date.

Harangue Funèbre de Madame Chrestienne de France, Duchesse de Savoie et Reyne de Cypre Prononcée par le R. P. De Barenne de la Compagnie de Jésus, Paris 1664

La Mendicité Abolie par un Bureau de Charité à Toulouse, Toulouse 1692

Ministero dell'Agricoltura Industria e Commercio, *Statistica del Regno d'Italia. Censimento degli Antichi Stati Sardi e Censimento della Lombardia, di Parma e di Modena*, vol.I, P. Castiglioni, *Relazione Generale con una Introduzione Storica sopra i Censimenti delle Popolazioni Italiane dai Tempi Antichi sino al 1860*, Turin 1862

La Police de l'Aulmosne de Lyon, Lyon 1539

La Police des Paouvres de Paris, about 1555, published by E. Coyecque in *Société de l'Histoire de Paris et de l'Ile de France Bulletin*, 15 (1888)

Regole e Costituzioni delle Reverende Monache del Terz'Ordine di s. Francesco, dette Convertite del Monastero di sta. M. Maddalena nella città di Torino . . . confermate da Monsignor Illustrissimo e Reverendissimo Arcivescovo Michele Beggiamo . . ., Turin 1671

Ricci G. B., *Istoria dell'Ordine Equestre de' SS. Maurizio e Lazzaro col Rolo delle Comende*, Turin 1714

Rouhault P. S., *Osservazioni Anatomico-Fisiche*, Turin 1724

Tesauro E., *Istoria della Venerabile Compagnia della Fede Cattolica Sotto l'Invocazione di S. Paolo*, Turin 1654 (enlarged edition 1701)

La Virtù Educata in Corte, Perfettionata nel Chiostro, Descritta dal Padre Fr. Alessio di Santa Maria, Carmelitano Scalzo, nel Doppio Stato Secolare e Religioso della Venerabile Serva di Dio Suor Anna Maria di S. Gioachino, nel Secolo Donna Caterina Forni, Turin 1692

Vives J. L., *De Subventione Pauperum*, Bruges 1526

Wyts G., *De Continendis et Alendis Domi Pauperibus et in Ordinem Redigendis Validis Mendicantibus*, Anvers 1562

Works of reference

Abrate M., *L'Istituto Bancario S. Paolo di Torino*, Turin 1963

'Elementi per la storia della finanza dello stato sabaudo nella seconda metà del XVII secolo', *BSBS*, 68 (1969)

Popolazione e Peste del 1630 a Carmagnola, Turin 1972

Allegra L., 'Modelli di conversione', *QS*, 78 (1991)

Anderson P., *Lineages of the Absolutist State*, London 1974

Andrew D., *Philanthropy and Police. London Charity in the Eighteenth Century*, Princeton, N.J., 1989

'Two medical charities in eighteenth century London', in J. Barry and C. Jones (eds.), *Charity and Medicine before the Welfare State*, London 1991

Appleby A. B., 'The disappearance of plague: a continuing puzzle', *EcHR*, second series, 33 (1980)

Arro F., *Del Diritto Dotale Secondo i Principi del Gius Romano e della Giurisprudenza dei Magistrati*, 2 vols., Asti 1834

Assereto G., 'Pauperismo e assistenza. Messa a punto di studi recenti', *ASI*, 141 (1983)

Assistance et Charité, Cahiers de Fanjeux 13, Toulouse 1978

Balani D., Carpanetto D. and Turletti F., 'La popolazione studentesca dell'Università', *BSBS*, 76 (1978)

Il Vicario tra Città e Stato. L'Ordine Pubblico e l'Annona nella Torino del Settecento, Turin 1987

Banker J. R., *Death in the Community: Memorialization and Confraternities in an Italian Commune in the Late Middle Ages*, Athens and London 1988

Barberis W., *Le Armi del Principe. La Tradizione Militare Sabauda*, Turin 1988

Barbero A., 'Savoiardi e Piemontesi nel ducato sabaudo all'inizio del cinquecento. Un problema storiografico risolto?', *BSBS*, 87 (1989)

'Una città in ascesa', in *Storia Illustrata di Torino* (ed. by V. Castronovo), vol. 2, *Torino Sabauda*, Milan 1992

Baron C. M., 'The parish fraternities of medieval London', in C. M. Baron and C. Harper-Bill (eds.), *The Church in Pre-Reformation Society: Essays in Honour of F. R. H. Du Boulay*, Suffolk 1985

Barry J. and Jones C. (eds.), *Charity and Medicine Before the Welfare State*, London 1991

Bataillon M., 'Juan Luis Vives, réformateur de la bienfaisance', *Bibliothèque d'Humanisme et Renaissance*, 14 (1952)

Beier A. L., 'Vagrants and the social order in Elizabethan England', *Past and Present*, 64 (1974)

Benedetto M. A., *Ricerche sui Rapporti Patrimoniali tra Coniugi nello Stato Sabaudo*, Turin 1957

Benedict P. (ed.), *Cities and Social Change in Early Modern France*, London 1989

Benigno F., 'La questione della capitale: lotta politica e rappresentanza degli interessi nella Sicilia del Seicento', *SS*, 47 (1990)

Bernard F., 'Les confréries communales du Saint-Esprit, leur lieux de réunions et leurs activités du Xe au XXe siècle dans la région Savoie Dauphiné', *Mémoires de l'Académie des Sciences, Belles-Lettres et Arts de la Savoie*, s.6, 7 (1963)

Bertelli S., *Il Potere Politico nello Stato-Città Medievale*, Florence 1978

Biraben J. N., *Les Hommes et la Peste*, 2 vols., Paris 1975

Bizzarri D., 'Vita amministrativa torinese ai tempi di Emanuele Filiberto', *Torino Rassegna Mensile*, 7–8 (1928)

'Vita amministrativa torinese ai tempi di Carlo Emanuele I', *Torino Rassegna Mensile*, 9 (1930)

Black C. F., *Italian Confraternities in the Sixteenth Century*, Cambridge 1989

Bloch C., *L'Assistance et l'Etat en France à la Veille de la Révolution*, Paris 1908

Blockmans W. P. and Prevenier W., 'Poverty in Flanders and Brabant from the fourteenth to the mid-sixteenth century: sources and problems', *AHN*, 10 (1978)

Blumenfeld-Kosinski R., *Not of Woman Born: Representations of Caesarean Birth in Medieval and Renaissance Culture*, Ithaca, N.Y. and London 1990

Bonenfant P., 'Les origines et le caractère de la bienfaisance publique aux pays Bas sous le règne de Charles Quint', *Revue Belge de Philologie et d'Histoire*, 5 (1926) and 6 (1927)

Hôpitaux et Bienfaisance dans les Anciens Pays-Bas des Origines à la Fin du XVIIe Siècle, Brussels 1965

Bonino G. G., *Biografia Medica Piemontese*, 2 vols., Turin 1825

Bordone R., '"Civitas nobilis et antiqua". Per una storia delle origini del movimento comunale in Piemonte', in *Piemonte Medievale. Forme del Potere e della Società*, Turin 1985

Borghesio G. and Fasola C., 'Le carte dell'Archivio del Duomo di Torino (904–1300) con appendice 1301–1433', *BSSS*, 106 (1931)

Bulferetti L., 'La feudalitá e il patriziato nel Piemonte di Carlo Emanuele II', *Annali della Facoltà di Lettere, Filosofia e Magistero dell 'Università di Cagliari*, 21 (1953)

'Sogni e realtà del mercantilismo di Carlo Emanuele II', *NRS*, 37 (1953)

'Assolutismo e mercantilismo nel Piemonte di Carlo Emanuele II', *Mem. Acc. Sc. Tor.*, series 3, T.II, 1953

'L'elemento mercantilistico nella formazione dell'assolutismo sabaudo', *BSBS*, 54 (1956)

Buttino M., 'Politics and social conflict during a famine: Turkestan immediately after the Revolution', in Buttino (ed.), *In a Collapsing Empire. Underdevelopment, Ethnic Conflicts and Nationalisms in the Soviet Union, Annali della Fondazione Feltrinelli*, Milan 1993

Caffaratto T. M., 'Mammane, levatrici, ostetriche', *Minerva Ginecologica*, 14 (1957)

'I primordi dell'insegnamento universitario dell'ostetricia a Torino e la figura di Michele Aliprandi', *Minerva Ginecologica*, 20 (1963)

Il Flagello Nero, Saluzzo 1967

'Storia dell'Ospedale Maggiore di Torino della religione e ordine dei SS. Maurizio e Lazzaro', *Ann. Osp. M. Vitt.*, vol. 22 (1979)

L'Ospedale Maggiore di San Giovanni Battista e della Città di Torino. Sette Secoli di Assistenza Socio-Sanitaria, Turin 1984

Calvi G., *Histories of a Plague Year*, Chicago, Ill. 1989

Carboneri N., *Ascanio Vitozzi. Un architetto tra Manierismo e Barocco*, Rome 1966

Carlin M., 'Medieval English hospitals', in L. Granshaw and R. Porter (eds.), *The Hospital in History*, London 1989

Carmichael A., 'Plague legislation in the Italian Renaissance', *BHM*, 57 (1983)

'Contagion therapy and contagion practice in 15th century Milan', *RQ*, 45 (1991)

Carpanetto D., 'La facoltà di medicina a Torino nel XVIII secolo', *Giorn. Acc. Med.*, 140 (1977)

'Gli studenti di chirurgia', in Balani, Carpanetto and Turletti, 'La popolazione studentesca'

Carutti A., *Storia del Regno di Vittorio Amedeo II*, Turin 1897

Casanova E., 'Censimento di Torino alla vigilia dell'assedio, in Regia Deputazione di Storia Patria, *Le Campagne di Guerra in Piemonte (1703–8) e l'Assedio di Torino (1706)*, Turin 1909, vol. VIII

Cavallo S., 'Assistenza femminile e tutela dell'onore nella Torino del XVIII secolo', *Annali della Fondazione Luigi Einaudi*, vol. 14 (1980)

'Strategie politiche e strategie familiari intorno al baliatico. Il monopolio dei bambini abbandonati nel Canavese, tra Sei e Settecento', *QS*, 52 (1983)

'Bambini abbandonati e bambini "in deposito" a Torino nel Settecento', in *Enfance Abandonnée et Société en Europe XVIe–XXe Siècle*, Rome, Collection de l'Ecole Française de Rome, 1991

'Conceptions of poverty and poor relief in Turin in the second half of the eighteenth century', in S.J. Woolf (ed.), *Domestic Strategies: Work and Family in France and Italy, 1600–1800*, Cambridge 1991

Cavallo S. and Cerutti S., 'Onore femminile e controllo sociale della riproduzione in Piemonte tra Sei e Settecento', *QS*, 44 (1980), reprinted in E. Muir and G. Ruggiero, *Sex and Gender in Historical Perspective*, Baltimore, Md. and London 1990.

Cerutti S., 'Corporazioni di mestiere a Torino in età moderna: una proposta di analisi morfologica', in *Antica Università dei Minusieri di Torino*, Turin 1987
'Cittadini di Torino e sudditi di Sua Altezza', in G. Romano (ed.), *Figure del Barocco in Piemonte. La Corte, la Città, i Cantieri, le Provincie*, Turin 1988
La Ville et les Métiers. Naissance d'un Langage Corporatif (XVIIe–XVIIIe Siècle), Paris 1990
Chaney E.,'"Philanthropy in Italy": English observations on Italian hospitals, 1545–1789' in T. Riis (ed.), *Aspects of Poverty in Early Modern Europe*, Stuttgart 1981
Chatelier L., *L'Europe des Dévots*, Paris 1987
Chiaudano M., 'La finanza del comune di Torino ai tempi di Emanuele Filiberto', *Torino Rassegna Mensile*, 7–8 (1928)
'La finanza del comune di Torino ai tempi di Carlo Emanuele I', *Torino Rassegna Mensile*, 9 1930
Chierici P. and Palmucci L., 'Gli Ospizi di Carità in Piemonte. Appunti per la lettura del fenomeno insediativo', in E. Sori (ed.), *Città e Controllo Sociale*, Milan 1982
Chiffoleau J., *La Comptabilité de l'Au-Delà: les Hommes, la Mort et la Religion dans la Région d'Avignon à la fin du Moyen Age*, Rome 1980
Chittolini G., 'Stati regionali e istituzioni ecclesiastiche nell'Italia centro-settentrionale del Quattrocento', in *Storia d'Italia, Annali 9, La Chiesa e il Potere Politico*, ed. by G. Chittolini and G. Miccoli, Turin 1986
'Cities, "city-states", and regional states in north-central Italy', *Theory and Society*, 18 (1989)
Ciammitti L., 'Fanciulle, monache, madri. Povertà femminile e previdenza a Bologna nei secoli XVI–XVIII', in *Arte e Pietà. I Patrimoni Culturali delle Opere Pie*, Bologna 1980
'Quanto costa essere normali. La dote nel conservatorio femminile di S. Maria Barracano a Bologna (1630–1680)', *QS*, 53 (1983)
Cibrario L., *Breve Storia degli Ordini di S. Maurizio e di S. Lazzaro Avanti e Dopo l'Unione Loro*, Turin 1844
Storia di Torino, 2 vols., Turin 1846
Cipolla C. M., *Public Health and the Medical Profession in the Renaissance*, Cambridge 1976
Claretta G., *Storia della Reggenza di Cristina di Francia, Duchessa di Savoia*, 3 vols., Turin 1868
Il Municipio di Torino ai Tempi della Pestilenza del 1630 e della Reggente Cristina di Francia, Turin 1869
Dell'Ordine Mauriziano nel Primo Secolo della Sua Costituzione, Florence 1890
Cognasso A., 'Cartario dell'abazia di San Solutore di Torino. Appendice di carte varie relative a chiese e monasteri di Torino', *BSSS*, vol. 44 (1908)
Cohen S., 'Asylums for women in Counter-Reformation Italy', in Marshall, *Women in Reformation and Counter-Reformation Europe. Private and Public Worlds*, Bloomington and Indianapolis, Ind. 1989
The Evolution of Women's Asylums since 1500, Oxford 1992
Cohn S. K. Jr., *Death and Property in Siena 1205–1800: Strategies for the Afterlife*, Baltimore, Md. 1988

The Cult of Remembrance and the Black Death. Six Renaissance Cities in Central Italy, Baltimore, Md. 1992

Comba R., *La Popolazione del Piemonte sul Finire del Medio Evo. Ricerche di Demografia Storica*, Turin 1977

Comoli Mandracci V., *Torino*, Bari 1983

Cooper J. P., 'Patterns of inheritance and settlement by great landowners from the fifteenth to the eighteenth centuries', in J. Goody, J. Thirsk and E. Thompson, *Family and Inheritance. Rural Society in Western Europe 1200–1800*, Cambridge 1976

Coppo S., 'L'edilizia assistenziale ospedaliera nell'urbanistica torinese del Sei e Settecento', in A. Cavallari Murat (ed.), *Forma Urbana e Architettura nella Torino Barocca*, 3 vols., Turin 1968

Cosmacini G., *Storia della Medicina e della Sanità in Italia*, Bari 1987

Courtenay W. J., 'Token coinage and the administration of poor relief during the late middle ages', *JIH*, 3 (1972–73)

Danna C., *L'Istituto Creato da Rosa Govona*, Turin 1876

Davidson N. S., 'Northern Italy in the 1590s' in P. Clark (ed.), *The European Crisis of the 1590s*, London 1985

Davis N. Z., *Society and Culture in Early Modern France*, Stanford, Calif. 1965
  'Poor relief, humanism, and heresy: the case of Lyon', *SMRH*, 5 (1968)

De Fort E., 'Mastri e lavoranti nelle università di mestiere tra Settecento e Ottocento', in A. Agosti and G. M. Bravo (eds.), *Storia del Movimento Operaio, del Socialismo, delle Lotte Sociali in Piemonte*, 2 vols., Bari 1979

De Gaudenzi T., 'Torino e la corte sabauda al tempo di Maria Cristina di Francia', *BSBS*, part 1, vol. 18 (1913) and part 2, vol. 19 (1913)

De la Roncière C. M., 'Pauvres et pauvreté à Florence au XIVe siècle', in M. Mollat (ed.), *Etudes sur l'Histoire de la Pauvreté*, 2 vols., Paris 1974

De Waal A., *Famine that Kills: Darfur, Sudan, 1984–85*, Oxford 1989

Dinges M., 'Attitudes à l'egard de la pauvreté aux XVIe et XVIIe siècles à Bordeaux', *Histoire, Economie et Société*, 10 (1991).

Donnison J., *Midwives and Medical Men: a History of Interprofessional and Women's Rights*, London 1977

Donvito L., 'La "religione cittadina" e le nuove prospettive sul Cinquecento religioso italiano', *RSLR*, 19 (1983)

Duparc P., 'Confréries du Saint Esprit et communautés d'habitants au moyen-âge', *Revue d'Histoire du Droit Français et Etranger*, s. 4, vol. 35 (1958)

Einaudi L., *La Finanza Sabauda all'Aprirsi del Secolo XVIII e Durante la Guerra di Successione Spagnola*, Turin 1908

Elton G. R., 'An early Tudor poor law', *EcHR*, 6 (1953)

Emmison F. G., 'The care of the poor in Elizabethan Essex', *Essex Review*, 62 (1953)

Erba A., *La Chiesa Sabauda tra Cinque e Seicento. Ortodossia Tridentina, Gallicanesimo Savoiardo e Assolutismo Ducale (1580–1630)*, Rome 1979

Erickson A. L., 'Common law versus common practice: the use of marriage settlements in early modern England', *EcHR*, 73 (1990)

Evans R., *The Fabrication of Virtue. English Prison Architecture, 1750–1840*, Cambridge 1982

Fairchilds C., *Poverty and Charity in Aix-en-Provence 1640–1789*, Baltimore, Md. 1976

Farge A., 'The honour and secrecy of families', in *A History of Private Life* (general editors P. Aries and G. Duby), vol. III, *Passions of the Renaissance*, edited by R. Chartier, Cambridge, Mass. and London 1989

Farge A. and Foucault M., *Le Désordre des Familles. Lettres de Cachet des Archives de la Bastille*, Paris 1982

Farr J. R., 'The pure and disciplined body: hierarchy, morality and symbolism in France during the Catholic Reformation', *JIH*, 21 (1991)

Fasano Guarini E., 'La politica demografica delle città Italiane nell'età moderna', in *La Demografia Storica delle Città Italiane*, Bologna 1982

Ferrante L., 'L'onore ritrovato. Donne nella Casa del Soccorso di San Paolo a Bologna (sec.XVI–XVII)', *QS*, 52 (1983)

'Malmaritate tra assistenza e punizione (Bologna sec. XVI–XVII)', in *Forme e Soggetti dell'Intervento Assistenziale in una Città di Antico Regime*, Bologna 1986

Ferrante L., Palazzi M. and Pomata G., *Ragnatele di Rapporti. Patronage e Reti di Relazione nella Storia delle Donne*, Turin 1988

Filippini N. M., 'Levatrici e ostetricanti a Venezia tra Sette e Ottocento', *QS*, 58 (1985)

'Gli ospizi per partorienti e i reparti di maternità tra il Sette e l' Ottocento', in *Sanità, Scienza e Storia*, 2 (1990) – 1(1991), *Gli Ospedali in Area Padovana fra Settecento e Novecento*, edited by M. L. Betri and E. Bressan

Fissell M., 'The "sick and drooping poor" in eighteenth century Bristol and its region', *SHM*, 2 (1989)

Patients, Power and the Poor in Eighteenth Century Bristol, Cambridge 1991

Flynn M., *Sacred Charity. Confraternities and Social Welfare in Spain, 1400–1700*, London 1989

Fosseyeux M., 'La taxe des pauvres au XVIe siècle', *Revue d'Histoire de l'Eglise de France*, 20 (1934)

Foucault M., *Folie et Déraison. Histoire de la Folie à l'Age Classique*, Paris 1961

Gabotto F., 'Le origini "signorili" del "comune"', *BSBS*, VIII (1903)

Gavitt P., *The Ospedale degli Innocenti, 1410–1536*, Ann Arbor, Mich. 1990

Gelfand T., *Professionalizing Modern Medicine. Paris Surgeons and Medical Science and Institutions in the Eighteenth Century*, Westport, Conn. and London 1980

Gélis J., *La Sage-Femme ou le Médecin. Une Nouvelle Conception de la Vie*, Paris 1988

Geremek B., 'Renfermement des pauvres en Italie (XIV–XVIIe siècle). Remarques préliminaires', in *Mélanges en l'Honneur de Fernand Braudel. Histoire Economique et Sociale du Monde Méditerranéen 1450–1650*, vol. I, Toulouse 1973

'La réforme de l'assistance publique au XVIème siècle et ses controverses idéologiques,' in *Domanda e Consumi Livelli e Strutture (nei secoli XIII–XVIII)*, Florence 1978

La Pietà e la Forca: Storia della Miseria e della Carità in Europa, Bari 1986

Ginatempo M. and Sandri L., *L'Italia delle Città. Il Popolo Urbano tra Medioevo e Rinascimento (Secoli XIII–XVI)*, Florence 1990

Granshaw L. and Porter R. (eds.), *The Hospital in History*, London 1989

Green M., 'Women's medical practice and health care in medieval Europe', *Signs*, 14 (1989)

Greenbaum L. S., '"Measure of civilization": the hospital thought of Jaques Tenon on the eve of the French Revolution', *BHM*, 49 (1975)

'Nurses and doctors in conflict. Piety and medicine in the Paris Hotel-Dieu on the eve of the Revolution', *Clio Medica* (1979)

Grendi E., 'Ideologia della carità e società indisciplinata. La costruzione del sistema assistenziale genovese (1470–1670)', in G. Politi, M. Rosa, F. Della Peruta (eds.), *Timore e Carità. I Poveri nell'Italia Moderna*, Cremona 1982

Gribaudi P., *Il Regio Educatorio della Provvidenza nei suoi Due Secoli di Vita (1735–1935). Notizie Storiche*, Turin 1935

Grimm H. J., 'Luther's contributions to sixteenth century organization of poor relief', *ARH*, 61 (1970)

Griseri A., 'Il cantiere per una capitale', in *I Rami Incisi dell'Archivio di Corte: Sovrani, Battaglie, Architetture, Topografia*, Turin 1981

Grosso M. and Mellano M. F., *La Controriforma nella Diocesi di Torino*, 3 vols., Vatican City 1957

Guichonnet P. (ed.), *Histoire de la Savoie*, Toulouse 1984

Gutton J. P., *La Société et les Pauvres: l'Exemple de la Généralité de Lyon*, Paris 1971

Henderson J., 'Piety and charity in late medieval Florence: religious confraternities from the middle of the thirteenth century to the late fifteenth century', unpublished Ph.D. dissertation, Westfield College, University of London 1983

'The hospitals of late medieval and Renaissance Florence: a preliminary survey', in Granshaw and Porter (eds.), *The Hospital in History*, London 1989

Himmelfarb G., *The Idea of Poverty. England in the Early Industrial Age*, London 1984

Horden P., 'A discipline of relevance: the historiography of the later medieval hospital', *SHM*, 1 (1988)

Hufton O. H., *The Poor in Eighteenth Century France 1750–1789*, Oxford 1974

Imbert J., *Les Hôpitaux en Droit Canonique*, Paris 1947

'La bourse des pauvres d'Aire-sur-la Lys à la fin de l'Ancien Régime', *Revue du Nord*, 34 (1952)

'L'Eglise et l'Etat face au problème de l'assistance', in *Etudes d'Histoire du Droit Canonique dédiées a G. Le Bras*, T.I, Paris 1965

Jacobson-Schutte A., 'Periodization of sixteenth century Italian religious history: the post-Cantimori paradigm shift', *JMH*, 61 (1989)

Jones C., *Charity and Bienfaisance. The Treatment of the Poor in the Montpellier Region 1740–1815*, Cambridge 1982

'"Professionalizing modern medicine" in French hospitals', *MH*, 26 (1982)

The Charitable Imperative: Hospitals and Nursing in Ancien Régime and Revolutionary France, London 1989

Joret C., 'Le père Guevarre et les Bureax de Charité au XVII et XVIII siècle', *Annales du Midi*, 1 (1889)

Jutte R., 'Poor relief and social discipline in sixteenth century Europe', *ESR*, 11 (1981)

Kent J. R., 'Population mobility and alms: poor migrants in the Midlands during the early seventeenth century', *Loc. Pop. St.*, 27 (1981)

King M. L., *Women of the Renaissance*, Chicago, Ill. 1991

Kingdon R. M., 'Social welfare in Calvin's Geneva', *AHR*, 76 (1971)

Kirshner J., 'Materials for a gilded cage: non-dotal assets in Florence, 1300–1500', in D. I. Kertzer and R. P. Saller, *The Family in Italy from Antiquity to the Present*, New Haven, Conn. and London 1991

Koenigsberger H. J., 'The Parliament of Piedmont during the Renaissance, 1450–1560', in *Essays in Early Modern European History*, Ithaca, N.Y. 1971

Laget M., 'Childbirth in seventeenth and eighteenth century France: obstetrical practices and collective attitudes', in R. Forster and O. Ranum (eds.), *Medicine and Society in France*, Baltimore, Md. 1980

Lallemand L., *Histoire de la Charité*, 4 vols., Paris 1906

Le Bras G., *Histoire du Droit et des Institutions de l'Eglise en Occident*, vol. I, *Prolégomènes*, Paris 1955

Leguay J. P. (ed.), *Histoire de la Savoie*, 3 vols., *La Savoie de la Réforme à la Révolution Française*, Rennes 1983–86

Leistikow D., *Ten Centuries of European Hospital Architecture*, Ingolheim 1967

Leverotti F., 'Ricerche sulle origini dell'Ospedale Maggiore di Milano', *ASL*, 107 (1984)

Levi G., 'Gli aritmetici politici e la demografia piemontese negli ultimi anni del Settecento', *RSI*, 86 (1974)

'Come Torino soffocò il Piemonte', in *Centro e Periferia di uno Stato Assoluto*, Turin 1985

Lindemann M., *Patriots and Paupers. Hamburg, 1712–1830*, New York and Oxford 1990

Lis C. and Soly H., *Poverty and Capitalism in Pre-Industrial Europe*, Brighton 1979

Lombardi D., *Povertà Maschile e Povertà Femminile. L'Ospedale dei Mendicanti nella Firenze dei Medici*, Bologna 1988

Loriga S., *Soldati. L'istituzione Militare nel Piemonte del Settecento*, Venice 1992

Mallé L., 'Appunti e revisioni per la scultura del '600 e '700 in Piemonte', in *Arte in Europa. Scritti di Storia dell'Arte in Onore di Edoardo Arslan*, vol. I, Milan 1966

Marshall S. (ed.), *Women in Reformation and Counter-Reformation Europe. Private and Public Worlds*, Bloomington and Indianapolis, Ind. 1989

Martini G., *Storia delle Confraternite Italiane con Speciale Riguardo al Piemonte*, Turin 1935

Martz L., *Poverty and Welfare in Habsburg Spain. The Example of Toledo*, Cambridge 1983

Massabò Ricci I. and Rosso C., 'La corte quale rappresentazione del potere sovrano', in Romano (ed.), *Figure del Barocco in Piemonte. La Corte, la Città, i Cantieri, le Provincie*, Turin 1988

Matta P., *Breve Monografia del Regio Istituto delle Rosine*, Turin 1889

McIntosh M., 'Local responses to the poor in late medieval and Tudor England', *CC*, 3 (1988)

Meersseman G. G., *Ordo Fraternitatis: Confraternite e Pietà dei Laici nel Medioevo*, Rome 1977

Miccoli G., 'La storia religiosa', in *Storia d'Italia*, part II, vol. I, Turin 1974

Monti A., *La Compagnia di Gesù nel Territorio della Provincia Torinese*, Chieri 1914–20, vol. 1

Naso I., *Medici e Strutture Sanitarie nella Società Tardo-Medievale. Il Piemonte dei Secoli XIV–XV*, Milan 1982

Navarrini R. and Belfanti C. M., 'Il problema della povertà nel ducato di Mantova: aspetti istituzionali e problemi sociali (secoli XIV–XVI)', in Politi, Rosa, Della Peruta (eds.), *Timore e Carità. I Poveri nell'Italia Moderna*, Cremona 1982

Niccoli O., *Profeti e Popolo nell'Italia del Rinascimento*, Bari 1987

Nolf J., *La Réforme de la Bienfaisance Publique à Ypres au XVIe Siècle*, Gand 1915
Norberg K., *Rich and Poor in Grenoble 1600–1814*, Berkeley, Calif. 1985
Norena C. G., *Juan Luis Vives*, The Hague 1970
Nutton V., 'The seeds that fell among thorns? The reception of Fracastoro's theory of contagion', *Osiris* (1990)
Okin S. M., 'Patriarchy and married women's property: questions on some current views', *Eighteenth Century Studies*, 2 (1983–84)
Olson J. E., *Calvin and Social Welfare. Deacons and the Bourse Française*, London 1989
Orselli M., ''Vita religiosa nella città medievale italiana tra dimensione ecclesiastica e "cristianesimo civico". Una esemplificazione', *AIIGT*, 7 (1981)
Palmer R., 'The Control of the Plague in Venice and Italy 1348–1600', unpublished Ph.D. thesis, University of Kent, 1978
  'L'assistenza medica nella Venezia Cinquecentesca', in B. Aikema and D. Meijers (eds.), *Nel Regno dei Poveri*, Venice 1989
Pancino C., *Il Bambino e l'Acqua Sporca. Storia dell'Assistenza al Parto dalle Mammane alle Ostetriche (Secoli XVI–XIX)*, Milan 1984
Panzac D., *Quarantaines et Lazarets. L'Europe et la Peste d'Orient (XVIIe–XXe Siècles)*, Aix-en-Provence 1986
Park K., 'Healing the poor: hospitals and medicine in Renaissance Florence', in J. Barry and C. Jones (eds.), *Medicine and Charity before the Welfare State*, London 1991
Park K. and Henderson J., '"The first hospital among Christians": the Ospedale di Santa Maria Nuova in early sixteenth century Florence', *MH*, 35 (1991)
Pastore A., 'Strutture assistenziali fra Chiesa e Stati nell'Italia della Controriforma', in *Storia d'Italia, Annali 9*
Paultre M.C., *De la Repression de la Mendicité et du Vagabondage en France sous l'Ancien Régime*, Paris 1906
Pedrini A., *Ville dei Secoli XVII e XVIII in Piemonte*, Turin 1965
Pelling M., 'Healing the sick poor: social policy and disability in Norwich, 1550–1640', *MH*, 29 (1985)
  'Illness among the poor in an early modern English town: the Norwich census of 1570', *CC*, 3 (1988)
  'Old age, poverty and disability in early modern Norwich', in M. Pelling and R. M. Smith (eds.), *Life, Death and the Elderly: Historical Perspectives*, London 1991
Perrero D., 'Il Conte Fulvio Testi alla corte di Torino negli anni 1628 e 1635', in *Documenti Inediti*, 78, Turin 1865
Peyronel Rambaldi S., *Speranze e Sogni nel Cinquecento Modenese. Tensioni Religiose e Vita Cittadina ai Tempi di Giovanni Morone*, Milan 1979
Pirenne H., *Histoire du Belgique*, vol. III, Bruxelles 1923 (first edition 1907)
Pollak M. D., *Turin 1564–1660: Urban Design, Military Culture and the Creation of the Absolutist Capital*, Chicago, Ill. 1991
Ponzo G., *Stato e Pauperismo in Italia: l'Albergo di Virtù di Torino (1580–1836)*, Rome 1974
Porter R., 'The gift relation: philanthropy and provincial hospitals in eighteenth-century England', in Granshaw and Porter (eds.), *The Hospital*
Pound J., 'An Elizabethan census of the poor: the treatment of vagrancy in Norwich, 1570–80', *Univ. Birm. Hist. Jl*, 8 (1962)

Prato G., *La Vita Economica in Piemonte a Mezzo del Secolo XVIII*, Turin 1908
'L'evoluzione agricola nel secolo XVIII e le cause economiche dei moti del 1792–98 in Piemonte', *Mem. Acc. Sc. Tor.*, series 2, vol. 110 (1909)
Problemi Monetari e Bancari nei Secoli XVII e XVIII, Turin 1916
'Risparmio e credito in Piemonte all'avvento dell'economia moderna', in *La Cassa di Risparmio di Torino nel Suo Primo Centenario*, Turin 1927
Prodi P. and Johanek P. (eds.), *Strutture Ecclesiastiche in Italia e Germania prima della Riforma*, Bologna 1984
Promis D., *Le Monete dei Reali di Savoia*, 2 vols., Turin 1841
Pullan B., 'The famine in Venice and the new Poor Law 1527–1529', *BISSSV*, vols. 5–6 (1963–64)
Rich and Poor in Renaissance Venice. The Social Institutions of a Catholic State, to 1620, Oxford 1971
'Catholics and the poor in early modern Europe', *TRHS*, 26 (1976)
'Support and redeem: charity and poor relief in Italian cities from the fourteenth to the seventeenth', *CC*, 3 (1988)
'Plague and perceptions of the poor in early modern Italy', in T. Ranger and P. Slack (eds.), *Epidemics and Ideas: Essays on the Historical Perception of Pestilence*, Cambridge 1992
Quazza G., *Le Riforme in Piemonte nella Prima Metà del Settecento*, 2 vols., Modena 1957
Radice G. and Marpelli C., *I Fatebenefratelli*, vol. V, *I Conventi. L'Ospedale del S. Sudario di Torino e di S. Michele di Asti*, Milan 1977
Ranger T. and Slack P. (eds.), *Epidemics and Ideas: Essays on the Historical Perception of Pestilence*, Cambridge 1992
Rapley E., *The Dévotes. Women and Church in Seventeenth Century France*, Montreal and Kingston 1990
Regione Piemonte, Assessorato all'Istruzione e Cultura, *L'Ospedale Maggiore di San Giovanni Battista e della Città di Torino*, Turin 1980
Ricci G., 'Povertà, vergogna e povertà vergognosa', *SS*, 9 (1979)
Romano G. (ed.), *Figure del Barocco in Piemonte. La Corte, la Città, i Cantieri, le Provincie*, Turin 1988
Rondolino F., 'Vita torinese durante l'assedio (1703–1707)', in Regia Deputazione di Storia Patria, *Le Campagne di Guerra in Piemonte (1703–8) e l'Assedio di Torino (1706)*, vol. VII, Turin 1909
Ronzani M., 'La "chiesa del comune" a Pisa nel '200–'300', in G. Rossetti (ed.), *Spazio, Società, Potere nell'Italia dei Comuni*, Naples 1989
Roper L., *The Holy Household. Women and Morals in Reformation Augsburg*, Oxford 1989
Rosa M., 'Chiesa, idee sui poveri e assistenza in Italia dal Cinque al Settecento', *SS*, 10 (1980)
Rossen G., 'Communities of parish and guild in the late Middle Ages', in S. Wright, *Parish, Church and People. Local Studies in Lay Religion 1350–1750*, London 1988
Rossi T. and Gabotto F., *Storia di Torino, Biblioteca della Società' Storica Subalpina*, vol. 82 (1914)
Rubin M., 'Development and change in English hospitals, 1100–1500', in L. Granshaw and R. Porter (eds.), *The Hospital in History*, London 1989

Rusconi R., 'Confraternite compagnie e devozioni', *Storia d'Italia, Annali 9*, Turin 1986

Russell A. W. (ed.), *The Town and State Physician from the Middle Ages to the Enlightenment*, Wolfenbuttel 1981

Russo S., 'Potere pubblico e carità privata. L'assistenza ai poveri a Lucca tra XVI e XVII secolo', *SS*, 23 (1984)

Schwarz R. M., *Policing the Poor in Eighteenth Century France*, Chapel Hill London 1988

Scotti A., *Ascanio Vitozzi, Ingegnere Ducale a Torino*, Florence 1969
'Malati e strutture ospedaliere dall'età dei Lumi all'Unità', in *Storia d'Italia, Annali 7. Malattia e Medicina*, Turin 1984

Semeria G. B., *Storia della Chiesa Metropolitana di Torino*, Turin 1840

Sergi G., *Potere e Territorio Lungo la Strada di Francia*, Naples 1981
'Le città come luoghi di continuità di nozioni pubbliche del potere. Le aree delle marche d'Ivrea e di Torino', in *Piemonte Medievale. Forme del Potere e della Società*, Turin 1985

Slack P., 'Vagrants and vagrancy in England, 1598–1664', *EcHR*, second series, 27 (1974)
'The disappearance of plague: an alternative view', *EcHR*, second series, 34 (1981)
The Impact of the Plague in Tudor and Stuart England, Oxford 1985
Poverty and Policy in Tudor and Stuart England, New York 1988
'Dearth and policy in early modern England', *SHM*, 5 (1992)

Solero S., *Storia dell' Ospedale Maggiore di S. Giovanni Battista e della Città di Torino*, Turin 1859

Spicciani A., 'The "poveri vergognosi" in fifteenth century Florence', in T. Riis (ed.), *Aspects of Poverty in Early Modern Europe*, Stuttgart 1981

Staves S., *Married Women's Separate Property*, Boston, Mass. 1990

Storia d'Italia, Annali 7. Malattia e Medicina, edited by F. Della Peruta, Turin 1984

Storia Illustrata di Torino, edited by V. Castronovo, vol. II, *Torino Sabauda*, Milan 1992

Strocchia S. T., 'Remembering the family: women, kin and commemorative masses in Renaissance Florence', *RQ*, 42 (1989)

Stumpo E., *Finanza e Stato Moderno nel Piemonte del Seicento*, Rome 1979
'I ceti dirigenti in Italia nell'età moderna. Due modelli diversi: nobiltà piemontese e patriziato toscano', in A. Tagliaferri (ed.), *I Ceti Dirigenti in Italia in Età Moderna e Contemporanea*, Istituto di Storia dell'Università di Udine, Udine 1984

Symcox G., *Victor Amadeus II. Absolutism in the Savoyard State, 1675–1730*, London 1983

Tamburini L., *Le Chiese di Torino dal Rinascimento al Barocco*, Turin 1968

Tawney R. H., *Religion and the Rise of Capitalism*, London 1926

Thompson J. D. and Goldin G., *The Hospital: a Social and Architectural History*, New Haven, Conn. 1975

Thomson D., 'The welfare of the elderly in the past, a family or community responsibility?', in M. Pelling and R. M. Smith (eds), *Life, Death and the Elderly: Historical Perspectives*, London 1991

Tierney B., *Medieval Poor Law: a Sketch of Canonical Theory and its Application in England*, Berkeley, Calif. 1959

Todd M., *Christian Humanism and the Puritan Social Order*, Cambridge 1987

Torre A., 'Il consumo di devozioni: rituali e potere nelle campagne piemontesi nella prima metà del Settecento', *QS*, 58 (1985)

Trexler R. C., 'Charity and the defense of urban elites in the Italian communes', in F. C. Jaher, *The Rich, the Well-Born and the Powerful*, Urbana, Ill. 1973

Troeltsch E., *The Social Teaching of the Christian Churches*, London and New York 1931 (German edition 1911)

Turletti C., *Vita di Rosa Govona, Fondatrice del Regio Istituto delle Rosine*, Turin 1896

Vallauri T., *Storia delle Università degli Studi*, 3 vols., Turin 1816

Vauchez A., 'Assistance et charité en Occident XIII–XV siècles' in *Domanda e Consumi Livelli e Strutture (nei secoli XIII–XVIII)*, Florence 1978
'Les confréries au moyen age: esquisse d'un bilan historiographique', in *Les Laics au Moyen Age. Pratiques et Experiences Religieuses*, Paris 1987

Versluysen M. C., 'Midwives, medical men and "poor women labouring of child"', in H. Roberts (ed.), *Women, Health and Reproduction*, London 1981

Viale Ferrero M., *Feste delle Madame Reali di Savoia*, Turin 1965

Viora M., *Le Costituzioni Piemontesi 1723, 1729, 1772*, Turin 1928

Visceglia M. A., *Il Bisogno di Eternità. I Comportamenti Caritativi a Napoli in Età Moderna*, Naples 1988

Vovelle M., *Piété Baroque et Déchristianisation en Provence au XVIII siècle*, Paris 1973

Walter J. and Schofield R. (eds.), *Famine, Disease and the Social Order in Early Modern Society*, Cambridge 1989

Wear A., 'Caring for the sick poor in St. Bartholomew exchange: 1580–1676', in W. F. Bynum and R. Porter (eds.), *Living and Dying in London, Medical History Supplement n.11*, London 1991

Webb B. and Webb S., *English Poor Law History*, part I, *The Old Poor Law*, London 1929

Wilson A., 'The politics of medical improvement in early Hanoverian London', in A. Cunningham and R. French (eds.), *The Medical Enlightenment of the Eighteenth Century*, Cambridge 1990

Woolf S. J., 'Sviluppo economico e struttura sociale in Piemonte da Emanuele Filiberto a Carlo Emanuele III', *NRS*, 46 (1962)
Studi sulla Nobiltà Piemontese All'Epoca Dell'Assolutismo, Turin 1963
The Poor in Western Europe in the Eighteenth and Nineteenth Centuries, London and New York 1986

Zarri G., 'Aspetti dello sviluppo degli ordini religiosi in Italia tra '400 e '500. Studi e problemi', in P. Prodi and P. Johanek (eds.), *Strutture Ecclesiastiche in Italia e Germania prima della Riforma*, Bologna 1984
'Monasteri femminili e città (sec. XV–XVIII)', in Chittolini, *Storia d'Italia, Annali 9, La Chiesa e il Potere Politico*, Turin 1986
'Le sante vive. Per una tipologia della santità femminile nel primo Cinquecento', *Annali dell'Istituto Storico Italo-Germanico di Trento*, 1980, reprinted in *Le Sante Vive. Profezie di Corte e Devozione Femminile tra '400 e '500*, Turin 1990

Index

271

Cambridge History of Medicine

Health, medicine and morality in the sixteenth century *edited by* CHARLES WEBSTER

The Renaissance notion of woman: A study in the fortunes of scholasticism and medical science in European intellectual life IAN MACLEAN

Mystical Bedlam: madness, anxiety and healing in sixteenth century England
MICHAEL MACDONALD

From medical chemistry to biochemistry: The making of a biomedical discipline
ROBERT E. KOHLER

Joan Baptista Van Helmont: Reformer of science and medicine WALTER PAGEL

A generous confidence: Thomas Story Kirkbride and the art of asylum keeping, 1840–1884
NANCY TOMBS

The cultural meaning of popular science: Phrenology and the organization of consent in nineteenth-century Britain ROGER COOTER

Madness, morality and medicine: A study of the York Retreat, 1796–1914 ANNE DIGBY

Patients and practitioners: Lay perceptions of medicine in pre-industrial society *edited by*
ROY PORTER

Hospital life in enlightenment Scotland: Care and teaching at the Royal Infirmary of Edinburgh
GUENTER B. RISSE

Plague and the poor in Renaissance Florence ANNE G. CARMICHAEL

Victorian lunacy: Richard M. Bucke and the practice of late-nineteenth-century psychiatry
S. E. D. SHORTT

Medicine and society in Wakefield and Huddersfield 1780–1870 HILARY MARLAND

Ordered to care: The dilemma of American nursing, 1850–1945 SUSAN M. REVERBY

Morbid appearances: The anatomy of pathology in the early nineteenth century
RUSSELL C. MAULITZ

Professional and popular medicine in France, 1770–1830: The social world of medical practice
MATTHEW RAMSEY

Abortion, doctors and the law: Some aspects of the legal regulation of abortion in England 1803–1982 JOHN KEOWN

Public health in Papua New Guinea: Medical possibility and social constraints, 1884–1984
DONALD DENOON

Health, race and German politics between national unification and Nazism, 1870–1945
PAUL WEINDLING

The physician-legislators of France: Medicine and politics in the early Third Republic, 1870–1914
JACK D. ELLIS

The science of woman: Gynaecology and gender in England, 1800–1929 ORNELLA MOSCUCCI

Science and empire: East Coast fever in Rhodesia and the Transvaal PAUL F. CRANEFIELD

The colonial disease: A social history of sleeping sickness in northern Zaire, 1900–1940
MARY INEZ LYONS

DATE DUE

10-13-09

PRINTED IN U.S.A.